*Hudson **Sound*** *of 2,577 gross tons was completed in 1950 for the Hudson S.S. Co. Ltd., London. Though built as a collier, oil firing and derricks made her suitable for other trades.*

Downshire *of 398 gross tons was built by Scott & Sons, Bowling for the East Downshire S.S. Company of Dundrum and regularly carried coal cargoes to her home port until the 1950s.*

Also in this Series ___ _ _ _ _ _ _ _ _ _ _ _ _ _ _ _ _ _ _ _

MARINE and LOCAL HISTORY; SOIL SCIENCE.
All books are large format (A4), 21 x 30 cms, (8.5" x 12").

MARINE.

Marine Art & Liverpool. Painters, Places & Flag Codes 1760 - 1960.
by A.S.Davidson.   *ISBN 0 905184 10 6.   171 pages.*
   The result of many years study of Liverpool artists and ships they painted. The text covers 69 painters especially Jackson, Salmon, Collins, Jenkinson and James; Miles and Samuel Walters; Heard, Dove, Hughes, McFarlane, McMinn, Waldron, Desilva and Ogilvy. The Yorkes, Witham, Greenwood, Hall, A. de Clerk, Stevens and finally The Brownes, Rosenvinge, Mann and Ellis. There are lists of works plus 43 colour and 26 black and white photographs, sketches and charts. The author also describes with the aid of diagrams how old code flags in paintings can be used to name a vessel and includes a compilation of ships names and corresponding numbers for Watson's Liverpool Code and Marryat's Code.

Estuary & River Ferries of South West England.
by Martin Langley & Edwina Small.   *ISBN 0 905184 08 4.   148 pages.*
   The many creeks and rivers of the area had rowing and sailing ferries which were later replaced by paddle and screw steamers or steam chain ferries in a number of cases. Full histories of some 139 ferries are supported by sketch maps, plans and photographs from the River Severn in the north to the River Stour, Christchurch and Poole in the south.

Steam Coasters & Short Sea Traders.
by C.V.Waine.   *ISBN 0 905184 04 1.   157 pages.*
   The history of the British steam coaster covering, building, repairing, engines, early designs, Clyde 'puffers' and the various engines-aft types, including the big east coast colliers. Also covered are those with engines amidships and coastal tankers. An account of the various owners, their fleets and trades is also given, with 68 plans and 29 colour profiles selected with the modelmaker in mind plus 89 black and white sketches and photos.

British Steam Tugs.
by P.N.Thomas.   *ISBN 0 905184 07 6.   222 pages.*
   The history covers early tugs, wood, iron and steel paddle tugs; harbour seeking and coastal screw tugs and ocean tugs. Thames craft, tenders and passenger carrying tugs, naval and wartime tugs. Tug owners and builders. Tug construction, engines and deck gear. Over 1000 steam tugs, 100 builders and 400 owners are covered. The plans from 1833 to 1956 will be of interest to modelmakers. More than 90 photographs, sketches, funnel colours and 29 colour profiles.

Old Time Steam Coasting
by O.G.Spargo & T.H.Thomason.   *ISBN 0 905184 05 X.   138 pages.*
   An eye witness account of life in Liverpool steam coasters in the 1920s and 1930s. An important contribution to the maritime social history of the period in which the operation and handling of the vessels, crews and cargoes are fully described. Six colour plates, four plans and numerous sketches, photos and voyage charts.

SOIL SCIENCE.

Handbook for Soil Thin Section Description.
by P.Bullock, N.Fedoroff, A.Jongerious, G.Stoops and T.Tursina. Additional Contributor: **U.Babel.**
Collaborators: **J.Aguilar, H.-J.Altemüller, E.A.FitzPatrick, St.Kowalinski, G.Paneque, G.K.Rutherford**
and **E.A.Yarilova.**   *ISBN 0 905184 09 2.   152 pages.*
   This standard work was prepared under the auspices of the International Society of Soil Science by an International Working Group set up to develop a comprehensive descriptive system covering the approach to thin section description, basic concepts, general descriptive criteria, microstructure, basic mineral components, basic organic components, groundmass and pedofeatures. Illustrated with 126 colour and 97 black and white photomicrographs; 146 diagrams.

LOCAL HISTORY.

The Wandering Worfe.
by D.H.Robinson.   *ISBN O 905184 06 8.   130 pages.*
   An environmental and historical study of an east Shropshire river and its tributary streams, which flows into the River Severn near Bridgnorth. It describes the water and other mills and the uses to which they were put, reservoirs and other water sources and their place in local history. Two coloured maps and 89 black and white photos, sketches and maps.

The Sleepy Meese.
by D.H.Robinson   *ISBN 0905184 11 4.   105 pages.*
   A further book about the local history of Shropshire based on the area drained by the River Meese around Newport. Fully illustrated with colour and black and white photos, maps, sketches and plans.

2. **Cliff Quay** 3337/50, *first of the large steam colliers for the British Electricity Authority.*

THE STEAM
COLLIER FLEETS

J. A. MacRae & C. V. Waine

Illustrated by C. V. Waine

3. Weardale loading at Blyth c.1870.

 WAINE Research Publications

To the Steam Collier men of Britain.

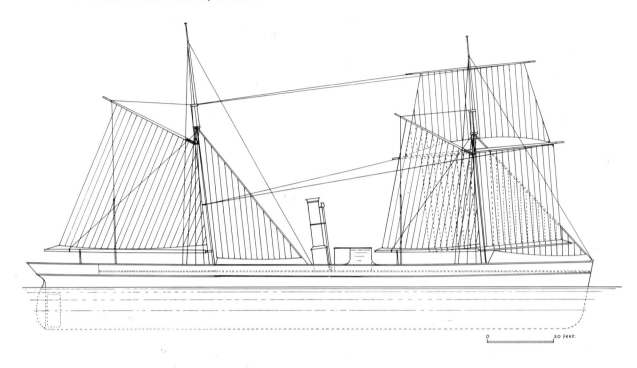

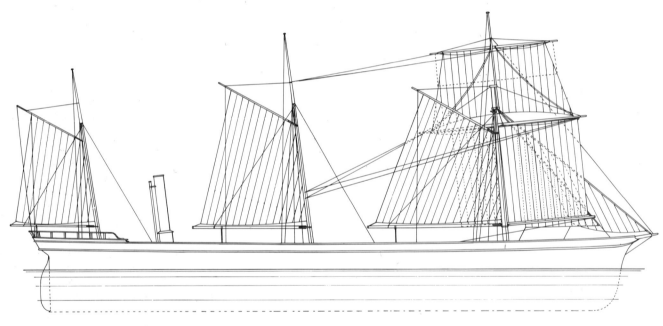

4. Lambton (top) was built by C. Mitchell of Newcastle in 1857 for the Earl of Durham and had the registered dimensions 168.0' x 26.6' x 13.6'. The yard also built the engines-aft collier **Helios** (above) for the Hamburg Gas Company. This type was much used by London owners in the early years.

Courtesy Tyne & Wear Museums

© The Authors

Published by:
Waine Research,
Mount Pleasant,
Beamish Lane,
Albrighton,
Wolverhampton.

First Published 1990

ISBN 0 905184 12 2

Printed & Bound in England.

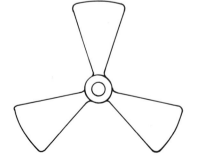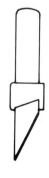

4. *Early propeller c.1860.*

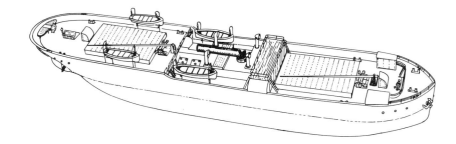

Preface

5. *Radcliff* from a model, Science Museum, London.

This book was begun by Captain MacRae some 20 years ago while master of the Thames up-river collier **Hackney** (204). He served in the flatirons for much of his career including the Second World War. He had been working on the project for some time when I published 'Steam Coasters and Short Sea Traders'. On his retirement, we got together with a view to producing a companion volume on colliers. With the untimely death of Captain MacRae, the family invited me to take over his papers and carry on the project.

Completion of the work has been made possible with the help of our many friends who have contributed extra research to complete unfinished parts of the story, especially P.N. Thomas, Pat O' Driscoll, John Bartlett, Edward Paget-Tomlinson, Roy Fenton, Robin Craig and Alan Pearsall, while on the marine side Captain O.G. Spargo, Alan Dowsland, Mr.R.H.Hughes, Captain J.B. Roberts, Mr.R.C.March and Mr.C.L. Lovell have all made valuable contributions. Thanks are also due to the various archives and museums especially Adrian Ostler and the Tyne & Wear Museums. Fortunately Captain MacRae had already drafted his introduction:

When the notion of writing the history of these fleets was first thought of, it was intended to be an account of the ships well known to the writer who had either sailed in them, or knew them and the men who manned them, by more or less constant contact over thirty years or more. However during conversations which invariably included the phrase "Do you remember old so and so on the such and such?" names of ships and men came tumbling out of the past, demanding to be at least mentioned, if not fully accounted for.

A new difficulty now presented itself, for what, exactly is a collier? The Oxford Dictionary defines a collier as 'a coal ship or a sailor thereon'. This latter is not perfectly correct, as the men who man the colliers are always referred to as 'collier men', a race apart and withal proud of the name. A coal ship? In the past, especially during the great depression of the early thirties, many ships at some time or other carried a whole or part cargo of coal.

The true collier is a ship designed and built with the carriage of coal, in bulk, as its sole or main aim, easily and quickly loaded and discharged, and of such a speed that under normal circumstances she can pass between loading and discharging ports without having to spend time at anchor awaiting the tide to her berth. During the time covered by this book there were many firms whose ships carried coal and little else, and many carried coal as return cargoes. To complicate matters there were ships during the two world wars which carried coal and nothing else between the coal ports of the North East and South Wales to the Thames and South of England, but were not colliers at all. A perfect example were the lake boats, brought over from the Great Lakes of North America to make good earlier losses. The task of covering the hundreds of ships involved in the period of Britain's greatest prosperity, has led the writer into some strange byways, and it soon became obvious that not only the ships but also some of the main ports at which they loaded and discharged would need to be accounted for.

At one time, on a voyage from the Tyne to London River, the watchkeeper on the bridge of a collier would have had in sight at any one time at least twenty ships, half bound in the opposite direction for ports between the Wash and Methil. By the 1970s the loneliness was awful, perhaps the whole watch of four hours passing without seeing anyone one knew. One year, 1948, needed 24 pages to record the ships stemmed to load at one berth in the River Tyne. The last three recorded years, 1960-61-62, are all contained in less than 2 pages. Most of these loading berths, like the ships, have long since fallen into disuse if they have not actually disappeared.

Talks with the older hands soon bring out hair-raising tales, some humourous, some inevitably of tragedies which could have been avoided. These were the characters who brought fun and colour into our lives, far too many to mention in detail, but there are some who must be told about. They cannot be left out of the collier story, for they were the colliers.

This has been an enjoyable task, though demanding at times, involving months of research into firms and ships long since gone from the scene, with perhaps little or no information about the ultimate ends of ships at one time famous names on the waterfront at many ports. If the reader, wandering down the years between 1852 and today, finds himself meandering up a creek away from the main stream, to read of things not too important, of ships, men and places remembered in 35 years spent in coastal colliers, they will perhaps forgive me and enjoy reading as much as I have enjoyed writing, this account of what a gentleman once called, with truth, my 'beloved' colliers.

The late Captain J.A.MacRae and C.V.Waine
Albrighton, 1990.

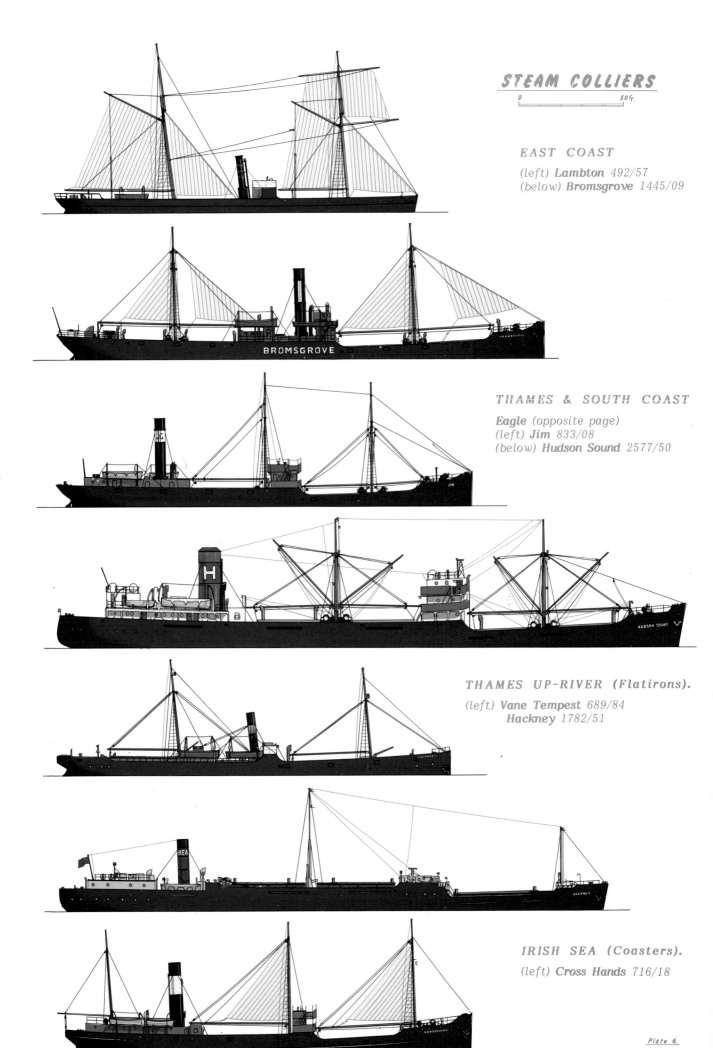

STEAM COLLIERS

0 ———— 50 ft.

EAST COAST

(left) **Lambton** 492/57
(below) **Bromsgrove** 1445/09

BROMSGROVE

THAMES & SOUTH COAST

Eagle (opposite page)
(left) **Jim** 833/08
(below) **Hudson Sound** 2577/50

HUDSON SOUND

THAMES UP-RIVER (Flatirons).

(left) **Vane Tempest** 689/84
Hackney 1782/51

IRISH SEA (Coasters).

(left) **Cross Hands** 716/18

Plate 6.

CONTENTS

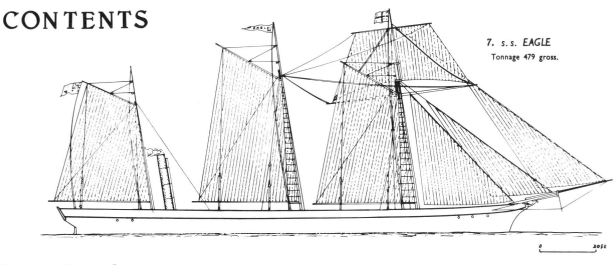

7. s. s. EAGLE
Tonnage 479 gross.

NOTES: Figure numbers correspond with page numbers. All the plans are from the original shipyard
drawings unless otherwise stated. Ships' names are followed by gross tonnage / year of build.

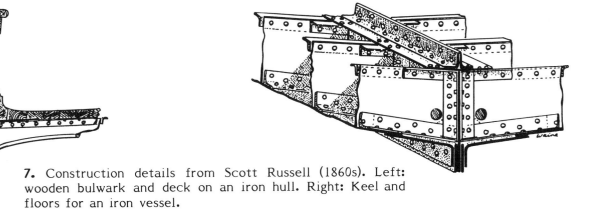

7. Construction details from Scott Russell (1860s). Left:
wooden bulwark and deck on an iron hull. Right: Keel and
floors for an iron vessel.

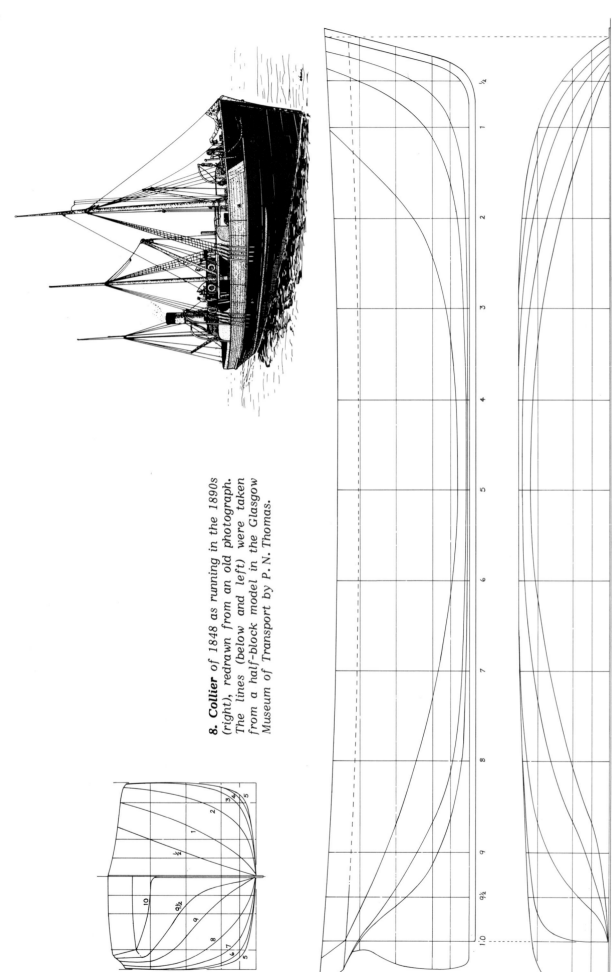

8. Collier of 1848 as running in the 1890s (right), redrawn from an old photograph. The lines (below and left) were taken from a half-block model in the Glasgow Museum of Transport by P. N. Thomas.

THE IRON STEAM SCREW COLLIER, "Q. E. D."

1.

From the
'Illustrated London News'
Courtesy John Bartlett.

THE "Q. E. D." SCREW STEAM COLLIER.

A perfect novelty in the coal trade arrived in the river Thames, at the close of last week, and took in her moorings at the tier off Princes Stairs, Rotherhithe, where she has attracted considerable attention and curiosity. This was an iron vessel of handsome appearance, barque rigged, with taunt masts and square yards, the masts raking aft in a manner that is seldom seen except in the waters of the United States. The hull was built by Mr. Cootes, who is the owner, at Walker's-quay, near Newcastle, and is of peculiar construction, with a 20 horse power engine, by Hawthorn, which turns a screw propeller (a compound of several inventions), having four flies or flaps a right angles with each other, the bend of each flap at an angle of 45 degrees from the centre. Her length over all is 130 feet; breadth of beam, 27 feet 6 inches; tonnage by admeasurement, 273 tons, but capable of carrying 340 tons of coals, and with this weight her draught of water is 11 feet 9 inches abaft, and 10 feet 3 inches forward. Her hold is divided into separate chambers (so that injury to the bottom in one chamber will not affect the others), and each chamber has a false floor of sheet iron hermetically closed; and between the bottom and these floors are spaces to be filled with water by means of large taps, for the purpose of ballast—so that her only ballast is the liquid element which may, if required, be pumped out again in a very short time by the engine. Her bows are like the sharp end of a wedge rising to a lofty billet-head, and her overhanging stem projects much more than is customary; but, though low, the flatness of what is usually termed the counters must lift her to every swell, so as to render it next to impossible for a sea to break over the taffrail; but we fancy that when struck as she scuds aft, the concussion must be very great. On her stern is an armorial bearing, with the motto, "Spes mea Christus," and beneath these appears her name, the "Q. E. D., of Newcastle."

The cabin is commodious, with a raised roof surrounded with window-lights, enabling persons below to see what is passing upon deck. There are four sleeping apartments and a state-room for the Captain; a swinging compass is suspended, having a magnet on each side, and one before it, to counteract the attraction of the iron. Her shrouds are wire-rope served over, with a strong double screw to each shroud to set it up when slack without the smallest difficulty and with scarcely any labour. Her mainmast from the step to the cap is 65 feet in altitude, her mainyard 52 feet in squareness, and from the keel to the royal-truck the height is about 130 feet; the other masts and yards are in proportion, the mizenmast being of iron, and hollow, so as to form a funnel for the engine-fire, and it is not the least curious part about her to see the smoke issuing from the mizenmast head. This vessel was launched on St. Swithin's day (15th July), took in a cargo of coals at Newcastle (from 18 to 20 keels), but getting aground on the Hook of the Gunfleet Sand, in the Swin, was obliged to heave two or three keels of coals overboard. She laid ashore several hours, but sustained no damage. We are informed that she steers with ease, sails remarkably well, and when tried with the screw propeller, rather exceeded expectation. Much ingenuity has been displayed in putting her together, and we feel confident that the time is not far distant when our ships of the line will be fitted with engines and screw in a somewhat similar manner. Of the success of the constructor's experiment we trust that he may hereafter be enabled to say Q. E. D.

Pioneer Steam Colliers

Coal made the industrial revolution possible, and Britain fortunately had extensive deposits. Some 300 million years ago much of the country was covered by a shallow sea into which a large river delta fringed by great swamps slowly advanced. The plant debris from these tropical forests accumulated and advanced seawards. From time to time the sea spread over the swamps due to storms, the land settling or a rise in sea-level, burying the swamp in sand and silt. If this happened frequently then the coal seam was thin and poor, but if accumulation continued unhindered for thousands of years then a thick seam formed. Even so only about 5% is coal, the remainder is sands, silts or clays. The whole was buried under thousands of feet of material so that the organic debris was compressed to become coal. About one foot of peat makes about one inch of coal. The varying forms of organic material and the varying temperatures and depths of burial produced considerable variation in the nature of the coal.

Around Newcastle, in the Northumberland and Durham coalfields, the coals are mainly bituminous. This is the common household coal which is easily lit. Other types of bituminous coals include the coking coals. As the coals are followed southwards to the Durham area there is a gradual change to those suitable for gas making, and those on the western side were found to be especially suitable for making coke. This is made by heating coal to about 1000°C to drive off gas and other volatile constituents in specially designed ovens. The coke was much in demand for iron and steel making furnaces. Another variety of coal produced around Newcastle was the dull black (splint) coals. These were soon used as steam coals as they do not fuse into a solid mass of clinker in boiler furnaces and so would allow air to reach all parts of the fire. In addition they did not produce much fine ash to clog the boiler tubes. In these coals there is only about 20% volatile matter and so they are harder to light but burn with little smoke and soot, making them ideal for steamships. This type of coal is a particular feature of the South Wales coalfields, indeed the phenomenal development of this coal went hand in hand with the increase in steamships, railways and industrial use. A special feature confined to the South Wales coalfield was the production of anthracite, which contains the least amount of volatile matter (less than 10%). Anthracite is the result of bituminous coals being buried to even greater depths or hotter conditions which drive off the gaseous and liquid components, leaving mainly carbon. It burns slowly with little or no smoke and was much used for hot water boilers. In contrast, gas coals contain more than 40% volatile matter sufficient to make it worth extracting, selling the gas and producing coke as a valuable by-product. The Lancashire and other coalfields offered a similar mix of bituminous gas and steam coals.

Steam coal had been shipped in increasing quantities to London and the trade had become such that the Woodmongers changed their name to the Society of Coal Merchants in 1605. As the ships grew larger they could not get alongside the small quays and had to discharge into lighters. The lightermen came to control the trade and the Government acted to allow other wharfingers to freely handle coal. The coal itself was sold by coal factors who undertook to sell the entire cargo on commission for the master or coal owner. They also paid the tax due on the coal which was determined on weight, so there were officials of the City Corporation who supervised the weighing of the cargo from the ship to lighters. There was an extensive network of restrictive practices, for example a cargo had to pass through the hands of a factor on the coal exchange before it could be passed on to a coal merchant even if he had ordered the cargo direct from the northern mines. As soon as the factor had sold the cargo it could be discharged, but as factors could limit the number of cargoes sold on the market, ships could wait for weeks to discharge. Even when discharge began the lightermen, whippers and coal heavers limited the rate of discharge so that it took about five and a half days, but they would discharge the ship in about three days if extra was paid. Newcastle coal owners even attempted to restrict the supply of coal to keep prices up, but with new mines opening up elsewhere this proved impracical and coal owners relied on the restrictions of the factors to protect them from losses. Shipowners became keen to avoid purchasing a cargo of coal when there was a strong possibility that the price obtained in London could easily be less than they had paid, so they became carriers of coal, chartered by the coal owner for the voyage or longer periods. To secure ships many coal owners became shareholders in ships, as did London coal factors, leading to the establishment of shipping companies of merchants and factors such as William Cory & Son and Stephenson Clarke. This was a small step as the factors acted as ships' agents.

Ships on arrival at Gravesend in the early part of the 19th century sent their papers ashore; the fitter's (loading agent's) certificate for the cargo and customs papers. The papers were sent up by the Gravesend office of the Coal Factors Society to the Coal Exchange in strict rotation, based on time of arrival. Vessels were given numbers on arrival which had to be displayed and the Meter's Office had their own Inspector of Colliers at this time to regulate the matter. The Meter's Office was also involved where the cargo was to be weighed out and their turn list for accepting colliers was used as the basic sales list by the factors at the Coal Exchange. As the Gas Companies did not require their coal to be metered, it was passed through the market at a nominal fee as soon as the ship arrived if discharging at berths, or at the end of the day if discharging to lighters. The other colliers moved to lie in the collier tiers at Greenwich, Blackwall, Bugsby's Reach or that in the Pool of London itself. When the cargo was sold the vessel moved to a discharging berth or had lighters sent alongside to receive the cargo.

Because of the congestion, the Port Committee, as early as 1825, resolved that no more than 250 vessels were to lie in the Pool at one time and the Harbourmaster was to hoist a red flag at Blackwall to prevent colliers proceeding up the river. This control became more important as enclosed docks were built as the entrances needed to be clear of moored colliers. In the 1830s the flag-pole was in use at Greenwich. The work of the harbourmaster and the turn system were completely integrated by 1842 and collier tiers were arranged in seven sections between Blackwall and Northfleet, each berth indicated by a numbered pile. Colliers remained in the holding tiers pending sale of the cargo and the subsequent move to the Pool of London for discharge, which extended from London Bridge to Limehouse and had berths for 243 vessels.

During the 1840s the price of coal fell from 15 shillings per ton delivered at the loading staith to 7 shillings loaded on board ship and many of the small, less efficient collieries collapsed, but the lower price meant that more coal was used. In 1850 the collier dock was established at Poplar where coal could be discharged by hydraulic cranes to wagons of the North London Railway Company.

Improving the efficiency of coal discharge had been resisted by the coal whippers, gangs of men, engaged by the captain on arrival to discharge his vessel. They shovelled the coal into baskets and hauled it out of the ship's hold. The foreman of the gang then took charge of the basket and tipped it down a chute into a lighter alongside in most cases. About 1850 a portable steam-powered winch which was moved from ship to ship operated fairly successfully discharging up to 130 tons a day. Dock developments overtook the whippers and eliminated the lighters as hydraulic cranes were installed at Regents Canal Dock, Dudman's Dock, West India and Victoria Docks. With these discharging improvements already in use the stage was set for the introduction of steam colliers, the last link in the chain of coal supply to London to become mechanised by the use of steam power, for the collieries relied on steam to hoist the coal out of the mines and steam railways to carry it to the harbours. The hydraulic cranes used for discharge obtained their power from steam plant which supplied the water under pressure.

By 1850, the development of the screw steamer had advanced considerably from the first tentative steps of the previous decade which had seen the successful trials of the 239 ton Archimedes. She had been completed in 1839 for the Ship Propellor Company by Henry Wimshurst at Millwall. This company was established by Francis Smith who took out the first patent for a stern mounted propellor in 1836. Interest was initially aroused among the steam packet companies who were looking for a more economical vessel with better cargo capacity than paddle steamers. Though paddle steamers had been in widespread use for some 30 years they had never been able to overcome the disadvantages of their heavy machinery amidships taking up much of the prime cargo space. Their coal consumption also tended to be high so further space had to be given over to bunkers. The steam machinery was by now fairly reliable but the paddle wheels were easily damaged by floating debris. These disadvantages meant that even after 30 years of progress they were confined primarily to the passenger trades where reliable quick passages were more important than cost so that even by 1850 there were only 320 steam vessels in the home trade compared with 8830 sailing vessels.

Initially there were problems with the propellers which required study to determine the most efficient blade shape in order to obtain a smooth flow of water over the blades. This in turn meant work on the lines on the hull aft so that would assist the smooth flow of water to the propellor. Various experiments were made and Beattie patented the arrangement of the screw aft of the rudder which was found to reduce vibration problems which had been encountered with the rudder behind the propeller. Beattie's design also made possible the lifting of the screw (11) and allowed the vessel to revert to sail in favourable winds. However, this arrangement had two drawbacks, firstly the screw was very exposed and more prone to damage and this also applied to the rudder as It had to be below the propeller shaft. In this position it was difficult to make it of sufficient area and so screw steamers were built with the conventional arrangement of propellor opening in the stern frame and rudder aft of the propeller. This also improved steering as the rudder was now able to fully direct the flow of water from the propeller. A typical design of propeller in use in the 1850s is illustrated in Scott Russell's 'Treatise on Naval Architecture' (4). Research on propellor design has continued to the present day with the blade area tending to increase and the blade section becoming more and more complex.

Progress with screw steamers was rapid in the liner trades. This is clearly shown by a government survey carried out in 1852 of leading steam packet companies operating to and from the Thames. Their fleets contained 59 wood paddle steamers, 52 iron paddle steamers and 23 iron screw steamers. Iron was used for nearly all the newer vessels. While the General Steam Navigation Company continued its policy of operating paddle steamers, the General Screw Steam Shipping Company had been set up in London and their first screw vessel, **City of London**, was built at Blackwall in 1845. A small vessel, she was 118'6" long and could steam at about 7.5 knots, but had sufficient sails to increase this to 9 knots in favourable winds. By 1848 they had **Earl of Auckland** which was 150' in length and could maintain 9 knots by steam alone. In 1852 she was operating on their Rotterdam service.

During the 1840s experiments were carried out around Newcastle with iron screw vessels exclusively for the coal trade. Almost certainly the first iron screw steam collier was **Bedlington** of 1841 which was built for the Bedlington Coal Company. Their colliery lay West of Blyth Harbour, but was separated from it by land belonging to rival colliery owner, Sir Matthew W. Ridley of Blagdon and,

11. Hold water ballast steamer with lifting screw designed by Scott Russell; probably the **Imperial** *of 1854 (152.0' x 27.0' x 14.8'), 408 tons gross.*

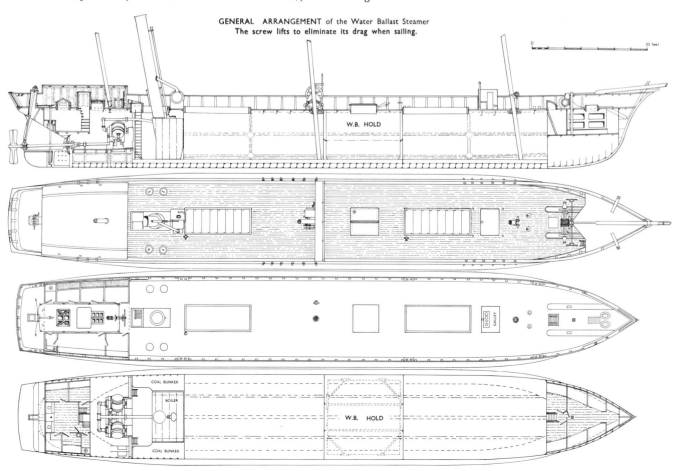

GENERAL ARRANGEMENT of the Water Ballast Steamer
The screw lifts to eliminate its drag when sailing.

not surprisingly, he would not allow them to build a wagon-way over his land to the harbour. The company at first used keels to carry their coal down to the harbour or round to the Tyne as they could reach the Bedlington Iron Works Jetty further up the River Blyth beyond Sir Matthew Ridley's land, though this was only possible at high tide and with favourable winds. As local coal sales were very limited the company had to develop access to the seaborne coal trade, especially the London market. The wind and tide problems were preventing this development and so the company were forced to try the radical approach which resulted in the special design of **Bedlington.**

Thus in March 1841 **Bedlington** was launched from Mr. T. D. Marshall's shipyard at South Shields An iron twin screw steamer of 214 registered tons, she had a 60 h.p. side lever engine which drove the screws via gearing. Steam was supplied by a boiler at the forward end of the vessel. This arrangement was adopted so that the vessel would be on an even keel when empty and so be able to navigate the shallows of the Blyth river more easily. The loading arrangements were very advanced for the time, the vessel having its own derrick to lift coal wagons directly from the quay on to the three lines of rails laid in the single large open hatchway. The coal was discharged into vessels in Blyth or South Shields harbour by hoisting the truck directly over the hatch of the waiting collier brig. The derrick was driven via a gear from the main crank shaft and while this was in use the propellers were disconnected. Water ballast tanks were incorporated in the design for the return voyage. Coal was taken for shipment in Shields Harbour as Blyth Harbour was unimproved at that time and the larger brigs could not load there.

The total cost of **Bedlington** appears to have been almost £5,000 and on arrival at Blyth she proceeded up river to load coal which she then carried down to **Agenoria** waiting at Blyth. Maintenance costs proved heavy with repairs frequent, but the company pressed on as it was their only link with the London market. The heavy maintenance work was the result of the vessel having to lie aground and the frequent groundings on the shoals in the river. Because of the shallow water the dimensions, particularly the depth, was restricted to 8'6" while the beam was 25 feet and the length 134 feet. Thus the hull could have very little depth to resist bending and iron was almost certainly adopted in an effort to overcome this problem. However, the 110 tons or so of coal and wagons still placed considerable loads on the hull, hence the regular need for new rivets, bolts and at times new plates. Repairs would have come under the watchful eye of Lloyd's surveyors who also supervised the building. Finally disaster struck in February 1846 when **Bedlington** grounded fully laden with coal and for practical purposes broke her back. The vessel was patched up and salvaged but apparently did no further work. Eventually she was sold in 1851 to Leith owners who had her towed there. The company was linked to Newcastle by rail in 1849 and so was able to use the loading facilities there.

No doubt the comings and goings of **Bedlington** had been observed by other owners and builders such as Mr. Coutts who had a shipyard at Walker capable of building in iron. **Q.E.D.**, an iron screw steamer, was completed in 1844 at the yard for Mr. Coutts own account and rigged as a barque. The engine of just 20 h.p. was probably enough to drive the vessel at about 5 knots on a calm day. The choice of name is interesting as Q.E.D. are the initials for 'quod erat demonstrandum' which was traditionally written at the end of mathematical proofs. The meaning translates as 'that which was to be demonstrated' and suggests that Coutts' associates may have suggested that he should put his ideas on iron steamers to the test, but on the stern was the motto 'Spes mea Christus' which translates as 'my hope in Christ'. **Q.E.D.** certainly made one coal carrying voyage to London as the 'Illustrated London News' of the 28th of September 1844 carried an account (9).

Shortly afterwards she was wrecked on the coast of France at the entrance to the River Seine. Her small engine would probably not have been able to overcome the wind resistance of masts, spars and rigging if the sails had carried away. She may well have been operating in the more profitable regular general cargo trade and carrying a few passengers as the description suggests she had been fitted out with this in mind. Screw steamer developments were continuing apace in this trade and the Cork S.S. Co., had their first screw steamer built at Cork in 1846 and were soon ordering more, but the largest vessels were those built by Malcolmson Brothers of Waterford. Their first screw steamer was **Neptune**, built at Waterford in 1847, 200 feet in length, 1,000 gross tons, and operated between London and St. Petersburg. No doubt those engaged in the coal trade had noted the good cargo capacity and the reliability of the screw steamers. It is also probable that coal had been carried in some of these steamers when there was insufficient work for them in the regular general cargo liner trade. In 1845 attempts were made to set up a steam collier company to carry coal from Sunderland to London and further colliers were built such as **Experiment** of 1845 and the iron **Conside** 259/47 which was tried on the trade.

Thus by 1850 the development of iron shipbuilding and advances in the screw propeller and suitable steam engines to drive it, opened the way for a successful steam collier to be built. Such a collier would also require equally efficient shore facilities for loading and discharge, so it was essential that the steamer was not kept waiting by the slow 'turn' system operated extensively in the Port of London, particularly for household coal. Vessels delivering to gas companies with their own wharves could avoid these delays. Charles Palmer, with his interests in collieries and shipping, would no doubt be aware of this, but first he needed a shipyard to build his iron ships and so it was that he founded Palmer Bros. & Company in 1851. On the 30th of June 1852 their second vessel was launched and named **John Bowes** just two months after the keel was laid. The launching was carried out by Mrs. C. K. Palmer and a bottle of red wine was used to christen the ship **John Bowes**, after the high sheriff of the county. John Bowes was a large coal owner and Charles Palmer held a share in John Bowes and Partners, and probably persuaded John Bowes to support the venture, the latter having some months previously agreed to Stephenson Clarke, a leading London coal factor, becoming his sole agent. Stephenson Clarke had strong contacts with the gas companies, for whom the ship would be suitable.

The vessel had the registered dimensions 148.9' x 25.7' x 15.6', 375 nett and 485 gross tons. The machinery was designed to give a speed of 9 knots but to occupy as little space as possible. This was achieved by fitting two simple (single cylinder) engines side by side geared to a single shaft. This worked well enough for a time but was replaced by a two cylinder simple engine with the cylinders in line, in 1864. This engine had about the same horse power (70 nominal) with each cylinder being 34 inches in diameter by 26 inches stroke. This new machinery, built by Thompson & Boyd (13), had no separate thrust block to absorb the push of the propeller, the crank shaft simply worked against a large collar on the after end of the bed-plate. The air pump for the condenser was at the front of the engine, low down under the forward end of the crank shaft.

She was rigged as a topsail schooner, but the sails were intended as an auxiliary and fuel-saving feature only. She was able to load 650 tons of coal and loading was greatly facilitated by a single hatch 60 feet long which allowed the coal to be loaded very easily into most parts of the hold directly from the coal chute just by moving the vessel along under the chute with very much less work needing to be done by hand, though coal trimmers were still needed to stow coal at the ends of the hatch and under the side decks. This was perhaps the most important feature of the design and also greatly facilitated discharge.

As might be expected there was considerable interest in her maiden voyage. She was fitted out and completed in less than a month and arrived in London on the 29th of July 1852, 48 hours after leaving the Tyne, with a full load of coal. The coal was discharged in 24 hours and she was back in the Tyne 48 hours later. So in less than a week **John Bowes** had done the work normally done by two brigs in a month but she had cost much more than two brigs at £10,000 but could offer customers a regular delivery of coal and not need to wait for the wind.

The first steam collier to be registered in London was probably **Haggerston**. She was entered on the register as belonging to the Port of London on the 30th of August 1852. Her registered particulars were 159.0' x 24.7' x 15.0', nett tonnage 329, gross 415, owner T. C. Gibson. Meanwhile, with tensions rising in Europe a Government committee was appointed to examine the state of merchant steamers with a view to arming them should the need arise. Though unimpressed with what they found they carried out detailed surveys of numerous steam vessels and recorded these particulars in their report. They examined **Haggerstone** (sic) which they noted was under the management of J. Gibson, shipowner of Gracechurch Street, London, trading between London and Newcastle and built in Liverpool in 1852. The dimensions they determined to be 163'0" by 25'3", 327 registered and 487 gross tons. They did not measure depth of hold, but noted that the loaded draught was 12'0" forward and 13'3" aft. They reported that **Haggerstone** "was a very strong built vessel with an inner bottom

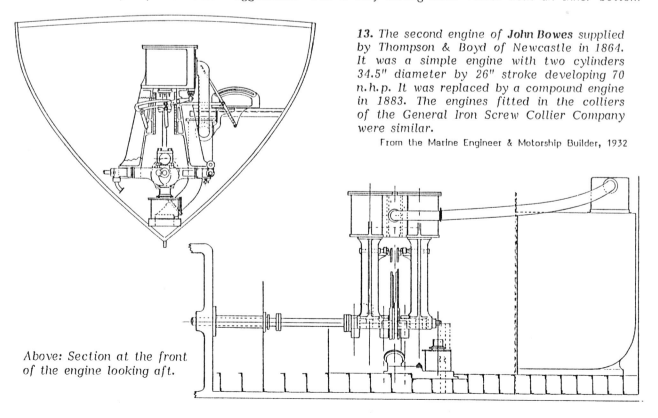

13. *The second engine of **John Bowes** supplied by Thompson & Boyd of Newcastle in 1864. It was a simple engine with two cylinders 34.5" diameter by 26" stroke developing 70 n.h.p. It was replaced by a compound engine in 1883. The engines fitted in the colliers of the General Iron Screw Collier Company were similar.*

From the Marine Engineer & Motorship Builder, 1932

Above: Section at the front of the engine looking aft.

divided into tanks containing 80 tons of water ballast when her cargo of 600 tons of coal is delivered". The ship was propelled by a 114 h.p. direct acting engine by James Watt & Co. which was below the single continuous deck, though the steam chest (or dome) of the boiler protruded above deck. Fuel consumption was stated by the owner to be 10 tons per day. The bunker capacity of 20 tons therefore gave two days steaming at the service speed of 8.5 knots and with sails set the speed could be increased to 10 knots. Thus under steam alone the range was about 400 nautical miles while the distance from London to Newcastle is about 316 nautical miles so **Haggerstone** could make the journey under steam alone and have some bunkers in hand should bad weather be met with. Haggerston was the name of one of the old Gas Light and Coke Company's plants in London and the vessel may well have been named after it as their business would have been of particular interest to a steam collier owner.

The next collier to be added to the port of London some four and a half months later was **Lady Berriedale** 393/52 (14). She was registered in the name of Prior with the dimensions 122.5' x 27.0' x 15.0', 262 registered and 393 gross tons. This is apparently the collier referred to in John Scott Russell's 'Treatise on Naval Architecture', published in 1864, though he records slightly different dimensions. The oscillating machinery and boiler was apparently more compact than **Haggerston's** and was easily accomodated below the single continuous main deck.

*14. Plans, believed to be of **Lady Berriedale** from Russell's 'Treatise on Naval Architecture'. The sail plan is stated to have been similar to **Eagle**, see page 7.*

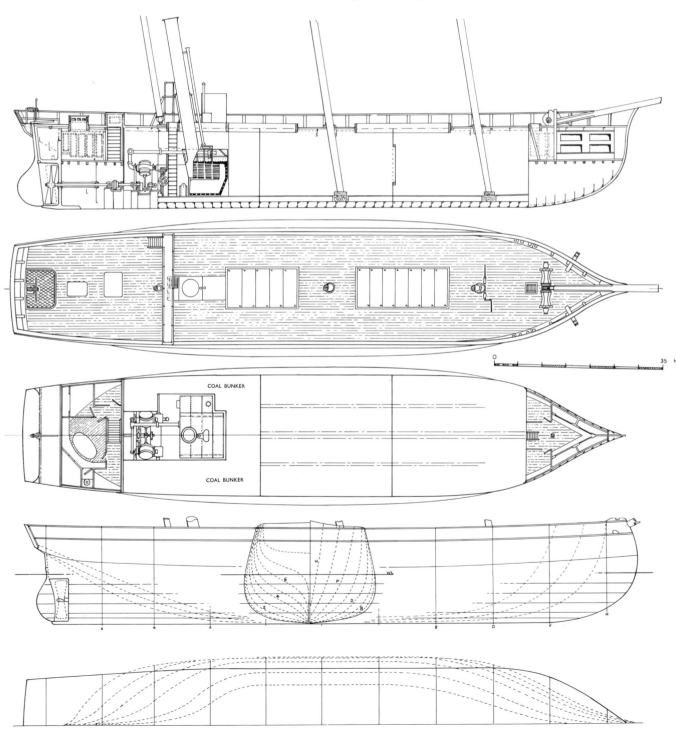

The arrangement of **Lady Berriedale** was typical of the earliest colliers. Though built largely of iron for strength and lightness, the layout still owes much to the collier brig in having a relatively deep draught and rather beamy form. The hull and frames up to deck level were completely of iron, but the deck and bulwarks were completely of wood, supported on iron deck beams. One of the early weaknesses of this arrangement was the contrast between the strong iron and the weaker flexible wood deck and bulwarks which rested on iron deck beams only. By this time builders had been alerted to this weakness by failures in earlier vessels. The top strake of plating could actually crack in a seaway and the topside plating was strengthened by iron angles or plates along the top of the iron deck beams (7a). The bottom construction was similar to later practice which indicates how good the design of iron hulls had become (7b).

Scott Russell states that the owners of the **Lady Berriedale** initially considered her rather long at 125 feet, though they were later happy to take a longer vessel, and that she was built after considering the following factors. Firstly, she must frequently take the ground and so need flat and easy floors (bottom). Secondly, she must be easy and stiff when under sail, light and not need any ballast. She must also be manageable under steam when empty with the weight of engine and boilers keeping rudder and propellor covered. He found that the depth of hold had to be limited or the coal cargo lay too deep in the hold and when full would leave too little freeboard for her to be 'wholesome and weatherley'. The depth of 10 feet contained engines, boilers and outfit and wastes no room, allowing her to be completely filled with coal. He felt that this resulted in rather ugly and unusual lines. He notes that the light displacement as 359 tons (empty weight of the ship) and with cargo and bunkers added (333 tons) the total weight fully laden was therefore 692 tons.

The vessel was registered in the name of J. Ricketts in 1855 and was still on the London register in 1862. She seems to have been fairly successful and was followed by **Eagle** which was registered on the 19th of July 1853 in the name of W. Gooch. The registered dimensions were 152.8' x 26.7' x 15.0' and 480 gross tons. Some 30 feet had been added to the 125 ft. design on the basis of the registered dimensions used by Russell. Lines, rig and equipment were all similar to the earlier vessel except a parallel sided midship section had been added. The machinery remained the same but the boiler tubes were increased from 270 to 288 which raised the heating surface area from 1125 to 1225 square feet and the grate surface of the furnace from 42 square feet to 50 square feet and engine speed was raised from about 85 to 90 r.p.m. Nonetheless the extra 100 tons of cargo this longer vessel could carry reduced the service speed from 9 to 8 knots. Several vessels were built to the design according to Russell and vessels appearing on the London register which fit the design included **Falcon** registered on the 14th December 1853 in the name of Russell and **Hawk** registered on the 7th of February 1854 in the joint names of Gooch and Russell. The names follow a theme, in this case birds of prey. Names with a theme were to be a feature of the new collier fleets.

Russell's success was completely overshadowed by that of Charles Palmer and his associates for they had set up one of the more significant shipping ventures of the decade under the guise of the General Iron Screw Collier Company. The directors included William Prinstep of the London Gas Company and Thomas Miers of the Commercial Gas Company. The new venture secured long term charters with the gas companies. The gas companies by this time were placing very large contracts with collieries, sometimes for as much as 100,000 tons at a time. It was a logical step forward for them to contract for a reliable means of delivery which steam colliers could provide. Palmer and his associates, from the experience gained with the **John Bowes**, were able to offer a very favourable low freight rate based on a slightly larger vessel carrying about 750 tons deadweight, but the demurrage was set at a high rate to ensure that the gas company discharged the vessel promptly as the profit in the venture depended on making as many voyages as possible in a year. The vessels were all given London registry and were built with great rapidity, financed from the company's capital which was set at £250,000. In just 18 months at least 10 vessels were completed. They were:

Date Registered	Name	Registered Dimensions	Nett Tonnage	Gross Tonnage
8.3.53	**William Hutt**	164.5' x 26.1' x 14.9'	425	530
25.6.53	**Northumberland**	163.2' x 26.2' x 15.3'	438	520
26.7.53	**Sir John Easthope**	163.6' x 26.1' x 15.3'	428	520
30.8.53	**Durham**	163.7' x 26.4' x 15.2'	428	531
14.11.53	**Jarrow**	164.0' x 26.4' x 15.2'	414	531
9.2.54	**Marley Hill**	164.3' x 26.4' x 15.0'	399	508
18.5.54	**Ross D. Mangles**	156.6' x 26.5' x 14.4'	430	531
3.6.54	**Nicholas Wood**	157.3' x 26.6' x 15.0'	430	530
28.8.54	**Black Prince**	157.0' x 25.7' x 14.0'	405	502
30.9.54	**Firefly**	157.2' x 25.7' x 14.1'	404	500

Extracted from Returns of Steam Vessels, 1855.

So progress of the steam collier had been phenomenal, in just two and a half years some 36 steam colliers had been completed and entered service, 23 of them in the period 1853-4 according to E. E. Allen who presented a paper to the Institute of Civil Engineers in February 1855. Such a large building programme, particularly that of the General Iron Screw Collier Company, represented a major financial and technical undertaking for the period. The colliers in service by 1855 were using several different ballasting methods and Allen commented on these as well as operating costs in his paper. He also calculated that during 1853 about 70,408 tons of coal was brought to London by 13 steam colliers which made 123 voyages bringing an average cargo of 572 tons. By the end of 1854 the figures were even more impressive: 202,607 tons in 348 voyages. He noted from these figures that sailing vessels made about 10 voyages per year while screw colliers were making 30 and could be expected to make as many as 36 provided no delays in the form of a 'turn' system was placed in their way. For return voyages some form of ballast was generally considered necessary. Though water ballast had been used in the earliest vessels, owners did not look kindly on ships which had space wasted in the form of ballast tanks or on the extra cost and weight of the material used in them. Some accounts suggest that **John Bowes** was built without ballast tanks and that initially some chalk ballast was loaded for the return voyage as was normal practice in the collier brigs. This was found time consuming both to load and discharge. The accounts suggest that barrels were loaded and filled with water to save time, but these had to be emptied and removed from the hold and then the water pumped out. At the suggestion of Mr. McIntyre, manager of Palmer Brothers' yard, permanent ballast tanks were fitted in the bottom of the hold and in the aft peak. Perhaps this rebuilding is reflected by the vessel being re-registered in Charles Palmer's name on the first of October 1853. At this time **John Bowes** probably came under the management of James Hall who had been associated with Palmer, Beckwith & Co., from 1841 and was the managing partner in the partnership he and his brother John Hall had formed with Charles Palmer.

The tanks fitted to **John Bowes** soon became known as McIntyre Tanks after the inventor. Essentially he laid a number of longitudinal plate keelsons on top of the existing frames and then plated the area over. An aft peak tank was fitted to improve screw immersion. The vessels built by Palmer Brothers for the General Iron Screw Collier Company were built with ballast tanks, though of slightly different form. However, it was then a short step to the double bottom in which the frame and keelsons were made the same depth and combined rather than being placed one above the other as in the McIntyre tank. The double bottom form of construction was being widely advocated by Graham and Croome and was tried by the General Iron Screw Collier Company beginning with **Black Prince** and **Firefly**, below.

Though this system worked very well and also contributed to the vessel's strength, Scott Russell was among those reluctant to accept the loss of cargo space they represented. Dr. D. B. White had proposed fitting collapsible water bags of tarred canvas in the bottom of the holds. His system was tried out in the sailing collier **Temperance** trading between Maryport and Belfast. Scott Russell adapted this for his colliers **Eagle**, **Falcon** and **Hawk**. The arrangement gave them 108 tons of ballast and when empty they lay along the bottom of the hold protected from the coal cargo by a timber covering. However, the bags were easily damaged and leaks were frequent and led to them being abandoned. Theoretically it would have been ideal as it did not permanently reduce the cargo capacity. Scott Russell tried another approach in the form of the water-ballast hold (11). The plan of the steamer shown with this arrangement, published in his book of 1864 may probably represent **Imperial** which was registered in his name in 1854 and had dimensions which fit the plan. The arrangement would appear to be the answer but in practice with the tank placed amidships, strain on the bulkheads and at the junction with the hull, especially when the ship was in ballast probably caused leakage problems. The "hold" type of tank was abandoned but various transverse tanks were often fitted in the area below the bridge of later ships to simplify coal trimming. So the permanent bottom tank remained as the only solution and was steadily improved upon for the next 100 years.

In retrospect it can be seen that Palmer Brothers' shipyard had produced a durable as well as practical design. The **John Bowes** was to continue in service for many years. She was sold to B.G. Barnett (later Barnett Brothers) of London in 1873 and remained with them until 1896. They even felt it was worth fitting a more modern two cylinder compound and boiler in 1883. She passed to John Mackenzie of Dublin, who resold her in 1897 to C.H. Pile of London, who was a ship sale and purchase broker. He soon found a Scandinavian owner for her. Later she continued under the Spanish flag until November 1933 when she sprang a leak in a gale while carrying a cargo of iron ore, and sank shortly afterwards. She was 81 years old.

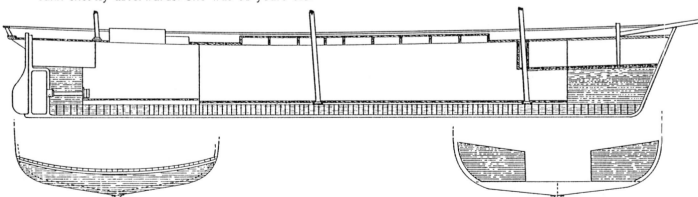

16. *Above and left, the double bottom and fore and aft peak ballast tank arrangement used in the General Iron Screw Comnpany's* **Black Prince** *and* **Firefly**. *The section, lower right, shows the partial tank to aid trimming of coal which was tried in the* **Chester** *and* **Tyne** *by the General Iron Screw Collier Company. From E. E. Allen's paper of 1855.*

Interestingly enough Allen in his 1855 paper, read to the Institute of Civil Engineers, looks upon **Northumberland**, completed in June 1853 with the dimensions 160' x 26' x 16.5' and a draught of 13 feet, as the first truly viable collier. She was fitted with a two cylinder engine 34" in diameter by 26" stroke using steam at 12 lbs. per square inch. This engine developed 120 nominal horsepower at 66 r.p.m. Allen probably selected this vessel as she would have incorporated the lessons learned from **John Bowes** and **William Hutt**.

It was not just London and Newcastle who were investing in early steam colliers. **Hunwick** was registered at Hartlepool in the name of Ralph W. Jackson on the first of March 1854. The dimensions recorded for **Hunwick** were 139.5' x 24.6' x 15.0', 334 nett, 409 gross tons. The deadweight was stated to be 480 tons by Allen in his paper and he felt the trials of this vessel and of the smaller **Lady Berriedale** were not very conclusive. However Mr. Jackson seems to have been satisfied as he added two further screw steamers to his fleet in 1854. Jackson was Chairman of the West Hartlepool Harbour and Railway Company and was keen to promote coal shipment from the expanding dock and railway system, but soon turned his attention to operating general cargo services to the continent.

The Lambton collieries were also among the pioneers and had been brought to prominence by John George Lambton who was created Earl of Durham in 1833. The second Earl continued to develop collieries which operated as part of the Lambton Estate. It was Henry Morton, the Lambton Estate Agent, who suggested the move into steam so that they could deliver their coal more efficiently to the London market and quote prices for regular contracts including delivery to London, as they were major suppliers of gas coals. **Lady Alice Lambton** was the result, registered at Wisbech on the 5th of April 1853 in the name of the Earl of Durham. Dimensions registered were 158.8' x 17.1' x 15.1', 429 nett, 572 gross. They were obviously pleased with the results from her, as a second vessel, **Earl of Durham**, was registered in the joint names of Morton and Lambton at Sunderland on the 13th of December 1854 with the dimensions 162.9' x 28.0' x 16.4'. This appears to have been considered the optimum size for the period and it is interesting to note that Nicholas Wood registered two steam colliers a few days later of a similar size. They were **Cochrane** and **Black Boy**.

Most of the early colliers were of engines-aft design, but **Lambton**, built by C. Mitchell and Co. of Newcastle, for the Earl of Durham's fleet had engines amidships (4). By this time Mitchell's yard was also building colliers for foreign trade such as **Helios**, built for the Hamburg Gas Company (4). Other ports were also setting up their own collier fleets and the Union Steam Collier Co., registered 7th of October 1853, was formed in Southampton. By the end of 1854 they had three colliers. The aim of the company was to ensure a regular supply of Welsh bunker coal to Southampton. The Crimean war and the consequent increased demand for steamers led the company into the liner trades, leading to the formation of the Union S.S. Co., which later merged with Castle Line to form Union Castle, famous for its South African services.

The tendency for early colliers to be quickly lost to the liner trade was lamented by Scott Russell at the time, as he felt they did not remain on regular coal runs long enough to obtain a clear idea of how reliably they could operate. But, of course, they were well built vessels and owners placed them in the most profitable trades they could find. For example, **John Bowes** was taken up to assist with laying a telegraph cable between Dover and Ostend in 1853. **Collier** herself, completed in January 1849 (8) and though presumably intended for the coal trade, after changing principal owners a number of times in her early years, even made a voyage to Australia in 1855, but was subsequently used by H. P. Maples for the Newhaven to Dieppe service he operated in association with the London, Brighton and South Coast Railway and was apparently fitted with some passenger accommodation by this time. She was lengthened 32.7 feet in 1857 and by 1861 was back registered in Glasgow.

One further experiment was **Connector** of 1863. The proposal was for the bow and fore hatch to be detachable from the midship section which also had a hatch, the machinery in the stern and bunkers made up the third section. The arrangement was intended to facilitate loading and discharge of part cargoes at different wharves, but does not seem to have proved very practical.

Although sails were considered auxiliary they were still an important feature of the design. In his treatise on sail-making of 1866, Robert Kipping describes the types of sail that were fitted to these early steam colliers. They were commonly rigged with three light masts. The foremast generally had a fore-topmast and topgallant mast made in one piece while the main and mizzen masts were often one piece pole masts. The rig was usually completed by a short bowsprit sometimes with a jib-boom. The bowsprit was rigged like that of a schooner and had a fore-staysail and jib, and sometimes a larger outer jib for fine light winds. The masts were supported by wire shrouds and stays. There were four shrouds on the main and foremast, while the mizzen had three shrouds on each side. A few vessels had two shrouds less per mast.

The yards on the foremast were usually square and lightly made for carrying a square sail, set flying, a topsail, and sometimes a topgallant sail. **Eagle** and **John Bowes** show the usual arrangement. Some vessels also had lower and topmast studding sails. The fore-and-aft sails were as large as could be easily worked and lowered down, and if they were left up did not cause too much obstruction if steaming head to wind.

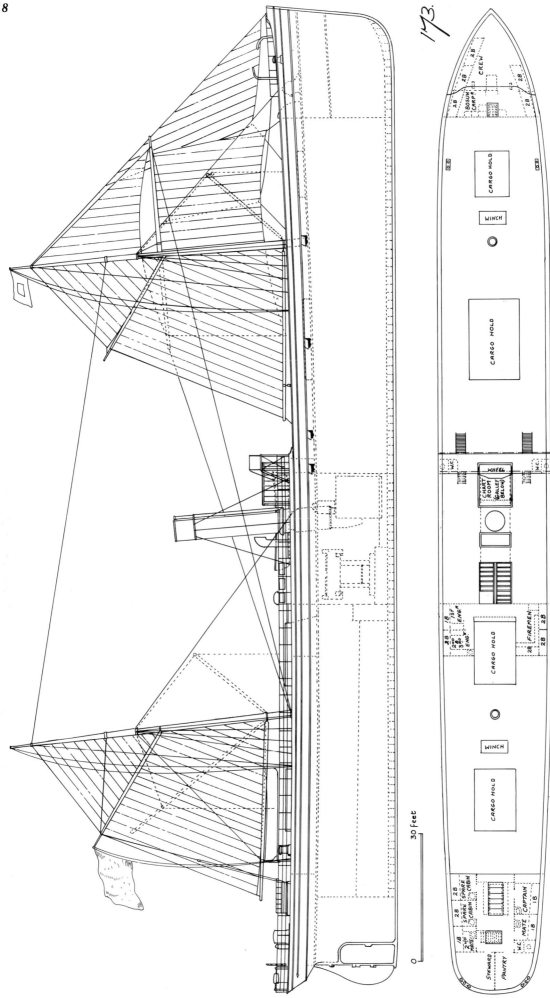

30 feet

18. Hugh Taylor built by C. Mitchell of Newcastle for the Taylor's coal trade. She is an example of one of the early well deck steamers: Built 1869 with the dimensions 224.5' x 29.2' x 17.6'. Courtesy Tyne & Wear Museums

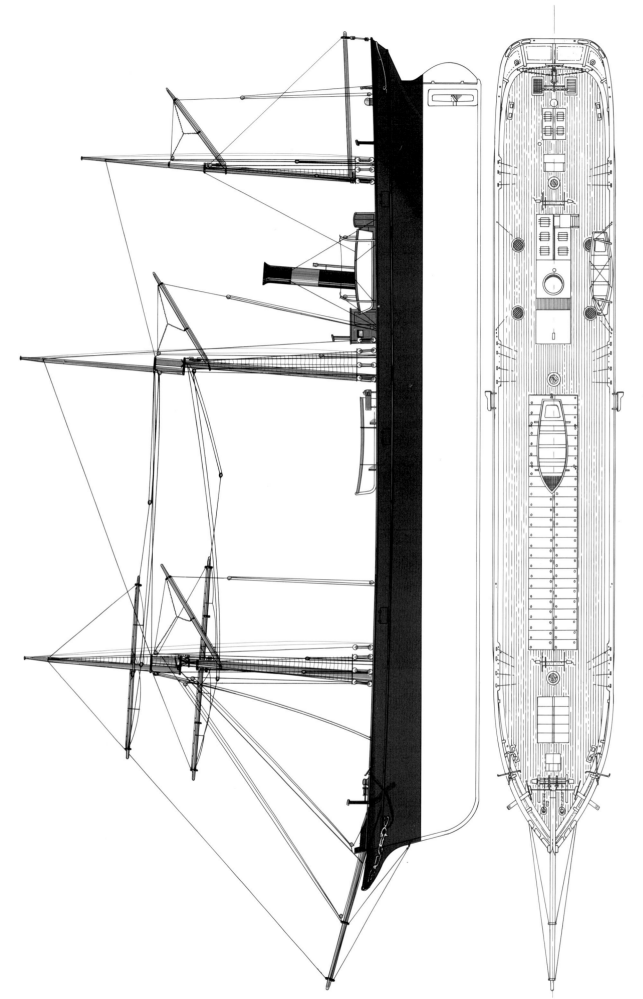

19. John Bowes, (148.9' x 25.7' x 15.6'), was built in 1852 by Palmer Brothers of Newcastle. Drawing from a model in the Science Museum, Newcastle.

19

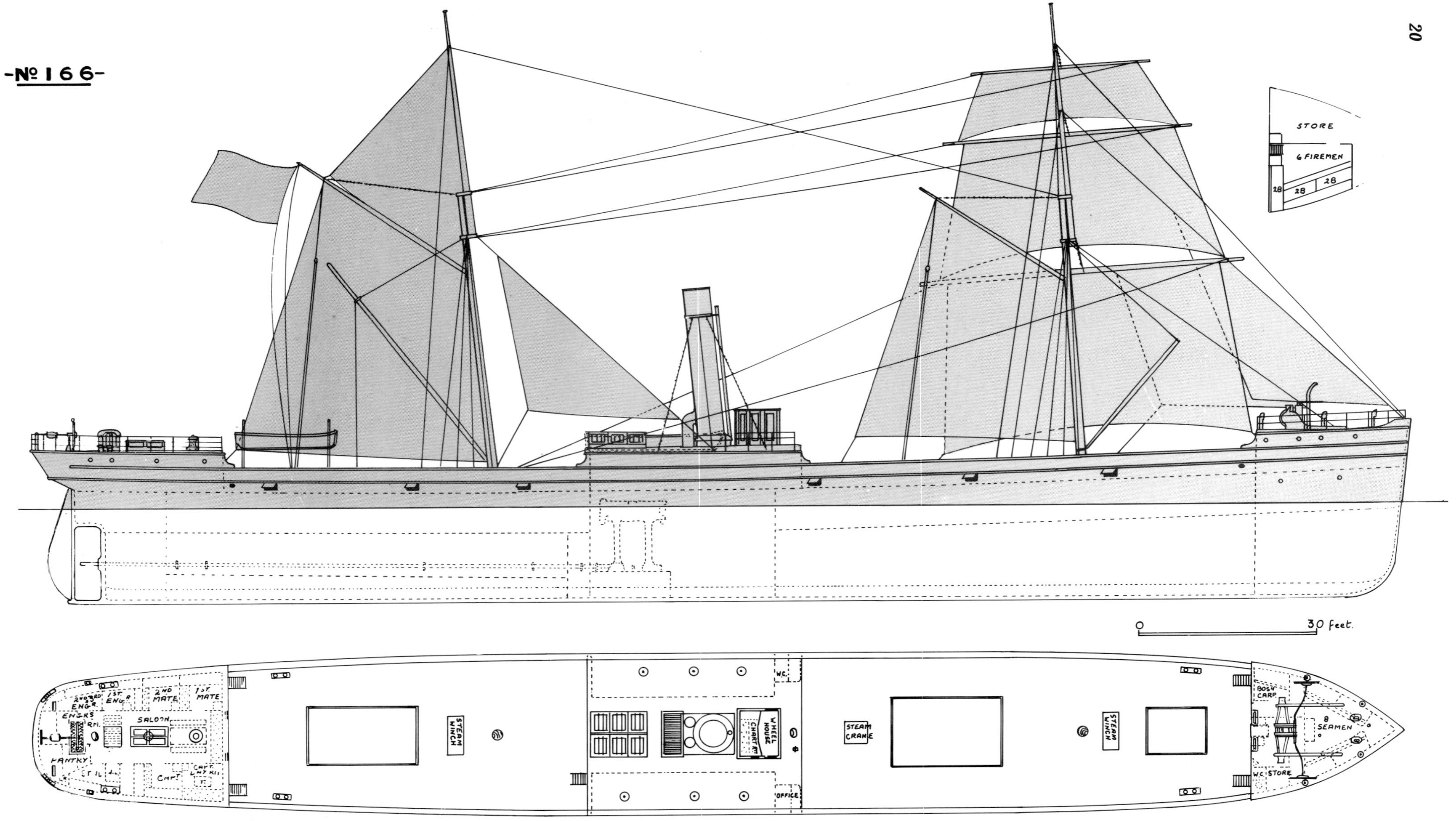

-№ 166-

STORE

6 FIREMEN

28

28 28

30 Feet.

BOSN
CARP

8
SEAMEN

WC
STORE

STEAM
WINCH

STEAM
CRANE

WC

WHEEL
HOUSE

CHART RM

OFFICE

STEAM
WINCH

1ST
MATE

2ND MATE

2ND/1ST
ENGR

SALOON

3RD
ENGR

CAPTAIN

CHIEF

PANTRY

GALLEY

20. Fenham, built in 1868 by C. Mitchell of Newcastle. She is of almost the same dimensions as **Hugh Taylor,** but of the earlier flush deck design and with a more extensive sail plan suggesting longer voyages to the Baltic or Mediterranean were to be undertaken.

Courtesy Tyne & Wear Museums

2.

21. France, Fenwick collier at Dunston Staiths circa 1925.
MacRae collection

New Harbours & Fleets on the East Coast

It was soon evident that if steam colliers were to achieve their full potential then harbours and loading facilities would need to show the same degree of improvement as the steam collier was to the collier brig. The main developments took place in the latter half of the 19th century hand in hand with the growth of the local collier fleets. One of the first of the truly mechanised coal drops was at Wallsend. The loaded chaldron truck ran out on to the platform and was then lowered down to the ship's deck by gravity controlled by a cleverly arranged weight and pulley. A man, whose job it was to "unhasp" the bottom door of the truck, travelled down with it. The system was invented by one William Chapman of Newcastle who patented it in 1800. His invention was ignored for fourteen years, until a 'drop' was built and successfully operated at Coxlodge Colliery, (27). From then on designs steadily improved (35). Within a few short years every creek, river, estuary and dock, large or small, in or near the great Northern coalfields, had coal handling appliances built or building. In the North East the massive and imposing timber staiths predominated. Every port from Amble to Hartlepool had these high wooden structures, with their gravity spouts augmented in the 20th century by electrically driven belts, often for use when loading deep water ships that were too high for the gravity spouts when the tide was in.

The Tyne

Railways were well developed in the Tyne area by the time the steam collier appeared in the river and so the delivery of coal to the riverside was quite efficient, but the problem began when the river was reached. There was no dredged channel and the rivermouth sandbar had only about six feet of water over it at low water; many vessels were forced to wait in Shields Harbour for a favourable tide and wind. Improvements were not begun until 1861 following the report of the Royal Commission of 1855. The usual method of loading had been to fill keels at the staith which then carried the coal to the waiting ships. Keels had been in use for centuries for this work on the Tyne. Initially they had belonged to the collieries and a Chief Keelman was placed in charge of delivering the coal, which had been sold to the shipmaster, to his ship. By the 19th century, independent keel owners provided the keels but arrangements for delivery were now in the hands of factors or fitters who acted as colliery agents, selling the coal produced and they usually owned the keels. They employed the keelmen on a yearly bond. Keels by the 19th century were built to contain a little over 21 tons and were officially marked with a load line corresponding to this amount. In time the capacity related to the number of wagon loads of coal they could accept measured in chaldrons. They were broad beamed flat bottomed boats with a simple squaresail. They carried the coal downstream to the waiting collier brigs which generally lay in Shields Harbour, where there was often considerable congestion. Newcastle had a low bridge so keels had to be used to bring coal down from pits situated west of the bridge, but below the bridge improvements were made to the staiths nearer the river mouth so they could load coal directly into colliers.

Initially the coal was taken to the nearest staith partly because land transport, especially on the wagonways using horse haulage, was expensive compared with water transport. When the wagonways were converted to steam haulage the cost was reduced. As these railways merged and expanded more distant transport was possible directly to staiths built for, or adapted to accept ships which, even in the 1860s were still largely sailing ships. Apart from better accessibility to ships, a further natural advantage which the staiths nearer the river mouth benefited from was the high ground close to the river. This meant that the coal trains or wagons arrived at a height suitable for tipping their loads down shoots and only short elevated sections had to be built to connect the riverside staith to the railway. By the 1860s railway transport to the downriver staiths had virtually eliminated the keels. The keelmen put up strong resistance to this loss of employment and on at least one occasion burnt down one of the new wooden staiths. Their strong resistance delayed staith development for a time. The formation of powerful railway groups led to them promoting lines to staiths in order to increase their business and then to the building of railway financed staiths.

The impetus for docks came from the Tyne Improvement Commission which was the result of the River Tyne Improvement Act of 1850. The Commissioners took over responsibility for the river from Newcastle Corporation. The Commissioners were made up of shipowners, coalowners and merchants together with members representing the Corporations of Newcastle, Gateshead, Tynemouth, South Shields, Jarrow and Wallsend. One of their first tasks was to obtain Parliamentary approval in 1852 to build the massive north and south masonry piers to protect the harbour mouth, and prevent the drift of shoreline sand across the entrance. The North pier was just under 3,000 feet in length while the South pier was just under a mile. The large enclosed water area gave the river a fine protected approach. The construction of the Tyne piers was formally completed in 1895, though the North Pier was breached in 1897 and the outer portion had to be reconstructed, work continuing until 1909.

The first enclosed dock where ships could load afloat was the Northumberland Dock, completed in 1857. Powers were obtained in 1852 for its construction and the dock was made enclosing a curve in the river by building a long pier across the curve and an entrance lock, see map (26). There were already several staiths at this point on the river many of which were served by lines of the North Eastern Railway and it was these staiths which were the reason for the dock. By the 1920s there were eight staiths in use. The Hartley Main Collieries owned three, the East Holywell Coal Co. Ltd one, and the remainder belonged to the London and North Eastern Railway Company. The maximum years shipment was 2,681,994 tons. The number of staiths and their owners varied over the years and prior to 1895 there were more inside the dock. An old chart of the period shows from west to east: Cramlington Coal Co. [1-3], North Eastern Railway [4-6], Seaton Burn Coal Co. [7], Seaton Delaval [8-9], Cramlington Coal Co. [10-11], North Eastern Railway [12-13], East Holywell Coal Co. [14]. The Cramlington Coal Co., also had a staith just beyond the west end of the dock, which was known as the Cramlington River Staith and was taken over by the Hartley Main Collieries Ltd. These berths were particularly used to ship the Northumberland steam coals around the world, but the North Durham coalfields to the south were not long in getting improved shipping facilities, and Tyne Dock on the south bank of the river was opened in 1859. This major undertaking was built by the North Eastern Railway Company. The southern end of the dock had four massive staiths capable of accepting 16 ships at one time. By the end of the 1920s some 313 million tons of coal had been shipped from the dock and the record for a day's shipment was almost 38,000 tons. There were 42 spouts in use allowing two or more to be used per vessel. The staiths were so designed that all movements of coal wagons were by gravity. The wagons themselves had bottom doors which allowed the coal to drop between the tracks and so slide down the spouts into the holds of the ships below.

As the Royal Commission of 1855 noted, the river was essentially in its natural state and very little re-alignment of the banks or dredging had been done even though the shipping had steadily increased. However, with the completion of the docks, river improvement was imperative and in 1861 a comprehensive scheme was embodied in a Bill which was passed by Parliament that year. By 1865 depth at low water over the bar was 15 feet and ten years later there was a depth of 20 feet from the mouth to Newcastle. Work continued so that there was 25 feet at Derwenthaugh some 14 miles inland and 30 feet to Northumberland Dock prior to WWI. All this dredging was possible because the river bed was of sands and clays which could easily be excavated. By 1929 the Commission had dredged some 156 million tons from the river and dumped it out in the North Sea. To this the collier brigs probably added considerable amounts of ballast quietly dumped over the side to save discharging time at the ballast quays. This source of silting was eliminated with the coming of steamers as they were fitted with water ballast tanks.

Collieries and coal shipments continued to develop and with this the demand for further coal staiths. Whitehall Point staiths Nos. 1 and 2 were opened in 1874 by the Tyne Improvement Commission on the north bank of the river and primarily for large vessels either wishing to load coal as cargo or bunkers, or coke without entering the docks. Further staiths, Nos. 3 and 4, were opened in 1891 and No.5 in 1904. The latter was destroyed by fire the following year and was not re-opened until 1908. Hydraulic lifts taking 20 ton wagons well above staith level enabled coaling to proceed of large steamers even when high out of the water, on the highest tides. All had electric coal conveyors installed and additionally an anti-coal breakage device was installed at No.5 staith. Two berths were also available in Albert Edward Dock, though this dock was mainly used for the general export and import trade.

Apart from the coal export trade the Tyne had developed some of its imports and gained part of its character from the bunkering trade. It was a distinctive feature of the Tyne coal trade and as a bunkering port the River Tyne had many competitors, but few rivals. As the coal trade expanded so did the bunkering trade as many vessels bunkered for the round trip back to the Tyne. The trade was also assisted by the fact that the Tyne became an important harbour of refuge with the completion

23a. Broomhill built in 1878 by T. Wingate & Co., Glasgow, measured 174.7' x 29.0' x 10.4'
She is shown in the colours of Broomhill Collieries entering the harbour at Warkworth.

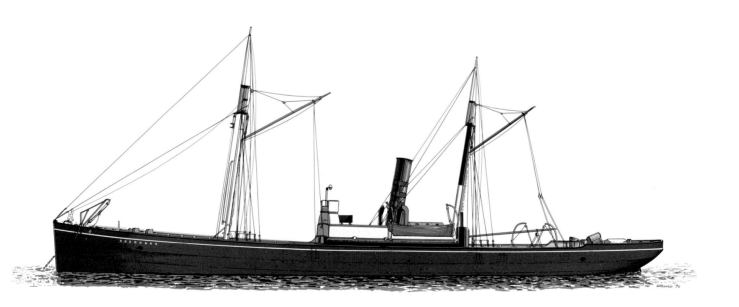

23b. Sherburn (187.0' x 28.9' x 16.7') of 1866 alongside Lambton Drops. She belonged to
H. T. Morton & Co., who managed the Earl of Durham's colliers and carried the Lambton
funnel colours.

of the Tyne piers. Thus vessels which made for the port in stress of weather often needed to bunker and this was generally the case when visiting the Tyne for repairs. Tyne steam coals were exported for bunkering purposes, particularly to the Baltic and nearby continent where, because of the longer shipping distance, South Wales bunkers tended to be more expensive.

An important feature in the development of the Tyneside coal trade was that facilities for shipping coal were provided at points on the river most convenient to the collieries thus allowing the shortest possible railway haul from pit to shipping point. This was an important factor in turn-round of wagons and loading costs. For example, prior to 1893, collieries in west and central Durham had to send their coals to Tyne Dock by a circuitous route which was expensive since part of the line was single track. Loading of steam colliers at staiths beyond Newcastle had become possible when the old low stone bridge was demolished and replaced with a swing bridge in 1876, and the river was soon dredged to a depth of 25 feet suitable for large ships. What coal owners needed was direct access to the river. Eventually the North Eastern Railway obtained powers to construct a line from Annfield Plain to the Team Valley main line near Birtley and then a short line from there to Dunston (26).

The coal staiths at Dunston on Tyne were built by the North Eastern Railway between 1892 and 1896 to meet the growing output of those mines to the west of Newcastle. In common with most of the staiths on the East Coast, they were constructed almost wholly of wood. Work on the outer staith (facing the river) was started in January 1892 and in operation by 1893. The inner staiths were completed at a much later date. There were six berths at Dunston, three outside and three inside the basin. All had gravity spouts, and, in addition, the three outer berths were equipped with electrically driven conveyor belts. The berths were numbered, on the outside from the bottom berth upriver Nos.1&2, 3&4, 5&6; and on the inside they were 7&8, 9&10, 11&12. The riverside berths offered about 25 feet at low water and the inside berth about four feet less. The last of these was never very popular as the water ballast could not be pumped out until there was a substantial proportion of the cargo aboard, and the vessel down by the stern, with, of course, the vessel afloat. This was because the shoot could not be lowered enough for the coal to run into the hold at or near high water. It was at the lower western end of the staith and there was not always enough difference in height between the staith and ship for the coal to slide easily into the ship's hold.

Loading at Dunston was always fast, a record for one day's shipment being 25,139 tons, whilst a years tonnage amounted to a staggering 5.5 million tons. Almost all the ships loading at Dunston were either self or easy trimmers, meaning they had wide hatch coamings with narrow decks on either side, fore and aft. In 1962 there were approximately 2,700 ships who, when they loaded in Britain, were classed as self or easy trimmers. It was important for a collier to be on this approved list in order to avoid higher trimming charges. More often than not, all that was required of the trimmers was that they levelled off the coal in each hold so that the hatches could be closed and the ship made ready for sea. There were times when extremely hard work had to be put in trimming out awkward and hard to handle cargoes of coke and large coal. The ship's bunkers, if she was a coal burner, sometimes presented difficulties which caused a lot of hard and dirty work, for the designers often seemed to have put the bunkers in an awkward spot.

Inside the basin at Dunston there were four lay-by berths at the dolphins, each capable of accommodating at least two and sometimes four ships awaiting loading turns. There were more buoys outside in the river, where ships could lie safely, these having been provided by the River Authority after the shippers at Dunston had threatened to send no more ships to Dunston on and after the 1st June 1894, until some arrangements were made for the provision of Mooring Buoys. The buoys referred to were not very convenient for crew members wanting to go ashore, for there were few safe landing places in the vicinity, and it had been known for over 90 ships to be waiting for berths.

The crews of these ships, if they were British, and hailed from the North East Coast, were generally on what was known as the Watch Aboard Watch Ashore system. In effect, it ensured, in theory at least, that there were always enough hands available to shift the ship wherever necessary, load her and prepare her for sea. This was essential as loading could be a very spasmodic affair in later times, the coal coming down in dribs and drabs from each of the fifty or so collieries that served the staiths. Often ships were warped or towed into a berth, loaded with 500 tons of their cargo, all that was available at the time, and returned to their lay-by berths in a day. There were at least three tugs, one each from Lawson & Batey; Ridley's; and France Fenwick's more or less permanently stationed at Dunston, returning to South Shields only over the weekend, being back ready for work early Monday morning. There were other small tugs available, including one belonging to a man named Nelson.

H.M. Customs were very much in evidence, for many of the ships coming to load were foreigners from the continent or even further afield. The Customs Office was a large brick building at the head of the basin which had been manned night and day during the busy years. There had been three launches stationed at Dunston, which also attended to newly arrived ships at the C.W.S. Flour Mills, West Dunston and Derwenthaugh staiths, as well as to any smaller craft going to some of the little berths further up the river. Reading through a list of the mines who supplied Dunston loading ships with their coal is mining history. The names have a poetic ring about them; Holmeside, Annfield Plain; Townley; North Walbottle; Addison; Stargate; Ryton Emma; Chopwell; are but a few of the many who sent coal to Dunston.

The six loading berths at Dunston were, by 1911-12 becoming overtaxed with the vast increase in coal shipments from 1,300,000 tons in 1894 to 3,523,000 in 1911. Permission to build additional staithing at West Dunston was sought and obtained with little trouble, and construction was well on its way to completion when the outbreak of the first world war brought it to a halt. At the conclusion of hostilities there was still considerable export and coastwise trade, justifying completion of the staiths, and they were officially opened on Monday 12th November 1923, demonstrating their efficiency by shipping nearly 34,000 tons in the first week. In addition to the usual gravity spouts (21), each of the three berths were fitted with electrically operated belt conveyors, which enabled the coal to be carried to much greater heights for delivery into the holds of bigger ships, thus obviating the delays caused by high tides when the slope of the gravity shoots was insufficient.

The coal was delivered to the loading points in bottom opening trucks, dropping on to the belt through a hopper, the supply being regulated by means of a steel door controlled from the deck of the staith. The construction of the shoot was unique in at least one respect. It was capable of being slewed eight feet either side of the centre line, thus reducing the number of times the ships had to be shifted in the berths. Anti-breakage devices were not available and the staiths were used less and less as coal shipments declined, the local mines being worked out and abandoned. They were finally closed in 1934, and demolished in 1936.

The most easterly of the main staiths were those at Derwenthaugh, on the south bank of the River Tyne about a mile below the Scotswood Bridge. They were built by the Consett Iron and Coal Company in 1893. There were two berths, one at the original wooden staiths and the other at the newer reinforced concrete staiths just east of the wooden one. Each was capable of loading at about 500-600 tons per hour, and during the heyday of the coal exports they were kept fully employed. It was a costly business keeping the channel to these berths dredged and when finally it became apparent that coal shipments were soon to be drastically curtailed, the T.I.C. shortened the life of the staiths by allowing the river to silt up again. The staiths were finally closed in 1960.

In addition to the large staiths mainly built by the Tyne Improvement Commission and the Railways, there were private staiths. There were smaller and fairly efficient staiths at Benwell and Elswick which because of their size and the limited depth of water available handled coastal colliers. There were various other staiths over the years, mainly belonging to coal companies and often connected directly to the colliery by their own private railway. Those in use in 1933 are noted on the map (26,27).

Speed of loading was often achieved by long working hours in the 1920s, usually from 6 a.m. to 10 p.m. on weekdays, with overtime to midnight if required. Saturday it was 6 a.m. to 12 o'clock noon, but extensions were available to 10 p.m. if necessary to complete loading and obviate the vessel being detained in port over the weekend. Continuous loading day and night was available at the main staiths of Tyne Dock, Dunston and Derwenthaugh. In addition to coal, coke shipments were also made, produced from the Durham coking coals. Various brands were produced and shipped to a variety of destinations, particularly to Germany, Belgium and France. Over one million tons were shipped for the first time in 1923.

Shipments from the Tyne tended to slump for a few years after 1923, but by 1929 had risen again to just under 20 million tons, a figure first reached in 1911. The main growth in the trade had taken place with the improvements of the 19th century, growing rapidly from an average of 4 million tons in the 1850s to about 17 million tons by the 1900s. Most of the growth was in exports in large ships so that in the peak year of 1923 only 3.3 million tons was carried by coastwise colliers. Most of the remainder was exported in short sea traders with almost half going to France and Germany in peak years, which had always been important markets. Exports to Scandinavia, Holland, Belgium, Spain and Italy varying more widely, especially after the First World War.

To maintain the trade more modern berths were built. Howdon Staith, with a riverside jetty over 900 feet long was opened in 1932. It had two berths and was equipped with conveyors which delivered the coal to two towers which could travel sideways and so obviate the need to shift the vessel loading, as had to be done with the old gravity spouts. Each tower was capable of loading 500 tons per hour. A similar arrangement was fitted to the Jarrow Staith, opened in 1936, which had three radial shipping towers for loading the coal.

Early Newcastle Shipowners and Ships

Some of the records of ships entering the Northumberland Dock have survived and for the period 19th August 1869 to the 28th November 1873 about half the 50 or so Newcastle registered cargo steamers loaded coal there, mostly for London or the south coast. By this time the size had increased to between 190 and 225 feet in length and about 28 feet breadth. The depth of hold was 15 to 17 feet which broadly corresponds with draught. The **John Bowes**, still owned by Charles Palmer, was thus one of the smallest vessels engaged by this time and the oldest. The next oldest was the 195 feet long **Carbon** dating from 1855 and owned by T. & G. Hedley who had coal interests and were also soap manufacturers. In general the pattern of ownership is very complex with each ship being divided into 64 shares as had been laid down by Parliament so each ship was in effect a separate shipping venture. Nearly all the shareholders in the Newcastle registered vessels were the leading coal owners, fitters (colliery agents), merchants and shipbuilders, with few shares held outside the Newcastle district or London. The London shares tended to be held by merchants or factors who would

MAP OF THE RIVER TYNE

SHEWING THE
COAL STAITHS ETC.

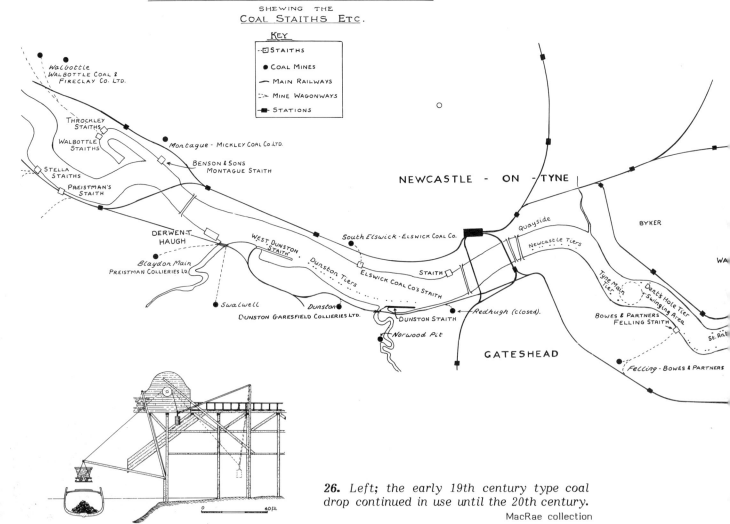

KEY
- ◫ STAITHS
- ● COAL MINES
- ━ MAIN RAILWAYS
- ⋯ MINE WAGONWAYS
- ■ STATIONS

Walbottle
WALBOTTLE COAL &
FIRECLAY CO. LTD.

THROCKLEY
STAITHS

WALBOTTLE
STAITHS

STELLA
STAITHS

PREISTMAN'S
STAITH

Montague - MICKLEY COAL CO. LTD.

BENSON & SONS
MONTAGUE STAITH

NEWCASTLE - ON - TYNE

BYKER

DERWENT
HAUGH

WEST DUNSTON
STAITH

South Elswick - ELSWICK COAL CO.

Quayside

Newcastle Tiers

Dunston Tiers

Elswick Coal Co's Staith

STAITH

Blaydon Main
PREISTMAN COLLIERIES LD.

Swalwell

Dunston

DUNSTON GARESFIELD COLLIERIES LTD.

Norwood Pit

Dunston Staith

Redhugh (closed).

GATESHEAD

Tyne Main Tier

Dent's Hole Tier
Swinging Area

BOWES & PARTNERS
FELLING STAITH

St. Ant

Felling - BOWES & PARTNERS

26. *Left; the early 19th century type coal drop continued in use until the 20th century.*
MacRae collection

be receiving the cargoes, especially in the case of the six colliers associated with Cory and Fenwick. J. & E. Joicey, the big coal owners and fitters, held some shares in all the colliers with which Cory and the Fenwicks were involved, and that probably accounts for **Beckton** 857/69, **Magna Carta** 764/65, **New Pelton** 630/65, and **Northumbria** 856/69 (29) being registered in Newcastle, particularly **New Pelton** in which they owned half the shares and was named after one of their collieries. However **Mary Nixon** 758/65 was named after a member of J. Nixon's family who owned collieries in South Wales.

The biggest owning group was headed by T. E. Smith who was a local M.P. and President of the North Shields and Tynemouth Chamber of Commerce, with G. Luckley and J. Southern of London. They were equal partners in **Wynyard** 528/70, **Wentworth** 397/65, **Dudley** 825/65, **Bradley** 576/66 and **Black Swan** 650/64. The latter vessel sailed with coal for Hamburg on 23rd August 1869 from Northumberland Dock. **Wentworth** also loaded coal there for London in 1869. The vessels probably did some liner trading as T. & W. Smith were operating the Blue Cross Line to Italy in the 1870s. The name was taken from their funnel colours which were a blue "X" which extended from top to bottom of a white band on the funnel. The houseflag was the same blue saltire on a white flag. They held 16 of the shares in **Gosforth** 1064/66 which sailed with coal for London from Northumberland dock in February 1870. The other major shareholder was R. Gray [8] who had colliery interests at Blyth and it was placed under the management of Watts, Milburn and Co., of Newcastle and Blyth whose principals held 11 shares. The remaining shares were in the hands of smaller investors. The vessel was named after T. E. Smith's home, Gosforth House. The partners held 8 shares in **Claremont** 1023/66 with R. Gray of Blyth holding 8. There were several smaller holders, 3 of which were the coal fitters Robert Hindhaugh, R. Rowell and J. Middleton, E. N. Watts [6] and W. Milburn [4], acted as managers. Mr. Gray was also an important shareholder in **Fenham** 880/68. Turnbull's list of 1871 shows the shareholders were as follows: John Middleton [4], J. W. Richardson [4], J. Scott [4], T. Stokoe [3], R. Gray [8], E. H. Watts [4], H. F. Swan [8], T. Crawford [4], B. C. Crawford [4], J. Ormston jr. [4], W. Dobson [2], W. Tate [2] and W. Milburn [13]. Watts, Milburn & Co., probably acted as managers. H. F. Swan was a regular shareholder in Watts, Milburn managed vessels. R. Gray became the managing owner in 1872 when the vessel was registered in London. William Milburn at this time separated from E. H. Watts, both subsequently developing their interests in the ocean trade.

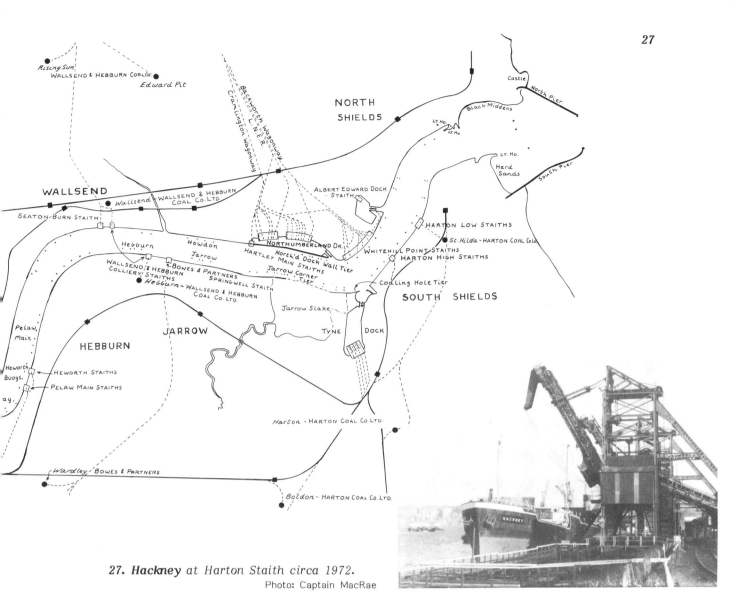

27. Hackney *at Harton Staith circa 1972.*
Photo: Captain MacRae

The steamer, built by C. Mitchell, was a typical engines amidships design suitable for the longer voyages to the continent, Spain and the Baltic (20). The coastal coal trade was not increasing much at this time, but exports were growing steadily. The vessel had a single deck with forecastle, bridge and poop erections on it. The forecastle housed the seamen while the firemen were below the main deck forwards. Ventilation was by the then newly introduced cowl ventilators. The anchor windlass is typical of those in sailing vessels and hand operated. There was no provision for driving it from the steam cargo winches, by chain as was the later practice, so the sailors had just as much work raising the anchor aboard **Fenham** as in sailing vessels. The small hatches also made for plenty of work loading coal and discharging it. From the builders point of view it made for a much stronger ship and the wooden hatches themselves were always a weak point. Though the hatches were small the steam winches serving the fore and aft hatches plus the steam crane at the main hatch speeded discharge. Steam cranes were not normal but were fitted to vessels aimed at the more lucrative general cargo liner trade, but even so these vessels often carried coal on their outward voyage. **Fenham** loaded a full cargo of coal in the Northumberland dock and sailed for London on the 7th of January 1873. This may have been a seasonal cargo, London always having a higher winter demand for coal. Other factors influencing the cargo available to these ships was the number of new, slightly larger vessels, which were being built for the Baltic and Mediterranean trade. At the same time the size of cargoes acceptable to London merchants also increased, so smaller ships like **Fenham** tended to move into the London trade even if they had been built with more distant voyages in mind.

The layout of much of the vesel was still strongly influenced by that used for centuries in sailing ships, such as the officers' accommodation in the poop. It had been handy in sailing vessels steered from aft, but by this time the steering position had been firmly established amidships for a number of years so that if the captain's advice was required in a hurry he was not easily accessible to the officer of the watch and the seaman at the wheel. A further disadvantage was the considerable vibration often experienced in the stern of the ship from the propellor. The engineers were also accommodated aft directly above the propellor and so they must have had many wet dashes forward at the changing of the watches. The change would not have been made any easier by the fact that the entrance to the accommodation was on top of the poop rather than via a door in the front bulkhead of the poop so they had to climb the companionway and then decend to the main deck level again to go forward. The spread of canvas was typical of vessels intended for the longer continental voyages. The galley was probably in a similar position to that on the plan of **Hugh Taylor** (18).

The **T. E. Smith**, Luckley and Southern partnership were also involved in **T. E. Forster** 810/66. There were also two vessels in which the Smith, Luckley, Southern partnership were involved in a small way, viz: **Hotspur** 1081/68 and **Iouna** 860/68, which were managed by Elliott, Lowry and Dunford. Other significant shareholders were M. J. Johanasson [7], who was a coal owner and fitter, and W. Hunter who was also a fitter. Perhaps the most interesting small shareholder was H. T. Morton who managed the Earl of Durham's fleet from Sunderland. Elliott, Lowry and Dunford owned **Monkseaton** in partnership and **Jesmond** 894/69 with George Luckley who had 21 shares. Their vessels were more wide ranging in their trading pattern. **Jesmond** was completed in July 1869 and entered the Northumberland Dock on the 3rd of September to load coal for Kronstadt, sailing on the 7th. This was probably the ship's maiden voyage.

The other major owning group comprised the Strakers, who were coal owners and also fitters (Straker & Love), Hugh Taylor (Hugh Taylor & Partners) who mined Ryhope and Hartley steam coals, and shipbroker A. C. Pring. J. Straker of Tynemouth was the sole owner of **Weardale** 514/67 which loaded 273 chaldrons of coal in the Northumberland dock and sailed for London on the 29th November 1869, a cargo of about 725 tons. The Strakers held 52 shares and J. Straker of Tynemouth also held 8 jointly with A. C. Pring in **Brancepeth** 761/64. The Strakers also held controlling interests in **Joseph Straker** 719/63 with H. Taylor and A. C. Pring. The vessel loaded 342 chaldrons (906 tons) for Hamburg in Northumberland dock and sailed for Hamburg on the 5th of September 1869. The **Stagshaw** 941/70 was just under their control [32 shares], the other major shareholder being the fitter J. Liddell of Benwell [16]. J. Coppin of North Shields was also a small shareholder in this and other vessels associated with the Strakers and managed by A. C. Pring. **Stagshaw** probably loaded her first coal cargo for London in March 1870 in the Northumberland Dock, sailing on the 1st of April with a cargo of 478 chaldrons (1267 tons) as she is noted in the Harbourmaster's book as a new vessel.

The **Charles Mitchell** 738/65 was also managed by A. C. Pring but J. Straker of Tynemouth owned less than half the shares. The other main shareholders were the fitters E. O. Lamb [8] and J. Liddell [12], and H. Taylor [8]. The vessel sailed for Portsmouth with a full cargo of coal on the 28th April 1870. The shareholders were similar in the **Swan** 710/67 with the addition of S. R. Streatfield. This vessel also sailed for Portsmouth from Northumberland dock in December 1870. S. R. Streatfield also held 8 shares in **Hugh Taylor** 974/69. The other main shareholders were T. Straker [16], J. Liddell [16] with Coppin, Pring and H. Taylor each with 8 shares.

As might be expected, with the shareholders strongly involved in coal, the **Hugh Taylor** (18) was designed with the coal trade very much in mind. The vessel had identical dimensions to those of the **Fenham** already described but was laid out rather differently. Perhaps the most important feature from the point of view of the coal trade was the additional hatch for the after hold which would greatly facilitate loading and discharge. Also of almost equal importance for coal carrying, the vessel had the bridge deck and poop deck combined extending from the engine room aft to compensate for the loss of stowage space taken up by the propellor shaft tunnel running through the after hold. Thus when coal, a uniform bulk cargo, was loaded the vessel would trim on an even keel when full. Without the raised deck level aft there would be more coal forward of amidships than aft and the vessel would trim by the head so single deck vessels like the **Fenham** were unable to fill the forward hold full if they were not to be down by the head and so make the vessel difficult to handle in a seaway. However, single deckers continued to be built even for the coal trade as owners often were not prepared to meet the extra expense of a well deck vessel like **Hugh Taylor** or put out a specification for tender which asked for little more than the ability to carry a given deadweight on a certain draft at a specified speed. Prospective builders, mindful that owners would probably give the order to the builder offering the lowest price, submitted the cheapest design. Captains then found themselves with ships which could not be filled forward leaving the danger of cargoes which could shift in heavy seas. Charles Mitchell was a particularly good shipbuilder and would be well known to all the shareholders in **Hugh Taylor** and he probably pointed out the advantage to them of his design.

The crew accommodation in **Hugh Taylor** was similar to that in **Fenham** with the captain and officers aft in the poop, but not the engineers who have been moved amidships with their engines. The first, second and third engineers are arranged just aft of the engine room on the port side of the hatchway at main deck level. The accommodation was apparently entered from the engine room which had a combined engine room skylight and companionway. The six firemen had berths on the starboard side opposite the engineers, rather than the more usual forward accommodation. The space vacated aft by moving the engineers amidships provided two two-berth spare cabins. These were probably used by a few passengers, mostly those needing to travel on business, often associates of agents or shareholders. This could expand into a fairly regular passenger service if the shipping agents found they could always fill the spare berths. This happened in the case of William Dickinson's steamers which began carrying coal out to Spain, returning with iron ore. As the trade became more regular, larger vessels were ordered capable of carrying quite a number of passengers.

29. Northumbria after transfer to Cory's fleet. She was built by Palmers in 1869.

The remainder of the crew accommodation in **Hugh Taylor** was similar to **Fenham** with the seamen in the forecastle along with a cabin for the bosun and carpenter. The galley was placed at the after end of the well deck under the bridge and chart room, with W.C's for the crew and engineers placed at the ship's sides slightly forward of the galley. No doubt in heavy weather the water closets saw plenty of water as seas breaking on to the foredeck would run aft until stopped by the adjacent bulkhead of the bridge deck, the steward would also have needed some good seaboots in the adjacent galley. He had the further problem of carrying cooked food all the way aft for the officers. On occasion he was probably reduced to providing cold food, but at least this was easy as the pantry in the accommodation aft was adjacent to his cabin. The sails were of a much simpler plan than **Fenham** again pointing to the shorter voyages **Hugh Taylor** was intended for. Adam Bros. & Co., Newcastle, managed the vessel for a number of years around 1890 and she probably made some voyages to the Mediterranean when new. As with many ships of the period, the machinery was the weak point and new engines and boilers were installed by Hawthorns in 1877. Engine performance and reliability were being rapidly improved upon.

Shipbuilders also owned a few vessels, for example **Constantine** 798/66, which was controlled by Charles Mitchell. Apart from **John Bowes**, of which Charles Palmer was the sole owner, Palmers Shipbuilding & Iron Co., owned **Clotilda** and the large steamers **Grinkle** 833/67 and **Mulgrave** 707/63. Various other groups controlled single ships.

There was a steady build-up in the number of Newcastle registered steamers and colliers reflecting the prosperity of the coal export trade which was expanding steadily. Further steamers were added to the home trade as the collier brigs were steadily replaced. W. Benson acquired **American** which had been built in Southampton. She was rebuilt at Newcastle in 1870 and renamed **Allerwash** 285/61. William Benson had coal interests in the area, and he named her after his home, Allerwash House. She measured 131.0' x 25.3' x 11.6', rather small for the coal trade by this time and this is probably why she was lengthened to 167.6' in 1876.

Shields Shipping

The only other port on the Tyne which had sea-going steamers on its register was North Shields, as at this time South Shields was limited to tugs. The largest ocean going ships belonged to the Northumberland S. S. Co., who had four steamers, leaving 15 steamers suitable for the intermediate trade, and of these five of them loaded coal in the Northumberland dock during the period 1869-73 according to Captain MacRae's notes extracted from the Harbourmaster's books. Most prominent of the local owners in 1871 was James Hunter who owned two ships jointly with Hugh Taylor, the colliery owner. These were **Chipchase** 664/64 and **Tyne** 612/63. They traded as the Shields S. S. Co., and were sold in the early 1870s, by which time Taylor was involved with ships managed by A. C. Pring and Elliott, Lowry and Dunford, who were both Newcastle based. **Chipchase** was named after the home of Hugh Taylor, Chipchase Castle, and loaded coal on at least two occasions in the Northumberland dock for London, sailing for that destination on the 21st September 1869 and 15th August 1873. **Tyne** loaded coal for Hamburg and sailed on the 4th September 1869. James Hunter also had 8 shares in the **Bolivar** 479/66 and 16 in the **Blyth** 687/70 with other local investors.

William Johnson seems to have engaged his ships in the coal trade. He owned 53 shares in **Bamborough** 925/70 and 12 jointly with George Luckley in **Lindisfarne** 913/70. The sisterships were built by T. and W. Smith of North Shields and had registered lengths of around 216 feet. R. C. Carr had 2 shares in each ship and perhaps this accounts for their visits to Northumberland dock as John

Carr & Son were fitters who shipped coal at Northumberland Dock. **Bamborough** loaded 418 chaldrons (about 1108 tons) and sailed for London on the 19th March 1871. **Lindisfarne** sailed for Hamburg on the 12th of March a year earlier. This may well have been her maiden voyage as she is noted in the harbourmaster's book as a new vessel. Lloyd's Register noted that she was intended for the Black Sea trade. By the names, it seems likely that **Galatz** 884/70 managed by Thomas Sutton and **Galeed** 950/70 managed by J. F. Middleton were also intended for this trade. **Galeed** is of interest as John G. Hill of Sunderland had 9 shares. He later went on to build up his own fleet which eventually came under the management of Witherington and Everett in 1903.

The only other North Shields vessel to visit Northumberland Dock in the period 1869-73 was apparently **Thetis** 830/66 managed by J. & J. Wait which loaded 412 chaldrons (1092 tons) for London and sailed on the 12th of December. Lloyd's Register notes Black Sea as her intended trade and so the voyage to London was perhaps just a winter cargo when the London coal trade would be looking for extra ships to keep up with demand. There was no real differentiation between coastal and foreign trade and it was not until 1894 that the home trade limits were introduced which required extra crew and more highly qualified masters for voyages outside the Elbe-Brest limits. Vessels tended to settle into the coastal and near continental trades or foreign trades following the Act.

The Northumberland Dock records also indicate the beginning of the steam coasting trade in which steamers begin to replace sailing vessels supplying coal merchants in the small coastal harbours. The first coaster noted by Captain MacRae was **Lincolnshire** 88/67. This little iron steamer had been built by Mitchell at Low Walker and probably passed into the control of J. Y. Hawdon of Blaydon when registered at Newcastle in 1870. She loaded 43 chaldrons of coal (about 114 tons), which was a fair cargo for a vessel with the registered dimensions 76.3' x 20.1' x 8.5', and sailed for Boston on the 10th of April 1871. An even smaller vessel, managed by J. Y. Hawdon, was the wooden steamer **Gitana** 58/68 built at Friars Goose, Durham. This vessel measured just 69.6' x 18.5' x 8.1' and loaded 32 chaldrons (85 tons), sailing for Scarborough in 1871. Another small steamer was **Jane & Hannah** 57/72, built of wood and with the dimensions 67.4' x 19.7' x 7.7', this screw steamer belonged to Robert Foster of Willington Quay and loaded 85 tons of coal for Montrose, sailing on the 8th of August 1873. Several other small steamers seem to have loaded similar cargoes from time to time, but on the whole the usual steam coaster, some 110-150 feet in length, was not yet being built in any numbers.

Blyth

The mouth of the River Blyth lies about eight miles north of Newcastle and was used for shipping coal from the middle ages, but much of the early coal production was used by the important local salt-making industry to heat and evaporate the water out of brine.

The first real improvements for the shipment of coal were the work of the Ridley family who were local landowners. They built quays and in 1765 the first breakwater, North Dyke. This was followed by a staith which could accept the horse-drawn chaldron wagons and tip them directly into waiting ships. To guide the ships in, the high lighthouse was erected in 1765 also, and continues in use. The rather difficult approach to the harbour, which meant coming inside the Sow and Pigs rocks, and the proximity of the shore meant collier brigs were often unable to get in or out and the first tug was hired from Newcastle in June 1819 to get loaded brigs on their way.

Collieries continued to be opened locally and the Cowpen Colliery had pits adjacent to the harbour. Railway developments followed and in 1849 the Tyne and Blyth Junction railway was completed utilising a number of colliery wagon-ways and building a staith on the south side of the river. The first steam collier to load at Blyth for the Cowpen Coal Co., was probably **Weardale** (3) in 1868, which had been completed in July 1867 for J. Straker of Tynemouth. She had been built by J. Laing of Sunderland and measured 202.2' x 28.2' x 15.5' and carried about 724 tons of coal. Coal shipments had increased from about 250,000 tons in 1850 to 343,000 tons in 1873. The collieries sending coal from Blyth at this time were Bebside, Bedlington, Cambois, Choppington, Cowpen, North Seaton and Seaton Delaval collieries. But the shallowness of the river was preventing the larger steam colliers from loading. Harbour improvements had begun in 1854 with the formation of the Blyth Harbour and Dock Co. under an Act of Parliament and chaired by Sir Matthew White Ridley. Powers were granted to the Company to build a breakwater, dock and half-tide basin. The capital of £150,000 proved inadequate because of engineering dificulties and higher construction costs, mainly because much of the river bed was rock. Dues were raised but trade was steadily lost to the Tyne where lower freights of larger vessels compensated for the longer railway journey, particularly for the collieries further out from Blyth.

The directors of the private harbour company decided the only way forward for the Harbour was to follow the example of the Tyne and Wear and form a Trust with Commissioners. This required Parliamentary approval which was obtained in 1882. At this time there were two coal berths offering about 9 feet at low water on the north side and two on the south side under construction with about 15 feet of water, in addition there were four small berths. The first staith built at the Port was at South Blyth in 1788. This was added to and improved over the years, the main extensions being completed in 1888 by the North Eastern Railway, which provided two new berths and coal shipments exceeded a million tons for the first time. These sturdy timber staiths stood up to the ravages of time and weather, and though they were ultimately condemned as unsafe, it was not until 1964 that they were finally closed down and, shortly after, demolished.

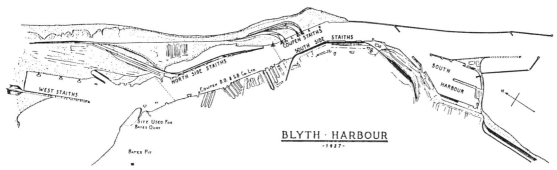

BLYTH · HARBOUR
-1927-

As the coal trade flourished and new collieries opened north of the river, more and more staiths were built by the North Eastern Railway (who had come to an agreement with the Commissioners). Four berths opened in 1896. In 1899 the south harbour was completed with jetties used as waiting berths. Shelter for the harbour was improved with the completion in 1908 of an extension to the east pier. Deepening of the river had continued with the removal of large quantities of rock. The Cowpen Coal Company and its successor the N.C.B., built and operated staiths on the north side of the river for 100 years from 1868 to 1968, when they were sold and demolished to make way for a modern discharging berth for Alcan in 1972. The remainder of the staiths at North Blyth were built by the North Eastern Railway (31) and played an important part in achieving the astonishing total output of not far short of 400,000,000 tons of coal shipped between 1896 and 1972, when the last cargo was loaded there.

Powers to develop staiths at West Blyth were obtained in 1912 and these staiths were also built by the North Eastern Railway. Though the superstructure was completed in 1915, the stringent economies resulting from the First World War prevented any further work on the construction of the actual staiths until 1926. The first shipment was made in 1928.

Bates pit at Blyth was opened in 1934 and started shipping coal at once. The dredging of the upper harbour for the west staiths enabled the Cowpen Coal Company, owners of the pit, to build a new private staith. The belt conveyors at this berth were built by Messrs. Turnbull's of Heaton, Newcastle on Tyne, a firm famous for this type of appliance. In addition to these two new berths the Cowpen Coal Co., continued to use the four gravity spouts they owned on the north side of the harbour until 1968. The London & North Eastern Railway had 8 spouts on the south staiths to handle loading of coal for the other collieries in the district. The coal shipments continued to increase throughout the 20th century, exceeding 6 million tons in 1934, in 1950 and 1951, and again in 1966, but by 1971 they were down to 2 million tons. This was due in part to reduced shipments to southern power stations, but it must not be forgotten that the two power stations (Blyth 'A' and 'B') consumed huge quantities of coal, including the whole output of one pit close to them.

No time was lost in getting loaded ships out of the berths, and a start made on the next ship. It was usual to find a second ship lying outside the ship in the loading berth, ready to slip into the berth as soon as the completed ship pulled out. Then one of the waiting ships in the lay-by berths in the Import Dock or other place, cast off and steamed into place as second bottom, thus ensuring continuity and no waste of time. All the waiting berths were occupied by coastal colliers, middle traders and, sometimes, big deep sea tramps loading for ports even further afield. The generating stations in the South of England used Northumberland steam coals, especially those in the Thames area. They had voracious appetites for Blyth coal, one, Deptford, burning nothing else for many years.

The almost inevitable delay in loading whilst waiting for a berth made Blyth a favourite port with North East Coast collier men. Being on the Watch Aboard/Watch Ashore system, those of the watch ashore welcomed any delay in loading which gave them a few extra hours with their family or friends. The watch aboard, usually of three men, one of which was nightwatchman, simply attended

31.
North Blyth Staiths.

to routine duties such as adjusting the ladder or gangway, and the moorings as the tide rose and fell. At times of neap tides this was as little as seven feet but could exceed fourteen feet on spring tides, necessitating rather more work. They also loaded the ship, shifting her back and forth as required and, as each hold was filled, battened it down and generally made ready for sea.

During the exceptionally cold spell that hit the whole country in 1962-63, loading at Blyth, in common with every other coal port, was extremely slow and hazardous. The contents of each wagon was frozen solid, and called for considerable effort by the teemers, the gentlemen who normally knocked the bottom doors open, and then watched the coal drop out of the wagons into the chutes on its way to the ship's holds. With it frozen they had to break it up into small enough lumps for it to clear the bottom doors of the wagons and the trimming doors of the chutes themselves. The language used should have melted the ice quite easily, but the cold was too intense even for that. Some extraordinarily hard work had to be put in to get the ships loaded and away.

South Blyth was always a favourite loading place with the North East Coast crews, for they could retreat to a very well known pub called the Dun Cow, from the windows of which many a collier was loaded. A practice frowned upon by the owners, but they did little to stop it. Next in order of popularity were the North Blyth berths. At one end of the staiths was one of the finest clubs in the country, whilst at the other south end there were two pubs, one at the Jubilee Staiths and the other further south. That at the Jubilee shared the same fate as the Cowpen Staiths and was demolished to make room for the Alcan berth, whilst the Seven Stars, at the south end, was abandoned by 1975.

Amble and Warkworth Harbour

Like Blyth, Warkworth came under the jurisdiction of North Shields for customs purposes and served the northernmost part of the Northumberland coalfields. The Harbour Commission was established by Act of Parliament in 1847. The harbour is about 20 miles north of the Tyne at the mouth of the River Coquet and has an anchorage partly sheltered by Coquet Island. The important Trinity House lighthouse on the island was a convenient landfall for vessels making for Warkworth. The harbour was tidal and protected by two substantial masonry piers, the one on the north side extends 800 yards in an easterly direction, and the other on the south side extending northwards to leave an entrance about 80 yards wide. Vessels drawing 15 to 16 feet of water could use the harbour at neap tides and up to 20 feet on spring tides. In the 1880s the depths had been about two feet less over the bar (33).

By this time H. Andrews of Eastfield Hall was the proprietor of Warkworth and he was colliery agent (fitter) for Broomhill and Grey's Hartley collieries. He had extensive interests in sailing vessels before the building of **Warkworth** in 1874. **Broomhill** of 1878 served the coal trade from Warkworth for some 30 years. Other local collieries active in the 1880s in the vicinity were Dand's and Radcliffe Colliery. The Radcliffe Coal Co., had loading berths in the harbour but had ceased operations prior to the First World War. At the turn of the century there were five coal loading staiths in use, capable of loading 250 - 300 tons per hour. It was left to the Broomhill Coal Company to develop the coal mining and shipping fleet to such an extent that the fleet became synonymous with Warkworth. By this time the Broomhill colliery had a number of riverside staiths and in all there was some 2,000 feet of quay space. The company also operated a tug from early times to assist colliers to berth.

In 1904 the fleet consisted of **Broomhill** 562/78 (23), the slightly longer **Ringwood** 905/89 and **Turrethill** 691/95, which had been built by Doxford's to their turret design. These unusual vessels had a central trunk which incorporated the hatch coamings running completely fore and aft so that looking bow-on the sides of the ship appeared to have a step inwards about half way up. The ships were particularly good for bulk cargoes such as coal as it was unable to shift sideways even if the cargo had settled due to motion in a seaway. She was regularly employed carrying coal to London and also visited Great Yarmouth delivering steam coal for bunkering the local fishing fleet and gas coal for the local gasworks. The collieries output was essentially steam and household coals and so it was likely that the gas coal was probably loaded from another colliery. This independent operation of the ships was normal practice and in the 1930s recognised by the formation of a separate associated company, Broomhill Steamships Ltd., but it continued to have the same offices as the colliery itself: "D" Floor, Milburn House, Newcastle.

The coal trade continued to improve at the beginning of the 1900s and the company invested in new colliers for their fleet. First to be delivered was a new **Broomhill** 1329/09 which was built for the company by Irvine's Shipbuilding and Dry Dock Company of West Hartlepool. She measured 243.3' x 36.0' x 14.8' and followed the engines amidships design used for the earlier **Broomhill**. She had machinery by Richardsons Westgarth & Company Ltd., Hartlepool. The triple expansion engine (18.5", 30", 50" by 36" stroke) used steam at 180 lbs from the twin scotch boilers. The same machinery was also used in the sisterships **Axwell** 1442/09 and **Bondicar** 1441/10 which had a deadweight of 1,975 tons. This included coal bunkers of up to 134 tons so they were suitable for the near continental coal trade. Though the same engines were used, the boilers were given more heating surface and so they were better able to maintain a good service speed. They were also slightly shorter and had a loaded draft of 15'1" as compared with the **Broomhill's** 15'8" which undoubtedly was useful when getting over the bar into Warkworth harbour on less favourable tides. **Axwell** and **Broomhill** left the fleet after about a decade of service but **Bondicar** was to continue for 37 years, making

33. Warkworth Harbour from a lithograph of 1889.

her last voyage from Warkworth for Broomhill Collieries in March 1946, with a cargo of coal for Greenwich.

Various vessels were purchased at the beginning of the 1920s as there was a general surge in demand for coal. A German vessel, part of the war reparations, was obtained and renamed **Broomhill** 1247/14. It was a most unusual twin screw vessel and soon returned to Germany. A much more suitable purchase was **Laura** which had been built by Verschun & Co., of Amsterdam in 1920. She was renamed **Amble** 1162/20. Her dimensions were 230.7' x 34.3' x 13.2' and she could carry 1,829 tons on a draft of about 15 feet. Unlike other vessels in the fleet, she had machinery aft. The company had not had her long when she went ashore at Alnmouth during a gale on Sunday December the 20th, 1925. After several attempts the vessel was refloated on December the 30th and was found to be leaking so badly that she had to be taken into Warkworth harbour and beached so that temporary patches could be placed on the leaking areas. When this was completed she was towed down to Smith's Dock at North Shields where she arrived safely on January 3rd. The rudder had been lost and all the propellor blades had snapped off at the boss, but the full extent of the damage was not revealed until the dry dock was emptied. The double bottom was extensively damaged from stem to stern and across the whole width. In addition over 80 feet of the bottom had been pushed upwards and was clear of the blocks in the bottom of the dry dock. Nearly all the double bottom of the ship had to be removed and replaced, a most expensive and difficult repair.

A programme of building was also undertaken, the order going to the Furness Shipbuilding Co. First to be delivered was **Chevington** 1537/23, following the pattern of engines amidships, but with a continuous deck on which were placed poop, bridge and forecastle. The next to be delivered, **Togston** 1547/24, was similar but with a raised quarterdeck and a deadweight of 2,510 tons, 15 tons less than **Chevington**, but drawing just under 16'6" as compared with the 16'8" of the **Chevington**. **Hauxley** 1595/25 reverted to the more cheaply constructed single continuous deck formula used for **Chevington** but the draft was reduced to 16'3" and deadweight increased to 2,538 tons by increasing the breadth 1'5" to 39'5". Owners and builders were always searching for the best carrying capacity given the restrictions of the harbour they were working from and the price they were prepared to pay for the ship.

So in 1927 the fleet consisted of the old **Bondicar** along with **Amble, Chevington, Hauxley** and **Togston**. They were generally employed carrying the Broomhill Collieries output of steam coal to the power stations of southern England. The fleet soon found themselves under attack at the beginning of World War II and **Amble** was sunk by a mine eight miles ENE of Whitby on the 16th December 1939, followed by **Togston** which was sunk by a torpedo from a German E-boat on a voyage from Blyth to London on the 8th March 1941 off Smith's Knoll. Later that same year the **Chevington** was torpedoed and sunk on the 12th October by a German E-boat east of Haisborough Sand.

By the summer of 1943 the only original member of the Broomhill fleet sailing out of Warkworth was the old **Bondicar**. In that year she loaded 26 cargoes at Warkworth, half of which went to Barking Power Station and a further third to Greenwich and the remainder to Woolwich. The collier **Miervaldis** 1265/04 was also working from Warkworth at this time. This collier belonged to the Ministry of War Transport and management was given to Broomhill Steamships Ltd., and she was employed running coal to London power stations alongside **Bondicar**. Though **Miervaldis** had come from Latvia she was returning to the trade for which she had been built as she was originally **St. Edmund** of Stephenson Clarke. She was sold by them in 1922 and sailed out of Cardiff as the **Kingsdon** until sold again in 1929 to Stahl & Co., of Riga. She continued running from Warkworth after nationalisation of the coal industry on the 1st of January 1947. **Bondicar** had been sold by the time Hudson S. S. Co., were appointed managers of **Miervaldis** in 1948, but their management lasted only a few months as she was laid up and then used to dispose of war stocks of poison gas ammunition by loading her with a full cargo and scuttling her in the Bay of Biscay. The colliery company was finally wound up in 1953. The harbour continued in use for coal shipments until September 1969.

Sunderland and Seaham

The prominent shipowning coal owners were the Earl of Durham of Lambton Castle (Lambton Collieries), the Londonderry family; Earl Vane (Londonderry Collieries) and the Wood family, Hetton Hall (North Hetton Coal Co.). Most active in the seabourne coal trade originally were the Londonderry family and initially they developed their coal shipments through their own harbour about 14 miles south of Sunderland as the most direct route. Seaham Harbour was promoted by Charles William the 3rd Marquis of Londonderry and his wife Frances Ann. Work on constructing the harbour was begun in 1828 reputedly with just £1,500 available immediately. The village of Seaham consisted of a few houses when the project was begun but by 1841 the population was over 2,000 such was the work and prosperity brought about by the coal trade for the new port which began shipping coal out in 1831. Further extensions were made in 1845 so that the harbour consisted of the North Dock, the South Dock and the Tidal Harbour. Much later the present South Dock, about twice the size of the original South Dock was constructed at the turn of the century. The harbour was well able to accommodate the collier brigs and loaded them with coal primarily produced by the Seaham, Dawdon, Vane Tempest and the Easington, Horden and Blackhall mines.

The harbour proved inadequate for the increasing output of the Seaham, South Hetton and Murton Collieries. Full use of steam haulage on the Londonderry Railway made the better harbour facilities at Sunderland the obvious choice. Developments at Sunderland had been begun rather later. The first enclosed dock was completed for the Wearmouth Dock Company in 1837 on the north side of the river. However, riverside coal drops and staiths had been used for many years. The Wearmouth staiths on the north side were used by the Wearmouth Colliery and those on the south side were used by the Hetton Coal Co., served by the Hetton Colliery Railway, and adjacent to these were the extensive staiths of the Earl of Durham's Lambton Collieries served by the Lambton railway.

The most important development of Sunderland as a port came in 1846 when the Sunderland Dock Act was passed, authorising the Sunderland Dock Company to construct wet docks and other works on the south side of the rivermouth. Work progressed fairly rapidly and in 1850 the Hudson Dock was opened followed by an extension southwards in 1855. The final step was taken towards full development of the river as a whole with the incorporation of the River Wear Commissioners who took over the Sunderland Dock Company. However the North Dock, belonging to the North Eastern Railway, did not come under their jurisdiction until 1922, (35).

The Hudson Dock was well placed to handle coal for the Londonderry colliers and the Londonderry Railway was extended up from the south to carry coal to the dock for loading. In 1860 Lady Londonderry (owner of the colliery) was allotted staiths numbered 21 and 23 (35) to 29 while the North Eastern Railway had those numbered 16 to 18. As it seemed likely that Londonderry coal shipments would increase she was also allowed to retain the use of No. 19. However by the end of 1860 the Commissioners resolved that No. 18 and 19 drops were to be appropriated as soon as possible for use of large vessels and access was to be by the Londonderry railway or the North Eastern Railway. To achieve this the North Eastern Railway built a spur just south of Hendon Station. Loading did not always go as planned and on New Year's Eve 1867 there was an accident in which some wagons ran off the top of the staith on to a ship in the dock, doing £25 of damage to the staith and the cost was recovered from the Londonderry Railway Company. Coal shipments were continuing to rise and Earl Vane (Marquess of Londonderry) in February 1869 applied for an additional two drops as his shipments from the Londonderry Collieries greatly exceeded the quantity which entitled him to 11 drops under the Board of Trade rulings at that time. After due consideration the Commissioners asked if he would accept two spouts instead of drops and he agreed to this at the end of March. He and his Company now controlled about half of the loading appliances in the dock, but the situation had been improved by the opening of the Hendon Dock directly to the south of the Hudson Dock the previous year.

Though much of the coal was shipped in chartered vessels, the Londonderry family were investors in sailing vessels and brigs for their own harbour and were among the first owners of steam colliers to be registered at Sunderland, as Seaham came under the jurisdiction of that port. The loans used to pay for the construction of Seaham had been repaid by 1855 and so the enterprise was in a strong position to finance this new venture. By 1857 the **Londonderry** (150.0' x 26.0' x 14.8') 393/57, was in service but the fleet was not expanded rapidly, and in 1871 the steam yacht **Cornelia** 212/68 was the sole additional vessel, and of course was not used in the coal trade. During the early 1870s further, often secondhand, tonnage was acquired and the fleet was steadily increased with vessels such as **Maglona** 626/71, purchased by Earl Vane in October 1872. Shipping continued to prosper and shipowners were making good profits and this was probably why Earl Vane (Marquess of Londonderry) began to add new larger vessels to his fleet. The price for a collier similar to **Hugh Taylor** measuring 220 x 31 x 16 feet was about £20,000, a not inconsiderable sum, even for the Marquess. Investment in shipping shares was generally becoming known and the Marquess took advantage of this to finance his fleet. Thus by 1884 the fleet was one of eleven steamers, **Harvest Queen** 555/60, **Lady Aline** 600/75, **Londonderry** 393/57, **Maglona** 626/71, **Marchioness of Londonderry**, and **Viscount Castereagh** 694/78, of which he was the sole owner. In addition there were the joint stock steamers in which he personally owned a third or less of the 64 shares in each vessel. These were **Kronos** 1071/72, purchased secondhand, which retained Hartlepool as its port of registry, and the new steamers **Garron Tower** 650/76, **Wynyard Park** 693/78 (named after the Marquess' home) **Seaham Harbour** 1904/80, and the newly commissioned **Longnewton** 1878/84. Other prominent share-

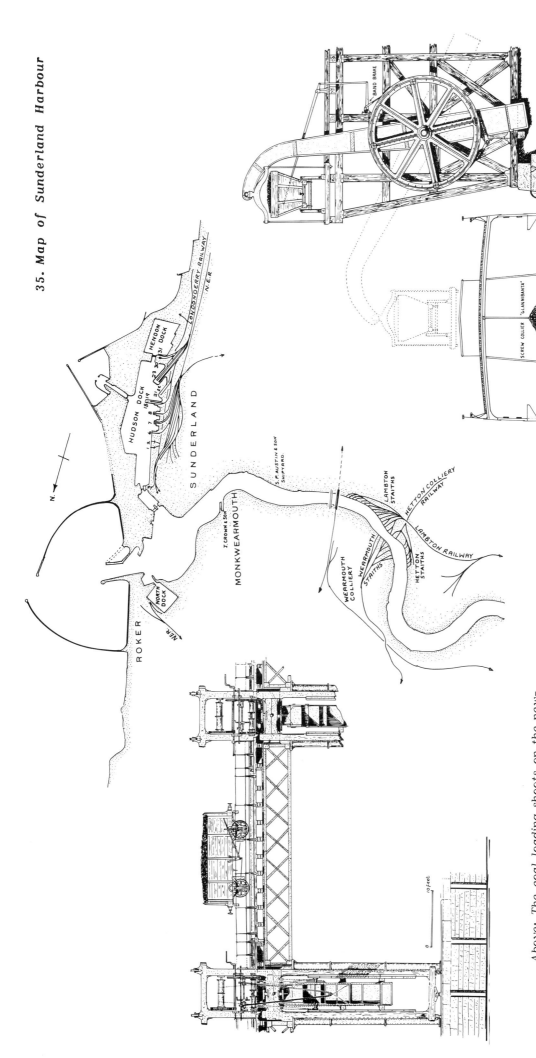

35. *Map of Sunderland Harbour*

Above: The coal loading shoots on the newer staiths in the Hudson and Hendon docks. The shoot is shown removed on the right.

Right: The later design of coal drop used in the Hudson dock and still in use in 1897.

New Harbour and Dock Works

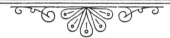

... BELONGING TO THE ...

Seaham Harbour Dock Company.

THE old docks were acquired from Lord Londonderry, and were built some seventy years ago, and the Company is now adding a new ten-acre deepwater dock and entrance, and throwing out two protective piers to shelter the approach from the sea.

The new works were commenced in the early part of 1899, and are now nearly completed.

In the early stages of the work considerable difficulty was experienced in enclosing and reclaiming the necessary land required for the new dock and quay space, as at that time little or no protection was afforded by the piers, they not being far enough advanced. This was, however, eventually done, and the site of the new dock deepened some twelve feet into the magnesian limestone rock by the aid of steam navvies and blasting. The walls of the new dock are constructed of concrete faced with masonry above water level, and finished off with a cope of Norwegian granite. They are 35 feet high above dock bottom level, and there will be 27 feet 6 inches of water in the dock at H.W.O.S.T. The length of the dock is 1000 feet and breadth 450 feet.

The new entrance is constructed of concrete faced with masonry, and is 65 feet wide with a depth of water of 25 feet 6 inches on the cill. There are two pairs of gates fitted (the outer to act as storm gates) constructed of karri wood from Western Australia. They are worked by hydraulic rams fixed in machine pits at coping level, and supplied with pressure from a hydraulic installation working at 700 lbs. per square inch. Two five-ton capstans are also fitted at the entrance.

The approach channel to the entrance has at present been deepened to a minimum depth of 22 feet at H.W.O.S.T., and will, as soon as the weather permits, be further deepened by dredging to a depth of 24 feet 6 inches at H.W.O.S.T.

A system of gravity coal staiths is provided along the west side of the new dock, so arranged that the full coal wagons run down by gravity from the storage sidings, pass over the spouts, and the empty wagons pass away to low level sidings. It is anticipated that some two million tons of coal will be annually dealt with in this dock.

The protective piers are 1,383 feet and 878 feet long on respectively the North and South sides. They are built up of concrete blocks weighing up to 28 tons and faced with masonry. These blocks were formed in moulds in the block-yard, allowed to harden for some six weeks, and then set in position by a Titan Crane capable of dealing with a load of 30 tons at 60 feet radius. The foundations for the piers are on rock throughout. Sand overlaid this in places, and was cleared away by means of a grab and diving bell. Mass concrete put in place by divers was used to level up the surface of the rock, and the blocks were placed on this and secured to one another below low water level by means of concrete joggle bags. Above low water the blocks are set in cement mortar.

The North Pier is 25 feet and 30 feet wide on top at its inner and outer ends respectively, and the South Pier 20 feet and 25 feet. The ends are finished with roundheads on which lighthouses are being erected, with a subway running through the piers to give access in stormy weather.

The contractors for the work are Messrs. S. Pearson & Son, Ltd., of Westminster.

November, 1905.

holders in the vessels included S. J. Ditchfield, manager of the fleet for the Marquess, who held 4 to 9 shares in each vessel, Thomas Elliott, fitter at Seaham for the North Hetton Coal Co., and the Belmont Coal Co., and J. O. Clazey who was the Marquess's fitter in Sunderland. The remainder, mostly in lots of one or two shares, were held quite widely. All had to sign an agreement to sell their shares if the Marquess decided to sell his. This allowed him to sell to a new owner without restriction, should he wish to do so. The new vessels, including the **Wynyard Park**, were photographed about 1880 and the sloping hatch sides to make them among the first 'self trimming' colliers can be clearly seen (37).

Perhaps the most interesting addition to the fleet was **Vane Tempest 689/84**. This raised quarter-deck collier with the dimensions 185.0' x 30.0' x 13.5', was specially built with folding masts and funnel to pass under low bridges (38). As the Londonderry Collieries produced considerable quantities of household coal and had a wharf at Nine Elms, above the Thames fixed bridges, they decided to supply the wharf directly using an up-river collier similar to those pioneered for the nearby gas company some five years earlier, see page 54.

By the 1890s the size of colliers coming into general use were becoming too big to be easily accommodated in Seaham and although some half million tons were being shipped still more capacity was needed. Thus in 1898 the Marquess sponsored the Seaham Harbour Dock Act which empowered the newly created Seaham Harbour Dock Company to construct new harbour works and staiths. Details of the work carried out were given in a leaflet (36) produced when the new dock (the South Dock) was opened by the Prime Minister, Mr. A. J. Balfour, on the 11th November 1905. The South Dock was built and extended later by the addition of the 'extension' at the south end. The Castle-reagh staiths, of reinforced concrete, were built in 1923 to handle increasing shipments and further staiths on the eastern side of the extension were completed just before the Second World War.

These improvements made all the difference and the port became even busier, if that were possible. On one memorable occasion in 1950 there were 19 ships jammed into this comparatively little harbour, some loading, some waiting to load and others weather bound, unable to get out when a heavy swell was running, and the lock gates could not be opened. Though they were referred to as 'lock' gates, the correct name for them was 'dock' gates, for their purpose was simply to impound the water in the Dock. There were two sets of gates, one, the inner, opening inwards, and the other outer set opening outwards. When these were shut they were reinforced by stay gates to assist them to withstand the enormous pressures and surges of a rough sea outside. If any sort of swell, even a quite moderate one was running, and ships were able to use this entrance, the wave surge into the dock was considerable and necessitated the use of coir springs to try and take some of the strain off the wire springs and moorings. At times this surge was so great that though a light ship of comparatively shallow draught could enter the port to load, she could not leave until the swell had died down and the Harbour Master allowed the gates to be opened.

Paddle tugs were always available, and had to be used by the bigger ships using the port. They were never very powerful and only the original steam paddle tugs such as **Granville** and **Seaham** were built for the old organisation and the new Dock Company. All the other tugs were second-hand, two of them becoming more or less famous and immortal. **Eppleton Hall** made the passage from Britain to the United States under her own steam (after conversion to oil fuel) and the **Reliant** forms an attraction at the Neptune Hall section of the National Maritime Museum at Greenwich, London. By the 1970s the port was handling about 4 colliers a week but an astonishing variety of other imports and exports, including timber to Sweden, kept the port busy and well employed.

37. The Londonderry colliers in Seaham Harbour circa 1880.
MacRae Collection

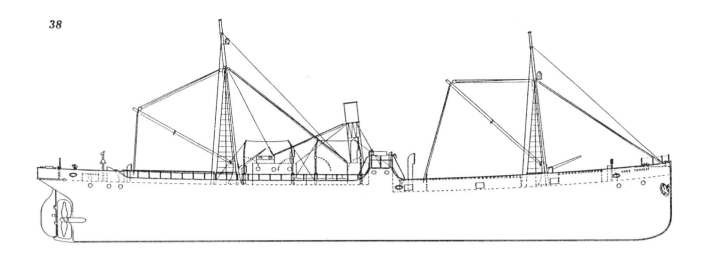

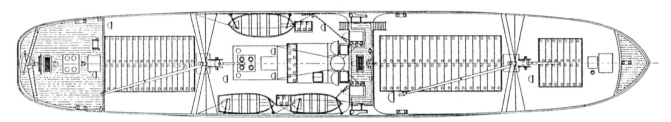

38. *The Marquis of Londonderry, seeing the success of the first Thames up-river colliers, decided to build a similar vessel to carry household coal directly to his wharf at Nine Elms. The result was* **Vane Tempest.** *Drawing by P. N. Thomas from a model in Glasgow Museum of Transport.*   Courtesy P. N. Thomas and Glasgow Museum of Transport

At the height of its prosperity, when coal was the fuel for all industrial purposes, the five coal berths were always occupied and loading operations seemed non-stop. Household, steam, manufacturing, and gas coals were all shipped out of Seaham, and were carried in ships belonging to the Gas Light and Coke Company (later to become the North Thames Gas Board), the Wandsworth and District Gas Company and the South Metropolitan Gas Company (later to be part of the South Eastern Gas Board on nationalisation) as well as in the ships belonging to the collier companies, great and small. Of course the first fleet involved with the port was the one for which it was built, the Londonderry fleet, which carried the coal not only around the coast of Britain but to places very much further away. The fleet was reduced in the latter part of the 1880s and 1890s reflecting the lower profits to be made in shipping and the ease with which vessels could be cheaply chartered to carry coal. New tonnage was again added in 1904/5 in the form of **Maureen** 2476/04 and **Lord Stewart** 1445/05. Further tonnage was added in the period prior to the First World War and this was retained during the war when rates were high and ships difficult to charter, but as rates fell at the end of the war the fleet was steadily reduced and was down to three vessels by 1926, and all were disposed of by the 1930s.

Returning now to Sunderland, development there also continued with the opening of the Hendon Dock in 1868 which added two more coal loading berths. The entrance to the River Wear was initially protected by two short piers each with lighthouse, built around the end of the eighteenth century, but to offer a safer entrance and protected anchorage the construction of the Roker pier to the north of the entrance was begun in 1885 and the southern protecting pier in 1893. Building was a major undertaking and each took about 20 years to complete. Coal shipments steadily increased and were about 5,300,000 tons in 1928, only a quarter of that from the Tyne. Developments had generally followed the Tyne pattern with coal conveyors replacing staiths and coal drops.

The private staiths were responsible for major shipments of coal especially those belonging to the Lambton family (Earl of Durham). These were located on the south side of the river. The first member of the family to develop their coal business was John George Lambton who purchased existing collieries and was active in sinking new pits. To achieve the rapid expansion he borrowed heavily and on his death in 1840 owed over £647,000. However the foundation he had laid down in coal mining was developed by his heirs and the debts met. To handle the output the Lambton Railway was built to carry the coal to drops which lay on the south bank of the river immediately to the west of the Sunderland Bridge which was sufficiently high to allow navigation of rigged vessels and some eleven drops or shoots (39) were eventually in use.

The Earl of Durham became a pioneer steam collier owner when **Lady Alice Lambton** was registered at the port of Wisbech on the 5th April 1853, but a few years later re-registered at Sunderland. The vessel, of 572 gross tons, had the dimensions 158.8' x 27.1' x 15.1' and thus was similar to **John Bowes** in size. She had been built for the Earl of Durham at the instigation of H. T. Morton, who was the Lambton estate agent, essentially the manager of the estate and its business. A second vessel soon followed, **Earl of Durham** 554/54 was registered on the 13th December 1854 as owned by

Messrs. Morton and Lambton. Henry Morton often appears as part owner or sole owner subsequently, though as far as is known all the vessels carried the famous three red rings on a black funnel, said to represent the 'Lambton worm' referred to in a popular local folk-tale. Bearing in mind the debts of the estate and the success of the first collier, Henry Morton was probably happy to invest in the Earl's ships which he would be managing. **Viscount Lambton** 616/56 was probably the first vessel in which H. T. Morton held a controlling interest. The fleet grew rapidly and at the end of 1861 consisted of **Lady Alice Lambton** 589/53, **Viscount Lambton** 615/56, **Lambton** 492/57, **Countess of Durham** 539/55, **Earl of Durham** 566/54, and the new **Earl of Elgin** 608/61. Though the **Viscount Lambton** was 190 feet in length the later vessels were rather smaller at 177 feet long. **Lambton** (4) certainly had engines amidships and this design was generally used for the fleet. Much of the coal carried was for gas works on the south and east coasts and on the continent. The Lambton staiths used to load colliers all through the night though between the wars there was only one coal trimmer until the day shift came on at 6 a.m., so the ship needed moving during the night.

Expansion of the fleet continued throughout the 1860s and Turnbull's Shipping Register of 1871 lists the following Sunderland registered vessels for the Earl of Durham; **Lambton** 576/57, **Earl of Durham** 593/94, and **Lady Beatrix** 625/63. These were managed by H. T. Morton of Biddick Hall who traded as H. T. Morton & Co., Lambton Offices, Sunderland. He owned several ships in his own right. These were **Frankland** 706/69, **Finchale** 714/69, **Harraton** 654/67, **Houghton** 763/70 and **Countess of Durham** 412/55. He also owned the majority of shares in **Kepier** 703/69, **Lanchester** 735/70, **Langley** 707/68 and **Sherburn** 644/66 (23). In all these vessels he owned 48 or more of the 64 shares but in the case of **Biddick** 640/64 he owned only 32. His associates in this vessel were John Murray of Kerksnow and Charles Robson of Sunderland. Other associates in the above vessels included J. Straker of Tynemouth and John Laing had 8 shares in the **Lanchester** which he built. The overseas trade was expanding and the Lambton Collieries with their shipping facilities took full advantage of the trade opportunities. The ships traded to the Baltic, often returning with timber for the local timber importers. This trade continued to prosper and by the time the 1884 edition of Turnbull's Register appeared the fleet had increased considerably. The Earl of Durham had added **Dora** 645/73, **Lady Eleanor** 764/65, **Lady Katherine** 945/81 and **Matin** 560/73 and retained the earlier vessels. H. T. Morton had followed a similar pattern, retaining all the earlier vessels which were modernised, for example the **Biddick** was lengthened in 1878 (see photo 40). However the old **Countess of Durham** had been lost in 1881. The additions to the fleet were; **Cleadon** 760/71, **Consett** 807/73, **Cornwall** 677/72, **Douglas** 768/61, **Heathpool** 999/78, **Lady Ann** 1082/83, **Lumley** 753/72, **Ottercaps** 977/78. **Douglas** of 1861 had originally been built by Marshall Bros., South Shields for a group of shareholders headed by William Stobart, who was also associated with the Lambton estates. The vessel was lengthened to 211.0' x 29.0' x 17.2' by J. Laing in 1871 for W. T. Bell and Stobart. The long lives of the early Lambton colliers is a tribute to both builders, managers and crew in a period when marine losses were high.

The late part of the 1880s and 1890s was a period of less favourable freight rates and the fleet saw an overall reduction by 1902. Most of the earlier vessels had been built by John Laing but S. P. Austin became the main builder after 1880, contributing **Offerton** 744/85, **Hedworth** 1078/84, **Northdene** 1356/93, **Linhope** 1338/94, **Gregynog** 1699/99, **Sunningdale** 1798/99 for example. The emphasis was now on longer 4-hatch colliers in the building programme, but several were quickly sold. Changes in policy were to be expected as there was a new man at the helm. In 1890, H. T.

39. Coal shoots at Seaham Harbour (left) showing balance-weights on doors used to deflect coal into the required shoot. At Lambton shoots (right) the truck ran parallel with the shoots rather than at right-angles to them. Both arrangements had a hinged extension which reached out over the ship.   Drawing: Captain MacRae, Photo: MacRae collection

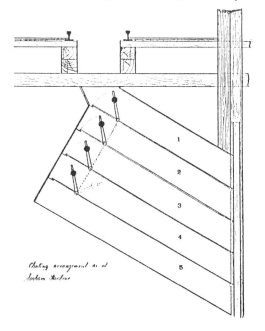

40. **Biddick** *alongside Lambton Staiths in 1891. Her original dimensions were 185.7' x 28.9'*
x 16.6', but by this date she had been lengthened by inserting a 25.3' section into the hull
directly in front of the bridge.   Photo: F.Depeaux, courtesy Tyne & Wear Museums

Morton & Co., had ceased as a separate entity and all the ships passed to the Earl of Durham,
giving him a fleet of 22 colliers and three paddle tugs. In 1896 the Earl sold his coal interests to
Sir James Joicey, who thereafter continued acquiring collieries. He registered his new acquisition
as Lambton Collieries Ltd. This company was merged to become the Lambton and Hetton Collieries
Ltd. when he acquired the latter and finally became the Lambton, Hetton and Joicey Collieries in
1924. In addition the Silksworth Colliery had been acquired from the Marquis of Londonderry.

After the Joicey takeover the shipping operations were controlled from Newcastle and managed
by Mr. E. T. Nisbet. Some of the old steamers were retained into the 20th century, **Langley** 702/68,
950 deadweight and **Biddick** 788/64, 1,090 deadweight, were both considered self-trimmers and had
their machinery renewed between 1868 and 1878 respectively and new boilers in 1886. **Sherburn**
retained her original machinery. Her speed was about 8 knots and she was not considered a self-
trimmer. Later vessels could manage about 9 knots and the large recently delivered **De Fontaine**
1716/01, 2,600 deadweight, could manage a service speed of 10 knots. More of these large colliers
were added to the fleet prior to the First World War and the older smaller vessels disposed of.

During the war all the fleet were fully employed in the war effort and several were lost, **Lady
Ann** 1082/83 and **De Fontaine** 1716/01 to mines, **Herrington** 1285/05 and the **Gregynog** 1698/99 to
submarine attack. Following the ending of hostilities the Tanfield S. S. Co. Ltd., was formed, with the
Joicey family providing three of the five directors along with E. T. Nisbet and J. R. D. Bell. The
capital was £250,000 and of this £133,925 was subscribed by the Lambton, Hetton and Joicey Collieries, thus leaving the fleet under colliery control and the houseflag and funnel colours unchanged. A
programme of renewal was begun as soon as the price for building new ships had fallen sufficiently.
In 1924 **Hetton** 2714/24 and **New Lambton** 1709/24 joined the fleet and **Harraton** 2795/30. The
general pattern of trade was for the ships to be employed in the coal trade to London during the
winter months and usually the Spanish iron-ore trade in summer, though this latter trade was not a
pleasant one for the Lambton colliers during the Spanish Civil War of 1937. Voyages further afield
to the Mediterranean were also usual during the 1920s and 1930s. Usually in winter at least three
of the colliers would be chartered to carry coal to Beckton Gas Works. As the Works had just two
berths, there was alway a great deal of keen competition for the berths between the Tanfield ships
and those under Stephenson Clarke. Mr. W. B. Nisbet, who had taken over as Manager, allowed
his masters who liked the Beckton trade, to put in for it each winter. He would always impress on
them to run no risks, nevertheless when going down to Bordeaux or Bilbao the passage was always by
the shortest route viz Yarmouth Roads, the Downs, the Fair Channel, Raz du Seine.

During the 1930s trade continued to improve and two ships were purchased from the Burnett S. S.
Co., also of Newcasle, **Heworth** 2855/24 and **Marsden** 2874/24, which, as they already had appropriate
local names, were not re-named. New vessels were also ordered. About 1933 some completely
new summer employment appeared in the form of Russian time charters. These were very lucrative
and the Tanfield ships ideal with their good ballasting. It was known as the Kara Sea Expedition by
Sovfrecht and was a convoy from Murmansk to Igarka of 12 ships. Captain Judge aboard **New Lambton** 2709/24 was designated lead ship for the voyage to the mouth of the River Yenesi for the
500 miles or so down the river to the town of Igarka. Captain Judge had a conference with the other
captains who were Swedish, Finnish, Latvian and British, before leaving Murmansk, and a speed
of 8.5 knots was decided upon. The Russians provided Captain Judge with an Ice Advisor who turned
out to be a bear hunter who could speak no English, so communication was by means of carefully
drawn sketches, details of which were then radioed back to the following ships. These sketches were
essential as the standard compass gave an alteration in deviation whenever the firemen swung
the vents in search of a breeze. All went quite well and after 12 hours pushing through ice out of

the 12 ships only three had very slight damage due to running against old winter ice which had been swept out of the Rivers Ob, Yenesi and Lena, which being freshwater ice was harder than sea ice. A single pilot came aboard at Golchika for the remainder of the voyage to Igarka. This meant good station keeping by the following ships, which was achieved. The season was short and only one trip per year was made in the months of July and August.

Lea Grange was completed in December 1939 and had already been allotted a collier number (80) on the 17th of July, so provision was made for coal to London. She survived the war but **Heworth, Hutton** and **New Lambton** were all lost to enemy action in the later part of 1940 while on the East Coast Coal run. As a partial replacement the Company were allowed to build **Lambtonian**, completed by S.P. Austin's yard in January 1942. Both survived the war and were sold in 1953 to Stephenson Clarke and became full time colliers. Meanwhile the Scandinavian type war built steamer **Van Ostade** (ex **Empire Toiler**) was purchased in the latter part of 1950 with a view to the Baltic, Bay and Mediterranean trades and renamed **Etal Manor** after Lord Joicey's home. However with the traditional coal cargoes now under the control of the National Coal Board and little coal being exported, prospects were not good and **Etal Manor** was sold to the Pelton S.S. Co., to become **Moto** in 1955, thus ending over 100 years of enterprise in the coal trade by the Lambton and Joicey families.

The Hetton collieries, which were taken over by Sir James Joicey in 1911, had their staiths just a little up-river from the Lambton drops and had been brought into prominence by the Wood family of Hetton Hall which lay to the south of the river. They too were pioneer collier owners, indeed the first steam collier to be registered at the port of Sunderland was apparently the **Hetton** 560/54 registered in the name of William Armstrong and others. The vessel measured 163.8' x 28.0' x 16.2' and within a month two further vessels were registered in the name of Nicholas Wood. These were **Cochrane** 528/54 (164.9' x 26.4' x 15.5') and **Black Boy** 537/54 (164.0' x 26.5' x 15.7'). By 1861, apart from **Cochrane** and **Black Boy** Wood was associated with **Killingworth** 567/55, **Seaton** 552/57 and **Lyon** 435/57. Ten years later the Wood family still had **Black Boy** 504/54, **Cochrane** 508/54, which was owned in partnership with A. H. Cochrane among others, **Killingworth** 578/55 and **Lyon** 604/57. They also owned some shares in the newer ship **Fatfield** 658/65 in which C. R. Fenwick and W. T. Bell also had shares. Their holding in **Elemore** 706/70 was minor and it was managed by Robert Sharp of Sunderland who was agent for the Hetton Coal Co. By 1884 **Cochrane, Lyon** and **Seaton** were listed under the North Hetton Coal Co., and by 1888 just **Lyon** remained. The family then appear to have dropped out of collier owning on their own account.

The Wearmouth Coal Company were ideally placed to exploit the coal trade with London as their colliery was on the north bank of the river and was the nearest of all the collieries to the river. They had their own drops opposite those of the Lambtons. The Stobart, Fenwick and Bell families were all involved and were to remain so until the colliery was nationalised after the Second World War. W. T. Bell acted as fitter and managed **Belmont** 777/65, **Douglas** 768/61 and **Ocean King** 699/63. C. R. Fenwick, as London agent for the collieries, registered two steam colliers to handle the trade as early as 1855 and was also involved with Stobart in the later, locally registered vessels. William Stobart of Cocken Hall was also closely involved in the Earl of Lambton's coal trade. He was the leading owner in **Fatfield** 658/65 in the 1870s as well as **Amy** 808/70. Later he partnered Fenwick in the London firm of Fenwick Stobart & Co., which eventually became William France, Fenwick & Co.

Though more than half the 60 or so ships registered in 1870 were still directly owned or controlled by the four large colliery proprietors, other owners not so closely connected with coal production began to appear. Perhaps the most significant locally was James Westoll who, backed by the Adamson family, began to build up a fleet of steamships. The Adamsons, William, John and Thomas had made money from their fleet of sailing ships and joined James Westoll in a steam venture in the 1860s. By 1870 they had 5 steamers, **Natalian** (1865), **Advance** 758/65, **Wear** 776/65, **Pyrrha** 1089/69 and **Edgeworth** 727/70. **Wear** for example measured 195.1' 28.8' x16.7' and loaded in the Tyne at Northumberland Dock and sailed for Kronstadt on the 7th of September 1869 with a cargo of 1,026 tons of coal. Growth of the fleet was rapid and by 1884 he was managing 22 ships mostly suitable for the continental or Mediterranean trade. Other names to become significant by the 1880s in Sunderland were Culliford & Clarke, whose fleet were mainly involved in more distant trades, but had some colliers, as did that of Dixon & Wilson. Small owners active in the 1880s included Freer & Dix, Richard Weatherley and John G. Hill who had begun investing in ships in the 1870s and by the mid-1880s was managing his own vessels **Bromsgrove** 667/68, **G. N. Wilkinson** 719/69 and **Vectis** 907/77. His fleet was to rise to prominence in the 1890s, and eventually came under the management of Witherington and Everett (42). W. A. Watson on the other hand never had a large fleet but it was a particular feature of the East Coast coal trade to the Thames.

In the case of colliers on a regular trade, ties between the ship's crew and the shore were often stronger at the port where the ships regularly discharged than the home port of the owner. This was often the case where the vessel was on time charter or repeated voyage charter to a particular merchant who would probably have coal of different grades loaded at different berths on the North East Coast delivered to his own discharging berth on the Thames or Medway. This was certainly the case with **City of Rochester** 1329/79. Though she was built for W. A. Watson and partners of Sunderland she was regularly to be seen in the Medway as she carried coal to W. Haymer and Sons of Rochester for over 30 years. She had been specially equipped with steam cranes probably with

42. *Vectis of Witherington & Everett, Newcastle, aground at Ardurn Point off Plymouth. She had left Plymouth bound for Cardiff in ballast in fog and snow and was wrecked in the Christmas Gale of 1912.* From a photo, MacRae collection

a view to discharging into lighters alongside when lying in the Medway. Throughout much of her 30 years service on regular charter to Haymer's she was under the command of Captain Robert Hardy. The association betwen Messrs. Watson and Haymer must have been established at some time prior to the building of **City of Rochester** as Captain Hardy had commanded Watson's smaller **Dunelm** 782/77 on the same run and first became a regular visitor to Rochester in command of **Jubilee** a few years earlier. Captain Hardy became part of the social scene of Rochester and was an active member of the Rochester Conservative Club. Though his family home was in Sunderland, on his death at the age of 67 the Club and other organisations remembered him with flags at half mast, as did ships in the Medway. At that time a local newspaper credited him with carrying over a million tons of coal to Messrs. Haymers.

The design of the **City of Rochester** was fairly typical of 1879 with compound engines amidships and with forecastle, bridge deck and raised quarterdeck aft on registered dimensions of 240.0' x 33.0' x 18.9'. The steam cranes, similar to those fitted to vessels in the liner trade at that time, were fitted one on the foredeck between Nos. 1 and 2 holds and one on the afterdeck between Nos. 3 and 4 holds adjacent to the mast.

She was built by Osbourne, Graham and Company and the 1884 Turnbull's Register shows the 64 shares in **City of Rochester** were held quite widely with northern investors predominating: W. A. Watson [9], R.Hardy [2], R.T.Greenwell [6], J.Parker [2], C.Dinham of London [2], J.Cutter Patterson [1], R.W.Farrow of Easington Lane [2], J.Raine [2], R.Neilson [3], C.Johnson of South Hetton [1], W.T.Grieve [1], R.Grieve and W.Wilson, Langholme, Dumfries [1], G.E.Wood [10], L.Raine of Cockermouth [1], H.Taylor [2], C.Craig [2], M.Hudson [1], G.Butchart junior [2], W.A. Wilson and G.Buchart [3 jointly], Janet Swallows [3], Eleanor J.Walthews, Whitstable [6], Sarah Eilly and George Buchart junior [2 jointly]. The shareholders are of Sunderland unless otherwise indicated. W. A. Watson's management must have been successful at this time as the **Dunelm** built two years earlier had many of the same shareholders.

Captain Hardy also had an eye to another profitable employment for coastal colliers regularly moving along busy shipping lanes, that of salvage. On the 7th of February 1903, while proceeding north in ballast from Rochester to Sunderland, he rendered assistance to the new collier **Battersea** 860/02. **Battersea** was also bound northwards from the Nine Elms Gas Works to the Tyne and was on approximately the same course about a mile distant. The wind was about gale force from the S.S.W. The tide was on the flood and so was against the wind, giving a steep confused sea. Vessels in ballast tend to lift their screws out of the water in these conditions. The engine then races as there is no load on the propellors and as the bow begins to rise the screw is plunged back in suddenly, slowing the propellor shaft and in the case of **Battersea** sufficient to fracture it. The engineers were probably not quick enough to cut the steam to the engine or were relying on a governor to control engine speed. The fracture had probably been getting worse over hours or even months and finally spread right across the shaft. The Captain immediately hoisted the signal N.C., the international distress signal and blew the ship's whistle to attract the attention of other vessels nearby. **City of Rochester** immediately altered course towards **Battersea** which was about half a mile off the Shipwash Lightship When she was within hailing distance the master of the **Battersea** asked to be taken in tow for the Tyne and put out his boat to carry a heaving line to **City of Rochester**. This line was then used to haul the 3.5 inch steel wire hawser of **Battersea** aboard **City of Rochester**. At about 5.45 p.m. towing began with about 100 fathoms of the hawser between the two ships. The first task was to bring **Battersea**'s bow round which was pointing towards the shore. Unfortunately the tow soon parted because of both vessels rolling and sheering in the rough sea. As it was too rough and dark to lower a boat **City of Rochester** backed down to **Battersea** and after several attempts got a heaving line on board and another 3.5 inch wire was passed from **Battersea** and shackled on to the broken end of the first hawser. In order to get more spring in the the tow a coir hawser was attached to the wire hawser aboard **Battersea**, which had a crew of 17 hands all told. They now had about 140 fathoms of tow line and by the time towing could again be commenced at 6.15 p.m. **Battersea** was about a mile to the S.E. of Orfordness. At about 8.30 when almost 3 miles off Southwold the coir hawser broke aboard the **Battersea**. After several attempts a heaving line was got aboard **Battersea** by **City of Rochester** and the two steel hawsers which had been recovered by the **City of Rochester** were hauled back again and attached to the chain cable of **Battersea** which gave about 200 fathoms of scope. In addition one of **City of Rochester's** wires was shackled on to the shackle where the two wire hawsers were joined. This wire was taken to the port quarter of **City of Rochester** and made fast to act as a bridle.

At about 10.15 p.m. towing resumed at a speed of 6.5 knots, the vessels having been driven past Yarmouth Roads. A NNE course was followed and at 11.45 p.m. the Cross Sand Lightship was passed. The wind by this time had veered WNW and was blowing hard and squally and the course was altered to the north west so as to get under the lee of the land. At 10 a.m. the following morning the coir hawser again parted due to the short confused sea and gale force conditions. However, the tow was reconnected and though the captain of **Battersea** suggested sheltering in the Humber, **City of Rochester** pressed on through heavy squalls, especially in the afternoon. At 8.30 p.m. they arrived off the Tyne where the tow was handed over to the tug **Devonia** at the request of the **Battersea** which was taken to the middle docks. They had covered 230 miles in 38 hours. At the time of the salvage **City of Rochester** was said to be worth £12,000 and **Battersea** £14,000. The values suggest that, as would be expected, the owners of **Battersea** tended to undervalue their vessel to reduce the claim on themselves, while Watson had rather over-valued his ship in order to get more risk money from the salvage claim.

City of Rochester herself got into difficulties on the north east coast a few years later in 1908 when she ran ashore on Redcar Beach (43) while on a voyage to Middlesborough with chalk. By this time she had shortened topmasts and much reduced capacity to carry sail. She was successfully refloated and again carried out some salvage. The following year, at 2.30 p.m. on the 24th of July, on a voyage from Blyth to Rotterdam with coal she was proceeding through a south westerly gale when she observed **Ocean Prince** blowing her whistle and flying the signal 'My screw is lost or out of order'. **Ocean Prince** was of 5,101 gross tons and was bound from Rotterdam and in ballast. The propellor had worked loose and jammed against the rudder post and she had anchored, but was in danger of breaking her cable in the wind and sea. Owing to the severity of the conditions **City of Rochester** was forced to stand-by and anchored until conditions improved. By the following afternoon conditions had moderated sufficiently to send a boat to the **Ocean Prince** and ask if she wished to be towed and where to. He replied Yes, to Rotterdam. The **City of Rochester** then anchored ahead of **Ocean Prince** and allowed her small boat to drift down to **Ocean Prince** to pick up her 4 inch wire. This was successfully got on board **City of Rochester** which because of the size of **Ocean Prince** could make only about 3 knots and also was making considerable leeway. They took 8 hours to cover the 30 miles to the Hook of Holland where **Ocean Prince** anchored. The Dutch pilot, on board **City of Rochester** by this time, insisting on this, as the pilotage regulations prohibited such towing in the river.

Having survived many such incidents in her long life in the North East coal trade she was finally to meet her end on the 24th September 1909. The vessel was usually employed carrying coal between Seaham and Rochester but had been making a few trips to the continent as the summer demand for coal was insufficient to keep the steamer fully occupied on her usual run. She had sailed from Shields Harbour about a week previously with a cargo of coal for Hamburg. On the return voyage to Seaham all went well until the ship encountered fog off the Dogger Bank. At about 11 p.m. a collision occurred with **Director Rippenhagen** 1683/93 which struck the port side of **City of Rochester** abreast the fore-hatch. The water rushed into the fore part of the ship and those members of the crew hearing and feeling the crash rushed on deck. By this time the vessel had begun to settle forward and then heel over. The only boat available was on the higher side and could not be launched, but fortunately **Director Rippenhagen** had swung round alongside after the collision and the crew scrambled on to the German steamer. One of the seamen was seriously injured, his leg being crushed between the

43. City of Rochester of 1879 stranded off Redcar in 1908 on a voyage to Middlesbrough with a cargo of chalk. Despite being almost 30 years old she survived and was eventually refloated and returned to service.   From a photo courtesy Tyne & Wear Museums

two vessels, but was successfully hauled aboard the German vessel. Meanwhile the two vessels had drifted apart leaving some crew members on the forecastle head. The German crew launched their boat and went to the forecastle of **City of Rochester**, which was by now practically down to water level and the remaining crew members, except for the steward were able to step into the boat. The latter was spotted on the after part of the ship. He was advised to jump but he did not come up again and was apparently sucked down into the sinking ship and drowned. **City of Rochester** had gone down in about 15 minutes.

The German vessel, which had been on a voyage from Hull to Stettin with coal had a large hole in her bows which was stuffed with a straw mattress. They then set course for the Tyne where the crew, nearly all from Sunderland, were landed. The German crew had done much to make the survivors as comfortable as possible and gave clothes to those who had been asleep at the time of the collision and who were forced to leave the ship before they could dress.

Mr. Watson now needed a replacement vessel and because of the specialised nature of the trade and its regular nature, he decided to have one specially built. The order was placed with Sir Raylton Dixon & Co. Ltd. The steam cranes were retained (45) but the opportunity was taken to incorporate the latest improvements in collier design. The machinery was placed aft with the bridge to leave a long unobstructed deck and hold which had one permanent bulkhead, but could be divided with wood bulkheads into five holds allowing up to five different grades of coal to be carried. Perhaps the most advanced feature of **Rochester City** was the topside water ballast tanks which meant that she was completely self-trimming and must have been one of the earliest colliers so fitted. Crew accommodation was also fairly well laid out with two bathrooms aft for the officers, but the remainder of the crew still had the rather sparse accommodation typical of the period. Though the new vessel was slightly shorter and of shallower draft, beam was increased by two feet and this gave a greater deadweight of 1,875 tons. The vessel was completed in 1910. Captain A. Hardy, who had spent many years in the previous vessel, supervised her construction and carried out her sea trials on the 1st of February. The vessel was sunk in the North Sea on the 5th of May 1916.

West Hartlepool and the Tees

The Tees in its natural state at the beginning of the 19th century was not very suitable for navigation as the wide lower reaches had numerous shifting sandbanks, and the upper part winding up to Stockton was also difficult. The nearest colliery was some 14 miles to the east in the southern part of the Durham coalfield. The packhorse transport used made the coal so expensive that it was often cheaper to ship it in for the inhabitants by sea from Newcastle. Change began to come about with the construction of the Stockton and Darlington railway which was supported in Parliament by Mr. Lambton, who felt sure that it could not compete with his colliery and railway, but just to be sure inserted a clause in the Bill which only allowed the railway a very low toll charge on coal for shipping. But the charge of half a penny per ton did not work and by 1826, after more staiths were built, over 50,000 tons of South Durham coal was shipped to London, even though the size of ship was much restricted. To get round this the line was extended from Stockton to Middlesborough. Further railways were built, of which the Hartlepool Dock and Railway scheme was the most important as new collieries were being opened on the eastern side of the Durham coalfield. Though their charges were high for carrying coal, the Hartlepool dock dues were low and the navigation in and out was quick and easy. The expanding network from Hartlepool soon captured the coal shipments being sent south to the Tees and the increase in trade led to the promotion of the West Hartlepool Dock in 1844. The new coal dock was opened in 1847. Further expansion of the docks westward continued, quarried out of the limestone in the 1850s. This dock company and its associated railway remained independent of amalgamation for many years, but management irregularities and the depression in the coal trade led to the company being taken over by its later rival the North Eastern Railway, in 1864. Dock expansion was undertaken in the 1870s and in 1880 a new entrance to West Hartlepool Docks was opened in the form of the North Basin, and the new Central and Union docks came into use.

Coal shipments from the port were important but were always small in comparison with Newcastle none the less they measured in millions of tons. The first steam collier to work from the port was **Hunwick** 409/54 (see p.17), but was not very successful and the company moved into the liner trade. However another local coal shipping venture under George Pyman was more successful. He came from a seafaring Whitby family and later sailed on board local brigs, rising to the rank of Captain at the age of 21 in 1843. At the age of 27 he gave up the sea and set up in West Hartlepool as a ship-chandler and later formed a partnership with Thomas Scurr to act as ship-brokers and coal-fitters for the South Durham and Weardale Iron and Coal Company's collieries. The business prospered, and on the death of Mr. Scurr the firm continued as George Pyman & Co. Having seen the success of steam introduced to the port by Jackson he ordered his first collier from the local yard of John Pile. The vessel, completed in 1865, was named **George Pyman** 610/65. Trade was generally improving and coal exports doing well. Further vessels soon followed, **Raithwaite Hall** 676/68 and **Lizzie English** 673/67. The latter vessel almost immediately began making quick and safe passages and was an example of the well deck steamer which was just coming into use. Whether George Pyman and the builders, Denton Gray's Shipyard, Middleton, can take the credit for this new design is uncertain, for the **Hugh Taylor**, built by Charles Mitchell in Newcastle was similar (18). The design proved successful and George Pyman continued to invest in new steamers. The enterprise grew rapid-

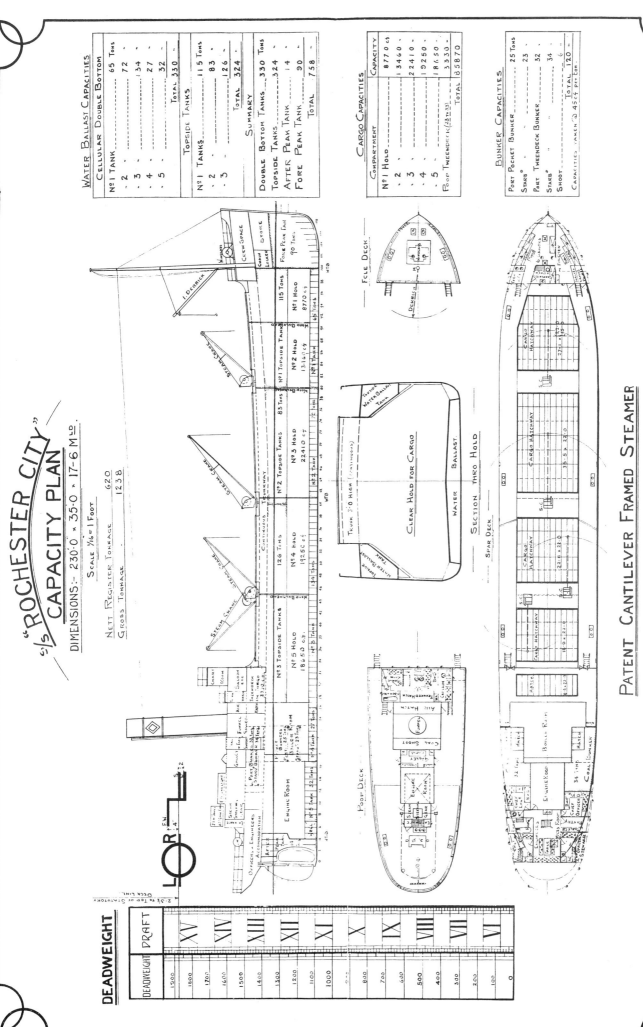

"ROCHESTER CITY"
s/s CAPACITY PLAN

DIMENSIONS:- 230·0 × 35·0 × 17·6 MLD.

SCALE 1/16" = 1 FOOT

NETT REGISTER TONNAGE - 620
GROSS TONNAGE - 1238

WATER BALLAST CAPACITIES

CELLULAR DOUBLE BOTTOM

No1 TANK	65 TONS
„ 2	72 „
„ 3	134 „
„ 4	27 „
„ 5	32 „
	TOTAL 330 „

TOPSIDE TANKS

No1 TANKS	115 TONS
„ 2	83 „
„ 3	126 „
	TOTAL 324 „

SUMMARY

DOUBLE BOTTOM TANKS	330 TONS
TOPSIDE TANKS	324 „
AFTER PEAK TANK	14 „
FORE PEAK TANK	90 „
	TOTAL 758 „

CARGO CAPACITIES

COMPARTMENT	CAPACITY
No1 HOLD	8770 c.f
„ 2 „	13460 „
„ 3 „	22410 „
„ 4 „	19250 „
„ 5 „	18650 „
POOP TWEENDECK (23 × 33)	3530 „
	TOTAL 85870

BUNKER CAPACITIES

PORT POCKET BUNKER	25 TONS
STARBD „	23 „
PORT TWEENDECK BUNKER	32 „
STARBD „	34 „
SHOOT	6 „
	TOTAL 120 „

CAPACITIES TAKEN @ 45 c.f per ton

FCLE DECK

TOPSIDE WATER BALLAST TANK

CLEAR HOLD FOR CARGO

WATER BALLAST

TRUNK 3'·0 HIGH (CONTINUOUS)

SECTION THRO HOLD

SPAR DECK

POOP DECK

DEADWEIGHT

DRAFT

PATENT CANTILEVER FRAMED STEAMER

BUILT BY SIR RAYLTON DIXON & Co LTD, MIDDLESBROUGH-ON-TEES.

No 544.

Courtesy Tyne & Wear Museums

ly. He soon expanded his coal exporting business to cover other ports, forming Pyman, Bell & Co., of Newcastle, Pyman, Watson of Cardiff and Pyman Brothers of London. The vessels traded widely and moved into the general tramping trades of coal out and grain, timber or other cargoes home. Other tramping companies such as Appleby, Ropner & Co., later to become Ropner & Co., were also developing in West Hartlepool at this time. The original Hartlepool Collieries Co. had the collier **Ludworth** 448/66, which was registered in London. The staiths at Hartlepool closed in 1970, suddenly no longer there, and took with them the long shoots that demanded that the smaller and medium sized colliers had to be held off by means of wires to buoys during the whole of the loading operations. They were heartily disliked by most of the collier men, for it meant that the watch aboard were kept fully occupied when the ships were sent there to load, tending the mooring lines.

Goole

Goole became an important loading port for Yorkshire coal, mainly as a result of the Aire & Calder Navigation, which made these rivers navigable. The Selby Canal had been constructed to give another outlet to the Ouse but this proved inadequate for the larger vessels and merchants began pressing for an outlet nearer the sea which would be suitable for longer ships. Eventually Parliamentary powers were obtained to construct a new canal from Knottingley to the Ouse at what became Goole. The canal was opened, together with the docks, on the 20th of July 1826. There were two locks admitting vessels to a small harbour, off which led locks into a ship dock. A barge dock and extension were made in 1838. The railway arrived at Goole in 1848 and to handle the expected extra traffic the Railway Dock was constructed. In the 1850s the Lancashire and Yorkshire Railway, which controlled the line, attempted to start the shipment of coal from the port, but not much trade was done until later.

The establishment of the coal trade was left to the Aire and Calder Navigation. W. H. Bartholomew patented a system using rectangular tubs called compartment boats which were marshalled just like railway wagons into 'trains' and towed by tugs. They were essentially rectangular iron boxes 21' x 15' x 8', each carrying 35 tons of coal and up to 40 could be towed at one time, though initially they were not towed but pushed in groups of 6. The whole system worked very successfully, especially as Bartholomew also designed a hoist capable of lifting a compartment boat and tipping its contents down a shoot into a collier. The first boat hoist was working in the Ouse Dock by 1868. More hoists were added and at its peak the system had over 1,000 compartment boats and five hoists working. The hoists were worked by hydraulic power and the opportunity was taken to mechanise the opening of bridges and locks from the same power source. One of the earliest users was William France of Leeds, who opened a service to London with his steamers such as **William Aldam** 283/54. There was never sufficient general cargo on the southward run and so he filled up his ships with coal, later moving to London and eventually selling the business to Fenwick, Stobart & Co. of London. The success of the compartment boats and the acceptance of Yorkshire coal by the London and later the continental markets, led to other local men founding shipping companies based on the new coal trade. One of the leading companies was the Yorkshire Coal and S. S. Co.,(46) who had three new ships in service by 1875, **Dinnington** 374/73, **Marianne Briggs** 630/74 and **Whitwood** 391/72.

Under Batholomew's supervision, the Aldam Dock was added in 1882 and a second compartment boat hoist completed in the Ouse Dock. However, as at other ports, the next step required river improvements and these became possible when the Aire and Calder Navigation obtained powers in the Ouse (Lower) Improvement Act to straighten and deepen the channel and construct training walls. This allowed the size of vessels loading coal to be increased from 500 tons up to 2,000 tons by the turn of the century. To handle these ships further coaling appliances were built, and during the 1880s the Railway Dock was extended and the 'New Extension Dock' as it was then known opened to traffic in 1891. It later became the Stanhope Dock. Goole's coal traffic had now become important and was similar in amount to West Hartlepool but only about 8% of that of the Tyne. None-the-less this was a considerable achievement considering the average cargo was only 350 tons in the early 1880s, compared with the Tyne where the average cargo was just over 900 tons.

3.

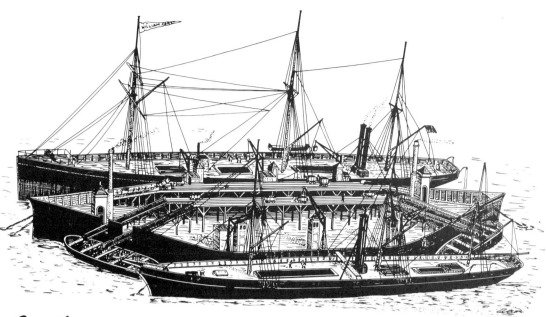

47. Cory's Atlas

Rise of the Southern Collier Fleets

As early as 1860 more than half the coal was being discharged by hydraulic or steam cranes. These were able to attain a discharge rate of about 60 tons per hour. This was achieved by loading iron tubs by hand in the ship's hold as the mechanical grab had not yet come into use. The coal whippers, discharging by traditional methods, were now much less in demand and in 1856 they were forced to take a cut in wages to compete with the cranes and the 'coal backers', men who shovelled the coal into bags and carried it ashore, from ships alongside the proliferating wharves.

One of the companies behind these improvements was William Cory and Son who had been leading merchants under various titles before the turn of the century. The present title was adopted when William Cory junior joined the firm in 1838. Richard Cory joined the firm in 1846 and by 1848 was a partner. Both sons were keen to try out new ideas and they possibly found it easier to do so when their father retired in 1854. They had shares in the new steam collier **Samuel Laing** 606/54 which was built by Palmer Bros. & Co. for a group headed by Hugh Taylor, the Newcastle coal owner, which included William Cory junior and John Fenwick. The vessel was some 30 feet longer than those Palmer was building for the General Iron Screw Collier Co, and had the dimensions 190.2' x 26.8' x 15.6'. Having purchased their big steam collier they had to discharge it efficiently when it arrived in London. To do this they built No.1 Jetty in the tidal basin of the Victoria Dock, which was completed in 1855. The jetty was fitted out with the most modern equipment of the times. Three hydraulically-powered cranes were installed, each capable of handling 15 cwt capacity tubs. These were tipped into large hoppers which were used to guide the coal into small railway trucks which were pushed and tipped by hand into large storage bins which had capacities of 750 to 1,000 tons of coal. The adjacent facilities were also developed by other coal merchants and factors so that in total there were 8 hydraulic cranes in use in the tidal basin of the Victoria Dock. By 1860 the dock was handling about 700,000 tons of coal per year, Cory's having taken over all the coal berths by this time. Mooring tiers were provided for the screw colliers in place of the smaller moorings used for brigs, though colliers arriving one day were usually away by the following night.

Similar developments were being made elsewhere on the Thames, such as Ratcliff Wharf. This was built by the Charringtons and was laid out to handle coal efficiently from ships and load wagons for despatch by road as well as barges. It was further up river on the north bank at Shadwell, not far from the Regents Canal Dock. John and Thomas Charrington purchased the old Bell Wharf and spent some £30,000 on the new facilities, which included two cranes. It was completed in 1857. However, these facilities were soon surpassed for convenience and speed by a completely novel approach to discharge taken by the Cory's. They had a large fleet of lighters but only acquired their first steam tug in 1859. This meant that barges would be much less dependent on the tide for movement and generally was to revolutionise the lighterage trade on the Thames. Originally there were a few steam tugs which towed long strings of barges on the wider parts of the river below Woolwich, but higher up they were navigated by lightermen using long sweeps and working with the tide.

Though the shore discharging facilities for coal installed by Cory's at the Victoria Dock were a success they could not be used at all states of the tide and there were still delays getting the steam colliers alongside and where coal was to be delivered to customers by lighters there was only need for shore facilities in the form of cranes for discharging. In the summer of 1860 William Cory purchased a large floating derrick which had been built for a group of investors who intended to use it for lifting vessels which had sunk. This group had formed the Patent Derrick Company, registered in 1857, and commissioned the Thames Iron Shipbuilding Company to build it for them, who completed it in 1859 as the Atlas. However it was not a success and they sold it cheaply to William Cory. In September 1861 Cory put down his ideas for use of the vessel in the form of a patent 'invention for improvements in vessels and machinery for unloading colliers and other vessels containing coals'. He removed the original derrick and replaced it with six hydraulic weighing cranes, powered by a central steam plant which provided the cranes with water under pressure. The new plant was included in the International Exhibition of 1862 and illustrated in the catalogue (47). The illustration shows the Atlas with **William Cory** 1578/57 alongside which was apparently known on the river as 'dirty billy'. It may be of note that the artist has depicted the collier with a plain black funnel. The arrangement of the Atlas allowed two large steam colliers to be rapidly discharged to lighters alongside. The plan to moor the Atlas in the river came under opposition from the owners of the Victoria Dock who were worried about loss of dock work, and the Coal Factors Society. The latter sent a deputation of factors to a meeting of the Thames Conservancy in October 1861, where they stated that discharging facilities were adequate and that no one firm should be allowed the large exclusive mooring space needed in Bugsby's Hole, where it was proposed to moor the derrick barge. The Conservators deliberated on the matter for some months, examining the submission of Cory and those of the objectors. Eventually they gave permission for the derrick to be moored in the river, but only after Cory gave notice of appeal to Parliament after the initial application was rejected. The Atlas came into operation in November 1862, just in time for the busy winter period, moored in Bugsby's Hole at the top end of Woolwich reach. The Conservators made certain stipulations. Firstly that a yearly rental of £300 in the first year, rising to £650 by the third and following years, be paid. Secondly, the discharging facilities must be generally available to the coal trade and thirdly that Cory's lighters coming above bridges must be towed by steam tugs. At this time no other firm was using steam in the upper part of the river for towing and this stipulation was probably made because of the traffic congestion which might arise. Cory's had about 250 lighters and often hired as many more again to handle their trade, which was about 1,000,000 tons in 1862 or nearly 28% of the total coal cargoes arriving in the Thames.

The Atlas soon proved a great success as each crane could discharge 60 tons per hour, and working two steam colliers, could discharge their 1,200 tons into lighters in 10 hours. Steam vessels were given priority in its use and night operation was facilitated by the gas plant fitted which supplied gas lamps to illuminate working. Even so, in terms of tonnage, the collier brigs were still delivering some 75% of the coal arriving by sea and so there was still a great part of the market to be exploited by the steam colliers. The opposition faded away and plans were soon put in hand for a second Atlas. Prior to the commissioning of the first Atlas, J. Adams had made proposals for two buildings at Prince's Stair which would provide rapid discharge for colliers coming to the Pool of London using hydraulic power. This proposal was probably overtaken by Cory and his project and so it was perhaps to avoid a conflict of interests that in September 1865 Cory and Adams jointly took out a patent for an improved version which used weighbridges rather than weighing cranes. Though the amount of coal arriving by sea was not increasing much in quantity, steam colliers continued to replace collier brigs wherever shore facilities were available for rapid loading and discharge, and the costs of constructing such vessels was also falling, so there was a need for a second Atlas.

The new coal discharging float was built on the Tyne and towed down to the Thames to be moored a little up-stream from the original Atlas, which became Atlas No.1, while the new vessel became Atlas No.2. Atlas No.2 began work in 1866 and by the mid-1870s the two floats were handling about 1.3 million tons of the 2.75 million tons of sea coal for London, or just under half the trade. When Atlas No.2 was being planned there were discussions with the Coal Factors Society with the view of forming a separate company to own the derricks. Stephenson Clarke and C.M. Palmer both offered to make considerable investments in the project, but it came to nothing and Cory continued to own both. The floats, apart from discharging the coal, also had shoots which had a double purpose, they loaded the waiting lighters and graded the coal for size at the same time.

The coal business was in many ways a series of partnerships between coal owners, shippers, factors and merchants, and this is clearly seen in the Cory brothers arrangements of their trade. Having invested heavily in the Victoria Dock discharging facility, the steam colliers using the facility were not wholly owned by Cory's but were owned in partnership with coal suppliers and customers. The colliers were built by Palmer Brothers for a group led by Hugh Taylor of the Ryhope Coal Company of Newcastle, William Cory Junior and John Fenwick. The vessels were:

Date Built	Name	Registered Dimensions	Tons Gross
1854	Samuel Laing	190.2' x 26.8' x 15.6'	606
1855	Earsdon	171.1' x 26.4' x 15.7'	526
1855	General Codrington	163.0' x 26.1' x 15.8'	452
1855	George Hawkins	158.5' x 26.3' x 15.5'	466
1855	Sardinian	169.5' x 26.4' x 15.9'	520

The vessels traded quite widely and two were lost in the Baltic by 1860 (**Earsdon** and **George Hawkins**) and **General Codrington** was also lost after being sold to A. G. Robinson of London. The other two were much more successful, **Samuel Laing** sailing for Cory's until 26th of February 1901 when she sank off the Newarp Light Vessel after a collision with the steamer **Chamois**. The **Sardinian** did even better, lasting in the coal trade until February 1913, when she was sold to French ship-breakers for demolition at Boulogne. She had been sold to the Woods in 1874 and when broken up the registered owners were the Hetton Coal Co. Ltd.

Further vessels were built, the largest of which was **William Cory** 1578/57, purchased in association with Cardiff coal owner John Nixon. His steam coal was important, and with the expanding use of steamships and railways was used both at home and overseas. Further vessels were added during the 1860s and the investors were drawn quite widely from London and the North. By 1870 the Cory's had interests in quite a number of vessels. Most of these were slowly being registered with John Fenwick (later John Fenwick & Son) as the managing owners. Those registered in Newcastle were **Beckton** of 1869 (Richard Cory 16 shares, J. Fenwick 16 shares, J. Nixon of Cardiff 12 shares, J. & E. Joicey 6 shares each). The vessel was named after the gasworks and so it was probably the Joicey's coal which was intended as the initial cargo, rather than Nixon's steam coal. Shares were held in smaller groups in the **Magna Carta** 764/65 but again Cory, Fenwick and the Joicey's held 25 shares between them.

Mary Nixon 758/65 was built by Palmers for John Nixon of Cardiff who registered his ship at Newcastle with his partner Richard Cory, who held 12 shares. John Nixon was a steam engineer originally from London who had moved to Cardiff and sunk coal mines in the area when he saw what good steam coals could be mined in South Wales. The **Mary Nixon** served her shareholders well and joined the Cory fleet proper in 1891. She had at least one voyage from Northumberland Dock, and probably many more, sailing from there with 904 tons of coal for London on the 22nd of February 1871.

New Pelton 630/65 was half owned by Richard Cory with the other half owned by the coal owners J. & E. Joicey, and appropriately the vessel was named after one of the latter's collieries. **Northumbria** 900/69 was the largest of the Newcastle registered vessels in 1870, with the dimensions 221.1' x 28.1' x 17.4'. Her cargo capacity was about 1,070 tons. Richard Cory held 16 shares and other prominent shareholders were Fenwick, the Joiceys and Nixon. The old **Northumbria** (29), served her owners well until she failed to arrive in London having sailed from Leith on the 23rd of December 1915, almost certainly a victim of enemy action. The Cory Brothers, William and Richard, owned the Sunderland registered **Berrington** 629/65 in equal shares in 1870 but by 1875 management was in the hands of J. Fenwick & Son and she was lengthened. Fenwick also had other vessels in which the Cory's were not involved, and controlled a large fleet in the 1870s and 1880s.

A similarly complex picture existed with the London registered ships. In 1870 the Cory's were involved in **Samuel Laing** 606/54, **Sardinian** 566/55, **Henry Morton** 986/60, **Ryhope** 687/61, **Haswell** 706/61, **Tom John Taylor** 687/61, **Hawthorns** 752/61, **James Joicey** 695/63, **John M'Intyre** 985/63, **Despatch** 728/63, **Thomas Lea** 630/76, **J. R. Hinde** 740/64, **Orwell** 628/64, **Tanfield** 759/64, **Berwick** 537/55, **Usworth** 524/69, and **Fenella** 1097/70. Vessels as large as **Fenella** (246.6' x 29.1' x 17.5) would have been mainly involved in the Baltic and Mediterranean trades. Many of the vessels had long lives in the coal trade and thus a tribute to the shipyards and men who built them. Nearly all came from Palmer's yard at Jarrow and were mostly fitted with 2-cylinder simple expansion inverted engines. During the 1870s these were converted to compound expansion engines to improve efficiency and reduce coal consumption. This was often just to get a few years more service from the engine which were then replaced by more modern compounds in the 1880s.

Many of the early ships were registered in the name of H. Taylor & Co., who were the Ryhope Coal Company, and although his associates John Fenwick, who took over management of the colliers in the 1870s, and Cory, had about a third of the London coal trade, Stephenson Clarke was also a prominent figure for he represented another major northern coal owner John Bowes and partners. The family had been in the London coal trade for at least a century when Robert Clarke died in 1849 and handed over to his son. Stephenson Clarke did not go in for steam colliers but waited until 1865 when Palmers of Jarrow delivered **J. M. Strachan** 762/65, **C. S. Butler** 760/65, both just under 200 feet long and the smaller **M. E. Clarke** 656/65 which was 181 feet in length. He went back to Palmers in 1870 for **Lord Alfred Paget** 866/70. It was in this year that Stephenson Clarke landed the contract to supply 15,200 tons of coal to the Southampton Gas Works, with the monthly amounts varying from 2,400 in winter down to 800 in the summer months. This contract was to be renewed for almost 100 years, with the last deliveries in 1968 when the coal plant was closed. It may have been this contract which led to **Lord Alfred Paget** being lengthened by about 20 feet the following year to give the dimensions 243.8' x 28.2' x 17.3', though possibly it was intended for longer voyages such as the Spanish trade for which he had **Luis de Cuadra** 923/75 built four years later, followed by other vessels. In the interim the steamer **Shoreham** 791/72 was added to the fleet, probably for

49. Mary Nixon of 1865.
From a photo, MacRae Collection

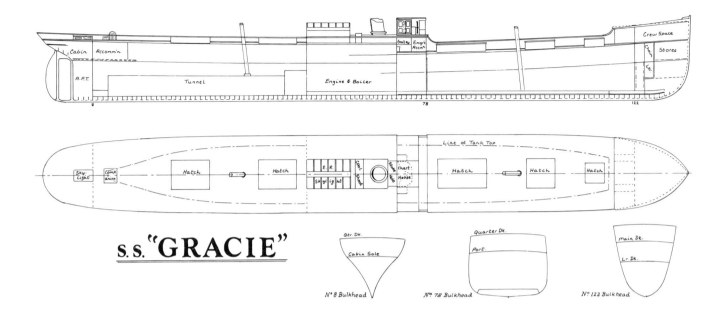

s.s. "GRACIE"

Qtr. Dk.
Cabin Sole
Nº 8 Bulkhead

Quarter Dk.
Port.
Nº 78 Bulkhead

Main Dk.
Lr. Dk.
Nº 122 Bulkhead

50. *General arrangement and machinery of Stephenson Clarke's collier* **Gracie** *of 1879 built by E. Withy & Co. She soon proved a very good ship and remained on the London coal trade for a number of years. Further similar vessels were built for the London trade and the* **Hadley** *of 1901, built for the Cory fleet shows how the design had advanced by the turn of the century. See page 57.*

Gracie from The Marine Engineer 1st June 1883

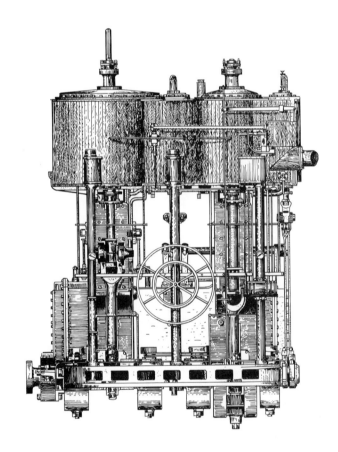

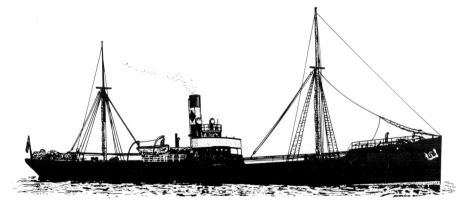

supplying the Brighton, Hove and Worthing Gas Company works, which was constructed in 1870. The name was to be a familiar one in the Stephenson Clarke fleet and reflected the Company's regular coal trade to the port. The problem with serving the port with steamers was the shallowness of the harbour, which only had about 15 feet of water and sometimes less, and a small entrance lock. The steamer's dimensions were 159.2' x 28.8' x 13.8' to allow for this. The vessel was lost on the 8th of January 1888 after colliding with the **Colstrup** 506/74 off the Kentish Knock Light Vessel while on passage from Shoreham to the Tyne in ballast.

During the latter part of the 1870s further steamers were ordered, the largest of which was **Gracie** 1312/79, which was described in the Marine Engineer of June and July 1883. She was built with considerable thought on the part of the owner's superintendent and E. Withy & Co. of West Hartlepool, the builders. The point which had been causing builders and owners problems was the raised quarterdeck which had been introduced in the early part of the 1870s and soon found to be a good feature from the shipowners point of view as it made the vessel easier to load and trim but more difficult to construct because of the discontinuity of the main deck. There were problems with the rivets working loose in the side plating where the deck changed from one level to the other, and although doubling plates were fitted to strengthen the sides, this had not proved sufficient to solve the problem. To achieve this Stephenson Clarke's marine superintendent and the builders made a working model and checked it for stiffness with various arrangements of fore-and-aft and athwartships stiffening plates. One of the features they noted was the stiffening effect of the vertical bulkhead between the two decks and to repeat this further aft they inserted a strong gusset plate vertically amidships between the main deck stringer, where it was supported by a bracket and against a strong engine room beam at the raised quarterdeck 4 feet above. This and other improvements sufficiently impressed the Lloyd's officials during construction that they later incorporated the improvements in the next edition of the rules for construction.

The general arrangement of the **Gracie** was similar to other vessels of the period (50). A particular feature was the good crew accommodation in the raised forecastle. The navigating officers and engineers were accommodated amidships, but the captain's accommodation was still aft, following the tradition established over hundreds of years for sailing vessels. The well deck forward was to lead to quite a serious incident: Because of her ample buoyancy provided by the extra height of deck aft and the forecastle forward, combined with the sheer, the freeboard measured at the after end of the well deck was only 2' 4". A Board of Trade official, on seeing her fully loaded with coal down to this freeboard at South Shields on the 20th of March 1883 considered her overloaded and placed a detention order on the **Gracie** despite the protests of John Brown, her master, that his ship was not overloaded. The master eventually sailed despite being served with a detention order, taking the luckless Customs official, Richard Harkness, with him. This led to the captain being fined £80 for breaking the detention order and £100 for carrying off the Customs Officer! Mr. Clarke, as owner, was also fined, but as he was in Spain at the time of the incident this was reduced to £1.

This was typical of the disputes that were going on about what constituted a safe load-line. Although Samuel Plimsoll's agitation for a proper load-line to prevent overloading had been incorporated in the Merchant Shipping Act of 1876 it did not get through Parliament, except in a much amended form. As passed, it was left to the discretion of owners, some of whom painted lines much too high on their ships. There is no doubt that overloading of colliers was taking place. The Board of Trade officials had the difficult task of trying to catch unscrupulous owners and captains and protect the lives of ordinary seamen with what was a very unsatisfactory law. The Board of Trade were, it seems, unwilling themselves to issue rules and the views of naval architects were also at variance. The 1882 Lloyd's rules on freeboard were considered by all parties to be very good and toned down all the defects of earlier tables. Eventually the Board of Trade called a conference with Lloyd's and other classification societies and finally in 1890 compulsory load lines corresponding with Lloyd's 1885 Rules were accepted, though the Board of Trade's load-line committee amended them somewhat later. In fact **Gracie** had been built in excess of the Lloyd's rules in force in 1879 and met the 1882 rules with a little in hand. The coefficient of fineness (block coefficient) was 0.77 for the hull below the upper deck and her surplus buoyancy was determined to be 26% while the new rules set a minimum of 0.76 and 25.5%. Her displacement was 2,949 tons and overall length 269.6'.

At least part of the extra strengthening was carried out because she was to be fitted with a rather more powerful machinery than was usually fitted to colliers at this time. The compound surface condensing type engines were supplied by J. Blair & Co., of Stockton-on-Tees. The cylinders were 36.5" and 68" in diameter and the stroke 42". They were fitted with steam and hand reversing gear and steam and hand turning gear to make examination of the crank pins and bearings a simple matter. The power developed when running light with 80 lbs of steam pressure was about 1,000 indicated horsepower. This was sufficient to give about 13.3 knots as indicated by 'Patent Log' when loaded with 1,840 tons of coal. The run from North Shields to London was done in good conditions in as little as 23 hours 30 minutes. In the first three years of full operation an average of just over 60 voyages per year was achieved. The extra speed was to catch an earlier tide, but as costs of bunkers and stokers wages increased, speeds of about 10 knots were reverted to after some years.

Other features included steam and hand steering gear by Wilson of Liverpool, which could be used from the bridge or from the flying or upper bridge. It was noted that the exhaust steam from the gear was fed back to the main condenser, unlike some steamers which exhausted to the air on the open bridge and could completely envelop the helmsman in steam, just when he needed to see where he was going, as to save fuel the gear was often only used when approaching land and docking. An engine room repeating telegraph by J. Humes & Sons of London was fitted, and a Durham & Churchill steam governor helped to prevent the Jackson's patent propellor racing when in rough seas it lifted out of the water.

The continuing replacement of the collier brigs by modern screw colliers of increasing capacity placed more demands on the discharging facilities. Discharging was finally fully mechanised in 1875 with the invention of the grab by Priestman, but tubs remained in use and the grab-crane did not come into service until the 1890s on the Thames. In 1870 a 31-year lease was taken on Prince's Wharf at Vauxhall and it became the base of Cory's subsidiary, the Sea Coal Co., under which name they sold coal in the retail trade. However developments continued with Atlas concept and the float **Atlas No.3** (52) was added, taking its place with **Atlas No.1** and **No.2**. To service these Cory built an enormous fleet of barges to take the coal from the 'Atlas' floats, and by about 1875 the barge building yard was producing almost one a week. By 1890 there was a fleet of some 500 barges with capacities ranging from 75 to 200 tons. However the expansion of the coal trade was always held somewhat in check by the City of London dues on seabourne coal, fixed at 1/1d per ton in 1831. These dues were devoted to various improvements of bridges and the construction of the Thames Embankment. They were reduced and finally abolished on the 5th of July 1890. The railways and canals were always free of any dues so there was now fair competition for all forms of coal transport.

Much of the 'sea coal' arriving in London was for household use but slowly the railway companies especially the Great Northern Railway built up a network of coal depots supplying Yorkshire coal. These were rented out to small merchants at favourable prices. They were much better placed to deliver coal to householders and so the colliers lost this trade to the railways. The Midland Railway too were active developing coal supplies from the Nottinghamshire coalfield. This was compensated for by the build-up in demand from industrial users, who became the main customers of the collier fleets by the end of the 19th century, and often had their own wharves.

Cory's were the largest single operator but many others were involved. The General Iron Screw Collier Company, after their original surge to prominence, tended to lose their position somewhat as merchants and factors took up the challenge of steamship owning. In 1862 their fleet consisted of vessels largely built in 1854 and 1855, with only **Brunette** 618/61 of later vintage. During the mid-1860s the fleet was renewed with slightly larger vessels so that by 1875 they had eight vessels, including **J. F. McConnell** 762/67, which loaded in the Northumberland Dock for London in 1873, as did the **Hutton Chaytor** 580/55, which loaded for Rochester and was the last of the original batch to serve the company. Though the early vessels were all built by Palmers on the Tyne, the vessels built during the 1860s came from a variety of builders.

Another company to come to prominence in the 1860s was the London S. S. Co. Ltd, which had offices in the Coal Exchange. Their vessels were longer than those of the General Iron Screw Collier Company and had names ending in 'a'. In 1874 they had 14 vessels probably engaged in the Baltic and Mediterranean trades in summer, but the more local coal trades in winter. **Sabrina** 819/65 (211.2' x 28.1' x 17.4') built by Palmer, loaded a full cargo of coal at Northumberland Dock on the Tyne and sailed for London on the 27th February 1870. There was also **Medora** 966/64 on the 13th of October 1869, for London, and **Miranda** 996/70 on the 31st October 1870. **Miranda** was typical of the slightly larger vessels which were added to the fleet, she measured 236.0' x 28.1' x 17.2', and was another product of Palmers Yard at Jarrow. **Roxana** 915/68 (219.2' x 26.3' x 17.4') also loaded in the Northumberland Dock in June 1871 and took a cargo of coal for Southampton. The fleet lasted until the mid-1880s when it came under the management of John Fenwick & Son.

Also based at the London Coal Exchange were Lambert Brothers, the vessels often being registered under F. D. Lambert. Both were members of the Coal Factors Society, but their vessels were registered in the north in the 1870s. **Bebside** 605/64 was registered in Newcastle, F. D. Lambert owning 14 shares and the Joblings 18 shares. It is possible that as A. C. Pring owned 6 shares he acted as manager, though in practice the vessel was probably handled by him in the north and the Lambert's in the south. They sold her to James Laing in the early 1870s, who continued to use

52. Cory's third and last derrick barge, Atlas No.3., discharging the collier Surf 1597/96 around the turn of the century.

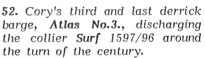
MacRae collection

her in the coal trade. They also owned **Lady Havelock** 570/61 with Lewis Ratto of London who owned 48 shares. **Jubilee** 790/64 made a voyage from Northumberland Dock to Southampton with coal in 1871. Their fleet was expanded steadily in the late 1870s and 1880s. Two notable additions to the fleet were **Medway** 944/79 and **Kent** 1045/81, both built for the company by Austin & Hunter with machinery amidships. They lasted until 1910 and 1911 respectively but by then were part of the Cory fleet. Lambert's also purchased **Burnham** 783/65 (ex **Upton**) and **Merthyr** 768/66, from fellow London collier owners Harris & Dixon. In the 1860s it was originally Dixon & Co., and operated from Gracechurch Street. F. W. Harris was a coal factor and had offices at the Coal Exchange. Between them they owned a dozen ships, most of which worked in the coal trade. Initially the partnership was known as Dixon & Harris. Two of their vessels, **Merthyr** 804/66 and **Bwllfa** 812/65 were named after Welsh mines. F. W. Harris and George Locket (later to merge with Charringtons) became involved with others in the sinking of pits at Cefin Bwllfa, the Rhondda and others including Locket's Merthyr Steam Coal. Co. The Bwllfa Colliery had a contract to supply Cie. Generale Transatlantique with bunkers for their Atlantic liners and the vessels were probably employed working to France where nearly all the output of the Bwllfa Colliery went in the latter part of the 1860s. Hastings was a visitor to Northumberland Dock and sailed for London with coal from there on at least two occasions in the 1860s and 1870s and probably many more, as did **James Southern** 801/65. Largest of the vessels and newest in 1875 was **Wimbledon** 1474/73 which was aimed at ocean tramping. Harris & Dixon went on from this to larger vessels and slowly dropped out of the coastal and continental coal trade by the end of the 1890s.

Another company to come to prominence at the beginning of the 1870s was the Commercial S. S. Co., of 32 Great St. Helen's Street. They had six vessels by 1875, often with names ending in 'on' such as **Brighton** 900/72. **Ann Webster** 771/70, **Pelaw** 793/69 and **Long Ditton** 813/70 loaded coal at Northumberland Dock for London, but **Long Ditton** was in the continental trade and as they built longer ships this was to be the pattern of their business.

Often, as might be expected, there were strong ties with the northeast coal ports. J. D. Hill, who was a coal factor on the London Coal Exchange, had an interest in Sunderland registered vessels including **Euclid** 686/66 and **Elemore** 706/70. Other shareholders were Robert Sharp of Gateshead and R. Weatherley. The latter expanded his interest in the 1870s, managing vessels such as **Dora** 645/73, and **Gilston** 557/72. Hunter & Co., had similar northern links and were associated with H. S. Pringle of Newcastle. They managed **William Hunter** 773/65, **George Elliott** 700/72 and **Charlaw** 901/72 which made voyages from the Tyne to London with coal in the 1870s.

Similarly C. R. Fenwick was an investor in the Wearmouth Coal Co. He was their London sales agent and traded as Fenwick & Co., and prior to 1861 as Fenwick, Laroche & Co. As the Wearmouth Colliery was on the north bank of the Wear, very close to the river, its coal had always been shipped to London and to facilitate this **Black Diamond** 588/55 and **Vedra** 588/55 were among the first London registered colliers. **Black Diamond** was still managed by C. R. Fenwick 20 years later, along with the newer and larger **Ernest** 726/70, **Nina** 783/70 and **Achilles** 1426/72 which was registered in Sunderland and probably intended for longer voyages. William Stobart held shares in this ship and this was later to lead to their interests being formally combined in Fenwick, Stobart & Co., in 1893. Apart from their coal trade Fenwick's had sailing vessels in the Tasmanian trade sailing outwards with general cargo and returning with wool. This return cargo was to bring them another partner in the coal trade who had also been trading to London for over 100 years. This was William France who traded between London and Leeds and who later moved to Goole as that northern port was improved. This was a regular service, but whereas the vessels could always be fully loaded with general goods from London, there was never sufficient for full cargoes southwards and so the ships made up a full cargo by loading coal. Thus William France's business, which operated from Stanton's Wharf, fitted in perfectly with Fenwick, Stobart & Co's for they could supply the northward cargo in the form of Australian wool and sell the coal brought south. A number of smaller companies owned one or two vessels such as the Patent Fuel Co. (Warlick's) Ltd., which owned **Retriever** 329/54 in 1875.

By far the largest manager in the 1880s was John Fenwick & Son, who, with Cory's fleet and others had over 20 ships and by 1891 this had risen to 32. They ranged from the old **Samuel Laing** of 1854 to the new **Urpeth** 1105/89. Most of the vessels were from 200 to 230 feet in length but larger vessels around 240 feet were added in the 1880s and 1890s. One of these vessels was **Langdon** 1262/82. Her registered dimensions were 240.0' x 34.2' x 16.1'. The main improvements for the coal trade were the large hatches (55) as compared with the **Hugh Taylor** built 13 years earlier. This vessel would be considered an easy trimmer and therefore quick to load. The raised-quarterdeck was now a much more substantial feature. This was helped by positioning the officers' accommodation at the after end of the well-deck so that there were two substantial bulkheads at the break of deck continuity. This was also helped by extending the main deck through on either side of the engine and over the boiler which was sufficiently compact to allow this. The engineers were neatly accommodated on this deck on either side of the engine so the Chief Engineer could always hear how things were going on in the engine room. The bunkers are arranged on either side of the boiler and filled from hatches on either side of the bridge deck. The only slight difficulty with the arrangement was that with the main deck extending through the coal bunker there was a little more trimming work needed to pass the coal down to the bunkers proper. Even on the shorter runs these 'tween decks bunker spaces would have probably been used as the compound machinery would have consumed more steam than the later triple expansion engines. The crew accommodation in the forecastle had changed little from earlier vessels and was not to change much for the next 50 years. One aspect of the accommodation was that the officers were now completely berthed amidships and the poop accommodation was reduced to a small store. The general layout was very modern in appearance but the low bridge and sails indicate age. A yard was still retained to set a square-sail and the masts were still in two pieces following sailing ship practice. Progress towards a modern wheelhouse was made with the protected steering position, but it was still rather low for easy navigation. The view forward was rather obstructed by the forecastle and so the flying bridge would have been in constant use.

The First Up-River Colliers or 'Flatirons'.

Perhaps the most novel development of the 1870s was the appearance of the collier with very low superstructure, broad beam and shallow draft designed to pass up the Thames under the fixed bridges and over shallows. The London Gas Light Company dissatisfied with the quality of coal arriving by barge at their Nine Elms Works asked for direct shipment. T. & C. Nicholls took on the contract and placed an order with Palmer's of Jarrow which resulted in **Westminster** 817/78 and **Vauxhall** 817/78. Their voyages to the London Gas Light Company's works at Nine Elms were so successful that the slightly deeper draughted **Lambeth** 923/79 was built measuring 220.5' x 32.2' x 14.5', an increase of 8.5 inches. The works were taken over by the Gas Light and Coke Co., who continued the charter of the vessels from River Steam Colliers Co. Ltd. (Managers: Escomb & Howard), London which had been formed to own the vessels in 1879. In 1884 **Westminster** was lost in collision with **Nerissa** off the Mouse Light Vessel when bound from the Tyne to London with coal. **Vauxhall** lasted until 1915 and the **Lambeth** until lost in a collision off Gunfleet Sands on December 7th 1899. A further vessel, **Chelsea** 1171/84 was built by River Steam Colliers for charter to the Gas Light and Coke Co. in 1884. Her dimensions were 230.0' x 33.2' x 14.9'. So a modest increase in size was achieved despite the limitations of river depth and the turning space available off the wharf. She served until lost 1903. They were single deck vessels with engines amidships on the basis of their register details. The design of these vessels was similar to the **Vane Tempest** built for the Londonderry fleet, see p. 37.

London and the South Coast.

The London factors and merchants often handled coal for ports along the south coast. Stephenson Clarke was particularly associated with Shoreham. In the 1880s there was little increase in the London trade and even a recession caused by over-tonnageing in the Bay trades and so Stephenson Clarke did not expand his Spanish interests but began to order steamers suitable for the Shoreham coal trade during the 1880s, which was developing. The size of vessel was limited by the lock which was constructed during the early 1850s and measured 175 feet in length and 31 feet in width and about 15 feet depth. Thus **John Grafton** 592/83 with registered dimensions 158.0' x 28.8' x 13.8' and **Portslade** 634/88 (161.7' x 29.9' x 11.9') were just able to fit into the lock, bearing in mind that the overall length would be some 6 to 7 feet longer than the registered length. A further very similar steamer, the **F. E. Webb** 585/91 was added in 1891. Unusually a return to sail was made in 1892 when four brigs were acquired from T. P. Cattey of Shoreham and a fifth purchased, but they were all old and traded for only a few years. The last to go was **Prospero** which was sold in 1899. No doubt they were cheap to buy and the steamers could be more profitably employed on other voyages, but were always available if a cargo was needed urgently.

Southampton had developed its collier fleet simultaneously with London. As already noted, the Steam Collier Company was registered on the 7th of October 1853. By 1862 they had the **Norman** 531/54, **Dane** 527/55 and **Celt** 551/55 in the coal trade to Southampton. The smaller earlier vessels had been disposed of. They dropped out of collier owning during the 1860s but two of their vessels passed to London owners Bremer, Bennett and Bremer of 61, Mark Lane.

Other collier owners appeared in the 1860s among which was the Southern Steam Collier & Coal Co., and their steamer **Basingstoke** 649/65 is noted sailing for London with 784 tons of coal on the 16th of November 1871 from the Tyne. However the main owner was W. Hill & Co., the vessels being registered in the name of James Ledger Hill. By 1875 his fleet consisted of **Hampshire** 625/66, **Henry Brand** 699/68, **Solent** 721/70 and **Ventnor** 857/72. The company subsequently had a long history in the Southampton coal trade. **Henry Brand** served the company well over the next 30 years or so and in 1904 the fleet was still the same except for **Solent**. Like most collier owners, they needed to find some other work for their colliers in summer and **Henry Brand** for example took a cargo of coal from Cardiff to Le Havre in May 1904 for 4/- per ton.

Amalgamations: The Great London Collier Fleets.

The 1890s saw considerable changes in the London collier fleets. This was partly due to the increase in consumption but also due to the larger steam colliers competing successfully with the railways to supply bulk industrial users, foremost of which were gasworks. Figures from the 1906 Royal Commission studying canals show that in 1880 37% of London's coal arrived by sea and represented 3,715,000 tons, but by 1900 the figure was 51% and the tonnage had increased to almost 8,000,000. This seaborne coal shipped to London had more than doubled, the greatest increase occurring during the 1890s. The tonnage brought by rail began to decline after 1900 but that by sea continued to increase.

Cory's continued to maintain their dominant position in the trade due to the determined efforts of C. F. Cory-Wright, a nephew of the first William Cory. He joined the company in 1860 and eight years later became a partner and took over the helm in 1888. He took up the challenge of selling

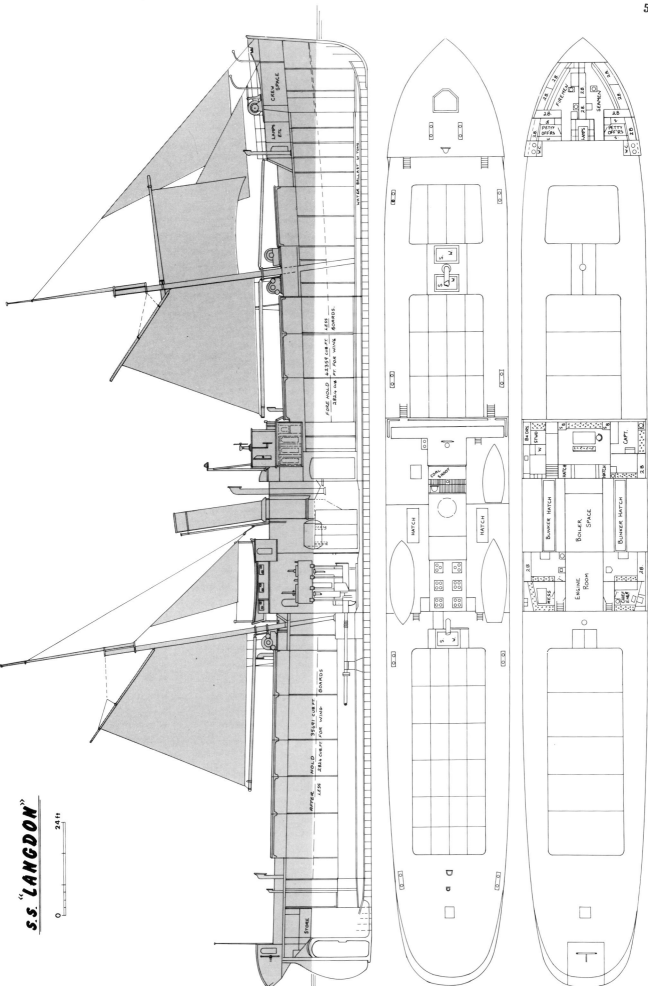

S.S. "LANGDON"

24 ft

0

STORE

AFTER HOLD 35691 CUB FT LESS 2824 CUB FT FOR WING BOARDS

FORE HOLD 42354 CUB FT LESS 2824 CUB FT FOR WING BOARDS.

WATER BALLAST 117 TONS

LAMPS ETC

CREW SPACE

COAL SHOOT

HATCH

HATCH

BLR.DRS
STWD
HATCH
BUNKER HATCH
BOILER SPACE
BUNKER HATCH
HATCH
CAPT.
2.8
2.8
MESS
ENGINE ROOM
CHIEF ENGR
2.8
2.8

W.C.
PETTY OFF'RS
LAMPS
FIREMEN
SEAMEN
PETTY OFF'RS
W.C.
2.8
2.8
2.8
2.8
2.8
2.8
2.8
2.8
S
S
S
S

Courtesy P. N. Thomas

55. *Langdon.* built in 1882 for John Fenwick & Son, London.

the Yorkshire coal which was being shipped from the expanding port of Goole. Though the coal burned well enough it was fragile and easily broken if care was not taken in handling, leaving small coal which was more difficult to burn and of lower market value. To save transhipment he decided to use sea-going lighters which would be towed down from Goole into the Humber, where they would be picked up and towed to the Thames by colliers. The plan was implemented in 1894 when a group of six 125' long lighters were delivered. Cory's first collier to be fitted for towing was **J. R. Hinde** 740/64. Initial results were satisfactory and a further four were acquired in 1896 but all were soon sold except for the one larger lighter, **Snark**, which was used until 1909. Cory's own colliers were not found powerful enough for the task and to overcome this they time-chartered **Lockwood** 1143/96 and **Rookwood** 1143/96, which were built for Steam Colliers Ltd., managed by Mr. H. C. Pelly. These vessels had been given particularly powerful engines but the fuel consumption offset any savings made on the quicker voyage. Cory's took them on consecutive time charters of from 5 to 7 years duration, both vessels being equipped with special towing gear similar to the tow hooks and beams fitted to deep sea tugs. For a number of years they towed **Snark** up and down the North Sea quite successfully. **Snark** carried about 1,000 tons of coal and had a small crew who looked after the towing gear and tended the donkey boiler which supplied steam for raising the anchor. Cory's paid an extra £20 to £25 per voyage depending on distance towed. Eventually it was decided the delays caused by having to pick up **Snark** from harbour tugs each end made the operation uneconomic and she was sold in 1909. Despite the towing both vessels managed 60 to 65 voyages per year for their charterers. To replace the barges, four 225' long colliers were built for the Goole trade: **Caenwood** 1191/02, **Brentwood** 1192/04, **Denewood** 1217/05 and **Hurstwood** 1229/06, all from Austin's yard.

The lighters were taken by river tugs on arrival in the Thames to Sheerness, Chatham or Rochester. The Yorkshire coal was a good free burning coal and was used domestically and in small size grades by some power stations. To promote the sale of the coal a branch office was opened at Gravesend in 1894. The winter of the following year saw all coal movement in the Thames virtually brought to a standstill by what is remembered as the great frost of February 1895. The Thames froze and the hydraulic powered Atlases could not use their hydraulic equipment as the water froze in the pipes. This was a recurring problem and led to its abandonment as efficient electric cranes were perfected. 'Hydraulic' equipment was to return many years later, but using oil rather than water. Cory's were placed in a difficult position and lost trade. Their reliance on the 'Atlas' floats had not helped the position but all this was to change in the following year when the company was completely reorganised. William Cory & Son was registered in 1896 as a public limited company with a capital of £2,000,000. The businesses of seven other companies engaged in the coal trade were taken over. The London coal businesses which were added to Cory's enterprise were Lambert Brothers D. Radford & Co., Beadle Bros. Ltd., J. & C. Harrison, Green, Holland & Sons, Mann, George & Co., and G. J. Cockrell & Co. Ltd. In addition those colliers in which Cory's had a major interest were taken into direct management and were no longer handled by J. Fenwick & Son. The latter continued to manage colliers on a much reduced scale and the last collier managed by the firm was absorbed by that of Lambton & Hetton Collieries at the end of the First World War. The black diamond on a white band was adopted for the amalgamated fleet to which Cory's contributed **Samuel Laing** 606/54, **William Cory** 1578/57, **Henry Morton** 986/60, **Ryhope** 698/60, **James Joicey** 695/63, **John M'Intyre** 985/63, **J. R. Hinde** 740/64, **Tanfield** 759/64, **Mary Nixon** 785/65, **New Pelton** 821/65. **Northumbria** 900/69 and **Eastwood** 982/70. The various interests were not entirely separated and **Hawthorns** 752/61 did not join the fleet from Fenwick management until 1904.

The Lambert Brothers London coal business was taken over but Lambert's retained their other

56. Nellie Wise *ashore off Hartlepool in 1908. When refloated she was broken up for scrap.*

Drawn from an old photo,
        MacRae collection

interests. Their ten coastal colliers joined the new fleet. They were Burnham 783/65, Pelaw 824/69, Merthyr 768/66, Vernon 982/78, Medway 944/79, Kent 1045/81, Walker 606/90, Cookham 1594/90, Ocean 1442/94, and Surf 1597/94. The company had begun having colliers built for the trade with the Medway and so brought more modern vessels to the fleet than did Cory, though the latter's vessels had been modernised over the years. Lambert's coal hoists were also taken over and incorporated with Cory's Albert Dock hoists.

Green, Holland & Sons had four secondhand colliers, three of which had been purchased just before the amalgamation; they were Sir Galahad 981/74, Leechmere 1120/76, and Walton 1069/77. The fourth vessel was Nellie Wise 1017/72 which had been purchased in 1888. (56). The only other company to have colliers to add to the fleet was J. & C. Harrison Ltd. They contributed Harberton 1443/94, Harpalus 1445/95, Harbury 1838/96. and Harbourne 1278/96, which were all new ships. J. & C. Harrison acted for the Cwmaman Coal Co., of Cardiff and arranged bunker supplies of their smokeless coal for ships calling at the Gravesend coal hulks. Harrison's retained their other interests in the coal and shipping trades and began operating coastal colliers again a few years prior to the First World War. None of the other firms operated colliers.

The amalgamation also brought with it a number of wharves on the Thames and Medway and the Atlas floats were slowly phased out. Last to go, Atlas No.3, was torpedoed during the First World War while being towed in the English Channel in 1915 while being taken to France. Modernisation of these shore facilities was put in hand prior to the First World War and new cranes were installed at Erith followed by electric transporters in the early 1900s. The Albert Dock facility was also modernised with hydraulic luffing cranes which were replaced by electric cranes just prior to the First World War. Meanwhile similar improvements were carried out at Rochester where a new ferro-concrete jetty was completed in 1910 equipped with electric cranes. During this period a further amalgamation occurred, including the addition of the Steamship Owners Coal Association Ltd.

The amalgamation of 1896 gave Cory's about 70% of the seaborne coal and 30% of all the London coal trade. To maintain their position a series of modern colliers was built. They were mostly given London place names beginning with 'H', like Hadley 1777/01 (50). There were six vessels in the series built between 1898 and 1901, all measuring about 268' x 37.7' x 17'. The seventh vessel Hendon 1809/99 differed in being slightly shorter but over 2 ft. broader beamed. A steady stream of new colliers joined the fleet from Austin's, largest of which was William Cory 2660/09, which was wrecked near Pendeen lighthouse in 1910 on a voyage from Uleaburg to Newport with pit props in September.

Five years after the Cory amalgamation William France, Fenwick & Co. Ltd., was registered on the 10th July 1901. This was the amalgamation of the interests of Fenwick, Stobart & Co. Ltd. which itself had been an amalgamation of Fenwick and Stobart interests. William France, which was a wholly owned subsidiary of Fenwick, Stobart and H. C. Pelly & Co. The latter company were the proprietors of the East London S. S. Co., and Steam Colliers Ltd. The capital was set at £300,000 and an agreement was entered into with C. H. Leslie to acquire the various businesses. The first directors were V. H. Smith, J. E. Champney, D. W. Stobart, R. E. Pattinson, H. C. Pelly and C. F. H. Leslie. The amalgamation gave the new company a fleet of 16 colliers. Fenwick, Stobart and their subsidiaries contributed Abchurch 1621/98, Arden 1517/01, Brenda 1152/99, Hylton 1484/97, Nina 1092/00, Northwood 764/89, Stanton 1097/99 and Wearmouth 982/94. Herbert C. Pelly contributed Poplar 830/86, Ratcliff 802/92 and Stepney 688/86, which belonged to the East London S. S. Co. Ltd. and Gwynwood 1084/99, Hawkwood 1155/00, Lockwood 1143/96, Monkwood 1141/00 and Rookwood 1143/96 of Steam Colliers Ltd., also managed by H. C. Pelly. The new company also inherited the barque Ethel 711/76 which was in the Tasmanian trade, but she was soon sold. The fleet was a varied one reflecting the variety of trades in which the partners had been engaged. Wearmouth was soon sold but the association with the Wearmouth Coal Co., in which both the Fenwick and Stobart families were involved, continued and when the tug and coal shipping arm was established as France, Fenwick Tyne & Wear Co. Ltd., acted as fitters for the company until the collieries were taken over when nationalised.

Hylton 1484/97 with her smaller hatchways was designed to operate in the London coal trade during the winter but to enter the Baltic timber trade or carry other cargoes such as iron ore from Spanish ports. Abchurch, named after the company's offices in Abchurch Lane, and Arden were similar, retaining extensive poop accommodation for the officers and a few passengers. They were considered large for the London coal trade and only suited to bulk trade to the larger gas companies. Stanton named after the wharf where the vessels loaded for Goole, carried about 1,600 tons deadweight. Like the Brenda, Nina and Gwynwood they had a full outfit of derricks, gaffs and steam driven deck cranes to make them suitable for the general cargo trade as well as coal carrying. Northwood and Gwynwood had been built for this trade and time chartered to Fenwick, Stobart & Co's subsidiary, William France & Co. Ltd. The southward part of the voyage was used to carry Yorkshire coal for Charrington's, and this business began in 1892. Charringtons continued to charter vessels thereafter. Northwood 766/89 ran for 20 years between Goole and Charrington's Ratcliff wharf and Gwynwood 1084/99, with a deadweight of 1,550 tons, was specially built with Charrington's Ratcliff wharf in mind and was the longest vessel which could berth there. The success of the venture over a number of years led to Fenwick, Stobart and Pelly amalgamating. Stanton and Gwynwood were kept going until the 1930s, despite high overhead costs, as they were so suitable for the Goole trade. Northwood, though dating from 1889, was built with particularly large hatches, with sloping end coamings, so that she was self-trimming. **Rookwood** and **Lockwood** were intended to make the voyage from South Wales to the Thames in four tides. As they would be loading and discharging at mechanised berths, and to save weight no cargo gear was fitted, a practice which was to become common later. They failed, but were often able to save a fifth tide in bad weather when less powerful colliers were delayed. When doing 12 to 13 knots their consumption of coal rose to as much as 30 tons a day and even at 7/6d per ton was too expensive. To make them more economic the valve gear was set to give a speed around 10 knots. They were let on 5 to 7 year charters to William Cory & Son to carry coal from U.K. ports to London, as were the **Hawkwood** and **Monkwood**, and this continued up to the first world war. The latter two vessels were intended as improvements on the earlier two. They were given more cubic capacity and less powerful engines to reduce fuel consumption. However, they too had problems, firstly the stability was not satisfactory and they had to be modified soon after delivery, resulting in the loss of cubic capacity. Also, as the donkey boiler was placed to one side it limited the space available for a side bunker and the bunkers on that side had about half the capacity of the bunker on the other side so the ship began to list as soon as coal could not be taken from each side equally. Masters compensated for this to some extent by loading the ship so that when they left port they had a list the opposite way, the vessel slowly coming upright and arriving with a slight list the other way on a long voyage. **Hawkwood** drifted ashore and was wrecked on the Yorkshire coast near Flamborough Head in January 1913, but should not have been. A trawler came upon the ship with a bad list, probably the result of cargo shifting. The lifeboats, which had been lowered, were nowhere to be seen and there was no sign of life on board. The weather was too bad for the small trawler to attempt to tow the ship and they had to leave her to her fate. The crew were never found, nor any trace of the boats. Had they stayed aboard there is no doubt they would have survived.

The vessels of the East London S.S. were built like 'flat-irons' with very low superstructure, not to trade above bridges like 'flatties' but up Bow Creek which had a low bridge also. The **Poplar**, **Stepney** and **Ratcliff** were chartered to the Commercial Gas Company. **Ratcliff** was under the command of Captain James Lowry who could not read or write but his memory and ability at mental arithmetic more than made up for this, and he dictated his portage bill to a clerk in the office and rarely made a mistake. Few coasting masters were certificated and pay was about £4.10s a week, while able seamen had about £1.8s a week. Working hours were whatever the master decided. Discipline was strict and sailing times never missed due to crew shortages, even though they had to provide their own food, cooking utensils and bedding. Turn-rounds were, in general, very fast so that if a vessel arrived in Tyne Dock to load on a Saturday afternoon the vessel expected to sail the same night and save an idle day on Sunday. Crew members were often very loyal to a ship. **Nina** 1082/00 had a seaman by the name of Ayre who worked his way up via boatswain, second mate, first mate and finally became master of her with a home trade certificate. The ship outlasted him by a number of years after he retired and was sold in 1930.

The first new ship for France, Fenwick was **Holmwood** 1327/02. She had been built as a speculation by the Northumberland Shipbuilding Company of Newcastle. She was a raised quarterdeck self-trimming collier of about 1,900 tons deadweight, which was about the largest which were normally built about that time. This was her only good feature for the ship had the absolute minimum of equipment when delivered but at a price paid by the company of approximately £15,000 there was no margin for extras and probably little or no profit for the builders. **Sherwood** 1353/04 was purchased in a similar manner and both, despite their lack of refinement for the trade, were profitable, especially the **Sherwood** which was sold to the Gas Light and Coke Company for £50,000 at the height of the First World War when self-trimming colliers were in short supply.

A series of six large self-trimmers was begun in 1904. First to be delivered was **Needwood** 2042/04 She had a deadweight capacity of over 3,300 tons and was considered large for a collier and only suited for charter by the larger gas companies who could handle such amounts of coal, and too large for the distributive trades which were only used to 2,000 ton vessels in many cases. However she had little time to demonstrate her worth as she was sold within three months of delivery at a small profit to the Union S. S. Co., of New Zealand. A replacement, **Needwood** 1985/06, was delivered from the same builders, Osbourne, Graham & Co. To offer a low price the builders had saved on ballast capacity which was only 487 tons with just 29 tons of this in the aft peak tank, compared with the smaller **Sherwood** which had 58 tons in her aft peak. The ships proved very difficult to handle

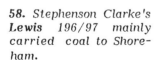

58. Stephenson Clarke's **Lewis** *196/97 mainly carried coal to Shoreham.*

Photo: World Ship Society

in bad weather when in ballast and were easily blown off course. Last of the six was **Ladywood** 1981/07. The price of the first vessel in the series had been £20,000 and by the time the last was delivered the price had risen to £24,000, reflecting the more buoyant shipping trade. Though six had been built, three were sold to the Union S. S., two not seeing any service with the company.

Raithwaite Hall 723/68 was purchased in 1906 for use on the Shatt-al-Arab waterway in the Persian Gulf and never worked on the east coast for the Company. The Company returned to Osbourne, Graham & Co., for an enlarged version of **Needwood** type, this was the second **Ladywood** 2314/10. She proved structurally weak and the propellor shafting was continually going out of alignment. The Company, after these experiences, changed builders going to Robert Thompson & Son of Sunderland for a raised quarterdeck vessel. Though much of the specification was left to the builders they produced a very well built vessel with better ballast arrangements and rather more power. These were **Wedgwood** 1674/10 and **Kirkwood** 1674/10. Two further vessels came from Thompson's before 1914 and a series of three from S. P. Austin's yard, first of which was **Portwood** 2248/13. The latter were of improved design and quality although the price was £32,000 for the first ship.

By contrast to William Cory and William France, Fenwick there were no major changes in Stephenson Clarke's business except that he had been succeeded by his two sons Colonel Stephenson Clarke and Charles B. O. Clarke. In 1900 the fleet consisted of the smaller steamers **John Grafton** 592/83, **Portslade** 634/88, **F. E. Webb** 585/91, **Ralph** 184/95 and **Lewis** 196/97 (58), which were mainly employed in supplying Shoreham with coal. **J. M. Strachan** 762/65, their first steam collier and now 35 years old, was still in the London trade which also supported **Gracie** 1312/79, **St. Dunstan** 1014/92 and **Erasmus Wilson** 806/76. The latter vessel inadvertently reduced the competition from Cory's fleet when she collided with the **Newburn** 680/61 and cut her in half in Thames Haven in 1897. Collisions between the by now numerous colliers were not uncommon in the East Coast Coal trade especially in fog, before the days of radar. Stephenson Clarke worked closely with the Gas Light and Coke Co., and their larger vessels were regular visitors to Beckton Gas Works. Further additions to the London fleet included **St. Agnes** 1195/03, **St. Edmund** and **Brook** 1436/06 which was running to the riverside wharf of the Brentford Gas Company who purchased the ship in 1919 but left it under Stephenson Clarke management.

The largest ship to be deliverd to the fleet prior to the First World War was **Minster** 2788/11, with the registered dimensions 314.0' x 45.7' x 20.9'. She was intended to handle the largest cargoes to the Thames and was a single deck design, probably because of her size and deck strength considerations (60,61). Although well designed for the trade she proved rather too big and was sold in 1914 to the W. J. Tillett S. S. Co. Ltd., (W. J. Tillett & Co., managers), Cardiff, who renamed her **Rosehill**. She was torpedoed and sunk off Fowey in September 1917 on a voyage from Cardiff to Devonport. Tillett's had probably purchased her for the Naval bunker trade as the expansion of the Navy just prior to the First World War had increased the demand for South Wales steam coal and the Admiralty were actively chartering colliers to cover their needs and the large hatches of **Minster** made her ideal. The **Abbas** 1430/11, delivered the same year, was much more successful. She was an engine aft design, and served the company for 34 years. The **Minster** was replaced by **Keynes** 1706/15 which had the dimensions 260.1' x 37.7' x 16.4' and so a rather smaller vessel.

The Gas Companies

For much of the 19th century the major users of seaborne coal were the gasworks of London. Their need was mainly for the gas coals from the Durham coalfields but the water companies needed steam coal for their pumping operations and a multitude of municipal and other services in the capital depended on coal-fired steam plant, as did the early electricity supply stations.

The Gas Light and Coke Company was the most important. The Company had been founded by Royal Charter in 1812, which gave the Company powers to supply gas lighting to the City of London, Westminster and Southwark. The whole project was a great success. The importance of the company to the London coal trade was recognised in 1826 when they were entered on the coal exchange as buyers. By 1827 they had their own agents in the north. The Company then moved into shipowning in a small way. By 1832 it had abandoned buying through the Coal Exchange and arranged contracts in the north directly with coal owners and fitters. Ultimately this led, in 1839, to a contract to take the entire production of the Pelton Colliery for 10 years. By 1839 some 340,000 tons of gas coal were being used annually.

The Gas Light and Coke Co., by the 1850s, were purchasing coal in very large quantities from a number of sources. The screw steamer was now viable and had been trading successfully for a number of years in the passenger and cargo lines. It is possible that the first screw steamer aimed at this trade was **Haggerston** 329/52, managed by J. C. Gibson, as it was named after one of the Gas Light and Coke Company's plants, see page 13. It is likely that some of these early London steam colliers were chartered. However, the main contracts seem to have been with the General Iron Screw Collier Company, which had close contacts with the Commercial Gas Company and the London Gas Company. The colliers **Caroline** and **Hawk** may also have been used for a short time before being taken up as transports for the Crimean War. Contracts with the General Iron Screw Collier Company continued and as the coal factors and merchants began to build suitable vessels they were also chartered.

In the late 1860s the Gas Light and Coke Company undertook the building of the Beckton Works,

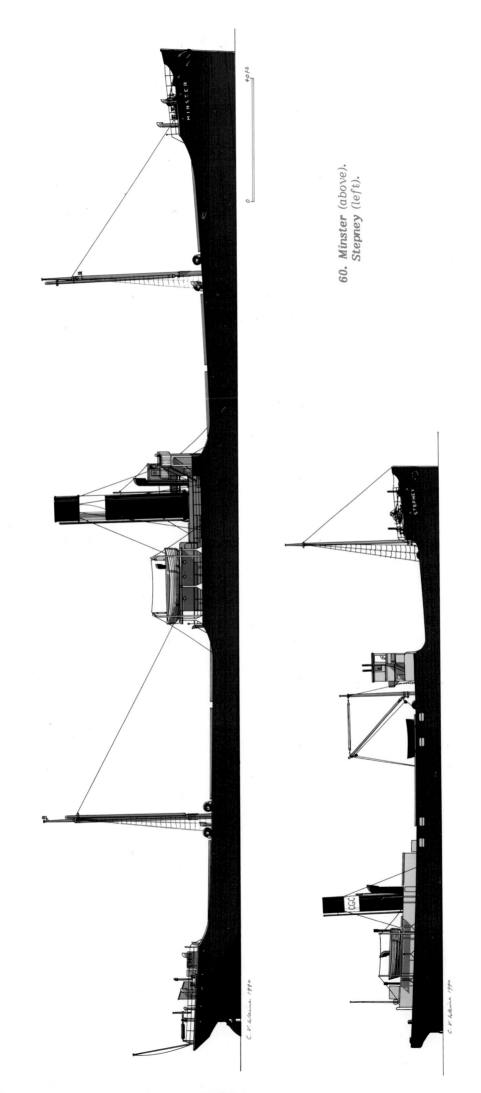

C. V. Waine 1980

C. V. Waine 1980

60. Minster (above).
Stepney (left).

Minster 2788/11 (314.0' x 45.7' x 20.9') was the largest collier to be built for the Stephenson Clarke fleet for many years. She was sold after a few years to Cardiff owners at the beginning of the First World War. The war was also responsible for the building of **Stepney** 808/16 (186.3' x 29.4' x 12.4'). The Commercial Gas Company had already purchased a similar secondhand Williamson built coaster and finding it satisfactory, ordered another to be certain of having ships available to carry vital supplies of coal to their gas works on the Thames during hostilities.

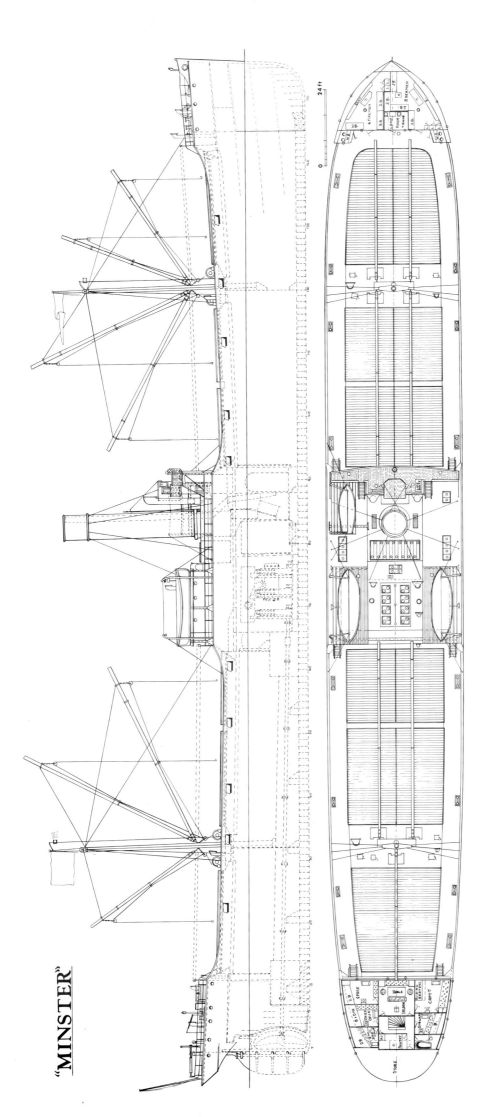

"MINSTER"

61. Minster with the dimensions 314' x 45.7' x 20.9' was by far the largest collier built for Stephenson Clarke when delivered by S. P. Austin in July 1911. She contained many features to make her suitable for the London coal trade, most prominent of which were the large hatches, the largest which could be safely fitted into the hull and still maintain hull strength. This latter consideration probably led to her single deck design which avoided introducing a point of weakness which was always a problem with raised quarterdeckers. The two long hatches had a fixed girder to strengthen them, splitting each hatch into two. In order to allow the fullest possible access to the No.2 hold, the bridge was made as short as possible and the officers accommodated aft, and the wheelhouse was extended aft and overhung the stoke hold gratings (compare with **Dulwich** 65). The bunkers were arranged alongside the boiler room to avoid taking potential hold space with a cross-bunker. The after hatches are the full length of the hold.

Courtesy P. N. Thomas

62. Fulgens (305.4' x 42.3' x 19.1'), first of the big engines-aft colliers for London owners.

which opened in 1870. This large plant was at Gallions Reach adjacent to the river. It was arranged to accept large colliers at the Company's own wharves for discharge directly into the works. The Company soon chartered more vessels, but apparently may not have been impressed with the terms offered as they applied to Parliament for an Act empowering them to operate steam colliers, which was granted in 1872. No vessels were purchased but the company's interests were safeguarded and they could purchase if need be.

Though the building of Beckton allowed many of the smaller plants to be closed, including their first works in inner London, some were still supplied by lighter, such as the five works which lay in the Regent's Canal. The Gas Light & Coke Company used to issue a schedule each July of the tonnages of the various coals, about 20 kinds, which they required lighters for during the next 12 months. The coal was discharged in the Regent's Canal Dock into lighters of Gardner Brothers. The ships agents were initially Alfred Steward & Co., but by about the 1890s Harris & Dixon had taken over. They supplied details of the ships to be discharged into lighters. Some of the colliers had large hatches, but other vessels put on the trade even had 'tween decks. All the coal was discharged by shovelling into large iron tubs which were lifted by hydraulic cranes, weighed by meters on a yardarm, and tipped down chutes into barges, which caused considerable breakage and dust. There was much trimming by hand and the men in the holds had to drag the tub underneath the side decks to reach the coal. The Commercial Gas Company also had a works adjacent to the Regent's Canal and this was also supplied by lighter.

The Commercial Gas Light and Coke Company was founded in 1837 by a group of dissatisfied East End consumers. The Company received its Act of Parliament, as all gas companies supplying the general public were required to do. The Company was very successful under C. S. Butler and took over other local companies. It is probably significant that Stephenson Clarke's first steam collier, built in 1865, was named **C. S. Butler**. The Gas Light & Coke Co., largest of the North London suppliers, offered to merge with them and the nearby Ratcliff Gas Company. In the end, after the take-over bid by the Gas Light & Coke Company failed, the Commercial Gas Company took over the Ratcliff Gas Company in 1874 and in 1878 a new works was completed on the River Lea at Poplar. It had been originally planned to have steam colliers delivering their cargoes directly to the plant. After deliberations on the matter the Company signed an agreement with F. Green & Co. for the charter of three steam colliers to carry coal from Newcastle. The first colliers to pass under Thames bridges had been built in 1878 and so the problems associated with such vessels were known. The colliers were of special design and apparently delivered in April and May 1886 as the dimensions of the vessels specified in the contract fit those of **Stepney, Wapping** and **Poplar**. They may well have arranged for the ships to be financed by a group including H. C. Pelly as he was specialising in letting colliers on long-term time charters, and certainly by the beginning of the 1890s they were under his name and by 1893 were registered under the East London S. S. Co. of which H. C. Pelly & Co. were managers. **Stepney** 658/86 carried about 1,050 tons, while **Poplar** 830/86 carried rather more at 1,200 tons. She had the registered dimensions 180.0 x 36.1 x 15.2 feet making her particularly broad in the beam in order to get a good deadweight in a relatively short ship. Voyages up Bow Creek to the Commercial works were begun in 1887 with **Poplar**. However, this did not last long as on one of these voyages **Poplar**, when returning down the creek in ballast, was just too high and struck Barking Road Bridge. The clearance had been reduced by a high spring tide and the damage to ship and bridge was quite extensive. It was decided to abandon further direct deliveries with **Poplar**. This was probably prior to 1892 when Pelly's built the slightly smaller **Ratcliff** 802/92 for this trade. She was 10 feet shorter and the registered depth of the hull was reduced to 13.6'. The **Poplar** was then returned to Pelly's, who placed her on the London - Goole trade of France, Fenwick.

By 1902 a new Barking Road Bridge had been built and this offered shipping using the creek much greater clearance. The Company now decided to build their own collier especially for serving their works via Bow Creek. This was **Commercial** 496/02 (165.3' x 27.1' x 13.3'). She was slightly shorter than the earlier vessels and of the conventional breadth to length and was therefore of considerably less capacity. The vessel served the company for only a little over a year before foundering off Whitley Bay on a voyage from the Tyne to London with coal. Fortunately the old **Poplar** 830/86 had been purchased in June 1903. The charters of **Stepney** and **Ratcliff** were ended about this time as a series of vessels came into service, all built by William Dobson & Co., Newcastle. They were **Limehouse** 562/03, **Bow** 565/04 and **Bromley** 565/04. The breadth was increased compared with **Commercial** to 30 feet. They were similar in design to **Ratcliff** with engines amidships. This arrangement reduced the problems of trim when empty to pass under the bridge as the vessel would be on an even keel. If the engines had been aft extensive ballasting would have been required in the bows. The ships worked successfully and the company went back to Dobson's yard in 1911 for a similar style vessel to serve Wapping, but in this case there was no requirement to pass under low bridges. The result was **Mile End** 859/11, with the dimensions 165.6' x 38.0' x 14.5'. The length was kept down but the deeper water at Wapping allowed the draft to be increased. The breadth is about that normal in a collier 260 feet long and though this gives a good deadweight of 1,100 tons, it needed about a third more power to push the ship through the water than one of conventional proportions.

The Wandsworth and Putney Gas Light and Coke Co., were in rather a similar position to the Commercial Gas Company though they had a Thameside wharf above the fixed bridges. This had been in use since the mid-1870s and took deliveries of coal in 200-ton capacity barges. However in 1906, with steadily increasing demand, they decided to try direct supply by up-river collier and purchased the old **Ratcliff** 802/92 from France, Fenwick. To make her suitable for passing under the seventeen Thames bridges she had to have some modifications. The initial trials were successful, but the coal was still discharged into barges initially, with the collier anchored in the middle of the river. After a period of experimentation **Ratcliff** was sold in 1908 and a collier ordered especially to serve the works. This was **Wandle** 889/09. Delivered in January 1909 she was just in time to help with the peak demand and was a product of Dobson's yard which had a few years before built similar vessels for the Commercial Gas Company. The dimensions were slightly greater (205.2' x 32.1' x 14.4') reflecting the better turning space in the river itself as compared with Bow Creek. **Wandle** proved successful and a further order was placed with Dobson's for a slightly larger vessel, this was to be the **Mitcham** 1125/13. She was a raised quarterdeck steamer with engines aft. To keep the bow down when in ballast and passing under the low bridges, the fore peak tank was given a capacity of 141 tons.

The only other gas company to purchase and register vessels in their own name at this time was the Gas Light and Coke Co. They had always chartered vessels, often on a long term basis, but as freight rates began to rise they decided to order a large collier which could be fully employed serving the large Beckton works. **Fulgens** 2512/12 was delivered from the yard of Wood, Skinner & Co. and had a deadweight of 3,700 tons fully laden (62). She was soon averaging 60 voyages a year to Beckton. Management was placed with Stephenson Clarke who had chartered their own vessels to the company for many years. The design of the vessel was of the raised quarterdeck engines aft style which was to become the standard design for colliers in the 20th century. Despite her modern appearance a foresail was still supplied and the four holds were each equipped with a steam winch and derrick in case they ever needed to find other work for her.

World War I

The situation was to change completely within weeks of the declaration of war in 1914. A large part of the navy was still coal fired and although the Admiralty already chartered colliers, with naval ships spending more time at sea on patrol, many more colliers were needed to supply the fleet. They were also taken up as general transports to move supplies and equipment to France. On land, many of the staff of the various merchants and shipowners joined the forces. Coal exports were diverted to the war effort. Coal supplies were limited throughout the war and were not to get back to normal until December 1919, over a year after the war had ended. Because of the shipping difficulties some of the trade was diverted to the railways, and this became considerable during November and December 1914.

The gas companies in particular were equipped to receive their coal by sea and so ships were essential to them and this led to the setting up of the Coal Advisory Committee in 1915 which was made up of representatives from the Gas Light and Coke Company, the South Metropolitan Gas Company and the main industrial and utility coal suppliers, Cory's, Stephenson Clarke, Hudson's and Gardner, Locket & Hinton. The gas companies generally arranged their own freights, purchasing their coal on a free-on-board basis in the north. The smaller users such as the electricity companies would contract with Stephenson Clarke for a certain tonnage at an agreed price delivered which left Stephenson Clarke to arrange the shipping, and other users would make similar arrangements

63. A dazzle painted collier photographed by Leut. Roper of R.A.F. Felixstowe on the 23rd of September 1918.

with their suppliers. The work of the Committee was to see that as far as possible sufficient colliers were available for essential users. Efforts were also made to protect colliers by naval patrols and dazzle painting to confuse German U-boats about the size and shape of the vessel (63).As submarines made attacks on the surface using their guns rather than their much more expensive torpedoes, efforts were made to arm the colliers. There was considerable resistance in the navy to introducing convoys and these were only introduced later in the war. The effects on the seaborne coal trade were dramatic, in 1913 some 9 million tons of coal had been imported into London by sea, but by 1918 it was down to just 3.5 million tons.

The gas companies, facing escalating freight rates brought about by the shortage of ships, began buying second-hand tonnage. However, this was not too easy as the increase in freight rates had pushed up the prices. The Gas Light and Coke Co., purchased the up-river collier **Battersea** 860/02, which had been on charter for a number of years, and set about acquiring second-hand tonnage to serve Beckton. First to be acquired was **Capitol** 1298/06 which came from Swedish owners, though she had been built for the British Maritime Trust, which was part of Furness, Withy. In all, four typical four-hatch steamers with engines amidships were acquired of which one was mined and sunk during the year. Further similar vessels were purchased in 1916, but the most unusual purchase was **Ignifer** 1451/07. This was a Great Lakes type steamer with the bridge on the forecastle, which had been brought over by Common Bros., of Newcastle and passed on to the Company. She survived the war and returned to the Great Lakes afterwards. Further vessels were acquired in 1916 including an iron steamer which had been built as the **Universal** in 1878 and was thus 38 years old and had been owned throughout by Taylor and Sanderson of Sunderland. Several other old vessels dating from the 1880s were acquired and though this was probably dictated by availability and price, they may have also been influenced by the fact that the Admiralty tended to requisition more modern vessels. At the end of 1916 the fleet consisted of **Capitol** 1298/06, **Phare** 1282/06, **Battersea** 860/02, **Ignifer** 1451/07, **Lampada** 2220/89, **Ardens** 1274/78, **Suntrap** 1353/04, **Firelight** 1143/96, (purchased from France, Fenwick for £35,000), **Glow** 1141/00 and **Lanthorn** 2299/89. The ten vessels were needed to overcome loading delays and delays caused by naval orders regarding sailing. Further delays could occur if naval patrols were met as these might order a change of course or even send the collier to a nearby harbour if a submarine had been sighted in the area.

The Gas Light and Coke Company also ordered new ships from Wood, Skinner. These were of the engine-aft design, probably due to the managers, Stephenson Clarke's, experience of this design and builder. The first to be delivered was **Flamma** 1874/17. Delivered in June 1917, within weeks she struck a mine off Seaham. She was eventually salvaged and dry-docked in the Tyne. The main damage was to the fore part of the ship and to get her back into service as quickly as possible the forepart of her sister ship then under construction was used in the repair.

The South Metropolitan Gas Company, which was by far the largest of the companies south of the Thames, held an equivalent position on the south bank of the Thames to that of the Gas Light and Coke Co., on the north bank. The Company began to build its main plant at East Greenwich in 1881, which was slowly expanded over the years. A jetty was built to accept chartered colliers. By 1902 they were using about 1,200,000 tons, three quarters of which was used at East Greenwich. The company made no attempt to enter shipowning but were forced to by the war, and purchased four ships in 1915, **Amsteldam** 1233/07, **Effra** (ex Broompark) 1325/10, **Quaggy** 993/04 and **Togston** 1057/09. The Company had lost three of these vessels on the east coast by 1917, two to submarine attack and one to a mine. Nor were they alone, for the Gas Light and Coke Co., had similarly high losses. Though many of the colliers now had a gun on the stern for defence, this was not as effective as it had been initially, as submarines were using torpedoes rather than risking surfacing and being shot at. The Company managed its own ships and placed their first building contract with the Dublin Dockyard Co. This was **Dulwich** 1460/16 (65). The vessel was a typical engines amidships steamer with a raised quarterdeck, 91 feet long, and was very near a true quarterdeck. The step was often rather greater as for example **Dashwood** (157). Both vessels had a tank top extending at the height of the shaft tunnel over the after hold. This was fitted to make discharging easier as it was always difficult to get the coal out of the wedge shaped space between the steeply sloping side of the ship and the side of the shaft tunnel. This was particularly the case where grab discharge was used and to overcome this problem the bottom of the hold was levelled off in the aftermost hold (No.4). Grab discharge was always the bane of shipowners, as the grabs, especially when loaded, could strike the hatch coaming or other parts of the ship and it was usual for the mate and foreman in charge of unloading to agree damage, if any, to compensate shipowners for repairs. But the saving of time and labour of grab discharge far exceeded the occasional damage bills. Another feature to assist grab discharge was the elimination of hold pillars, the strength being obtained by fitting deep brackets between the strength deck and the sides of the ships. The shaft tunnel was left uncovered in No.3 hold where there would be flatter floors. The large hatches also assisted grab discharge. The accommodation was unusual as it was concentrated amidships. The firemen and seamen's accommodation was placed on either side of the engine and boiler casing, while the space below the bridge was available for cargo or bunkers if needed, but avoids being measured for tonnage by having tonnage openings in the fore bulkhead. The bunker beneath was reached by a trunk into the after end of the No.2 hatch and probably had enough capacity for the Tyne-London-Tyne run without having to be trimmed to the top after end, thus employing trimmers to shovel it there by hand, but it could be reached by the small coal hatches. The officers' accommodation, cook and deck-boy were on one side of the 52 foot long bridge deck and the engineers on the other, built out to the side of the ship.

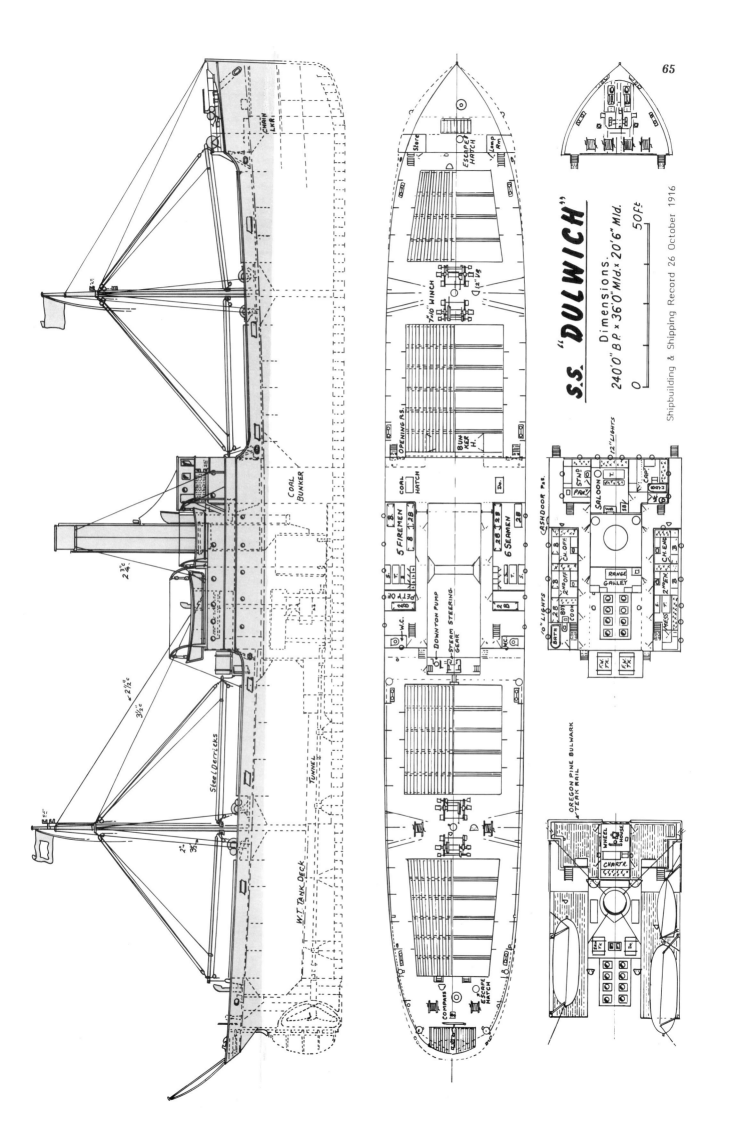

S.S. "DULWICH"

Dimensions.

240'0" B.P. x 36'0" Mld. x 20'6" Mld.

0   50 Ft

Shipbuilding & Shipping Record 26 October 1916

This gave the vessel's midships accommodation a rather short, slab-sided appearance. The saloon, captain and stewards' accommodation were placed below the bridge and wheelhouse, separated from the other accommodation. The deadweight was about 2,330 tons. The Company lost **Dulwich** on the 10th of June 1917 when she struck a mine off the Shipwash Light Vessel while on a voyage from Seaham to London with coal. Further vessels were ordered from the Dublin Dockyard and **Lambeth** 1536/17 was delivered in November 1917 and had a slightly increased deadweight. The raised quarter-deck was extended forwards 3 feet in later vessels. Depth and breadth were also slightly increased, giving the dimensions 240.3' x 36.3' x 18.4' for **Brixton** 1543/18. Deadweight was about 2,450 tons.

The Controller of Shipping who had been appointed to oversee shipbuilding and shipping, in order to maximise productivity, selected the design to be a standard ship of the Ministry of Shipping. The Dublin Dockyard were asked to supply copies of the design to a number of other builders and it was designated the C5 type. In order to simplify construction the shallow raised quarterdeck was eliminated and the dimensions increased to 240.1' x 36.3' x 19.1'. The first of the later series was laid down as **War Liffey** but by the time she was launched in February 1919 the war had been over three months and she was completed as **Bermondsey** 1561/19 for the South Metropolitan Gas Company. A further five vessels were in hand and the next three, **Catford** 1565/19, **Old Charlton** 1556/19 and **Brockley** 1559/20 were completed for the Company. The last of the series was **Jetblack** 1560/20, completed for the Gas Light and Coke Co. (66)

The smaller gas companies which both had experience of running their own vessels prior to the outbreak of war, began to purchase further vessels in 1915. The Commercial Gas Company purchasing **Ravonia** 703/08 from R. Williamson & Son of Workington, and were sufficiently impressed with the vessel to order a slightly larger version from Williamson's yard, this was **Stepney** 808/16, page 60. **Teeswood** 864/15, purchased from Constantine and Donking in 1917, was sold back to the Donking S. S. Co. Ltd., in 1923. The **Aberdale** 621/14 was also purchased in 1917. The Wandsworth, Wimbledon and Epsom District Gas Company acquired **Ewell** (ex Berne) 1011/06 and **Lightfoot** 1875/16 from Witherington & Everett in 1917, only to lose it the following year.

Most of the colliers requisitioned were involved as transports and fleet colliers but a few were taken up as Q-ships. Because of their hazardous mission they were taken over by the Royal Navy, and one such vessel was the **Penshurst** 1191/06, which had been built for the Power S. S. Co. Ltd., of London. The mission was to cruise slowly about in areas where submarines were known to operate. The vessel was equipped with carefully concealed guns and relied on the method of attack used by the early German submarines, which was to inspect the vessel carefully, surface if she appeared unarmed and then sink it by gunfire or even send a boarding party to sink the vessel with explosives, which saved expensive torpedoes. The early submarines often had to attack on the surface as they were not as fast as most steamers underwater. The Q-ships proved so successful that soon submarines were forced to attack with torpedoes from under water, and eventually they would not come close or surface.

The electricity supply companies were still quite small compared with the gas companies. They did not begin until the 1880s and initially supplied Theatres and other similar enterprises. At the beginning of the 1890s there were 14 stations within 12 miles of St. Paul's Cathedral, operated by 8 different companies. There was considerable competition to supply them among the coal merchants and Locket & Judkins, later to merge with Charrington's, were active supplying the stations with their steam coal requirements. One of their most important customers was the Westminster Electric Supply Corporation which had three stations. None of these companies was large enough to justify collier owning, but Locket & Judkins always had one or two vessels such as the **Marjorie** 1400/90 owned around the turn of the century. During the First World War, by which time the company had become Gardner, Locket & Hinton, the colliers were **Mid Surrey** 879/70 and **Camden** 1425/11. The former was lost in collision during the war but the **Camden** passed to Charrington, Gardner, Locket & Co. Ltd. when that company was formed in 1922. They also owned the old collier **Rose** 872/94 for a time.

66. Jet Black proceeding up the Thames and displaying her collier number on the bridge.
Photo: Alex Duncan

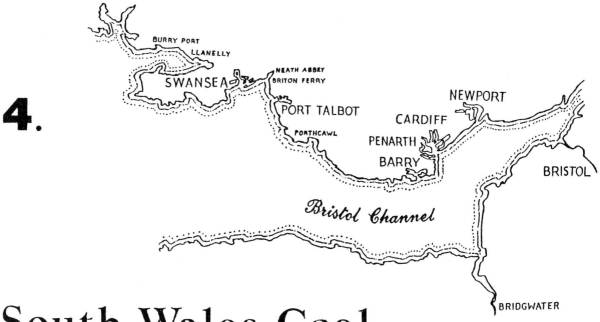

4.

South Wales Coal
& the Bristol Channel

Though coal had been known and used for centuries, it was initially not much used outside the area, but this was completely changed during the 19th century. This was largely the result of the efforts of the Second Marquis of Bute who developed docks to connect with the Glamorganshire Canal which linked the collieries of the Merthyr area with Cardiff. The first shipments of high quality steam coal from the locality were made in 1830, but it was not until 1839 when the first of the Marquis' docks was opened that the coal trade began to increase significantly and shipments from the Rhondda mines were also made. Much of the coal went to Bristol with smaller amounts to Ireland and nearby West Country ports, but all the new activity and improved docks attracted the attention of London merchants. Despite the influence of the North East coal owners, George Locket, later to become part of Charrington, Gardner & Locket went to Cardiff to see for himself, and according to family tradition was so impressed by the fire in his hotel room in Cardiff that he set off up the valley the following day to buy the whole of the output of the Colliery. However, as his travelling companion was Mr. Marychurch, who was a well known figure in the Cardiff coal trade and later in the Bay trade, it seems likely that a deal had already been discussed before the two journeyed together from London to Cardiff. He successfully concluded his negotiations and on his return sold the first consignment to the Mitcham Brewery. Interest in the almost smokeless high quality steam coal was stimulated by the London Smoke Act which had been passed to mitigate the effects of London's increasing industrialisation.

Coal shipments were a success and the East Bute Dock, which was designed from the outset to link up with the expanding railway network, was completed in 1859. The opening was probably of particular interest to William Cory and John Nixon as William Cory & Son had also become interested in Welsh steam coal, especially John Nixon's mines. John Nixon had shares in **William Cory** 1578/57 and owned **Mary Nixon** himself. Nixon's coal was also handled by George Locket, and at the beginning of the 1860s Nixon's Merthyr and Nixon's Duffryn was being supplied to Government Offices in Whitehall at £1 per ton, while Lambton's Wallsend commanded a slightly higher price at £1.2.6d.

The amount of coal arriving in London from South Wales is given as 126,789 tons for 1855, but had risen to 162,864 tons by 1857. However, this only represented 5% of coal shipments arriving in London. The trade of Cardiff developed on a much broader front, with much of the coal being exported in ocean going ships rather than on a coastwise basis. The ships of local owners were often employed in the 1860s and 1870s in the Spanish iron ore trade to South Wales, taking coal on the outward trip.

The return of steam vessels registered in the United Kingdom up to the 1st of January 1855 lists eight tugs and one steam packet and the picture was similar in the 1862 returns. It was not until 1865 that H. Vellacott purchased the new steamer **Llandaff** 411/65 and followed it with **Fairwater** 384/65. The vessels were probably engaged as coasting colliers, perhaps trading to France which was a good market for Welsh coals, or to Spain, as there were no home trade limits until 1894. By 1884 the much larger steamer **North Devon** 774/79 was owned by H. J. Vellacott. An early investor in Vellacott's ships was C. E. Stallybrass and by 1868 he was managing **Leckwith** 521/68 (171.6' x 25.9' x 15.7') and in the 1870s and 1880s operated larger tramps. This was the general pattern with few smaller vessels in the fleets. The high quality steam coal from the Welsh mines was much in demand all over the world and Cory Brothers set up an extensive network of bunkering stations. Other companies also supplied bunkers and large quantities were shipped to Plymouth and Portsmouth, the Navy purchasing over 200,000 tons by the end of the 1880s. Further extensions were made to the docks as the world-wide demand for Welsh coal continued to increase.

Newport

When the first steam colliers came into service in the 1850s Cardiff had not overtaken Newport in terms of tonnage shipped coastwise for in 1855 Newport's total was 506,000 tons and Cardiff 464,000 tons. The easy shipment of coal from Newport became possible with the completion of the Monmouthshire canal in 1799. Shipments steadily increased, resulting in the building of the Town Docks in 1842. Changes, concomitant with the coming of the railways, and the use of steam, brought another great upsurge of trade to Wales, while new port developments resulted in the remarkable achievement of 10 new docks at various ports between 1874 and 1909.

At Newport, the old Town Dock was unable to cope with the increase of trade, and a new Company, the Newport (Alexandra) Dock Company, opened their new dock in 1875. It became known as the North Dock, and even before it was finished it was obvious further extensions would be needed. In 1882 power was sought and obtained to build what was soon to become the South Dock. It was opened in 1893 and further extended, with the addition of what at that time were the largest locks in the world, impounding more than 95 acres of water.

Of the 7,000,000 tons of trade handled at Newport Alexandra Dock in 1913, 6,000,000 was coal being exported. The old Town Dock at Newport was eventually considered to be of no further use and powers to close it were obtained in 1929. The work of filling it in was started at once and completed about 1937. As the coal trade diminished after the Second World War, the coal tips in both the North and South Docks were dismantled one by one, some going to other ports, but most being scrapped. There were in all 14 tips in the port, operated by the Railways. Eight of them being capable of handling the newer 20 ton trucks. The five in the North Dock were all able to accommodate the 20 tonners. The remaining two were on the riverside coal quays, and were restricted to the old 12 ton wagons.

Barry and Penarth

Newport lies at the easternmost end of the coal field which was also served by the smaller ports of Barry and Penarth. These did not rely on canal development, but on the success of local railways. Barry's good sheltered position near to deep water was soon utilised as Barry Island shelters the entrance from the prevailing south westerly winds. This was enhanced by breakwaters on either side of the entrance, mainly to protect against easterly winds.

Dissatisfied with the high rates demanded at Cardiff a group of coal shippers and mine owners, under the leadership of Lord Davies, formed the Barry Dock and Railway Company and obtained permission to build a dock at Barry, 8 miles west of Cardiff, despite spirited and determined opposition by Lord Bute and others interested in the prosperity of Cardiff.

Work was started in 1884 and in 1889 the first cargo was shipped from the No.1 Dock. The increase in coal exports was so phenomenal - 3 million tons in two years, that it became necessary to open a new dock. The No.2 dock, 34 acres of it, was opened in 1898 and became an instant success, so that by 1913 11 million tons of coal was being shipped annually, mostly in ocean steamers, together with three quarters of a million tons of general merchandise and grain. The First World War played havoc with Barry as it did with all other ports, especially those involved with the export of coal as markets had been lost.

In 1963 it was decided to concentrate the shipment of coal from the remaining mines in South East Wales at Barry. Newport and Cardiff were stripped of the last remaining hoists and though

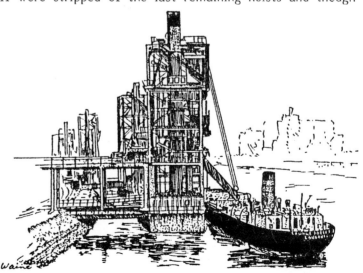

*68. The flatiron **George Balfour** 1570/37, loading coal in Barry No.2 dock in the 1950s.*

69. Goodwill of Bristol loading coal at Briton Ferry about 1930.

some were dismantled and shipped elsewhere and re-erected, they gave a lot of trouble. The number of tips in Barry Docks, which at the height of the hectic exporting days of the early 20th century was 28, and at times it seemed possible that one could walk across the No.1 Dock on the decks of ships waiting to load coal. By 1970 they had all but disappeared, the No.6 and No.8 hoists in No.1 Dock being the only two left. In fact No.6 was cannibalised to provide spare parts for No.8. In 1977 the British Transport Docks Board closed down the coal handling side of this port, which, less than a century before had been specially built for this very purpose.

The massive coal hoists of the Welsh and some Scottish ports had one great disadvantage. To board or leave a ship loading at them one had to use a plain ladder, without safety rails or ropes and sometimes of a great length. The butt was landed on a narrow wooden walkway at the side of the base that appeared to have been added as an afterthought. As loading progressed the ladder had to be drawn back at every 'shift ship' and then pushed out again to allow anyone who had business with the ship aboard. Stores had to be shipped via the ladder and could present some problems. Eventually the long sought permission to fasten a block and tackle on the latticework of the tip itself was granted. By means of this the ladder was hoisted more or less vertical and clear of the ship for each move. The provision merchants, lubricating oil and ship chandlers co-operated and delivered their goods when they could be carried across on a level platform easily and safely, and not carried by cursing and disgruntled seamen, up a dangerous and tilted ladder.

Captain MacRae further recalls that only one port made any realistic provision for a safe permanent gangway. This was at Preston in Lancashire, where a permanent gangway was secured to the telescopic 'fend-off' which was wound in or out as required by the loading conditions. Telescopic 'fend-offs' were also fitted to the coal tips in West Bute Dock, Cardiff and the South Dock in Swansea. They were used as gangways when extended during loading.

Between Barry and Cardiff lies Penarth which developed around the natural harbour formed by the river Ely. Development began in the middle of the 19th century when coal was shipped from the riverside wharf. The adjacent Penarth Dock was opened in 1863 and triggered rapid development of coal shipping from the port. It was always considered part of the Port of Cardiff. With the decline of export of coal the dock was closed for cargo handling in 1936. The riverside wharf continued in use, the four loading berths being suitable for coasters of not more than about 800 tons deadweight and capable of loading while aground. Tidal range varies from 20 to 30 feet and so required plenty of attention to moorings.

Port Talbot, Porthcawl and Briton Ferry

Between Barry and Port Talbot is Porthcawl. This little harbour was expanded by the Great Western Railway, who took charge under an Act of 1854. It was suitable for large coasters, the size being limited by the 26 feet width of the locks. Over 340,000 tons were shipped coastwise in 1888, often in the numerous schooners still operating in the coal trade to Ireland and the West Country. These schooners continued to be an important part of the coastwise trade to small harbours until the First World War.

The old docks at Port Talbot were opened in 1837, but prior to this coal had been shipped out of the natural harbour formed by the mouth of the River Afan. The major development of the port came in 1894 when the Port Talbot Railway and Docks Company was incorporated which opened the new dock in 1898. This led to a considerable expansion of trade from the port in the 20th century. It was particularly well placed for the shipment of Duffryn, Gorw, Ogmore, Llymin and Afan coals and also from the Rhondda, Neath and Aberdare districts. The port was built to accept ocean tramps drawing about 23 feet which entered via the mouth of the River Afan and an entrance lock situated on the east bank. Apart from the coal exports, considerable imports of iron ore for the steel works adjacent to the harbour were a feature of 20th century development.

Briton Ferry (69), lying between Port Talbot and Swansea is a small harbour entered off the River Neath. It never catered for ocean vessels but was suitable for coasters not drawing more than about 16 feet. Shipments of coal became significant in the latter part of the 19th century, some

176,000 tons being shipped coastwise in 1888. This trade continued into the 20th century, much of the coal going to the Channel Islands and local ports such as Bristol. By the 1930s one hydraulic coal tip which tipped the coal wagons down a chute was in use.

Swansea

Swansea, lying almost at the centre of the South Wales coalfield, was important for the shipment of local coal from early times and was largely developed as a centre for copper ore smelting at the beginning of the 19th century, which was followed by the iron, steel and tinplate industries. Some 200,000 tons of coal were being shipped coastwise at the beginning of the steam collier era and by 1888 this had increased to 341,000 tons, but had fallen well behind Newport and Cardiff. The small south dock was opened for traffic in 1859 and began coal shipments, but by 1900 was too small and had become a dock for deep-sea trawlers. There was also the small North Dock.

This change-over to new dock facilities became possible with the opening of improved docks. The Prince of Wales Dock on the opposite side of the River Tawe was begun in 1879 and was completed in 1881, but soon had to be extended to the size shown on the map (70). It was liberally equipped with coal hoists. To handle the increasing size of vessels, construction of the Kings Dock was begun in 1904 and completed in 1909. It was equipped with 8 coal hoists for ocean going vessels. The Queens Dock was opened in 1920 to handle the oil traffic of the Anglo-Iranian Oil Company, later to become British Petroleum. The port was especially well placed for shipping anthracite, a particularly hard coal low in volatile matter produced in the area. Even in 1884 there were few steamers registered in Swansea and most were tugs to handle the numerous sailing ships. Probably the first to operate colliers was William Pockett who by 1884 had acquired **Collier 205/48**, which he was to use in the coal trade to Bristol for many years. The vessel was to serve him well. He operated a steam packet service to Bristol and other ports from Swansea and may have used her on this initially before **Collier** became a regular vessel on the coal trade to Bristol. There were seven other steamers, one of which was **Equity** which, though registered at the port, was managed by F. F. Langstaff of Le Havre and was probably engaged in the coal trade to that port.

Llanelly and Burry Port

The harbour was progressively developed during Victorian times, and the whole was consolidated under the Llanelly Dock Act of 1904. The North Dock belonged to the Harbour Trust and was equipped for coal loading, primarily steam coals and anthracite. Similar facilities were available in the Great Western Railway Dock. The Great Mountain Colliery maintained tidal coal stages. The largest vessels which could load at the turn of the century were about 3,000 tons deadweight. Further west there was Burry Port which, though mainly associated with metal and tinplate works, could load coal in the small East Dock. The harbour was controlled by the Burry Port and Gwendraeth Valley Railway Co., which became part of the Great Western Railway which eventually became associated with all the South Wales ports so far mentioned.

Loading Methods

On the East Coast the coal drop or staith was almost universal and really came about as an accident of the local geography. In South Wales the situation was rather different. Firstly, the new docks were on relatively low ground, and secondly they were built rather later, by which time technology had moved on and coal hoists predominated. Cardiff's hoists, built in connection with the Bute Docks, were of the balance type. They were then replaced with hydraulic powered hoists built by Sir W. G. Armstrong-Whitworth & Co. In these, as can be seen from the photo (71a) the railway wagon was placed on a platform which could be hoisted up inside the tower and when in line with the shoot, the end door of the wagon opened. Then to tip the contents out, the back of the platform was raised via chains attached to a second hydraulic ram. The early ones were fixed and it was necessary to move the ships considerably. To speed up loading the Roath Basin at Cardiff was equipped with movable hoists, invented by Mr. George Taylor. They were built by Armstrong's to replace the original fixed hoists. These were the first moveable hoists erected and were the outcome of a suggestion of Sir W. T. Lewis, worked out and patented by Mr. Taylor in 1885. To

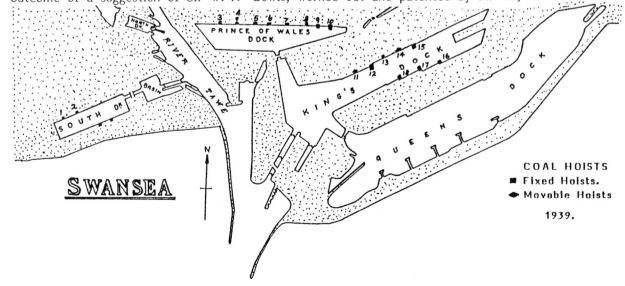

SWANSEA

PRINCE OF WALES DOCK

KING'S DOCK

QUEENS DOCK

COAL HOISTS
■ Fixed Hoists.
◆ Movable Hoists
1939.

71a. *Armstrong-Whitworth coal hoist after completion at Cardiff during 1911. The platform with a truckful of Nixon's Navigation coal (NN) has been raised ready for tipping by the vertical hydraulic ram at the back of the tower which hoists the platform via four chains. A second ram raises the back of the platform to tilt the wagon and empty it down the shoot.*

Photo courtesy Vickers Engineering Group Ltd.

get the coal rapidly to the hoists extensive railway sidings were laid out for each hoist, some for full wagons and some for empties. Various appliances were used to prevent coal being broken by the fall down the shoot into the ship's hold.

In the South Wales ports the coal hoists were nearly all built by Vickers Armstrong at Elswick, Newcastle on Tyne. They were designed to cope with the trucks of about 14 to 16 tons then in use, but were speedily converted to handle the new 20 tonners. However, washed duffs, as the small coals for the newer Electricity Generating Stations were known, are difficult to dislodge and tended to stick up in the ends of the wagons, a fault further aggravated by the slightest frost. So the hoists had to be modified by the addition of a device called the 'Norfolk Spade' to a selected few. It was fitted above the highest level to which the loaded trucks needed to be lifted and the truck containing the duff reluctant to leave the far corners was lifted up to it. It was uncanny to watch the hefty scraper blade dislodging and pushing out the coal in a truck about thirty feet away from the operator but it did the job well and ensured the fullest advantage of the rebates offered was taken and the new railway trucks really emptied (71b). Various appliances were used to prevent the coal being broken as it fell down the shoot into the ship's hold.

Of all the anti-coal-breakage appliances used throughout Britain, the escalator must be by far the most well known and widely used. Yet it was one of the most cumbersome to work with. It was extremely heavy and difficult to place correctly, and reduced the arc over which the chute could swing to almost nothing. The actual loading operations were slowed down, but as this was a common fault of almost all the A.C.B's it should be discounted. Perhaps the only one which did not cause an unduly prolonged loading time was the Lewis-Hunter system, described later.

Generally referred to as the Handcock anti-breakage appliance, the escalator consisted of an endless belt about 50 feet in length, running in an enclosed runway, the top being open to receive the end of the chute, and the bottom open to allow the coal to fall for a few feet to the tank

71b. *'Norfolk Spade' being used to push the remaining coal out of an Ebbw Vale coal wagon, see text above.*

top or coal already loaded. The motive power was supplied by the load of coal lying on each blade, as in the sketch (72), it's weight being enough to pull the belt over the end barrels.

Another A.C.B. appliance was the Morrison Leonard telescopic tube device (72). This had a platform with wheels adjusted so as to fit on top of the hatch coaming plate of smaller ships and capable of being secured anywhere. It had a telescopic tube hanging below it, and a small hopper above. Coal was sent down the shoot into the hopper and so into the tube, which at the start of operations was lowered right down to the bottom of the hold. The tube was allowed to fill up with coal and then the bottom section was slowly raised and the coal allowed to flow out and spread over the tank top. The tube was kept filled the whole time, either by the continued supply of coal being tipped into the hopper, or by raising or lowering the bottom-most section, as was necessary, thus avoiding damaging the coal and reducing it's value to shipper and consignee. At the same time it reduced the risk of explosion from gases released by breaking the coal, accumulating in the enclosed space of the hold.

Possibly the most effective of all the A.C.B's was the Lewis-Hunter appliance in Roath Dock at Cardiff. The Railway Company operating the Dock, the Great Western, claimed to have the sole right to this system. Unlike most of the other A.C.B's, which could be lowered into the holds without it becoming necessary to unship all the beams, use of this device called for the removal of all the beams in every deck hatchway. The so-called 'box' was big and, with it's 20 ton load of coal, became a hefty chunk of machinery, which, should it come into violent contact with the comparatively fragile hatch beams (designed to counter vertical stresses caused by heavy seas) could do an immense amount of damage. This equipment claimed to complete the loading of each hold with the minimum amount of trimming, meaning it could deposit coal anywhere in the hold. The loaded coal truck was drawn up to the stoppers swung across the rails, and the end doors released. When the empty box had been lowered into the pit, and the anti-spillage plates put into position the truck was tipped hydraulically and its load shot into the box. This was then lifted out by means of the hefty centre wire rope, and swung over the hold being loaded. It was then lowered

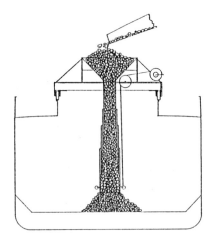

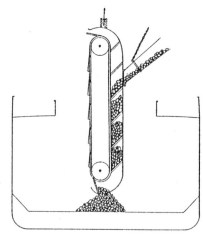

72. *Anti-coal-breakage devices. Left: Morrison Leonard telescopic tube. Right: Handcock escalator.*

From sketches by Captain MacRae

to within 3 or 4 feet of either the coal already loaded or the tank top itself if loading had just commenced. The sides of the box were then held by the two smaller wire ropes and the bottom allowed to open downwards. The whole was lifted slowly and gently and the coal remaining in the box allowed to run out, and having to fall a matter of inches, no further breakage occurred. This system was by no means new and was described in "The Stowage of Cargoes" by Robert White Stevens (Fourth Edition) published in 1867.

In September 1923, the Great Western Railway Company offered the coal shippers favourable terms to induce them to use 20 ton wagons for the carriage of their product from the pits to the docks. The first was to be a 5% rebate on carriage charges for coal carried in fully-laden 20 ton wagons, representing about one penny a ton off conveyancing charges. In addition they were granted a special reduction of a further one penny per ton in the tipping and weighing charges. Yet another attraction was a further quarter pence per ton rebate allowed on coal shipped for overseas destinations. So that all in all there was a distinct advantage of at least 2d per ton for shipping coal out of 20 ton wagons in the South Wales coalfield.

Shipowning made a rather slow start in the South Wales coal ports, largely because the established east coast shipowners, who had both ships and long experience in the coal trade tended to set up branch offices there, or at least send their vessels to load coal there. During the 1880s and up to the First World War local companies began to appear which were to become even more prominent in the 1920s and 1930s. Most expanded their interests into ocean tramping but the smaller ships of E. Jenkins & Co., of Cardiff were most suited to the trade with Spain and Portugal. In 1908 the company owned six vessels including the **Coventry** 1678/83, lost in October on a voyage from Newport to Oporto with coal. Trade with France was also very important and the French Navy had begun using South Wales steam coal even before the British Navy, taking their first shipments in 1842. Shipping coal to bunkering stations at Plymouth and Portsmouth was an important trade

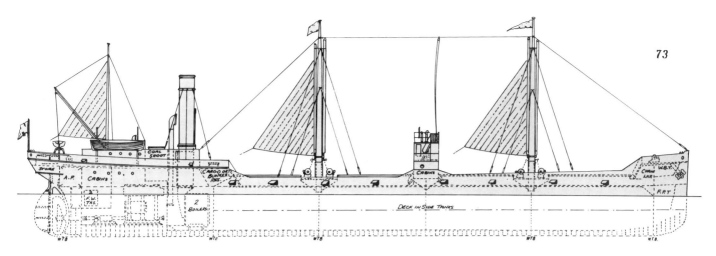

73. *Datetree 1850/14 was built for the Tree S.S. Co. Ltd., of Cardiff and had a deadweight of 2,670 tons on a draft of 16' 10.5".*
Courtesy P.N. Thomas

and often occupied large vessels up to 6,000 tons or so, as did the French trade. The French Railways and shipowners were also large users. One of the South Wales companies to specialise in supplying the needs of the Royal Navy and with close French ties was J. T. Duncan & Co. Mr. Duncan moved to Cardiff in 1883, commencing business as a shipbroker, and in 1889 became a partner with Mr. Valette to form Duncan, Valette & Co. Mr. Valette was French and an agent for French coal buyers. No doubt the connection offered some regular cargoes for **Benefactor** 1034/80. Mr. Valette left the partnership in 1895, in which year **Stokesley** 1047/83 was purchased. Mr. Duncan had invested in various other shipping ventures, most important of which was to be the Shamrock Shipping Co., for which he became representative in South Wales ports fixing coal cargoes for the Irish company's ships. The arrangement was to change Duncan's own shipping activities considerably as he agreed to operate only one of his ships in the French and Bay coal trade and so the older ship **Benefactor** was sold. The Company had also time-chartered their vessels as naval colliers and **Stokesley** had been on time charter to the Admiralty on several occasions. This side of the business was not restricted by any agreements and so in 1901 **Maywood** 1188/01 was delivered to the company and placed on a long-term charter to the Admiralty. Though mostly operated in Home waters, they did venture down to the Mediterranean on occasions. The arrangement proved so satisfactory that the much larger **J. Duncan** 1939/05 was delivered from the Ailsa Shipbuilding Company for charter to the Admiralty. The vessel was followed by the **Frances Duncan** 2384/07, again for charter as a collier to the Admiralty. She measured 297.2' x 41.5' x 20.8' and was equipped with electric light, a new idea then. The expansion of the Royal Navy prior to the First World War led to a request to the Company to provide colliers especially suited to the Navy's requirements. This led to the ordering of two engines-aft colliers with an unobstructed hold area to facilitate coaling, so the machinery was placed aft but a compact bridge was retained amidships. With dimensions of 306.0' x 43.2' x 20.1' **Agnes Duncan** 2512/12 and **Ethel Duncan** 2510/12 were amongst the largest engines-aft colliers of the period. They were both placed on charter to the Admiralty. The **Ethel Duncan** was lost off Orkney in October 1916. Her sister survived the war, during which she was modified by the removal of the intermediate bulkheads to produce one long unobstructed hold while the ballast tanks were modified to carry fuel oil, a sign of the Navy's change to oil fuel. Single-ship companies, generally incorporating the name of the ship in the title, were formed to finance each ship, (a practice largely abandoned by other owners), J. T. Duncan retaining management.

A Company which was to follow the engines-aft design, also at the suggestion of the Admiralty, was the Tree S.S. Co., managed by Howard-Jones & King of Cardiff. Starting with conventional engine-amidships colliers such as **Cedartree** 1780/13 built by J. Crown & Sons in 1913, they then went to the Antwerp Engineering Company for a very advanced design vessel incorporating much of what was to become standard practice in bulk carriers 60 years later. However, they were not the pioneers for that honour appears to fall to Henry Burrell of Glasgow, whose patent for an engines-aft 'straight-back' steamer was mentioned in The Shipping World for August 10th 1904. The name was derived from the fact that the single deck had no sheer and all accommodation was placed aft, including the bridge. Other advanced features included steel hatch covers and angled side tanks to run the coal or iron ore towards the middle of the hold where it could be easily reached by grabs, which he suggested should be on the ship's own electric deck cranes. He calculated that such a ship would reduce the round trip freight from Cardiff to Bilbao by over a shilling. He seems to have decided to put his theories to the test for **Ben Earn** is recorded as belonging to the Straight-back S. S. Co. Ltd., with H. Burrell of Glasgow as manager. The dimensions were 318.4' x 49.3' x 21.7', single deck, with poop 66 feet and forcastle 34 feet. The bridge was presumably right aft as depicted in one of his proposed designs dating from three years earlier. Another interesting feature was the hopper bunker.

In 1914 **Datetree** was completed for the company (73). Much of what had been advocated by Burrell was incorporated in the design, large unobstructed holds, single deck with no sheer, hopper coal bunker and poop accommodation. However, the bridge was placed amidships and the cargo gear was the more simple one of derricks and winches, though there were two to each hatch for quicker working. Though built with Admiralty collier requirements in mind, the beam was broader and the ends somewhat finer so that the vessel was sufficiently stable to carry a full cargo of timber without any ballast being needed for stability. The ballast was placed solely in side tanks which extended throughout the hold space which by their design were easily accessible with sufficient height for a man to walk through to inspect or for repairs. Though they would appear to reduce the capacity of the hold that is compensated for in part by the shallow floors as no double bottom ballast is needed, thus the stowage is very good, about 50 cubic feet per ton deadweight. The ceiling of the hold was of plain steel plates held by brass screws so they could be easily removed to repair grab damage or gain access to the bottom plating.

The engines were placed aft to eliminate the shaft tunnel and reduce the risk of grab damage when discharging and make available the best part of the ship for cargo. The nett register tonnage needed to be as low as possible for vessels in and out of port frequently, as harbour and other dues were calculated upon it. A figure of 32% less than the gross was obtained for the design as the side tanks, part of the gross tonnage, were deducted for the nett tonnage. The wings, which were part of the tonnage in an ordinary collier, but into which it was usually impractical to load coal, and thus were considered non-earning spaces, were also eliminated in this design. The sheer is dispensed with, which prevents the vessel trimming by the head when loaded due to the excess cargo carried forward in the case of engine-aft vessels with sheer. As this also brings the ends of the ship nearer the water, solid bulwarks were placed on the poop deck and similarly around the forecastle.

The ballast capacity was 1,060 tons and as the tanks were larger at the top the vessels roll was made easy in ballast trim. The tanks also had the advantage over conventional double bottom tanks in that they maintained capacity forward where the double bottom would be narrowing, reducing the tendency to trim too much by the stern as was a problem in conventional designs. The inner tank sides also passed up smoothly into the hatch sides and no beams, pillars or frames existed in the holds to reduce capacity or to sustain grab damage. The actual trim in ballast without permanent bunkers was 13 feet aft and 8 feet forward, the propellor being fully immersed when bunkers were in. The trim on a full deadweight with half bunkers was 3 feet by the stern but when required she could be brought on to an almost even keel by filling the forehold. Ballast was particularly easily discharged as much of it could be run out by gravity with only a little pumping, but of course the reverse applied when filling! The 6 ton derricks of good reach could be coupled in pairs for heavy lifts. Though the vessel was built in Belgium the machinery came from MacColl and Pollock of Sunderland who supplied a triple expansion engine 20" x 33" x 54" with 36" stroke and two 14 feet diameter boilers working at 180 lbs to give a fully loaded speed of 11.5 knots.

She had only been in service a few months when disaster struck, for on a voyage from Barry to Brest with coal she went ashore at Cape Cornwall on the 25th of June 1914 and became a total loss, despite her watertight bulkheads. She was valued at £75,000. However the company did not give up the design and ordered a larger version incorporating their experience from **Datetree**. The new vessel was ordered from John Priestman & Co., Sunderland. One change was to incorporate some sheer, even though this made the construction more complicated for the new ship which was named **Elmtree** 2686/16 (75). She could carry 3,800 tons on a draft of 19'6", compared with **Datetree's** deadweight of 2,700 tons on a draft of 17'1". Other changes included moving the captain and officers aft. The mizzen mast, complete with derrick to handle the work boat was retained, as was the large bunker hatch placed just behind the funnel. The smaller reserve bunker forward of the funnel was reduced in size to make way for the new accommodation. The 50 ft. derricks were retained with even more powerful winches. The vessel served the company thoughout the war and left the company, along with the remainder of the fleet, when the Tree S. S. Co. Ltd's ships were sold to the Maindy Shipping Co. (Jenkins, Richards & Evans Ltd.), Cardiff for £450,000 in the boom years at the end of the First World War. With the collapse of the freight market the Maindy fleet were slowly sold off, including the **Elmtree**, which had become the **Maindy Lodge**. Her new owners were the Interstate S. S. Company of Sydney, who re-named her **Iron Chief** and operated her in the Australian iron ore trade.

The partnership between Howard-Jones and King was dissolved after the sale and a new company Howard-Jones Ltd., was registered on the 5th of December 1923 to manage the Tree S. S. Co. Ltd., which returned to shipowning with the new steamer **Ashtree** 1581/24. She was a conventional raised quarterdeck steamer with engines amidships. The company operated her until 1935 when she was sold to William France, Fenwick & Co., and became **Kirkwood**. They had quickly expanded their fleet with the management of the Meadow S. S., which gave them a fleet of four steamers in 1931.

J. T. Duncan, in contrast, who retained his fleet at the end of the First World War, had **Agnes Duncan** 2512/12, **Frances Duncan** 2384/07 and **J. Duncan** 1832/14. The Admiralty coal purchases for naval use fell from 2.5 million tons in 1919 to 188,000 tons ten years later. Thus collier work for the ships was much reduced and by 1929 they were carrying coal in the Continental and Bay trades. It was while on a voyage from Barry to Rouen with coal that **Frances Duncan** 2384/07 capsized and sank in very bad weather off Land's End on 5th of December 1929. Sixteen of the twenty crew aboard were lost with the ship. When the market was at its lowest ebb **Parkhill** was purchased and re-named **Maywood** 1823/22 (116). **Agnes Duncan** was sold in 1934, and with rising freight rates the **Stokesley** 1149/22 joined the fleet but was to strike a mine in the Second World War, just three years later. The other ships survived the Second World War but with only small amounts of coal being shipped they were employed tramping with various cargoes. **J. Duncan** lasted until 1956 and

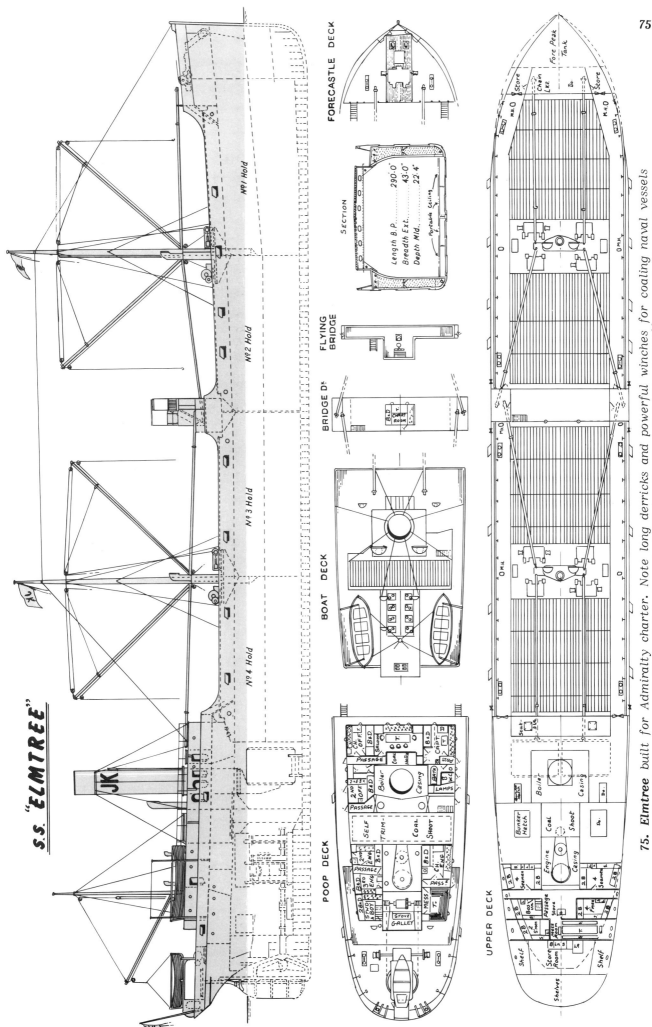

S.S. "ELMTREE"

FORECASTLE DECK

SECTION

Length B.P. .... 290·0'
Breadth Ext. .... 43·0'
Depth Mld. .... 22·4'

FLYING BRIDGE

BRIDGE Dᴷ

BOAT DECK

POOP DECK

UPPER DECK

75

75. Elmtree built for Admiralty charter. Note long derricks and powerful winches for coaling naval vessels using the ships own gear. Built by J. Priestman in 1916 for the Tree S.S. Co., Cardiff.

Courtesy P. N. Thomas.

the **Maywood** until 1959, when she was towed away from Penarth for breaking up. The firm continued as agents as there was little coal being shipped for export and the home trade, mainly to power stations, was in the electricity authority's own ships.

H. O. King of Cardiff was a director of the Power S.S. Co., with A. J. Power of London and W. E. Clare of Hove. The company was formed in 1906 and placed its vessels under the management of J. Power & Co. Their first vessel was the engine-aft collier **Penshurst** 1191/06 which was engaged in the French trade, probably running from Cardiff. By 1918 the Power S.S. Co., had three ships and H. O. King was managing the Redland Shipping Co. Ltd., which had just taken delivery of **Lord Rhondda** 1744/18. H. O. King was also associated with the Plisson S.N. Co. Ltd., which was formed in association with Plisson & Co., Paris, in 1913 and typical of the close commercial ties developed with French companies in the coal trade. This company operated from the same Cardiff offices and owned five steamers and two sailing vessels. King & Co. (Cardiff) Ltd. was registered in 1919 with H. O. King as managing director subscribing just over half the £100,000, the remainder being in the name of the Power S.S. Company. The new company acted as agents for Plisson & Co., of Paris and by 1922 **Lord Rhondda** 1744/18 had been joined by **Lady Rhondda** 1757/18 and by two large steamers under the Plisson S.N. Co. King & Co. (Cardiff) Ltd., had **Kingswear** 1457/09 themselves and had just become managers of the Haig Shipping Co. This latter company fully illustrates the difficulties which befell Cardiff owners, especially those who invested in ships at high prices towards the end of the First World War and particularly just after, when the high freight rates they initially obtained did not continue long enough to recover the high costs of the vessels they had purchased.

The Haig Shipping Company was registered on the 5th of September 1919 and in the first year they were able to pay a dividend of ten and a half per cent free of tax on the profits made by their steamer **Canterbury Bell**, of 970 tons deadweight, for which they had paid £55,000 and for which they had a bank mortgage of £29,803 secured on the steamer. By 1921 the first managers, W. H. Williams & Co., of Cardiff, struggling to operate the steamer, took Mr. King into partnership and handed over management to King & Co. (Cardiff) Ltd. For the first six months of 1921 **Canterbury Bell** showed a profit of just £46, the result of the collapse of freight rates, and in the latter 5 months the steamer was laid up. However, she returned to service in December and on the 5th of January 1922 was lost at sea. Among the shareholders was the Park Coal Company, but as there was a miners' strike, not even they were able to help with finding cargoes for her. The vessel was insured and the company almost immediately purchased **Polmina** 896/17 for which they paid almost £25,000, but difficulties continued and the vessel was sold by 1926. Accumulated losses were £3,476 and the bank was owed £5,715. H. O. King's own company King & Co. (Cardiff) Ltd., soon sold **Kingswear** and the Plisson S.N. Company also had no ships by 1925, but **Lord Rhondda** 1744/18 and **Lady Rhondda** 1757/18 were now directly owned and had mortgages of £30,000 on them.

Much the same sort of thing was going on at F. H. Green & Co., who managed the Neville Shipping Company Ltd. which was also formed in 1919. They faced up to the loss in value of their ships by writing down the £1 shares to 5s., a 75% reduction in value, in 1923. The company also reported that their seamer **Macville** 665/15 was laid up due to heavy operating costs. The company managed to make a small profit in 1923 but by 1926 losses were mounting again though the company continued to trade until the 1930s, while many of their contemporaries went out of business.

Some made quick profits, one such was the Gower Shipping Company Ltd., which was formed in September 1919 with a nominal caital of £100,000 to purchase coasters for the coal trade. Management was in the hands of Arthur Gibbs & Co., Swansea and Cardiff. The Gower Shipping Company had as managing director Mr. C. Arthur R. Gibbs of Porthcawl and acquired the steamers **Hampshire**, 1,080 deadweight (161) and **Sportsman**, 720 deadweight, as well as a similar sized steamer under construction. **Sportsman** was typical of the coasters acquired by South Wales owners or sent there by other owners looking for coal cargoes. The considerable industrialisation, coupled with the dwindling number of schooners trading to Ireland, meant that more and larger cargoes of coal travelled to small ports by steam coaster. A particularly popular destination for coasters was Northern France or Ireland. These ships could have uncertificated masters and less crew, provided they stayed within Elbe-Brest limits laid down in the Merchant Shipping Acts of 1894, and so were cheaper to run.

Sportsman was a typical larger coaster of the period and shows the transition from the older design with a low open bridge to higher bridge and shorter higher forecastle to allow the fore hatch to be as long as possible. The vessel was originally built for George Elsmie & Son of Aberdeen and designed for them by the Glasgow naval architect Mr. A. M. Gordon. There was a considerable coal trade to Aberdeen, and though not merchants themselves the ship was probably designed to take advantage of this trade. The long wide hatches with the sloping fore ends would keep coal trimmimng to a minimum and were convenient for rapid discharge. The moulded dimensions were 175' x 27' x 12.5' with an overall length of 183'6". She was designed to carry a cargo of 720 tons on a draft of 12' 10" at a speed of 10 knots. A feature of the design was the considerable sheer at the stern and this tended to be a characteristic of vessels built by the Ardrossan Dockyard at this time (77). In later vessels the engineer's space was taken up with increased ballast capacity as coaster owners found themselves making more passages in ballast. The engineers were then put in place of the galley and the galley moved forward over the boiler. Forward, the crew were packed into rather cramped quarters below decks. The two firemen sharing their accommodation with the cook and bosun. In later years it was placed on the deck above which allowed portholes and was not so prone to flooding in event of a collision which was always a thought uppermost in the minds of

The Steamers "Sportsman" and "Starbeam."

Built by the Ardrossan Dry Dock & Shipbuilding Co. Ltd.

"The Shipbuilder." October, 1914

seamen off-duty when proceeding in fog! The Captain and the mates had pleasant accommodation amidships with their bunks placed away from the cold outside steel plating, against the wood partitions separating them from the saloon with its welcoming stove. The flying bridge was also arranged with well placed poles to hold dodgers as well as a ridge pole to arrange some protection overhead. Owners tended to think that having an open bridge kept the officer of the watch and the seamen at the wheel awake, whereas they were often huddled against the dodger, too busy trying to keep warm to take that much notice. One possible benefit was that the severity of the weather would be all too apparent and shelter would be made for.

Just six months later an offer was made by the Fairfield Shipping Co. (1920) Ltd., to purchase the £1 shares for £1-17 shillings so the shareholders received almost £80,000 for their investment of £43,541. In addition the company had purchased the coaster **Arnhem** of 420 tons deadweight for £21,000 initially and re-sold her for £29,000. The deal may well have been at the suggestion of Mr. W. J. Stephen who was on the board of both companies. The manager of the Fairfield Shipping Company, H. Owen Jones & Co., Cardiff, soon found themselves in trouble and in the period July 1922 to December 1922 they made a considerable loss on trading. The company report sent out to shareholders in January 1922 shows all too clearly what had happened to them:-

"We beg to submit herewith profit and loss account of the company for the period of 15 months from July 22, 1921, to October 20, 1922, and balance sheet as on December 12, 1922.

"From these you will observe that the company has suffered a loss of £9,960 15s 4d. on trading, which is accounted for by the fact that owing to depression in freights and the heavy cost of insurance premiums on high insurable values, the vessels could not be run profitably and eventually had to be laid up from June last onwards.

"As was explained to you at the last meeting, the company paid £36,540 7s.11d on account of a new vessel building and the builders (Colby Bros. of Lowestoft) had gone into liquidation. The builders' assets proved insufficient to meet the claims even of their debenture holders, and in consequence your company has been able to secure nothing in respect of their claim, and after many negotiations and efforts to dispose of the same at an advantageous price, the materials appropriated at the builders' yard for building the company's ship and the portion of the hull which had been commenced had to be sold at the price of scrap.

"From the balance sheet it will be seen that the amount due to bankers on October 20, 1922, was £52,832. Though this had been reduced from about £70,000 yet the capital value of the company's vessels had decreased to an extent almost incredible, and although your managers endeavoured to get a good price for them they could not get even £25,000 offered for the two ships.

"Your directors made themselves personally responsible to the bank in respect of the company's overdraft and the position is such that the company cannot meet their obligations either to the bank or to creditors or to indemnify the directors under their guarantee.

"Experience in other cases has proved that it is useless to expect shareholders to put up further capital in an amount sufficient to save the situation and it is felt that there is no alternative but that the company should be wound up.

"The profit and loss account shows that the loss on voyages and laying up charges amounted to £5,899 14s 5d., and that bank charges absorbed £3,402 13s 5d."

The auditor, Mr. J. Pearson Griffiths, F.S.A.A., in his certificate, dated January 11, 1923, states: "In accordance with the provisions of the Companies Act 1908 to 1917, I beg to report that I have examined the balance sheet of the Fairfield Steamship Company (1920) Limited, as above set forth, and have obtained all the information and explanations I have required. The steamers shown in the accounts are not now in the possession of the company, the same having been taken by the mortgagees by arrangement under their powers." J. C. Gould was a member of the board and his own company also failed.

Though Cardiff was particularly heavily affected by speculation many companies opted for more cautious policies. One such was that set up by Frederick Jones, who formed Melrose Abbey (1907) Ltd., to take over **Melrose Abbey** 1211/77. The ship had sunk at a French port, been raised and declared a constructive total loss, but it seems Frederick Jones was an experienced marine superintendent who thought otherwise, purchased it and organised repairs himself. The vessel had been built for Pyman Bros., of Newport, an offshoot of George Pyman of Hartlepool, and registered at Cardiff. His next ship **Tintern Abbey** 1812/09 was built for him by Richardson, Duck & Co. The vessel was designed to be suitable for work as a naval collier and soon after delivery was voyage chartered to deliver coal to Oban and to Chatham. In between these were the usual coal cargoes out with iron ore or pit wood for the mines as return cargoes. From 1911 to 1914 the Admiralty time chartered **Tintern Abbey** but she was released just before the outbreak of the First World War and was trapped at St. Petersburg. During the war the fleet was increased by adding the captured German ship **Franz Horn** (re-named **Melrose Abbey** 1457/98), **Neath Abbey** (ex Kildare) 2410/03, and the new **Singleton Abbey** 2467/15, built for Admiralty collier work. All were more or less fully occupied throughout the war period as naval colliers.

Frederick Jones had gained his sea experience sailing in the steamers belonging to one of Cardiff's earliest steamship owners John Marychurch, and later with other owners including Hall Bros., of New-

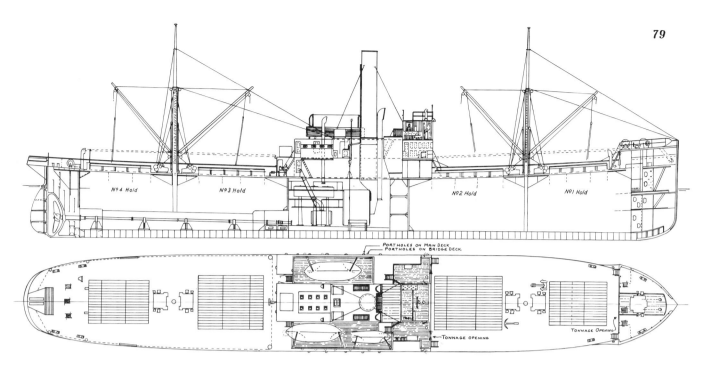

79. Hillfern 1535/20, was managed for most of the 1920s by McNeil & Jones of Cardiff but was sold in 1932 to John Kelly, Belfast.
Courtesy P.N.Thomas

castle. The ships, never a large fleet, were employed in the Mediterranean and Baltic trades with coal the outward cargo. By the late 1920s it had become known as the Abbey Line and successfully continued until 1957, the last steamer being **Tintern Abbey** 2471/39, built new for the company. A company with a similar trading pattern was the Portsmouth S.S. Co.,which was registered in September 1921. The main shareholders were members of the McNeil family. The company was managed by McNeil & Jones. McNeil, Hind & Co., had owned larger steamers and R. McNeil, who invested in the new company, managed the Portland S.S. Co., which had two steamers in 1922. The new company set about acquiring steamers as the prices fell, first to be acquired were the new **Hillglen** 1262/21 and **Tyne Bell** 1535/20. The latter vessel was one of the C5 standard vessels based on a collier design of the Dublin Dockyard Company. The vessel had been laid down as the **War Chelmer**. The company renamed her **Hillfern** 1535/20, (79). It was the only C5 type built by C. Rennoldson & Sons although seventeen were built by five different yards. The vessel built by C. Rennoldson was a simplified version of the original design illustrated by **Dulwich** (65). **Hillfern**'s hatches were reduced to make the vessel more suitable for general trading and the back of the bridge was altered to accept a bunker hatch placed over the cross bunker. However, space under the bridge deck was available for extra bunkers or cargoes if required. The arrangement of tonnage openings in the bulkhead meant that the space was exempt from tonnage measurement as are the passageways in the crew accommodation. The accommodation was similar, but wash-places have been added for firemen and seamen. The bridge deck accommodation was unchanged except for the engineers on the starboard side who have lost part of their messroom to allow an extra cabin for an apprentice. Perhaps the most prominent feature was the elimination of the raised quarterdeck. A deadweight of 2,400 tons was obtained on a draft of 18' 7". The company operated until the mid-1930s when they sold their last ships. **Hillfern** was sold to John Kelly of Belfast in 1932. There were mortgages of £39,000 in 1925 and the company were finding it hard to make ends meet. The largest of the vessels, **Hillcroft** 2268/12, was trading to the Mediterranean with coal and was not popular with her engineers as the winches were in bad condition, as was her other machinery, and it was a case of make-do and mend just to keep her running.

Another company to expand rapidly at the end of the First World War was Claude Angel & Co., who had managed larger vessels in earlier times. They had only the Marga S.S. Co. Ltd., in 1918 which operated the coaster **Clydeburn** 553/02, but in August the Manor Line (London) Ltd., was registered with Claude Angel subscribing £49,999 of the £50,000 capital and Mrs. P. M. Angel £1. The sole director was Mr. Angel. By 1922 the company owned **Horseferry** 1812/03, **Torquay** 870/14 and **Northquay** 730/20. **Torquay**, (117), which joined the fleet in 1921 was soon sold, as were the others, and replaced with larger more profitable vessels and by 1927 the fleet consisted of **Acton Manor** 1481/19, **Brompton Manor** 1735/14, **Chiswick Manor** 1480/19, **Drayton Manor** (ex Northquay) 730/20 and **Emsworth Manor** 1289/12. The latter ship was a regular visitor to Ramsgate carrying coal. The Manor Line continued to operate until the 1930s when the fleet was dispersed, but Claude Angel continued ship management with the Dillwyn Shipping Co. Ltd., which acquired two well known local sister ships about 1937, the **Madge Llewellyn** which became the **Dillwyn** 1451/20 and **Marie Llewellyn** which became **Killwyn** 1464/20. **Dillwyn** was soon to be lost in the Spanish Civil War. A separate management company, Angel, Dalling & Co.,was set up to manage the Bramhall S.S. Co., which by the beginning of the war was managing **Bramden** 1594/25 and **Bramhill** 1821/23. Claude Angel dropped out of managing ships in Cardiff about this time but the Dillwyn Shipping Co., continued, relocated in Swansea. The company operated through the Second World War and sold their last ship soon afterwards.

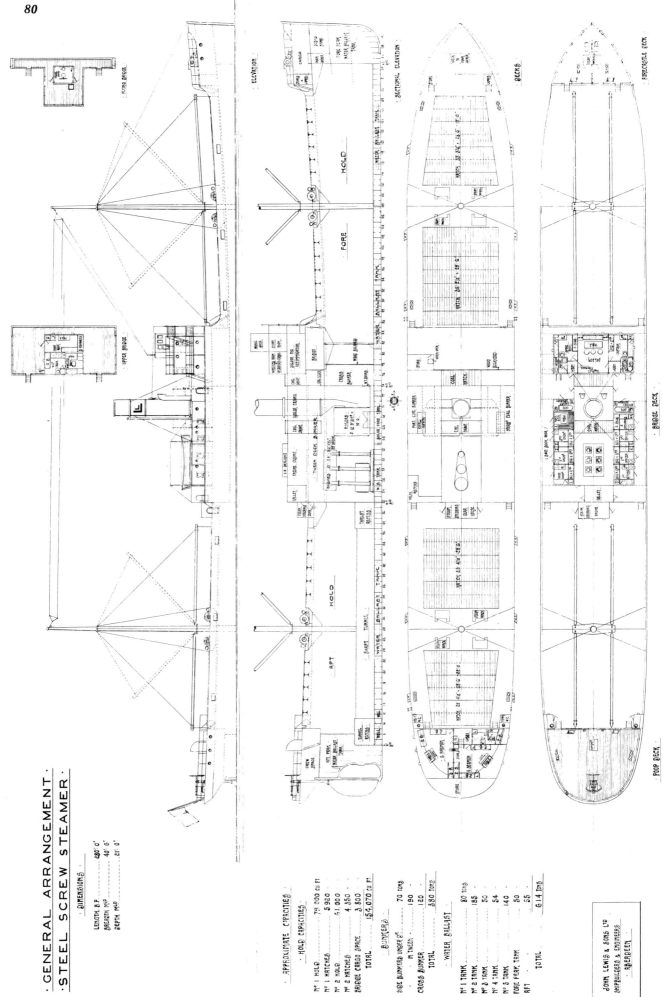

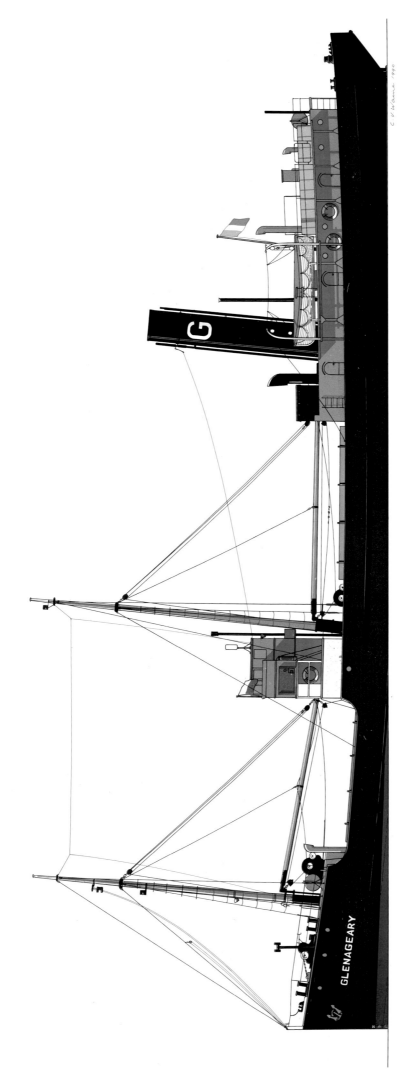

81. *Glenageary,* 464/20, (142.0' x 25.8' x 11.5'), and her sister ***Glencullen*** 466/21, were built for the Alliance & Dublin Consumers Gas Company and carried gas coal from Liverpool to Dublin for many years. They were both built at Lytham and closely similar to the series of coasters built for W. A. Savage of Liverpool (Zillah Shipping & Carrying Co. Ltd.) such as Beechfield and Briarfield. The drawing shows the ***Glenageary*** as she appeared in the late 1950s.

The Llewellyn sisterships were two of four sisters built for the Llewellyn Shipping Co. Ltd., of Cardiff. This company was registered in July 1919 and was one of several shipping ventures with which the coal magnate Sir David R. Llewellyn was connected. The family had important coal mining interests including North's Navigation Collieries (1889) Ltd., near Maesteg which, in 1940 were producing a million tons of coking and steam coals, and Craigola Merthyr Colliery which produced 550,000 tons of smokeless steam coal.

The sisters were all built by Lewis' Yard in Aberdeen (80). The first two appeared in 1920. They were **Madge Llewellyn** 1451/20 and **Marie Llewellyn** 1464/20, with **Maud Llewellyn** 1454/21 the following year. It was not until three years later that the last sister **Joyce Llewellyn** 1446/24 joined the fleet. Meanwhile **Madge Llewellyn** had sailed from Neath Abbey on the 16th of August with the largest cargo ever loaded there, 1,800 tons plus 100 tons bunkers which was bound for Northern France. They had the dimensions 234.5' x 35.6' x 16.5', with the engine room under the bridge deck amidships. Apart from the Llewellyn family other shareholders included W. B. Thomas, whose company W. B. Thomas & Co. Ltd., acted as managers and the Anglo-Spanish Coaling Company. This no doubt was the intended trade for the vessels, carrying steam coal for sale as bunker coal. Second-hand vessels were also purchased. The slump hit the venture hard and all the vessels were soon sold. The four sisters were all purchased by the Federated Coal & Shipping Co., and were traded without change of name from Cardiff. They were sold again in the 1930s, two of the ships remaining together in the fleet of the Cardigan Shipping Co. of Cardiff.

Another shipping venture which may have influenced the later formation of the Llewellyn Shipping Company was Sir David R. Llewellyn's major holding in Llewellyn, Merrett & Price Ltd., which was registered in March 1918 and managed by Merrett Brothers, who themselves owned a considerable number of ships for a short time around 1920. Sir David's shareholding was £259,612 of the total capital of £820,000, the other partners subscribing £174,144 (H. H. Merrett) and £112,492 (R. W. Price). The Vale of Neath Colliery Company also held a considerable number of shares. The initial profits were good and the company successfully operated a fleet of 12 vessels by 1921. This had increased to 21 by 1922, a short time before mounting losses forced the company to abandon shipping by the mid-1920s. The Maindy Shipping Company purchased a variety of large and small vessels including those of the Tree S.S. Co., which was taken over in 1919 when the Maindy Shipping Company was under the initial managers Jenkins, Richards & Evans Ltd. of Cardiff. The fleet eventually came under the personal control of Sir David R. Llewellyn in about 1922, by which time several new vessels had been delivered. Apart from the larger ocean-going ships such as **Maindy Manor** 3791/17 there was a series of single deck engines-aft colliers built by the Rennie, Ritchie & Newport Shipbuilding Company of Wivenhoe. The design (83) shows a layout which was to be adopted much later for motor ships; the enclosed poop deck containing all the crew accommodation aft of the engine room. There was space on either side of the engine room above the main deck for extra bunkers or cargo which was reached via the coaling hatches on the poop deck. The main cross bunker had a hatch on the casing above, directly in front of the funnel. Interestingly, the option of oil fuel was offered in the design. The single hold allowed 58,310 cubic feet of stowage or about 40 cubic feet per ton, rather less than ideal for the coal trade.

Engines-aft vessels always posed difficulties for designers, for although they had a large unobstructed hold there was always a fore and aft trim problem, usually when the vessel was fully laden, the addition of bunkers would set the vessel down by the stern, as was the case here, the ship having a mean draft of about 14'3" when fully laden with 1,425 tons. As the bunkers were burned the stern slowly lightened so that on arrival the vessel would be on an approximately even keel. This was not generally a problem as the coal loading ports had plenty of deep water and as the vessel would be on an even keel by the time it arrived at a shallower port to which the coal was consigned all would be well. Consideration had to be given to this as a vessel down by the head is difficult to steer and more vulnerable to heavy head seas. The enclosed poop deck helped to protect the stern from heavy following seas if the bunkers were particularly full when making a more distant voyage. The registered dimensions were 207.5' x 33.6' x 13.5' and a loaded speed of 9.5 knots was obtained using a triple expansion engine having cylinders 16.5", 27" and 46" in diameter by 30" stroke developing about 700 i.h.p. Steam was provided by two boilers 11'6" by 10'0" working at 180 lbs per square inch. The first vessel in the series was launched in March 1920 by Mrs. A. J. Richards, the wife of Mr. Richards who was a director of the managers and of the Maindy Shipping Company. She named the vessel **Maindy Transport** 969/20. The launch attracted considerable local interest as it was the largest vessel launched on the Colne. The second vessel, **Maindy Tower** 975/20 was completed in the same year and **Maindy Keep** 973/21 the next year. By this time the builders were in difficulties as were the owners, but **Maindy Cottage** was eventually completed by the receivers as **Stockrington** 973/22 for Australian owners appointed to take over when the shipbuilders failed. The hull of a fifth vessel lay rusting in the yard for some time before it too was sold, this time to Holland, where it was taken for completion. This type of vessel was never popular with Cardiff owners who operated larger ships on the whole, so when the Maindy fleet was sold off **Maindy Transport** became the **Ambleside** of the Quayside Shipping Co., (Connel & Grace) and **Maindy Tower** became **Gledburn** under Robinson, Brown management, both of Newcastle where large coasters were a feature of the Tyne coal trade.

It might be thought from this that coasters were not important in the South Wales coal trade, but in fact they were just as numerous as elsewhere but owned in other ports. Richard Hughes of

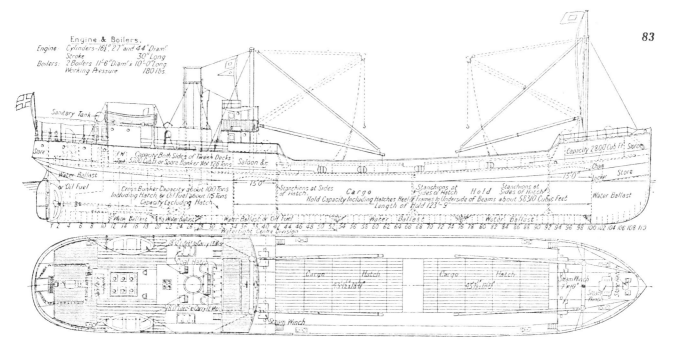

83. *Maindy Transport* launched in March 1920 for the Maindy Shipping Co. Ltd., Cardiff.
From the Shipbuilding & Shipping Record, 22 April 1920

Liverpool's large fleet of coasters had close local ties and was regularly employed. It included some large engines-aft colliers. Monks of Liverpool also ran their coasters in the trade. Other regular visitors were the coasters belonging to Irish merchants.

One coaster owner based in Cardiff was Gueret, Llewellyn & Price, another one of Llewellyn's. The company had its origins in L. Gueret & Co. Ltd., of Cariff which was formed to export coal. Mr. Gueret came from France, and as might be expected did considerable business with that country. The Gueret family had ships from about 1875 which were involved in the more distant and Bay trades, but with falling freights they dropped out of shipowning but continued as coal shippers, developing strong links with South America. At the end of the First World War they returned to shipowning, purchasing five of the numerous 'Kil' class patrol boats which were completed for them as colliers. They were **Mallock** 609/19 (86), **Mandrake** 606/19, **Mead** 606/19, **Mersdow** 615/19 and **Mington** 522/19. These vessels were only suitable for trade from dock to dock as they had to remain afloat because of the hull design and so were confined to trading to larger ports. This was a major limitation as colliers of this size were designed to lie aground when loading and discharging, and this was usually the case at smaller ports. The company acquired the foreign coal business of A. J. Pope in 1928. Much of his business was with Spain, but despite this there was not sufficient work for the ships and all were sold in the slump of the 1930s, **Mallock** and **Mandrake** being laid up in the River Fal for some time. The **Mallock** was eventually sold in 1934 to Italian owners who converted her to a motor ship. With the improvement in trade in the latter part of the 1930s **Merim** 1037/19 was purchased. A. J. Pope retained an interest in the Spanish trade and at the time of his death in 1937 during the Spanish Civil War, was operating three steamers and had a further eight on charter. A further offshoot Gueret, Llewellyn & Merrett Ltd., coal merchants and exporters, became part of the Powell Duffryn amalgamation of South Wales collieries including D. R. Llewellyn & Sons Ltd., Powell Duffryn Steam Coal Co., and the collier owners and merchants Stephenson Clarke.

A smaller empire was that built up by George F. Harrison, who began as a coal exporter in 1906 and was joined by his son to form Harrison, Sons & Co. Ltd. They initially ran one or two larger ships but in December 1914 they set up Town Line (London) Ltd., with a capital of £1,000,000 and this was the signal for spectacular growth during the First World War. They were mainly interested in the Bay and French trades and it was while returning from Oporto with pit props that **Newtown** 1153/15 was wrecked on Barricane Rocks, North Devon in January 1916. They had nine ships by 1918 all with names ending in town. The smaller ships **Denetown** 653/15, **Ennistown** 824/17 and **Woodtown** were on the shorter runs. By 1920 the company had its own coal mine and was still expanding with agencies in other ports. The company also had control of the Neville Shipping Co., and the Devon Shipping Co., which came under management by G. F. Harrison & B. C. Ridd. The Devon Shipping Co. was registered in December 1919 and Thomas & Ridd spent £188,000 acquiring the steamers **Wallacombe** (ex Lorient), 920 dwt., **Parracombe** (ex Yore) 670 dwt. and **Challacombe** (ex War Tamar) 670 dwt., or about £73 per deadweight ton. The company under the new management of Harrison & Ridd in the year ending December 1921 made a profit of £23,156, which was good considering they owed the bank £39,000 in mortgages. Mr. Thomas had resigned and Mr. G. F. Harrison became one of the managers, a confident move considering the company were already having difficulties keeping the ships running. The end came in 1924 when efforts to restructure the company failed and Barclays Bank, which was by this time owed over quarter of a million pounds, appointed a liquidator.

The Ashburnham Shipping and Coal Co. Ltd., appeared quite late on the scene and was registered on the 6th of April 1920 with Mr. P. E. Fry as manager. The main shareholders were the Rees family led by Sir Beddoe Rees who became chairman and subscribed almost half the £210,000 capital. £224,375 was spent on **Kenros** 823/18, **Pegham** 825/18 and **Algama** 774/04, which was lost about 1924.

The company did not prosper and management was transferred to P. C. Hull and with no improvement in trade or the leasehold mines the company had acquired, the last ships were sold by the 1930s.

The Cleeves' Western Valleys Anthracite Collieries Ltd., decided to become collier owners in 1916 when the shortage of tonnage and high freight rates produced by the First World War caused them difficulties chartering tonnage. In 1917 they purchased **Natuna** 757/98, **Beatrice** 719/90, **Fedelma** 495/99, **Hessle** 925/07 and the almost new **Wyndhurst** 570/17 from Newcastle owners. The latter was sunk by a U-boat on the 6th of December off St. Catherines Point. However the company's first new vessel, **Crosshands** 716/18, was delivered by A. Jeffrey & Co., Alloa, in February 1918, (84). She was named after their brand of anthracite mined at Crosshands near Llanelly, and was registered in Swansea, which was the usual loading port for the company's anthracite. The steamer was typical of the style of coaster being built by Jeffrey's yard at the time, especially the extension of the fore-castle on either side of the foremast to provide accommodation for the paint locker, lamp room and the second mate. Second mates were usually more fortunate, sharing a midships cabin with the mate. One compensating feature was the mess arranged adjacent to the galley. As it was placed over the boiler room this would always offer warm shelter in bad weather when it would be difficult to get forward. The engineers and cook also had good accommodation aft. She could carry about 850 tons deadweight on a draft of about 13'9" at a loaded speed of about 10 knots. The hold had a volume of about 42,000 cubic feet giving a stowage rate of about 52 cubic feet per ton and so she was able to load a full cargo even of the more bulky coals. **Crosshands** was almost lost in May 1918 when she was attacked by a U-boat in the Bristol Channel but fortunately she had been fitted with a gun and successfully repelled her attacker. With the fall in trade she was offered for sale for £9,500. Her good capacity and her solid construction caught the interest of Kelly's and she was sold to them in 1925.

A second vessel, **Tirydail** 650/18, was built for the company by C. H. Walker & Co., Sudbrook, and was named after another of the company's mines. She was sold in 1926. This did not signal the end of shipowning for the company, as it did with so many other coal associated companies, though shortly after the war management was taken over by Mr. V. M. Williams of Cardiff and Swansea. Not all the ships in the fleet were coasters. **Western Valleys** 3106/19 was built for longer voyages. She was wrecked off Heysham on New Year's Eve 1924 after being driven ashore with a cargo of iron ore from Casablanca. The last ship delivered to the company was the **Fred Cleeves** 1932/21 which was built by W. Harkess & Son of Middlesborough (86). This vessel too was almost lost, for the year after delivery she sank in the River Guadiana (Southern Spain) after striking rocks about 4 miles from Pomason. She was successfully salvaged by E. M. Z. Suitzee and returned to the company.

When Cleeves sold out to Amalgamated Anthracite Collieries in 1927 the old **Fedelma** 495/99 and **Fred Cleeves** 1932/21 were transferred. **Fedelma** was immediately sold to a Latvian firm and the **Fred Cleeves** in 1930. The vessel had been in trouble in the Atlantic in September 1928 with an engine breakdown and was towed in by the Dutch tug **Noordzee**. The company had a French associate, Cleeve et Jacqueline and apart from their own vessels had the French vessels **Fernande** 1311/09 and **Renee Marte** 1389/10 on time charter running between Swansea and Rouen, probably to comply with a requirement that French ships were to be used.

84. Crosshands of Swansea was the first vessel built for Cleeves' Western Valleys Anth-racite Collieries Ltd., and built by A. Jeffrey & Co., Alloa.   Courtesy P. N. Thomas

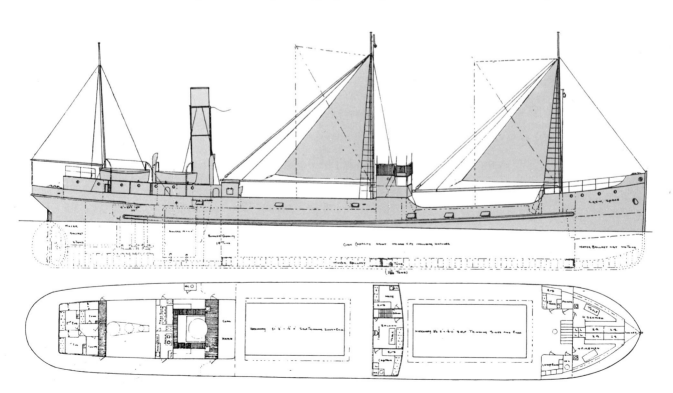

Swansea's big company was Letricheux & David Ltd., who mainly operated in the ocean trade but had the occasional smaller vessel such as **Milo** 1475/03 which worked as an Admiralty collier in the First World War and was sunk in collision while on passage from Rouen to Cardiff in ballast in 1917. Certainly the best known collier owners in Swansea were Harries Bros., founded in 1884. Mr. Harries slowly began to acquire a few vessels and was unlucky to lose the steamer **Musgrave** of 1871 with 9 crew on a voyage from Briton Ferry to Dundalk in 1892. During the 1890s vessels suitable for the Bay trade were purchased and by 1904 the fleet consisted of **King's Lynn** 556/80, **Ossian** 648/81, **Ravensworth** 801/83, **Eleanor** 544/94 and largest of the fleet **Lillian** 1219/89. The latter vessel took a cargo of coal to Bayonne in May 1904 at 5/9 per ton. The fleet continued to be built up by Thomas Harries, Hugh E. Harries and Owen L. Harries from their offices at 4 Cambrian Place, Swansea and by 1908, had **Burton** 649/89, **Glassalt** 621/83, **Kingsley** 633/81, **Lynn O'Dee** 497/83, **Peterborough** 590/77 and **Tanfordian** 921/98. Trade was slack at the time but by good management and their access to coal cargoes their ships were kept successfully employed. Many had seen considerable service, mostly with East Coast owners, and were no doubt purchased at favourable prices. The fleet successfully came through the First World War and by 1922 consisted of **Eleanor** 1277/12, **Gosforth** 1077/93, **Kingsley** 633/81 and **Hooton**, which had been re-named **Glanbrydan** 1892/12, **Glynmel** 1854/12 and **Manordilo** 1741/11. However **Eleanor** was wrecked a few months later when she lost her propellor on a voyage from Barry to Portsmouth with a cargo of coal. Unable to save herself, she drifted on to rocks off Godrevy Light and sank. The tendency was to purchase larger vessels as the company developed. With falling prices, a number of vessels were purchased in the 1920s such as **Bolbec** 1342/18 which served the firm until scrapped in 1958 (89). The company also had **Glanrhyd** 1525/24 built by Vickers at Barrow. She was a typical raised quarter deck collier 245 feet long with engines amidships. The company was reconstructed in 1927 when Harries Bros. & Co. Ltd. was registered with a capital of £100,000 by E. J. Tyrrell and J. J. Morgan. The 1927 fleet consisted of **Kingsley** 633/81, **Amiens** 1548/18, **Bolbec** 1342/18, **Glanbrydan** 1892/12, the almost new **Glanrhyd** 1525/24, **Glanmel** 1854/12, **Manordilo** 2741/11 and **Marlwood** 1988/06. The fleet was reduced in the 1930s and was down to three vessels by 1938, **Amiens, Bolbec** and **Glanrhyd**, which was lost in January when she foundered off Port Eynon on a voyage from Newport to Irlam with 2173 tons of coal. During the war years the company managed vessels for the Ministry of Transport. At the end of the war they purchased a war-built standard collier which was re-named **Glanowen** 2066/44, but with falling coal shipments and steamers becoming uneconomic the company ceased shipowning and became agents.

The smaller port of Llanelly, mainly developed for the shipment of anthracite and steam coals, was the home port for two shipowners who began in the 1890s as one. The senior partner was William Stone who set up in partnership with William Coombs at New Dock, Llanelly, and their first steamer was apparently **Electra** 495/76 which had the registered dimensions 176.6' x 25.4' x 14.8'. At the turn of the century both partners added a ship **Galtee** 565/81 by William Stone and **Jason** 798/78 by William Coombs, and this was to be the fleet for a number of years. About 1914 William Coombs left the partnership and a new partnership Stone & Rolfe was formed. With the strong demand for coal and shipping Stone & Rolfe prospered and by 1918 had **Gwladmena** 928/78, **Lizzie** 802/88 and **Morlais** 950/83, which had served the company from just after the beginning of the First World War. They also managed the coaster **Solway Prince** 317/90 which belonged to Channel Transport Ltd., William Coombs set up on his own in Llanelly and took with him **Galtee** and **Jason**. He also acquired the **Cardiffian** from Owen & Watkin Williams and renamed it **Afon Lliedi** 1015/04, which is Welsh for River Lliedi, and names of Welsh rivers were used for all further additions to the fleet. **Newglyn** 1250/17 was managed for Evans & Rogers. About 1919 the Afon S.S. Co. Ltd., was set up with capital of £200,000 by Messrs. Evans, Rogers and Coombs to finance the new steamers **Afon Dulais** 987/19, **Afon Gwili** 874/19 and **Afon Towy** 684/19. **Afon Lliedi** was initially included and then transferred to a further new company, the Afon Lliedi S.S. Co. Ltd., which was formed in the mid-1920s and included the ship named in the title plus **Afon Dyfi** 729/21 which was the second-hand Spanish coaster **Tarrasa** which was an unusual purchase for a British coasting owner. She returned to Spanish owners after a few years. By 1938 the fleet was reduced to the newer vessels of the Afon S.S. through they were now under the Afon Lleidi S.S. Co. Ltd. The fleet remained unchanged until the end of the Second World War when an 'Empire' coaster was purchased and named **Afon Morlais** 965/44, but with falling trade the company, which had become W. Coombs & Son in the 1920s, gave up shipowning in the mid-1950s.

Stone and Rolfe began replacing their fleet at the end of the First World War with the delivery of **Allie** 1369/19 and **Goodig** 749/19 which was named after Mr. Rolfe's home at Burry Port. In the following year **Wynstone** 637/20 was delivered and the partners entered on a new shipping venture when S. & R. Steamships Ltd., was registered on the second of January 1920 with Thomas Stone of Penmount, Sketty subscribing £40,000 and Joseph Rolfe of Goodig, Burry Port, subscribing £40,000. They then began to build up their fleet and the first vessel purchased was the old **Trostan** 1599/83, which was only kept a few years, and the **Eskwood** 791/11 was also purchased. But the major part of the fleet were much newer vessels, **Hubbastone** 873/21, **Monkstone** 867/23, **Runnelstone** 869/23, **Glynwen** 1076/23, and **Greenawn** 778/24. By 1938 these vessels were being operated with the addition of **Isadora** 1212/15, which was sunk in the Spanish Civil War, the much larger **Sarahstone** 2473/29, a 300 feet long three island steamer, and **Presto** 964/16 which had been acquired from Witherington & Everett in 1934. She had originally been built as the **Dunelm** and her large hatches made her particularly suitable for the coal trade (87). The stowage at around 49 cubic feet per ton meant she could

86.

Fred Cleeves *1932/21 on trials off Middlesbrough.*

MacRae collection

Mallock *609/19 of L. Gueret & Co., Cardiff approaching Bristol Docks.*

Photo: E.N. Taylor

Collin, *287/15, of A.J. Smith, Bristol in the Avon Gorge.*

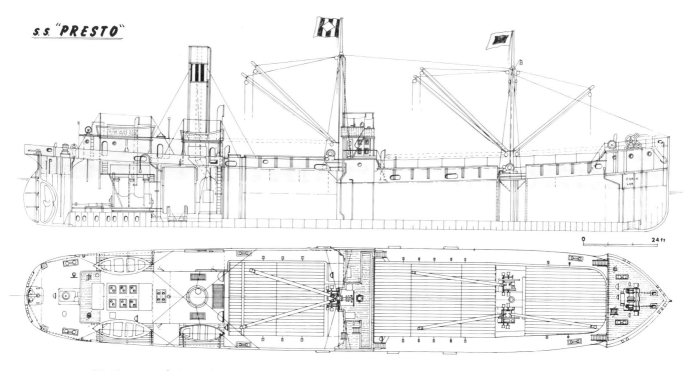

87. Presto of the Witherington & Everett fleet, joined Stone & Rolfe, Llanelly in 1934.

load a full cargo of lighter more bulky coals. The crew were accommodated forward in the forecastle and the donkeyman had a separate small cabin placed centrally at the after end of the forecastle with the entrances for the 4 firemen on the starboard side and the 5 seamen on the port side. The officers were accommodated below the bridge and engineers in rather small cabins in the after end of the engine casing. She was purchased by Stone & Rolfe in 1934 and by 1938 she had been allotted collier No. 214 by the Coal Factors Society and so remained in Thames coal trade.

The company continued through the Second World War managing a number of ships for the Ministry of War Transport including **Empire Harmony** 2906/43. The company became more Swansea-based and Thomas Stone (Shipping) Ltd., was based there when formed after the war. One of the company's first purchases was **Maystone** 2025/45 (ex Empire Wapping) soon followed in 1950 by **Avisbrook** which they had previously managed as **Empire Harmony**. She was renamed **Menastone** and had a deadweight capacity of 4,670 tons. The previous year **Maystone** had been damaged in collision while bound from Methil to London with coal. The company also purchased **Berylstone** 3538/45, another Empire ship. As the coal trade fell away even on the East Coast, the ships were employed tramping generally until the 1960s after which the company continued as agents in Swansea.

Some owners were also based at Newport, the most important of whom was probably Mordey, Jones & Co., who had **Auckland Castle** 661/83 and later added **Gwendoline** 933/82, which was registered in Newport in 1898. They were involved in the Spanish trade (coal out - iron ore home) but after the First World War Mordey, Son & Co., established the Mordey-Gwents Line with **Gwentgate** 1600/24 and **Gwentland** to Belgium from local ports. The outward cargo was usually coal and general cargo with steel the main return cargo. The ships were sold in the 1930s.

Almost a separate branch of the South Wales coal trade was that mainly confined to the Bristol Channel. Osborn & Wallis were initially involved in both the Bay and Bristol Channel trade. This was the result of the two partners' connections. William Osborn lived in Bristol while his cousin Humphrey Wallis had his office in Cardiff and was one of the founder members of the Cardiff Coal and Shipping Exchange. Osborn had an office in Bristol and sold coal there. Wallis was probably resonsible for the partners investing in tramp steamers in the early 1880s, such as **Alverton** 862/80, which traded to Spain with coal returning with iron or copper ore, which was the popular trade with Cardiff owners. Some of these cargoes were taken to Bristol where they were transhipped and carried up to the chemical works at Netham. The works made sulphuric acid from the sulphur rich copper ore. One of the small vessels involved was **Enterprise** 97/60. She measured 84.1' x 16.0' x 8.0' and was an iron screw steamer built at Bristol by Stothert who were leading shareholders in the vessel with Stephen Steeds and William Osborn. The spent ore was probably taken to Swansea which was a centre for copper smelting, using the steamer and returning with coal to Bristol from South Wales. Small sailing vessels had largely been engaged on this trade, and William Osborn had shares in several of them. However, by the 1880s small steamers were more efficient and slowly replaced sail, and William Osborn began purchasing further steamers. These included **Netham** 115/78 and **Clifton** 86/57 from coal merchant George Nurse, also of Bristol, and **St. Vincent** 115/66 which had been built and registered in Cardiff and was probably a regular visitor to Bristol with coal. She was solidly built, serving on the Bristol run until the 1920s. Their tramp steamers in the Bay trade were increased in the 1890s with second-hand vessels but all were sold by the beginning of the First World War except for **Eurterpe** 1522/83, which struck a mine in 1916.

A. J. Smith of Bristol had developed his coal trade to Bristol in a similar way using small steamers some of which were just as old, such as **Iron Duke** 146/57 and **John** 141/49 which had both belonged to J. B. Brain in the 1870s, also of Bristol. **Iron Duke** had begun life as a tug in the fleet of the Cardiff Steam Towing Company. By 1908 he had a fleet consisting of **Carbon** 126/92, **Iron Duke** 146/57, **John** 141/49, **Seaforth** 349/91 and **Tel-el-Kebir** 163/83. Osborn and Wallis had a slightly larger fleet consisting of **Clifton** 126/57, **Marion** 139/79, **Ocean** 140/93, **St. Vincent** 143/66, **Sneyd** 204/72 and **New Zealand** 309/86. They were basic vessels with a single deck and no forecastle or raised quarterdeck. A feature was masts and funnels which could be folded down so that they could pass under the low bridges giving access to the Avon from the docks and the various large works in the area. In favourable conditions they could tow a barge. The construction of the first Power Station for Bristol and another for the electric tramways increased the need for steam coal from the 1890s and the **Orb** 201/11 and **Ferric** 191/12 were built for the fleet. Those not supplying coal directly to consumers were used to keep up stocks for smaller users at the firm's coal yard off the upper harbour. The little steamer **Tanny** 154/90, acquired in the 1920s, often carried coal to Bude gas works. These small steamers were regular visitors to Lydney which sent out most of its coal in small coasters and schooners. Forest of Dean coal from Lydney was often mixed with Welsh steam coal for firing boilers. William Jones of Lydney had a few steamers including **Black Dwarf** 95/66 and had **The Forester** 191/10 built for the trade, which was sold in the 1920s.

A third important member of the Bristol Channel trade was James Wood Sully who was based at Bridgwater and the town's leading coal merchant. Bridgwater is almost opposite the South Wales coal field on the southern side of the Severn Estuary and well placed to distribute coal to the surrounding districts. This was helped by the Bridgwater and Taunton Canal which completed a dock at Bridgwater as the terminal of the canal in 1841. The trade was originally in sailing vessels. The first steamer, **Bull Dog** 149/66 was acquired about 1871 and was basically a twin screw steam barge. Later **Welsh Prince** 154/71, measuring 100.2' x 18.8' x 8.1' was acquired, probably from Bristol owners, and retained that port of registry. The first new addition to the fleet was **Katherine** 255/98, built for J. W. Sully in 1898, but the vessel was sold in 1907, possibly because with registered dimensions 113.0' x 23.9' x 9.7' and a proper coaster she proved rather too large. The barges were finally replaced with two second-hand coasters in the 1930s, **Crowpill** 190/11 and **Enid** 131/03 which served the company until scrapped in the 1960s.

Osborn & Wallis and A. J. Smith also added coasters to their fleets. A. J. Smith began around the time of the First World War with **Calcaria** 569/10 which was in the fleet for many years but generally he operated small coasters such as **Collin** 287/15 (86), which was acquired in 1932, in the local coal trade alongside the steam barges, and he continued to do so into the 1950s. Osborn & Wallis Ltd., was registered in 1921 with a capital of £40,000 of which £30,500 was subscribed by W. A. Osborn and I. D. Osborn, both of Bristol. G. A. Dearlove, a director of the firm, represented the Cardiff connection and was a small shareholder. The company had small coasters in the local trades from the 1890s with **Sneyd** 201/90 and **Blanche** 258/63 which were used on runs to France.

*88. **Lunan** 362/09. Note the unusual position of the bridge in the well deck. She was built as the **Inchbrayock** and later sold to Osborn & Wallis, Bristol.*

Courtesy P. N. Thomas

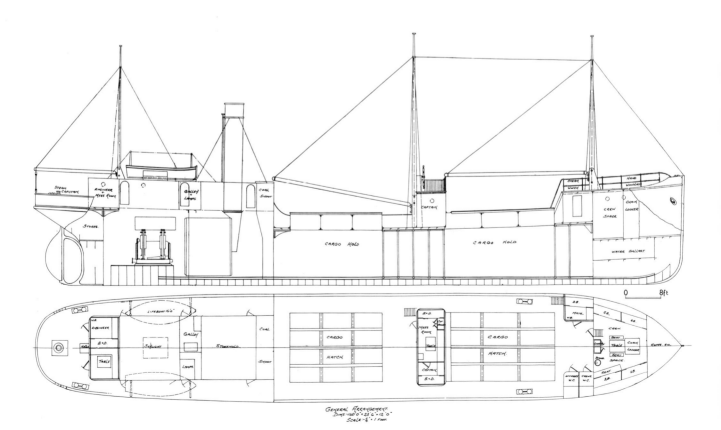

Their local coaster fleet was given a boost when the Portishead Power Station was opened in 1929 and the coal supply contract went to Osborn & Wallis who had been supplying the company's earlier power station at Bristol exclusively for many years. To meet the contract **Druid Stoke** 486/29 was specially built with a long single hatch for easy grab discharge. **Lunan** 362/09 was purchased as a running mate but was of the older style with two smaller hatches and the bridge amidships. She was one of the few coasters where the raised quarterdeck was not extended as far as the bridge amidships so the bridge sat in the middle of the well deck (88). The design had been tried out in the latter part of the 19th century but was not popular. At this time the company moved their offices and coal depot to Stothert's shipyard and used the drydock as berths for their colliers when discharging coal. The company moved on to motor colliers with the delivery from Hill's of **St. Vincent** 464/40. They also purchased two coasters from the Ald Shipping Co., which became **Rocklease** 486/24 and **Downlease** 486/24, and they were often to be seen loading at Penarth. The demands of the war for more electricity, coupled with the loss of local colliers to mine and other hazards, led to the Ministry of War Transport ordering some special colliers, two of which were managed by Osborn & Wallis. They were **Empire Runner** 313/43 and **Empire Townsman** 313/43. There were four others in the class and they were intended to carry steam coal from South Wales to the power station at Gloucester primarily but also worked to Portishead as required.

In the post-war period Osborn & Wallis continued to be very active in the coal trade and in 1950 the fleet consisted of **Downlease** 486/24, **Druid Stoke** 486/29, **Rocklease** 486/24, the steam barges **Ferric** 191/12, **Ocean** 140/93, **Orb** 196/11 and the motor coasters **St. Vincent** 484/40, **Salcombe** 590/38 and the newly delivered **Hotwells** 499/50. With the closure of the power stations at Bristol the small steamers were sold for scrap during the 1950s, but expansion of the Portishead Power Station and Yelland Power Station near Barnstaple led to the company adding two new motor ships to the fleet in the late 1950s, **Colston** 586/55 and **Brandon** 586/57. Last of the steamers **Druid Stoke** was scrapped in 1965. A few years later Mr. Osborn decided to sell up and retire, the ships passing to various owners at the end of the decade.

The Main Colliery Company of Neath and Bristol owned their own ships for a number of years. They had the collier **Main** 715/04 built in 1904 and she traded successfully until she was caught by a German submarine off Luce Bay, Wigtownshire, on October the 9th, 1917. The submarine made a surface attack using gunfire, during which twelve of the crew died, the vessel sinking. The company soon ordered a replacement which was built by W. Harkess of Middlesborough and completed in 1920, **Goodwill of Bristol** with registered dimensions 198.0' x 30.6' x 12.5', was a typical coaster type (69). They went into voluntary liquidation in 1934, one of the many victims of the 1930s slump which was so strongly felt in South Wales.

*89. **Bolbec** 1342/18 was purchased by Harries Bros., of Swansea during the 1920s. She sur-*
vived the Second World War and was eventually scrapped in 1954.   Photo: Alex Duncan

Irish Sea Colliers

90. *Point of Ayr colliery (see opposite).*

North Wales and Lancashire

One colliery company uniquely placed for access to the Irish Sea was that at Point of Air. The colliery is situated at the mouth of the River Dee and the pit shaft was within 40 yards of the sea. The original shaft was sunk by the West Mostyn Company in 1873, but was abandoned when they had problems with the flooding. The shaft lay derelict until 1885 when Point of Air Collieries Ltd., took over, successfully pumped out the shaft, extended it and found coal (the spelling was changed to Ayr in 1905). The colliery was progressively developed by the Batters family and by the turn of the century about one third of the mine's output was leaving by sea. The trade began almost as soon as the mine began producing coal as there was already a small quay used to ship Gwespyr sandstone. Much of the early shipments were made in Irish Sea schooners and ketches which often belonged to the masters themselves. The colliery soon developed their own quay to the southwest of the jetty first used for shipments and the photo (91) taken at the turn of the century shows the quay in full use. The small tug **Edward Batters** 34/08 came into use in 1908 to assist sailing vessels in and out as well as turning. The quay was linked to the Dee by a winding channel across the sands which were exposed for about a mile at low water. Efforts were made to prevent the gutterway from silting up by holding back water in a large pond adjacent to the quay and then releasing this water at low tide to flush out any silt which had settled. Some of the first steamers to work from the Point of Air colliery were those of Coppack Bros. & Co., from nearby Connah's Quay. The colliery company chartered vessels until the difficulties of the First World War forced them to become owners.

Their first coaster, **Clwyd** 289/09, was purchased from the Clwyd S.S. Co., of Liverpool which was managed by R. & D. Jones. She was lost in collision while returning to the colliery in ballast from Dublin in December 1917. **Paragon** survived the accident, which occurred off the Skerries, Anglesey. Many coasters would make this their landfall and then head along the coast to the Mersey or Dee. Fortunately the company were not left without a ship for a new vessel had been delivered by Crabtree's of Great Yarmouth. She was named **Talacre** 301/17, after the village near the colliery. The management was placed with J. W. Dishart and Alfred Stabback of Liverpool and that was also the port of registry. After a time the colliery took over management themselves. **Talacre** was typical of the single hatch coasters used in the coal trade on the Irish Sea. As can be seen from the plan (92) she had an open bridge, steadying sails and a single large hatch. The short 35' derrick soon proved inadequate and was replaced by one 50' 11" long in 1921. The work was carried out at Port Dinorwic which dry-docked and maintained many of the local coasters. The vessel was specially designed to withstand loading and discharge while lying aground and bulb angle was used for the frames and keelsons. She carried 300 tons at a speed of 9 knots on a loaded draft of 9' 11". In later years the open bridge was enclosed forming a charthouse and an upper open bridge added (92). A second-hand coaster of similar dimensions was added to the fleet in 1921. She had been built as **Solway Firth** for G. T. Gillie & Blair in 1921 and was sold almost immediately to become **Point of Ayr** 327/21. She was easily recognised as she had a chart room below the open bridge and for a time had a king post and derrick at the after end of the hatch. Both **Talacre** and **Point of Ayr** had separate stokeholds which were fed from a cross bunker placed on the fore side of the boiler. But there was a more compact arrangement, illustrated in **Tanlan** 293/14, which was purchased by the company in 1933. In this vessel (92) the boiler was stoked from the engine room side and the coal bunkers are placed on either side of the boiler. This arrangement was also popular with economy minded owners as the second engineer could also fire the boiler and reduce the number of firemen carried. As might be expected, the engineers did not like it, as apart from extra work for them there was more chance

*91. Point of Air Colliery about 1902 with some of Coppack's coasters loading and the top-sail schooner **Princess of Thule** on the bank. The colour photograph opposite taken on the 28th of August, 1955 shows **Point of Ayr** in the foreground and Coppack's **Indorita** and **Fleurita** already loaded and ready to sail beyond.*

of coal and ash getting into the machinery and causing the bearings of the engine to run hot. Coasters with this arrangemenmt could be spotted at a glance as the stokehold ventilators, always the most prominent of ships ventilators, were slightly behind the funnel rather than ahead of it as was the case for a vessel with a separate stokehold. The design of **Tanlan** was modern for the period when she was built (1914) as the original design incorporated a wheelhouse and steam steering gear for inshore work. The other vessels had hand steering gear only.

There was not sufficient water for the vessels to leave the colliery with full cargoes at times of neap tides and prior to about 1920 other cargoes were found for the vessels to keep them employed by Norris, Oats & Batters of Liverpool. In later years cargoes were often arranged by J. S. Jones & Co., the well known brokers in Liverpool. As soon as the tides improved the vessels would be back to the colliery. Common destinations were Londonderry, Newry, Belfast, Larne and Killyleagh, all in Northern Ireland. Ports often visited in Eire included Cork, Wexford, New Ross, Drogheda, Dundalk, Wicklow and Waterford. The trade to these ports was reduced for a period prior to 1935 as the Eire Government had imposed a five shillings per ton tax on English coals. At the end of the 1930s the annual output of the colliery was over 200,000 tons of household and steam coals. Vessels were regularly chartered such as those of R. Gardner of Lancaster, who was also a coal merchant. Gardner vessels chartered in the late 1930s and 1940s were **River Loyne** 153/16 and **Maurita** 201/20, and later the motor vessel **Calyx** 212/29 which carried slack (fine coal) to Story's of Lancaster.

The company's own colliers also regularly carried coal to Redruth and Mousehole in Cornwall, the smaller ports in Wales such as Bangor, and of course the Isle of Man. The River Dee is quite exposed to south westerly gales and a note in the 'Prestatyn Weekly' for January 24th, 1931 illustrates this: "The heavy gales during the latter half of last week, caused great inconvenience and delay to shipping. On Saturday the s.s. "Point of Ayr" arrived from Belfast. As she was nearing the quayside, the high winds and heavy seas, in spite of the efforts of her Captain, forced her well on to the bank at the side of the gutter. Up to Wednesday last she had resisted all efforts to refloat her, but it is confidently expected that the task will be accomplished in the course of a day or two. The s.s. "Talacre" which was due to sail for Wexford with a cargo of coal on Saturday morning, was delayed until Sunday, when the storm had abated somewhat." **Point of Ayr** was eventually refloated.

Docking was quite an interesting manoeuvre. When the ships arrived off the quay, they would turn away from it, putting their bows up on the mud bank opposite, the collieries boatman would then carry their hawser to the quay and the steam winch would then be used to haul the bow round. **Talacre** with the dimensions 130.5' x 23.2' x 9.5' was just largest of the company's ships and most of the chartered coasters were of a similar size. However, in the 1920s Neill's of Bangor used to send in their steamer **Whin** which had a registered length of 152 feet. This tricky manoeuvre was carried out on the top tide each month as Neill's had a contract to carry 800 tons of coal a month from the Point of Ayr Colliery to Quoile Quay, Downpatrick. Although their vessel was identical to those built for Clark's and Coppack's both these firms considered it too risky and would only accept cargoes for their ships if it was sent to Mostyn Dock a short distance up the river where there were better facilities. Coppack's had a contract to carry slack from the colliery and this was initially handled by **Trevor** and later by **Bolham**. The usual destination was Price's Candle Works at Bromborough. **Whin** survived her visits and was helped in this by the colliery tug.

The colliery's own fleet came through the Second World War safely although **Talacre** was machine-gunned on one occasion. Apart from carrying coal the vessels also helped lessen the effects of the food rationing caused by the war, particularly at Christmas. On voyages to Ireland the crew

S.S. "TALACRE"

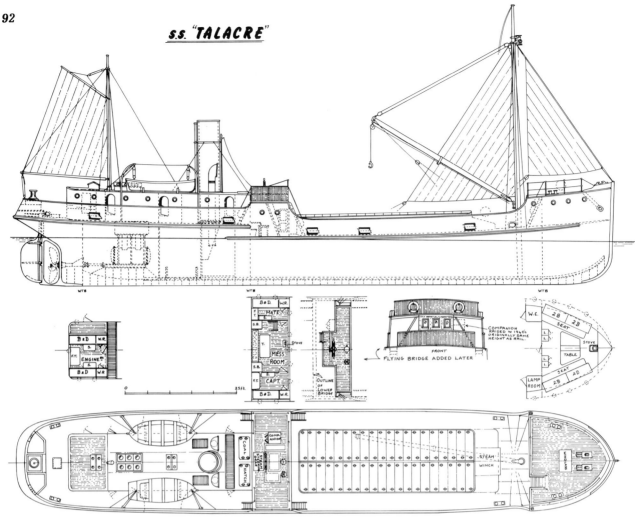

92. *Talacre* (above) *was designed for the Point of Ayr Collieries by Crichton, Thompson &*
Co. Ltd., a London firm of Naval architects. She was completed by Crabtree & Co., of
Great Yarmouth in 1917. The original plans were published in the Shipbuilding & Shipping
Record of February 27th, 1919. By the 1930s a flying bridge had been added and the
additional drawings of this have been prepared from photographs. **Tanlan** *(below) was*
added to the fleet in 1933 and was well equipped for a coaster built in 1914. P. N. Thomas

S.S. "TANLAN"

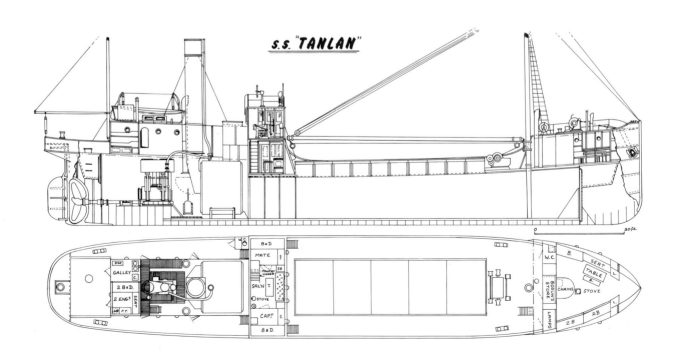

93. *Talacre* at Maid's Quay near New Ross, Southern Ireland on the 14th of August 1938. Between the Wars the fleet were painted grey rather than black.

Photo; the late Robert Shortall

returned with geese, potatoes and other foods in short supply. While waiting for the tide the supplies would be quietly rowed ashore and landed on Cockle Bank from whence they would be spirited away under cover of darkness. All ships were fitted with radio telephone equipment in 1946 and continued their regular coal runs. An enclosed bridge was fitted to **Point of Ayr** but **Talacre** retained her open bridge with wheelhouse below. The colliery was nationalised on the 1st of January 1947 but the colliers did not pass to the National Coal Board until a year later. The red funnel separated from the black top by a white band was retained, but the Coal Board flag was adopted as a house flag. The vessels lasted until the late 1950s and last to be scrapped was **Talacre**. Her final cargo was to Drogheda for Messrs. Cooney's and Finnegan's. In pre-war days the **Talacre** used to anchor in midriver there. Long planks were placed between the ships and the quayside and the coal shovelled into sacks to be carried ashore. Captain Lamb's last voyage in **Talacre** was then made when he sailed her to Dublin, arriving there on the 24th of April 1959, for scrapping by the Hammond Lane Foundry. Captain Lamb had been in command of **Talacre** (122) 26 years. Coppack's continued to ship out coal for a few more years in their motor coasters.

The Mersey ports were always the centre for coastal shipping but although Lancashire coal was shipped especially to Ireland it was never a major centre for the coal trade. As with all coasting fleets those of the Liverpool area were actively involved in the coal trade but also carried a variety of other cargoes. One of the most prominent fleets was that of Richard Hughes who employed his smaller ships in the china clay trade, but soon began to develop connections with South Wales and the larger ships, particularly between the wars, were employed in the South Wales coal trade to France. The company ordered a series of 1,500 to 1,600 ton vessels in the early 1920s for this trade, such as **Haig Rose** 1117/20, all with names based on First World War generals. Two vessels of 2,500 tons were delivered in the mid-1920s followed by a further four vessels at the end of the decade, by which time the company was in difficulties having ordered new ships just as the slump arrived. All was not lost, for the company was restructured as Richard Hughes (Liverpool) Ltd., in 1934 on the

93. *Tanlan,* making one of her last voyages, leaving Waterford on the 4th of May 1957 in ballast.

Photo; the late Robert Shortall

retirement of Mr. Richard Hughes. The company had been under the day to day management of Mr. Tom Tierney for some time. He had spent his early years in coal exporting from Cardiff and had joined the Cardiff office of R. Hughes & Co., in 1927 before taking over in Liverpool a few years later. He became Chairman and Managing Director, assisted by H. Sadler and J. R. Leed as directors. In 1938 there were 25 vessels in the fleet. The company came through the war, losing 6 to enemy action, and in 1950 had 4 of the larger steamers and 3 of the smaller type in the fleet. The following year it was taken over by Mr. P. E. Holden of Swansea, head of the British Anthracite Company. The company then became Hughes Holden Shipping Ltd. The steamers were slowly disposed of as the South Wales trade declined, though a new motor ship **Rambler Rose** 1422/54 was built for the company. The steamers were sold with the slump in freight rates of the late 1950s and **Rambler Rose** herself was last to go in the early 1960s. The design of the larger steamers was similar to the engines-aft raised-quarterdeck ships being developed for the London coal trade, as can be seen from the profile of **Louie Rose** 1596/24 (94). When **Fullerton Rose** 1596/24 was delivered she was painted grey, as were some of the others. It was suggested by some sailors that it was probably war surplus paint! Mr. Hughes had a reputation for not spending money on his ships and some went years after delivery without being repainted. He also removed the wheelhouse from any ship he purchased, believing in open bridges. Some of the vessels had their names painted on the side amidships in large letters, as was general practice for colliers in the London trade.

The Bramley Moore dock was most often used by coastal colliers when loading coal in Liverpool and regular visitors were the small colliers of the Alliance & Dublin Consumers Gas Co. Ocean going liners in the northern docks mostly bunkered from lighters, while vessels in the southern docks bunkered from the coal tips in the Herculaneum Docks, which also occasionally loaded cargoes. In Birkenhead there was a hydraulic coal tip and a conveyor in the West Float which was used to load coastwise cargoes. The East Float had originally two hand-operated tips but by the 1930s only one remained in use. It was so designed that it was quick and efficient in use.

Though quite large amounts of coal were loaded at Liverpool and Birkenhead much of this was

94. Louie Rose.

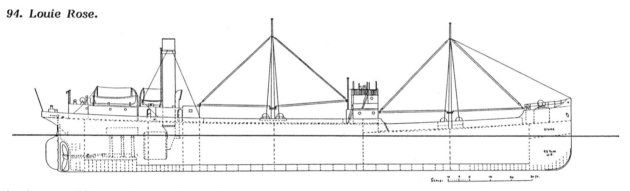

bunkers and it was the smaller docks of the Upper Mersey and Manchester Ship Canal which had a special place in the coal trade from the river. Much of the coal was shipped to Ireland, especially Northern Ireland. Foremost of these ports was Garston which lies about 4 miles south of Liverpool Docks and on the same side of the river. The first or old dock was constructed by the St. Helen's Railway & Canal Company under an Act of Parliament which was granted in 1846. The company was taken over by the London & North Western Railway in 1864. Under this company facilities were expanded and the North Dock was completed in 1874. This could be entered from a new entrance lock or via a passageway from the old dock. Coal exports still continued apace, as did a variety of imports, and this led to the opening of the Stalbridge Dock in 1909 which lay to the south of the old dock and replaced two small inlets from the river known as the Salt Dock and the Rock Salt Dock. Garston thus became the most important coal shipping port on the Mersey, handling millions of tons each year.

With the completion of this dock Garston had six moveable hydraulic hoists, each capable of lifting 30 tons and seven fixed hoists in the older docks of less capacity. Four of the moveable hoists were sited in the Stalbridge Dock, which could accept vessels up to 276 feet in length with a water depth of 25 feet. The remaining two moveable hydraulic coal tips were sited in the North Dock which also had four fixed high level tips of less capacity. The Old Dock had three fixed high level coal tips. The tips differed greatly from the Vickers-type coal hoists (95). Here the loaded truck ran out on to a platform which extended over the ship in the berth. Elsewhere conventional tips were erected by Vickers on the Manchester Ship Canal, at Ellesmere Port, Runcorn and Partington, where coal was loaded on both banks of the canal.

At Garston no charge was made on ships entering the old dock to load coal so trade to this dock was always strong. Quite a large amount of the coal was still shipped in schooners to the North Wales Coast or Ireland even after the turn of the century and it was only at the end of the First World War that the steam coasters took over the trade. The three docks were interlinked so that ships could move between the docks at all times unless different water levels were being maintained. Many of the Liverpool coasters were regular visitors to Garston but one firm which was particularly involved

95. *Coal loading at Garston. The loaded truck was lowered and then tilted by holding the inner end of the platform while the outer end was lowered further until the coal shot out of the end of the truck and into the ship's hold. The teamer who had opened the end doors of the truck checked that it was completely empty when it was hoisted to the horizontal, and the process was then reversed and the wagon hoisted and released on to the empties line.* Photo MacRae collection

was Captain E. W. Turner, later E. W. Turner & Son, who became established as owners and managers around the 1890s. One of Turner's first steamers was **Derwent** 264/84, but perhaps the most interesting were those the company managed for Wilson Bros.(Bobbin) Co.Ltd., of Garston and Todmorden, Yorkshire, who made wooden bobbins for the Lancashire Cotton Mills and soles of clogs. Their ships brought in beech logs for the company from Ireland and Scotland. Their connection with the coal trade was the outward voyage from Garston, when they loaded household coal for Ireland. One of their early steamers was **Ibis** 171/81 which had the dimensions 110.2' x 20.1' x 9.0' and was registered at Liverpool in 1896. These dimensions were fairly typical for local coasters. They subsequently acquired the appropriately named **Carlingford Lough** 245/91, which was registered at Liverpool in 1901. The company also owned schooners managed by J. C. Hornby. By 1918 Wilson Bros., had just the one coaster **Glencona** 282/07 which had been built for Newcastle owners. Following the end of the war they purchased **Mary Aiston** which was renamed **Glen Helen** 315/18. She was a typical coaster of the period with a long well deck and single hatch with a mast and derrick at each end. The **Glen Helen** and her sisters mostly carried cargoes of household coal from Garston to the small ports in Ireland: Wicklow, Bray, Wexford, Dundalk, Drogheda and Waterford were favourites.

One of the smaller ports was West Bank Dock, Widnes. This small tidal harbour handled over a quarter of a million tons in 1913, probably using four tips. Much of this was loaded into barges to be taken down to Liverpool for bunkering the Cunard liners. The coal came from the Carlton Main Colliery Company of Barnsley, Yorkshire, who had gained the bunkering contract. In the 1920s the trade was mainly in coasters and Kelly's were frequent visitors along with **Whin** 466/20 from Bangor, Co. Down. The dock was particularly busy during the high tides and from about 1926 onwards operated from 5 a.m. to as late as 9 p.m. for the Irish coal trade. Kelly's colliers were particularly active in the coal trade from Widnes to Ireland. Other local coastal fleets who regularly carried coal from the port were W. A. Savage Ltd., Monroe Bros., Ramsey S.S. Co. Ltd., often, as the latter name suggests, to the Isle of Man, and Thomas Bros. Sometimes the coasters had an inward cargo of stone for the Croft Granite Company. In the 1930s onwards, the coal carrying coasters usually arrived light at Widnes, often from Liverpool, Birkenhead or other coastal ports, but chiefly direct from Belfast, Dublin, other Irish ports, or the Isle of Man. There was an increase in shipments in 1940 which again was a peak year, achieved with only two tips.

Just across the river was Runcorn which was connected by rail and canal with the the mining areas. Collieries on the Bridgwater, Bolton & Bury, Leeds & Liverpool and North Staffordshire (Trent & Mersey) Canals could send their coal by canal for transhipment to coasters or larger vessels. Coal sent by rail could be loaded by balance tips in Runcorn Docks or by tip on the adjacent Manchester Ship Canal. The local shipping agents were Greenway, Millington and Clark & Grounds, who also had offices in Liverpool which managed their coasters.

Coal was loaded at a number of other places on the Manchester Ship Canal such as Ellesmere Port which had a typical coal conveyor installation (96), but the most important was Partington Coal Basin. It was the nearest shipping point for South Yorkshire collieries and the Lancashire collieries were within 10 miles by rail. The six hydraulic tips in use before the First World War were each capable of handling 300 tons per hour.

Richard Evans & Co. Ltd., who had extensive colliery interests at Haydock had their own wharf, Haydock Wharf, on the Manchester Ship Canal at Acton Grange. They used a steam crane to lift wagon boxes which were then tipped into the ships. The Wigan Coal & Iron Co. Ltd., had its own ships for many years. The company was registered about 1865 and in that year **Kirkless** 387/65 was completed by Bowdler's of Liverpool with a 2-cylinder engine of 60 horse power by Jones of Liverpool. She measured 150.3' x 24.0' x 12.6' and was named after the district where the company's coal mines were located. She traded for the company, mainly carrying coal to Belfast, until about 1886 when she was replaced by a new steamer **Balneil** 460/86. The vessel was named after Lord Balneil the son of the Earl of Crawford and Balcarries, whose family were the driving force behind the formation of the company. They had extensive colliery interests, and both railways and canal boats to handle the output from their mines in South Lancashire. The company also owned the larger **Balcarries** 1160/77. **Balneil** was typical of the engines-amidships steamers being built at the time for the coal trade, with two hatches forward and one aft. She was managed by J. & J. E. Carter, Liverpool, and had been built by MacIlwaine, Lewis & Co. Ltd., Belfast. She was replaced by **Balneil II** 628/09 and the old **Balneil** was sold to the Clydeside Shipping Co., of Glasgow. The collier became well known through her successful sinking of a submarine in World War One and to commemorate this a brass star was added to her plain black funnel. She continued trading for the company until the end of the 1920s.

Robert Gardner, whose vessels were regular visitors to the Point of Ayr Colliery, was based at St. George's Quay, Lancaster, where he was a coal merchant and also supplied the bunkers. He began owning motor and steam coasters in the mid-1920s and by 1927 the fleet consisted of two small motor coasters **Dela** 129/15 and **Dorit** 134/15 and the steam coaster **Grosvenor** 267/08. He later purchased **Mount Charles** 286/10 and the **Multistone** 296/10 which were to be active in the coal trade until the 1950s, though by 1956 only the small coaster **Calyx** 212/29 remained, and she was sold in the 1960s. The company became R. Gardner (Luneside) Ltd., in 1948.

The Isle of Man

The most prominent firm engaged in carrying coal to the Isle of Man, and based there, was The Ramsey S.S. Co. Ltd., which was begun by Mr. J. B. Kee. As the name suggests, it was based at the port of Ramsey and was also actively involved in the coal trade to the smaller ports in Ireland. The fleet began around the time of the First World War and in 1918 consisted of **Ben Rein** 212/05, **Ben Veg** 159/14 and **Whitestone** 198/14, which was later renamed **Ben Varrey**. The fleet continued with between two and four coasters throughout the steam era.

North Lancashire and Cumberland

Preston, on the Ribble, developed its dock facilities during the latter part of the nineteenth century. Improvements were progressively made to the River Ribble and, some 16 miles from the mouth of the Ribble, an enclosed dock was opened in 1892 and a 20 ton capacity coal hoist was used to load coasters. The most prominent port during the nineteenth century was Whitehaven which had a large general trade but also exported coal to Ireland. Coal was mined from early times in West Cumberland. Some 200,000 tons of coal were exported from Whitehaven each year from the 1850s onwards. The harbour remained tidal but in 1871 a Dock and Harbour Act was obtained and a wet dock was opened in 1876. The foundations of the rather small and inadequate dock shifted, eventually preventing the lock gates from shutting. In 1880 the docks were closed while repairs were made. Coal shipments were maintained, but during the 1930s the Whitehaven collieries closed for a time when the colliery company failed. Production was resumed in the latter part of the 1930s. Much of the early shipments were made in sailing vessels and steam coasters did not become active until the 1890s. Coal exports reached a peak in the 1920s. Ships up to 3,000 tons deadweight could berth but nearly all the coal left in much smaller vessels. The docks were modernised just prior to the Second World War.

96. *Coal conveyor, Ellesmere Port. The coal drops from the truck (left) into a hopper which feeds the conveyor.*   MacRae collection

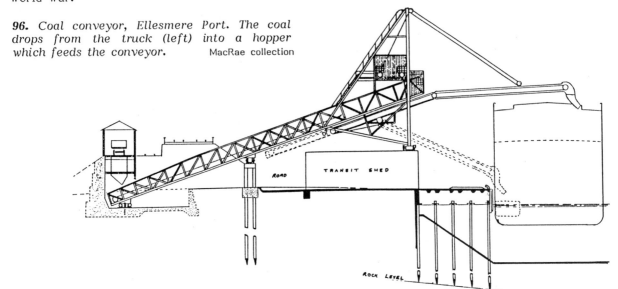

16 FEET

97. *Annaghmore* 583/24 (165.0′ x 27.0′ x 11.1′), in the colours of John Kelly Ltd., Belfast. With her sister *Annagher* she had originally sailed in the funnel colours of the St. Helen's Colliery & Brickworks Co. Ltd., of Workington which had the blue band replaced by a red band on the funnel. The shade of red was also lighter. Both companies were under the control of Sir Samuel Kelly and the two ships were transferred to the main fleet in 1935 where they joined two other sisters *Donnaghmore* and *Carrickmore* which had also been built by Lewis' yard in the early 1920s.

Further up the coast,Workington developed around iron works. The Lonsdale dock was equipped for loading coal and just before the First World War had a coal conveyor system capable of loading 400 tons per hour and could accept vessels up to about 2,500 tons deadweight, but the normal cargoes were of from 400 tons to almost 1,500 tons, the size of cargoes steadily increasing. The Lonsdale dock, lying on the north side of the entrance channel into the harbour, was improved and extended in the 1920s. The dock was re-opened in 1927 as the Prince of Wales Dock. The main shipper of coal was the St. Helen's Colliery & Brickworks Co. Ltd., which had an annual output of 350,000 tons during the 1930s. Two of Kelly's vessels, **Annaghmore** 583/24 and **Annagher** 586/23 were registered at Workington in the ownership of the colliery which was controlled by Sir Samuel Kelly from about 1920, but by 1935 they had reverted to the main fleet to join their identical sisterships. They were distinguished by slightly different funnel markings (97). However this move did not indicate any change in the pattern of shipments, which continued in Kelly's ships to Ireland. For example, in June 1938, of the 7,851 tons shipped, 5,143 tons were loaded in Kelly ships. There were 8 cargoes for Belfast, three for Dublin and one each for Bangor (Co. Down) and Warren Point. **Lagan** 393/03 loaded five cargoes, **Tynan** two cargoes and **Bellavale** 580/05, **Greenisland** 292/01, **Kerrymore** 509/21, **Tamnamore** 278/25 and **Moyallon** 257/26 one each. The colliers arrived light from various Irish ports, usually Belfast, Dublin, Drogheda, Carrickfergus or Bangor. Other regular visitors included Joseph Fisher coasters **Oak, Palm** and **Aspen** collecting cargoes for Dublin from other shippers. As might be expected the shipments were greatest in winter months. For example, in January 1939 eighteen different Kelly colliers loaded 11,120 tons of coal and made 24 voyages to Ireland, 15 of them to Belfast, 3 to Carrickfergus, 2 to Weston Point and one each to Bangor and Dublin. This represented 54% of the coal shipments that month, the remainder leaving in other colliers like **Downshire** and **River Humber** which sailed for Donaghadee with 290 tons of coal at the end of the month. She had been running regularly to Donaghadee from 1926, the year in which she was purchased by Charles Neill of Bangor. Occasional cargoes were taken by William Robertson's larger coasters which also brought in South Wales coal from time to time. Loading was fast and most vessels left the same day they arrived. The pattern continued into the war years, but as time went on the Kelly boats became less frequent visitors as coal shipments declined or were carried in larger ships.

The northernmost English harbour sending out significant amounts of coal was Maryport which became prominent in the latter part of the 19th century as the harbour was improved. W. E. Fisher & Son of Maryport managed **Holyhead** 196/98, which belonged to her skipper Alex Dempsey. She was typical of the small coasters which worked in the coal trade carrying about 180 tons. R. C. March recalls joining her at the end of 1939: "There was no log of either sort, no hand lead line and if there were charts aboard I never saw one used in the 15 months I was aboard. But there was no need for any of these aids to navigation. Soundings, when necessary, were taken using a heaving line with a shackle on the end and distances were calculated by the 'Old Man' with the aid of his 'turnip' watch. Apart from a few outside trips we were continuously in the coal trade from Cumberland and Scottish ports to the north of Ireland going to every harbour or 'hole in the rocks' from Drogheda round to the Bloody Foreland. Captain Dempsey knew all the courses and if he was told the time of high water at Liverpool could tell you instantly which way the tide was setting anywhere round the coast. He had no 'ticket' but I am sure he knew a lot more than some who had. Nearly everywhere the coal was dug out by hand into three tipping buckets which we carried, hoisting them ashore using our winch and derrick. The ordinary seaman and I drove the winch which we both enjoyed as it made us feel important, earned extra pay and very occasionally gave us the chance, by judicious delay, to cause the ship to miss a tide and get an extra night in port."

"The deck crew in **Holyhead** were the Old Man, the Mate, myself, the Able Seaman and one Ordinary Seaman. Below were the Chief, the Second who had been a Mate in other coasters, and a fireman. On this occasion we were on passage from the Irish side and the south easterly weather freshened into a gale and Dempsey decided to shelter in Loch Ryan. During the war you could not safely approach ports without showing recognition signals, flags by day and lights by night. Not having any for Stranraer we were abreast of the shore battery at Cairnryan when they fired a shot across our bows so we had to anchor at the mouth of the loch. As I lay in my bunk I could hear the anchor dragging on the rocky bottom followed shortly by feet overhead, the staccato creaking of the steam being turned on and the windlass heaving up. It was then that the mate almost cut one of his fingers off. It then came on to snow heavily so with lights out and those below warned not to make any smoke we steamed in past the battery without being seen. I was given a torch ready to flash S.O.S. if we had been challenged. The snowstorm persisted and daylight found us safely anchored in Wig Bay. As far as I know the shore battery never asked any questions." Silloth was also used for some coal shipments.

Ireland

Though Ireland throughout the 19th century was prominent in the development of steam navigation this was essentially confined to passenger and cargo liner services. The Irish Sea schooners, brigantines and barques were efficient and cheap to run and so there was no rush into steam on the part of Dublin coal importers.

Among the leading coal importers was R. Tedcastle of Great Brunswick Street. Robert Tedcastle, who was from Annan on the Solway Firth, moved to Dublin in the 1840s to represent a Cumberland colliery and commenced business in 1847 on his own behalf as a coal merchant, at which he was so successful that he purchased his first sailing collier in 1856 and was to operate many sailing colliers in the latter part of the century. In 1866 he ordered his first steamer from Messrs. Walpole of Dublin. This vessel was named **Dublin** 304/66. It was soon used to develop his passenger and general cargo trade to Liverpool. He then concentrated on developing the steam side of the fleet and his general cargo trade. By 1908 the fleet consisted of six steamers two of which, **Dublin** 711/04 and **Blackwater** 678/07 were designed with the coal trade in mind. The company had merged with John McCormick & Co., in 1897 who similarly had sailing colliers, and then entered the general cargo trade with steamers. The company sold its fleet to the City of Cork S.P. Co., in 1919 but the coal business continued without its own ships. W. O. McCormick & Co. Ltd., also began with an extensive fleet of sailing vessels and had the steamer **Dunleary** 470/05 built for his coal trade. The name perpetuated that of an earlier brigantine renowned for her fast passages. It remained their only steamer from 1905 until sold in the 1930s. Michael Murphy junior and W. Murphy of College Green, later Michael Murphy Ltd., had a few sailing vessels but were soon into steam. The company was founded by the third son of the head of Palgrave, Murphy and was closely associated with supplying Irish Railways and under the title of the Dublin General S.S. Co., the coal trade was developed, the company eventually moving to 94, North Wall, Dublin, where they had a well-equipped coal yard and developed an extensive coal and general cargo trade with South Wales ports, particularly Cardiff, where the business was carried on under the title M. J. Begg & Co. Ltd., who were coal exporters. At the turn of the century the Dublin company were operating three larger coasters with engines amidships suitable for coal and general cargo. **Beatrice** 712/90, **George** 511/94 and **Patricia** 843/01. They were a follow-on from the 'Captains' built in the 1870s such as **Captain Parry** 477/77 which foundered in 1893. Shortly after the death of Sir Michael Murphy a controlling interest was acquired by the British & Irish S.P. Co., (part of Coast Lines) in 1926.

Thomas Heiton began with sail in the 1850s and continued with sail until his death in 1877 after which the company was continued as a partnership, T. Heiton & Co., and three years later they purchased the old steamer **Arbutus** 356/54. This iron screw steamer had been built for William Whelan and was first registered at the port of Lancaster. By 1872 she was registered in Dublin so the vessel would have been well known to the partners. She traded for the company for five years, but during that time a new steamer was ordered from McIlwaine and Lewis, who delivered **Saint Kevin** 477/83 to the company. Further new building followed, all named after Irish saints. The company became Thomas Heiton & Co. Ltd., in 1896, by which time the fleet consisted of **Saint Kilda** 479/89, **Saint Margaret** 475/89, **Saint Mirren** 566/94, and **Saint Olaf** 568/96. Apart from coal the company were also merchants in iron, steel and building materials. The ships were used quite generally in the Irish Sea trade. The company continued to operate two or three steamers throughout the 1920s and 1930s when the first motor coaster **Saint Eunan** 436/37 was built, and this was the last ship to be sold in 1958 when the company gave up shipowning but continued as merchants.

Perhaps the most ambitious Dublin coal merchant was Owen Donnelly who purchased most of Richard Hughes fleet in 1920, but the deal collapsed and all the ships returned to Hughes in the space of a few months, though he did have the old coaster **Dinorwic** 276/92 and **Samoa** 370/90 in the coal trade in the 1920s. Captain Spargo recalls: coal was discharged by shovelling into tubs and as the colliers came alongside the river berths. The shore gang would come running with their shovels asking "which side did you load skipper?" On being told they immediately threw their shovels on that side to claim it, as they knew that the large lumps of coal shot across the ship when loading whilst the smaller coal dropped straight down and was easier to shovel!

The Alliance and Dublin Consumers Gas Company was forced into shipowning during the First World War and acquired **Braedale** 406/94. They decided to remain in shipowning and at the beginning of the 1920s had the **Glenageary** 446/20 and **Glencullen** 448/21 built at Lytham. They were the same design as those the yard built for W. A. Savage of Liverpool and were the maximum size for the Ringsend Dock lock gates at Dublin. The Gas Works were situated just off the Dock. They were typical of the small coasters employed in the Irish Sea coal trade. Originally with open bridges, they were eventually fitted with an enclosed wheelhouse and the forecastle accommodation moved up on to the main deck, and the fore winch was moved up to forecastle height (81). Their usual run was gas coal from Bramley Moore dock, Liverpool, but cargoes were also loaded at Partington or Garston. They both successfully survived the Second World War and were not scrapped until the 1960s. Two further steamers, **Glenbride** 440/19 and the new **Glencree** 481/34 (101) were purchased in the 1930s and were scrapped with the other steamers when the change was made to motor coasters in the 1960s.

Many other Irish ports had merchants with perhaps a ship or two and among these was Bray where Thomas Collier was based. He used names beginning with 'Brae' and owned a number of old coasters around the time of the First World War. One of the vessels **Braebeg** 165/78 was sold to John J. Murphy of Waterford, who was a coal merchant and also owned other old steamers such as **The Lady Belle** 331/00 and **St. Tudwal** 204/95. The fleet was sold in the 1920s after Mr. Murphy's death. In Wexford, J. J. Stafford had their own modern coal discharging berth from the 1920s but their ships were more involved in the general cargo trade. Most active in the coal trade was H. Wilson, who imported coal from Whitehaven, Garston, South Wales and sometimes from Blyth and supplied the Gas Works at Rosslare around 1900. A. Maloney & Sons of Dungarvan purchased **The Lady Belle** 331/00 in the 1920s and she regularly brought in their coal for many years. Cork was served by steam colliers

100. Glencree of the Alliance & Dublin Consumers Gas Company at their gas works adjacent to Ringsend Dock, Dublin.

MacRae collection

from the very earliest days. Mr. J. A. Harley entered shipowning in 1843 and employed his brigantines solely in the coal trade. He initially went into steam tugs. Later, after merging with fellow ship-owner James Scott & Co., the well deck collier **Scott Harley** 379/84 was built for the company in 1884.

R. McCowen & Sons of Tralee owned steamers to carry their coal from the 1890s. The new **Barrow Castle** 358/99 was joined by **Derrymore** 485/08. The firm was taken over by Kelly's about 1920 and they were to have just **Kerrymore** 509/21 until 1958. The ship was painted in McCowen's colours and registered at Tralee though cargoes were discharged at nearby Fenit. Mullock & Son at Limerick were established as early as 1778, becoming coal merchants and agents. In the 1920s they owned **Loop Head** 550/06 and **Kerry Head** 825/13. The latter was owned until the 1940s.

One of the more unusual Irish companies was the Shamrock Shipping Co. Ltd., of Larne which was set up in 1897 under Thomas Jack and the company immediately set about acquiring typical engines-amidships colliers. The vessels were widely employed, especially in the coal trade from Cardiff. The cargoes were fixed through J. T. Duncan & Co., of Cardiff, who were the company's agents in Cardiff. In return for this business Duncan agreed not to expand their own interests in the Bay trades. The venture prospered and by 1904 the fleet conisted of **Angus** 1238/83, **Inver** 1032/83, **Rochefort** 881/78, **Alacrity** 1080/83, all purchased in 1898, and the new ships **Clonlee** 1012/99, **Curran** 1106/00, **Glynn** 1106/99, **Gransha** 1192/01, **Raloo** 1012/98 and **Skeldon** 1337/03. The fleet was to remain at this size for the next 30 or so years trading to the continent, east coast, Mediterranean and Baltic. The coal strike of 1926 left them without English cargoes but they were soon employed in bringing coal in from the continent and this brought them to their port of registry, Belfast, where coal supplies were urgently needed. They were active again in the early 1930s when English coal was taxed in Eire so they brought cargoes from the continent again. The fleet was reduced somewhat in the 1930s but expanded again in the 1940s, purchasing larger vessels suitable for the more distant trades. In the 1950s their fleet of ageing steamers were rapidly scrapped as they looked to other trades.

The main locally operated northern fleets were based at Belfast, Larne and Newry and developed quickly with the industrialisation of the area towards the end of the 19th century. Howden Brothers of Larne trace their origins back to J. Smiley, who was a coal and grain merchant. The business eventually passed to nephews who were the Howden brothers. The first steamer was **Black Diamond** 259/64, which had been owned in Troon and probably was a regular visitor to Larne bringing in Scottish coal. The vessel was lost on Islandmagee on the 28th of May 1892. She was not replaced until **Ferric** 335/83 was purchased in 1899. With the deaths of the Howden brothers the business again passed to nephews when W. J. R. Harbinson and C. L. MacKean took over about 1903, but the name was not changed. The new management began adding to the fleet and by 1908 they had **Monarch** 310/84, **Roma** 181/03, **Kilcoan** 456/05 and the little wood steamer **Nellie** 109/95. In 1910 the company took delivery of **Carnduff** 257/10 which served them for 45 years. **Collin** 287/15 also had a long life. She was completed in 1915 by A. Jeffrey & Co., of Alloa for the company (102). The arrangement of the coaster was typical of the yard, with a long forecastle extended on either side of the mast. The forecastle was unusual in that the main deck was not extended through the accommodation but no doubt the arrangement makes for a more airy crew space which accommodates two firemen and two seamen. Aft, features to note were the absence of a wheelhouse below the flying bridge, the captain's cabin doubling as a chart room and the full stern. She served the company until 1918 when she was sunk in a collision with the **Esperanto**. She was subsequently raised and sold to Belfast coal merchant Alex King Ltd. They sold her on to Monroe Bros., in 1922 who in turn sold her to A. J. Smith of Bristol and so she continued in the coal trade. In the 1950s she was converted into a sand dredger and was not broken up until 1968. A series of eight further vessels were built by Jeffrey's for the company towards the end of the First World War, but two of the vessels **Sallagh** 325/16 and **Cargan** 274/16 were sold almost immediately so that in 1920 there remained **Straide** 326/17, **Dromaine** 234/17, **Falavee** 338/18, **Galgorm** 453/18, **Gracehill** 452/18 and **Finvoy** 374/20. The latter two vessels were the company's last ships when sold in 1957. In addition there were two vessels by other builders, **Carnduff** 257/10 and **Nellie** 235/21. The company became

Howdens Ltd, in 1933 though the Harbinsons' remained associated with the company and were joined by Arthur S.Davidson. The company became part of Kelly's about 1952. Howdens also managed three vessels which were owned by the Larne S.S. Company.

Kelly's came to dominate the Belfast coal trade and under his son, Sir Samuel Kelly, the influence of the fleet ranged far and wide in the coal trade and in coasting generally. Samuel Kelly built the business up from the 1840s, relying on sail, and with his death in 1877 his son John Kelly took over. He continued using sail and it was to be 1890 before steam entered the fleet in the form of **Susannah Kelly** 289/90, delivered from MacIlwaine & McColl, Belfast. She had a triple expansion engine and was soon doing quick passages between Ayr and Belfast. The steamer was so successful that the sailing vessels were all sold except one, which was fortunate for on June 15th 1897 their steamer developed a sudden list which continued to increase until the ship was on her side and she went down a few minutes later by the stern ten miles east of the Maidens Lighthouse. The ten crew all drowned. The cargo had shifted in the heavy weather. A larger replacement was obtained from the Ailsa Shipbuilding Co. She was named **Balmarino** 461/98, continuing the name of an earlier sailing ship. She was an eminently successful vessel. She lasted 59 years in the service of the company, finally being scrapped as the **Ballybeg** in 1957. On one occasion she managed five cargoes loaded at Ayr and discharged at Belfast in one week, under Captain 'Barney' Robinson. On the death of John Kelly in 1901 the business passed to Mrs. Susannah Kelly and she was assisted by her son Samuel Kelly in partnership. John Kelly Ltd., was formed in April 1911 with mother and son each taking up half the shares. The fleet then consisted of **Balmarino** 461/98, **Kelpie** 612/06, **Melissa** 520/08 and **W. M. Barkley** 569/98 which was the result of the new company taking over William Barkley & Son Ltd. who had been rivals in the coal business. Barkley had sailing ships for much of the latter part of the 19th century and purchased the steam collier **Pembury** 383/84 about 1890. The company was kept in existence under Kelly and continued to nominally own one or two ships. The First World War saw the newer ships being taken up for war service and some being profitably sold to Guinness to keep their supplies of the famous drink flowing to England. Kelly wisely purchased old secondhand ships which were not liable to be taken for Government service. Two fine new ships were ordered towards the end of the war. **Glenmaroon** 716/17 was duly delivered but the second vessel was cancelled. This larger vessel was often sent to the Thames for cement to Belfast. Four puffers were also acquired which may have been used for local coal movements round Belfast Lough or possibly for direct deliveries to some small quay, as puffers often ventured from Glasgow to Northern Ireland. The Belfast gasworks was on the river Lagan and may have been supplied in this way or by tug and barge, as Kelly had these available also. Kelly continued to expand by acquiring existing coal businesses; and acquired a controlling interest in R. McCowen of Tralee. He also acquired Charles M. F. Legg and Son Ltd., in 1918, which had long been established in Carrickfergus. This company had several steam colliers and owned **Lady Arthur Hill** 275/85 and **Carrick Castle** 223/91 as well as sailing colliers during the 1890s. Two new coasters were delivered in 1901, **Greenisland** 282/01 and **Jucar** 242/01. **Woodburn** 194/07 was built for the company in 1907. All the later coasters were small, **Woodburn** measuring just 101.6' x 19.7' x 8.3'. R. & D. A. Duncan was also acquired by Kelly. A number of vessels were also purchased and at the end of 1919 the capital was increased to £500,000. Though Sir Samuel Kelly and his mother subscribed all the extra capital in equal shares, the total actually suscribed was £476,658. The fleet was now some 23 vessels and the company were engaged in general coasting, particularly the South Wales coal trade to France. However, to enlarge the fleet high prices had been paid for old coasters.

A move to larger vessels was begun in 1921 with the purchase of two German war prizes which were put in the South Wales trade. **Albert Clement** 1187/04 was sold within a year and the **Cavehill** 1563/11 was lost on a voyage from the Tyne to Amsterdam with coal. New buildings continued to be added to the fleet which in 1927 consisted of **Ailsa** 325/94, **Balmarino** 419/98, **Carnlea** 579/13, **Clandeboye** 614/13, **Clewbay** 645/04, **Comber** 489/13, **Glenmaroon** 716/17, **Lagan** 364/03, **Melissa** 481/08, **Achill** 419/90, **Annagher** 596/23, **Aranisland** 275/95, **Bantry** 602/04, **Blacksod** 500/94, **Blackwater** 678/07, **Camlough** 540/20, **Carrickmore** 581/25, **Castlehill** 640/20, **Causeway** 463/94, **Clapham** 763/01, **Corteen** 530/20, **Crewhill** 695/23, **Crosshands** 716/18 (see page 84), **Fermanagh** 355/27, **Greenisland** 282/01, **Moyallon** 257/26, **Oranmore** 495/95, **Tamnamore** 278/25, **Tynan** 432/19. A fleet of 29 vessels including several new buildings, and further vessels were controlled through associated companies. Many of the firm's earlier vessels had come from the Ailsa Shipbuilding Company and

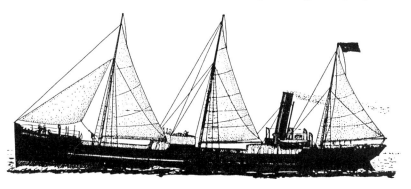

101. Lady Arthur Hill of 1885, from an old oil painting.

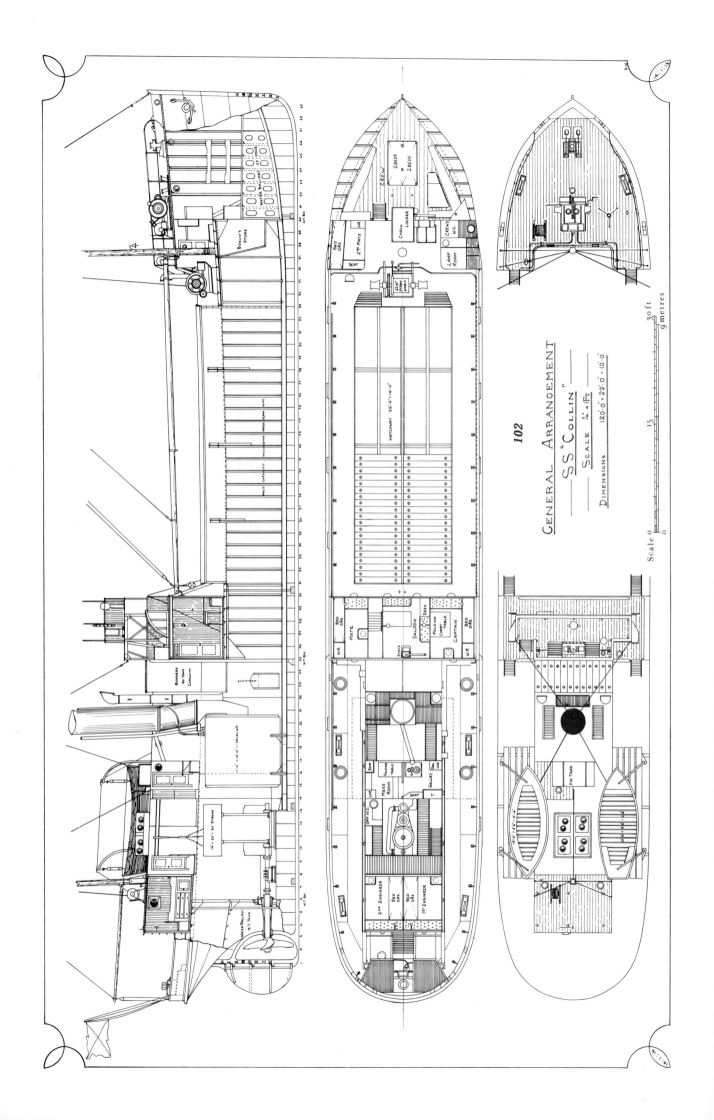

102

GENERAL ARRANGEMENT

S.S. "COLLIN"

SCALE ¼" = 1 Ft

DIMENSIONS 120'·0" × 22'·0" × 10'·0"

Scale 0   15   30 ft

0   9 metres

Scott's Yard at Bowling but in 1923 a new association with John Lewis of Aberdeen came to fruition. First to be delivered was **Annagher** 586/23 with the dimensions 165.2' x 27.0' x 11.2' and was followed by three sister ships, **Annaghmore** 583/24, **Donaghmore** 581/25 and **Carrickmore** 581/25. They proved themselves good sea boats and **Carrickmore** loaded four cargoes of coal at Rothesay Dock and discharged them in Belfast one Christmas week. The weather was bad and she was 40 minutes over her usual time passing Black Head inward to Belfast Lough. The crane men and the coal heavers at Abercorn Basin asked 'What kept you?!' By this time of course the crew had already taken off the hatch covers ready for discharge but even small delays could be costly with the shore gang hired in expectation of the ship being on time despite the weather. They were part of a series of at least eleven vessels built on the same basic hull lines by Lewis's yard. **Annaghmore** and **Donaghmore** were registered under the St. Helen's Colliery & Brickworks Co. Ltd., (see page 97). The design of the vessel was typical of the 1920s with the fore hatch slightly smaller than the main hatch and the foremast set well forward on the forecastle with the associated winch on the forecastle deck. This gave a larger deck which made a haven of shelter for crew members going forward in bad weather. The cargo capacity was about 770 tons including bunkers which gives a stowage of 45/46 cubic feet per ton depending on the amount of bunkers, which was suitable for the coal trade, as might be expected in a Kelly boat!

It is interesting to note that Lewis' yard No. 90, probably the last in the series, was delivered to D. R. Llewellyn, Merrett & Price Ltd., of Cardiff in the latter part of 1921, while those destined for the Kelly fleet, yard numbers 73, 75, 76 and 77 respectively, were not delivered until 1923. Perhaps he delayed delivery or took up hulls originally intended for other owners at a favourable price. This seems less likely as yard No.71 in the sequence was launched for the Allied S.N. Co., Hull, but named **Collooney** 577/20, this being the name of a small town in County Sligo, Eire. Kelly sold the vessel just prior to launching on a rising market in 1919 and the new owners in Hull did not change it. However, the layout of the vessel was slightly different from the later Kelly boats as it had a straight rather than curved bridge front and the lifeboats were placed aft of the funnel so that the position of the lifeboat and workboat were reversed. Willmott, Buttle & Co. Ltd., of Hull were the managers. The company sold the vessel to William Robertson in 1922. Sir Samuel Kelly seems to have been well satisfied with his purchases, though he continued to acquire second-hand coasters as they came on the market at favourable prices throughout the 1920s which were needed to replace a number of marine losses. One of the vessels lost was the almost new **Castleisland** 315/22 which was wrecked at the entrance to Belfast Lough. The vessel had got into increasing difficulties and finally grounded on Briggs Reef and was wrecked. She was only a year old, but the crew of 9 were saved. **Castleisland** was bringing coal from Maryport to Belfast. Oddly enough her sister **Coalisland** 314/21 was to be wrecked on the Mull of Kintyre in January 1925. During the coal strike of 1926 the ships were sent to the continent for coal, particularly Antwerp and Rotterdam, though eventually Sir Samuel Kelly, at the request of the Northern Ireland Prime Minister, secured supplies from further afield including Poland and the U.S.A. The strike, plus the failure of Kelly's Irish coal mining venture, may have caused most of the ships to be mortgaged to the Ulster Bank and the Bank of Ireland, but he continued to purchase vessels for the fleet at the low prices prevailing. Several older and smaller units of John Hay & Sons' fleet of Glasgow were purchased which were well known in the Irish trade. The large fleet were now widely employed in general coasting and in the east coast coal trade. Some cargoes were closely related Irish trades such as coal to Ireland and potatoes back to England. The smaller coasters could take coal into the out of the way places around the Irish coast and then load potatoes from farms in the area.

At the beginning of the 1930s there was a change of Government in the Irish Republic and a tax of 5 shillings per ton was imposed on English coal. This may well have prompted Kelly's to purchase some larger vessels more suited to importing Polish and other continental coals. The first was **Hillfern** 1535/20 (79), purchased from Cardiff owners, while **Islington** 1517/20 was purchased from H. Harrison (Shipping) Ltd. Both had been designed for the coal trade and were frequently employed in the South Wales coal trade to Spain. The Eire Government settled their differences with the British Government in 1935 and by 1936 the big colliers had been sold, **Hillfern** returning to Cardiff owners (the Bramhall S.S. Co. Ltd.) under the management of C. Angel. It was almost immediately sold on to the Derwent S.S. Co. of Newcastle and was later sunk on he 31st of October 1940 off Kinnaird Head while on passage from Sunderland to Cork north-about.

Beginning in 1933 a series of new larger coasters was ordered at a favourable price, (106). In all eight steamers were built, the orders flowing to Lewis' yard in Aberdeen as the trade picked up. First to be delivered was **Rosapenna** 869/33. The registered dimensions were 197.7' x 30.7' x 12.1' and so the design was suitable for the coal trade to Belfast and other ports which could accept larger coasters both in Ireland and the east coast coal trade to smaller customers and harbours like Shoreham, indeed **Rosapenna** was sold in 1937 to P. Hawksfield & Son of Dover who were the local coal merchants. The remainder of the series were **Portavogie** 869/34, **Baronscourt** 869/35, **Inishtrahull** 869/35, **Glendalough** 868/36, **Glengariff** 868/36 and **Saintfield** 867/37. All came safely through the war except for **Glendalough** which struck a mine off Cromer on a voyage from Shoreham to the Tyne in ballast. **Baronscourt**, **Glengariff** and **Saintfield** were all employed in the east coast coal trade during the Second World War.

Baronscourt was employed on the west coast and Mr. R. C. March remembers that it was with some

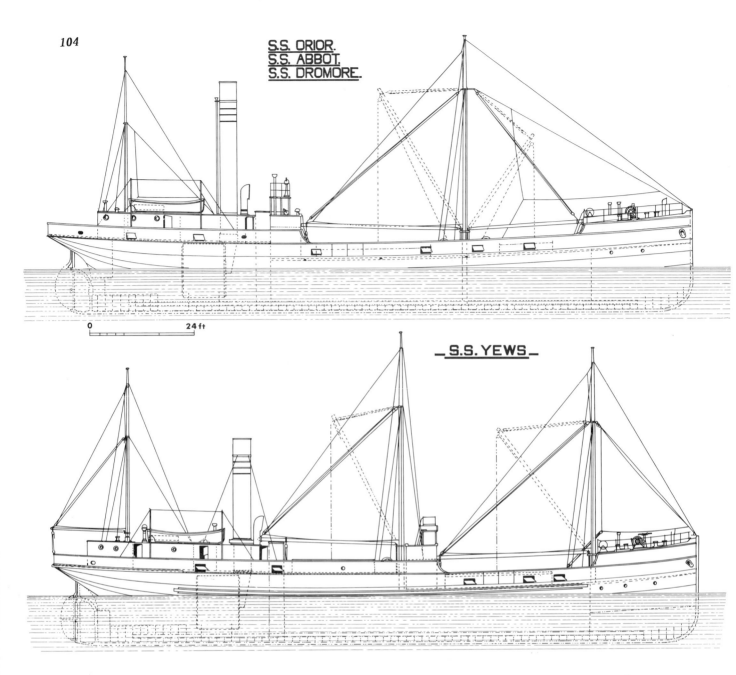

S.S. ORIOR.
S.S. ABBOT.
S.S. DROMORE.

0   24 ft

S.S. YEWS

104. *Rigging plans prepared by John Fullerton's yard at Paisley of four coasters built for Joseph Fisher of Newry (above) and below, the* **Alder** *341/09 (142.8' x 23.6' x 10.3') in the colours of Joseph Fisher of Newry.* **Alder** *was an improved version of the* **Yews** *of 1906.*

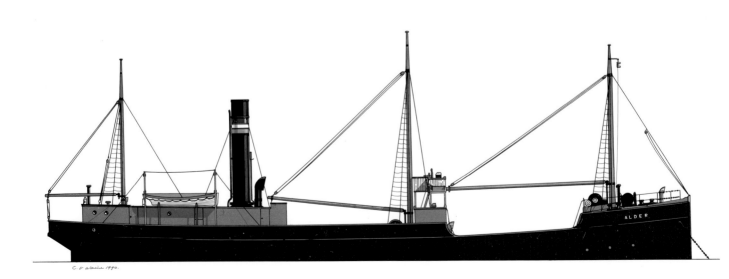

trepidation that he received the news that he was to join the commodore's ship as mate in June 1942. "Captain Foster had the reputation of being a difficult man to sail with, but I was so pleased to have such an appointment that I made it my business to get on with him. He had a reputation for interfering with the mate's work on deck, but for me it was a wonderful opportunity to see what standards could be reached. **Baronscourt** was the only ship in the fleet where the low gear on the winches worked, in all the others it had long since rusted up, and the same applied to the shackles in the derrick fall blocks. From September 1939 to April 1940 she had been on time charter to the Admiralty, lying anchored for weeks at Scapa Flow. There 'Gentleman Jim' as he was called, got her into great order, even chipping and painting the inside of the hatch coamings and beams. We often carried briquettes from Cardiff to Belfast which were clean and loaded by hand. The shore men set up a miniature railway in the hold and pushed small truckfuls about the hold until all were meticulously stowed. This took two whole days and gave us a night in port. For some reason the cargo was always 100 tons short of our capacity so I never needed to watch the load line. Discharge at Belfast was always by grab at Queens Quay and it shocked me to see the briquettes which had been so carefully loaded, being ground to dust before they even got over the ship's side! The crane drivers followed the directions of the hatchmen who gave them, by delicate movements of the hand (holding a rolled up newspaper if it was dark), until the grab was exactly over the right place, then there came a sweeping downward movement of the hand which was accompanied by a stentorian 'leggo!'"

Sir Samuel Kelly had died in 1937 and the business passed to Lady Mary Kelly, who invited her brother to take charge of the company. Captain Clint, who had looked after the fleet under Sir Samuel, continued to do so though now a director as well as superintendent. In 1937 the Kelly fleet consisted of 44 vessels and was one of the largest in the British Isles. Sales and losses then reduced the fleet during the war period and just prior to it. Some of the larger coasters were sold to east coast owners for their coal trade, such as to Culliford Shipping Co., and the Williamstown Shipping Co. However there was no repeat of spiralling prices and freight rates which had occurred in the First World War, as the Government set rates at a little above pre-war levels and these were reviewed from time to time. Kelly's coal business and remaining fleet of 31 vessels was sold in 1948 to William Cory and Stephenson Clarke. The larger vessels had from time to time worked for Stephenson Clarke who also handled coal exports from the Mersey, and so the link-up was a logical one to expand the east coast companies to the Irish Sea where nearly all the fleet were employed. The funnel colours were retained but the names were all changed to places beginning 'Bally' between 1951 and 1952. At the end of the war or just after, most coasters were equipped with radio telephone equipment and though it was supposed to be used for orders and important traffic, it was quite usual for the Kelly skippers to have a multi-way conversation to exchange news and views on the weather and other topics each evening!

Under the new management funds were provided for new larger colliers, prices having increased about three times from pre-war days, though the vessels were much better equipped. The new vessels were **Ballyhaft** 847/52, **Ballymoney** 1340/53, **Ballyhill** 847/54, **Ballylumford** 1147/54, **Ballymena** 1356/54 and **Ballylagan** 1208/55. It is interesting that they should have all been steamers, for Stephenson Clarke themselves were taking delivery of a series of similar sized motor ships for their own fleet, though steamers were easier and cheaper to build and Kelly crews had great experience of steam. However in 1953 a second-hand motor coaster was acquired and renamed **Ballyedward** 552/50. The change to motor began in 1958 when the sisters **Ballyloran** 1092/58 and **Ballylesson** 1092/58 were delivered from Alexander Hall, Aberdeen. The last of the original Kelly fleet to be scrapped was **Ballygarvey** 662/37, in 1964, and the last of the steamers was to be **Ballyhill** 847/54, sold for scrapping in 1973.

Ballyhaft 847/52 was transferred to John Milligen & Co. Ltd., another Belfast coal importer which Kelly's had gained control of during the 1940s, and wore Milligen's colours for some years. The company was registered in 1896, and by 1926 had a capital of £90,000 of which Sir Samuel Kelly held £6,000 with many smaller local shareholders. The company chairman was J. Taylor and directors J. W. Dunwoody and H. P. P. Newman. They had **Eveleen** 434/91 in the '90s, which was joined by **Kathleen** 738/02 and at 200 feet was the largest of the Belfast colliers for a number of years. A new **Eveleen** 502/20 was delivered from the Ardrossan Drydock and Shipbuilding Co. in 1920 and she served alongside **Kathleen** until the 1940s. Prior to the war **Eveleen** was running in Kelly colours and came under their management by accident as she was sunk in collision during November 1942 off Grey Point, Belfast Lough. She was salvaged by the Ministry of War Transport but was not refloated until November 1943, by which time ships were in such short supply that any which had been abandoned as constructive total losses were being salvaged if at all possible. Reconditioned, she was named **Empire Eveleen** and placed under Kelly management. In 1946 she was returned to John Milligen & Co. Ltd. and reverted to her original name and continued in the coal trade until scrapped at Troon in 1957.

Another old company in the Belfast coal trade to come under the control of Kelly's about the 1940s was Alexander King Ltd. Their first steamer, **Monarch** 316/85 was also the first iron steamer built by MacIlwaine & McColl. She was sold at the turn of the century to Howden's but they continued to own one or two colliers such as **Corbet** 468/09 which served them up until the Second World War. In 1942 Kelly's **Melissa** 520/08 was transferred to King's ownership, but was returned to the Kelly fleet in 1950.

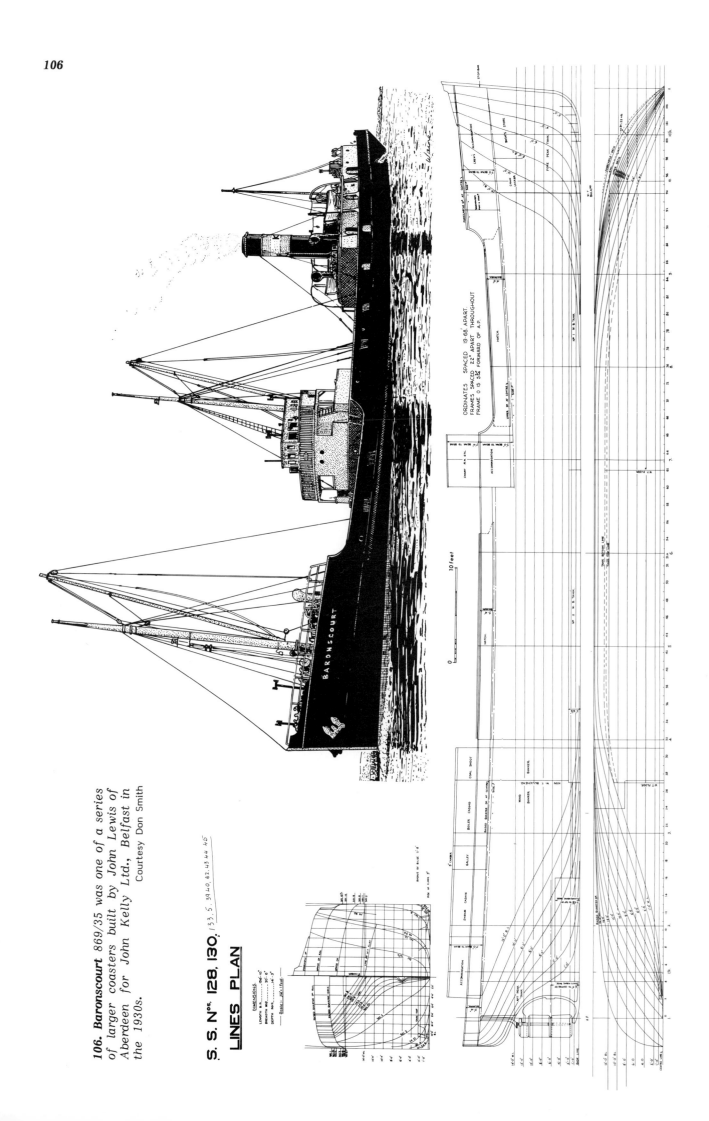

106. Baronscourt 869/35 was one of a series of larger coasters built by John Lewis of Aberdeen for John Kelly Ltd., Belfast in the 1930s.

Courtesy Don Smith

S. S. Nᵒˢ. 128, 130, 133, 5, 39 40, 42, 43 44 45

LINES PLAN

One company which did not succomb to Kelly's domination of the Belfast coal trade was Hugh Craig which began as coal importers in 1842. Mr. Craig's two sons took over the business and formed a partnership which lasted until 1927. Hugh Craig & Co. Ltd., was formed in 1938. Originally operating sailing vessels, their first steamer was the **Helen Craig** 417/91, built by Workman Clarke, Belfast. She was equipped with a towing hook so that she could assist sailing colliers, quite a common practice in those days. She served the company for 58 years and became an institution on the company's Belfast - Preston general cargo service and was eventually scrapped in 1959. In pre-war days she worked as a collier too. Further steamers were added to the fleet from the turn of the century so that by 1907 they had **Helen Craig** 417/91, **M. J. Craig** 691/98, **Alice M. Craig** 916/00 and **Ailsa Craig** 601/06, a fine modern fleet for the period. The company lost both **M. J. Craig** and **Ailsa Craig** in 1918, both torpedoed. **Clydebrae** 513/91 was purchased immediately as a replacement and at the end of the war new steamers were ordered so that by 1922 the fleet consisted of **Helen Craig** 417/91, **Alice M. Craig** 916/00, **Clydebrae** 515/91 and the new steamers **M. J. Craig** 605/21, **Cliffsider** 489/20, **Craigavon** 682/21 and **Craigolive** 605/21. The fleet was slowly reduced by losses and sales although no vessels were lost in the Second World War. By 1962 three ageing steamers were left, **Craigolive** 605/21, **Craigavad** 681/24 and **Craigantlet** 827/31, which were at the end of their days and so was the company, for they sold out to Cawood Holdings. The steamers were scrapped and replaced by a new motor vessel **Craigmore**.

Another firm of Belfast coal merchants taken over by Cawoods was A. S. Davidson Ltd., who purchased two engines-aft steamers in 1953 from Arthur Guinness of Dublin. Both had been designed as self-trimming colliers for Kelly but only **Clarecastle** saw service in the coal trade before their sale by Kelly, thus **Carrowdore** 660/14 and **Clarecastle** 670/14 finally returned to the Belfast coal trade for which they were intended. They served Davidson's until 1958 when both were scrapped and replaced by **Mayfair Sapphire** 1032/49, built as **Sapphire** for William Robertson of Glasgow. The vessel was named in part after the company's offices; Mayfair Buildings, and regularly carried cargoes from Preston, Merseyside and occasionally North East Coast ports. The company was taken over by Cawoods in the 1960s and finished her time in the Belfast coal trade in their colours.

The largest fleet of vessels in the Irish coal trade shortly after the turn of the century was that managed by Joseph Fisher of Newry. They had been long established at Newry importing coal, beginning in 1852 with sailing vessels. The first steamer to join the fleet was **Celtic** 197/82, purchased in 1889, which was soon renamed **Kilkeel**. A new steamer, the **Clanrye** 239/84 was also added, financed by the formation of the Newry S.S. Co. Ltd. The **Kilkeel** 197/82 was later transferred and in March 1887 the company changed its name to the Newry & Kilkeel S.S. Co. Ltd. Meanwhile **Clanrye** had foundered on a voyage from South Wales to Newry with coal. A further company was formed to own **Carlingford Lough**, the Carlingford Lough S.S. Co. Ltd. The vessel was built by John Fullerton of Paisley, who were to build 24 ships for Fisher-managed companies. Further vessels were added during the 1890s at about one per year, and to finance further growth the Frontier Town S.S. Co. Ltd., was formed in 1897 and took delivery of **Frontier Town** 294/98 and the larger **Cloughmore** 547/97 Newry was the main port for Northern Ireland until the middle of the 19th century, by which time Belfast was overtaking it. Newry countered this by continued improvement to its facilities, deepening and widening the approach channel to accept 5,000 ton ships. The sea lock at the entrance to the Newry Ship Canal could accept vessels up to 50 ft. wide and vessels of 3,000 tons could lie afloat in the Victoria Basin. Further up the Ship Canal the size of vessel was much more limited and in Newry itself the canalside quays offered a draft of about 10 feet while the Albert Dock could accept vessels drawing about 12 feet. This very soon led Fishers to standardise their fleet. Up to the turn of the century size of vessels had been slowly increased from **Mourne** 228/94 (125.0' x 20.1' x 9.3') to **Joseph Fisher** 292/96 (140.0' x 21.1' x 9.8') and one larger vessel **Seapoint** 593/99 (175.0' x 26.6' x 10.6'). However, from around the turn of the century the size became standardised on the maximum which could pass through the lock at Ringsend Dock, Dublin, but at the same time the draft was suitable for Newry and many other ports.

Typical of the early series was **Dromore** 286/03, **Abbot** 283/03 and **Orior** 284/03 which measured 142.5' x 21.3' x 10.2' with a loaded draft of 10'10". John Fullerton's general arrangement for the series (108) was typical of the short raised quarterdeck coasters he was building with a single mast placed between two hatches which were not very large and did not have sloping sides to aid cargo trimming. They were not particularly good with bulk cargoes like coal. The usual method of loading was to fill the main hatch and then put the remainder of the cargo in the fore hatch. However, as Captain Spargo notes in 'Old Time Sea Coasting', this could not be done with the **Letty** which was built to the same lines so it was probably not possible to load these vessels by that method either. Thus the cargo had to be heaped up in the middle of the ship and this could lead to loose surfaces at either end of the hold and the danger of cargo shifting. This may have accounted for some of the old type coasters foundering, as happened to **Orior** when heading for Newry with South Wales coal in 1908, but sails were still used to reduce fuel consumption and steady the vessel (104). The galley, housed in the long forecastle, was not usual. The small galley would have been difficult to use in any kind of sea and no doubt the engineers stove aft was resorted to quite often. Open forecastles could be an additional source of danger as water shipped in heavy seas could fill them and hold the head down. The crew accommodation followed the usual layout. Surprisingly there was no saloon or stove for the captain or mate, but typical of a vessel built to a cheap specification. The vessel had a flying bridge to give better visibility over the forecastle but the captain had only the engine room telegraph and no second steering position so orders had to be shouted to the seaman

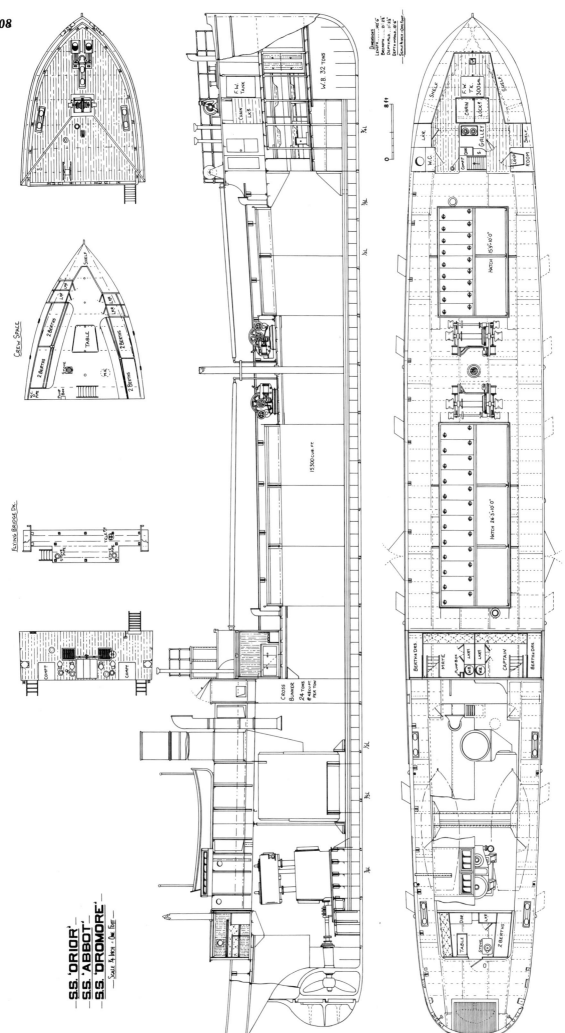

108. John Fullerton's earlier design of coaster for the coal trade of Joseph Fisher of Newry. The sail plan for this series of vessels is illustrated on page 104.

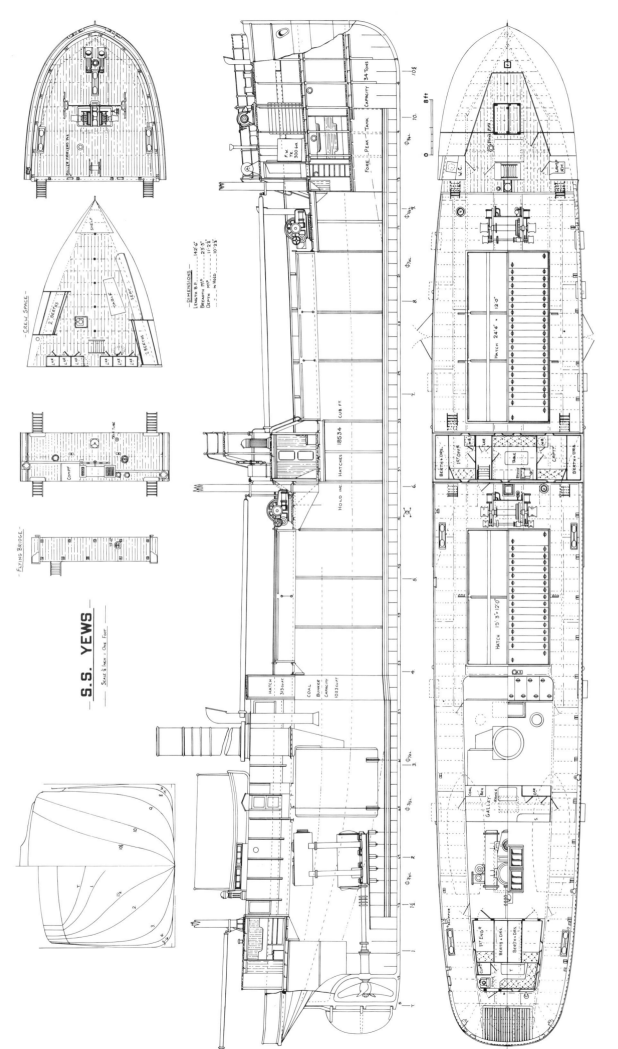

— S.S. YEWS —

Scale ¼ Inch = One Foot

DIMENSIONS
Length B.P. — 142'0"
Breadth m'LD — 23'5"
Depth m'LD — 11'2½"
˝ IN HOLD — 10'2½"

109. *The later design of coaster built by John Fullerton of Paisley for Joseph Fisher of Newry which made the vessel more suitable for coal cargoes and a better sea boat. Both designs are the same length.*

at the wheel below.

An improved design (109) appeared in 1905 with the commissioning of **Yews** 333/05 and introduced the use of names of different trees for vessels, although the plural was not repeated. **Yews** was lost in a collision off the Skerries in 1910. The main change in the design was an extension of the raised quarterdeck from 49 feet to 80 feet and the breadth was increased also to give the dimensions 142.6' x 23.4' x 10.1'. The extension of the raised quarterdeck allowed the draft to be increased to 11.6' and gave an additional 3,234 cubic feet of hold capacity. The machinery and boiler was also moved forward, probably to reduce the tendency to load by the stern. The machinery was identical, a compound engine with cylinders 16" and 34" by 24" stroke working at a pressure of 130 lbs giving about 47 registered horse power. Because of the increased dimensions, the speed was probably reduced to about 8.5 knots. Compound machinery was fitted because it was more compact and lighter, so although it burned more fuel this was offset against the increased earnings for the extra cargo capacity. However, as boiler and machinery efficiency was improved this size of ship was built with triple expansion machinery as standard by the 1920s. Bunker capacity was also slightly increased to allow for the slightly larger fuel consumption to be expected with the increase in beam and depth.

Forward there were various improvements in the forecastle. A bulkhead was now fitted closing off the forward part and so preventing water accumulating there. The ballast capacity was increased and the hold bulkhead moved aft one frame space, which reduced the risk of the vessel loading by the head. The number of crew bunks was reduced as it became usual to carry only two firemen and two seamen, with rising labour costs. Hatch width in proportion to width of the ship was also increased, which aided trimming coal cargoes. Amidships, the captain and mate now had a small saloon complete with stove. Above, the bridge layout was basically unchanged. Aft, a much larger and more convenient galley was arranged over the boiler, in the usual position. The engineers now had rather small but separate cabins which could be entered from the engine room. Beyond they had a small saloon which could only be reached by a quick sprint round the stern. The extra space was made by extending the engine room casing further aft compared with the earlier design.

From the company's accounts it appears that they were paying about £6,200 for the earlier design and about £6,500 for the improved design. The company seemed to have been well pleased with the extra investment and immediately ordered more of the later design so that by 1908 they had the largest fleet of colliers of the 142' long variety. The Newry & Kilkeel S.S. Co. Ltd., had **Joseph Fisher** 292/96, **Portadown** 291/00, **Rostrevor** 295/99 of the earlier type and the two year old **Oak** 346/06 of the later type. The Frontier Town S.S. Co. Ltd., had **Abbot** 283/03, **Dromore** 286/03 of the earlier type while **Yews** 333/05, **Elm** 349/06 and **Pine** 355/07 were all of the later type. The deck equipment was about the minimum with just two steam winches and no steam anchor windlass or steam capstan aft in both designs. No double bottom was fitted. This reduced the cost but when these vessels were light they could be difficult to handle and certainly the earlier design was so light that in a gale it was sometimes impossible to bring them round through the eye of the wind and there was then the problem of wearing the ship round and exposing the stern to heavy seas. Ballast was improved in the later ships and the fuller lines aft helped the stern lift in such conditions. The bow was also fuller so that if a heavy sea was met the ship tended to stop and ride over rather than slice through it. In the latter case it was up to the officer of the watch to grab the engine room telegraph and stop the ship burying herself completely in the next wave. The earlier design was quite popular never-the-less as in moderate seas they could make good progress without too much pitching. The later design with the long raised quarterdeck and the bridge amidships gave better freeboard, a good range of stability and propellor immersion. It was protected to some extent from heavy seas sweeping the whole length of the ship. At the time it was considered a particularly safe design for the worst weather conditions.

The older vessels were sold off and the newer type steadily built as replacements. Prices from Fullerton's tended to fall with **Alder** 341/09 costing £6,006 and having a fully equipped flying bridge and berths for two extra hands in the forecastle (104). There were subtle changes also elsewhere. The engine room had been extended forward by one frame space and this was carried along so that the raised quarterdeck was also extended by one frame space. Rather more obvious changes were made forward, the fore bulkhead was moved aft two frame spaces eliminating the unusable space under the foredeck, this also improved the ballast capacity to 45 tons. This bulkhead change had probably been incorporated as early as the **Oak** 318/06 as she also had increased ballast capacity. This latter vessel still had the foremast and winch in the well deck and this was later moved up on to the forecastle, which allowed a longer derrick and the winchman a better view and easier working on to higher quays. This design obviously proved ideal for the coal trade and both vessels were to serve the company for many years, **Oak** herself not being broken up at Llanelly until 1951.

The company lost a number of ships in collisions and founderings and continued to replace them by newbuildings from Fullerton's yard. The last to be built was **Aspen** 333/15, after which no new vessels were acquired for some years. The company may well have been feeling the effects of Kelly's rapid expansion. In 1924 the **Moygannon** 498/21 came from the Newry & Provincial Coal Co. and as she was put in the books at £10,500 part of the price may well denote the purchase of the company's business as well. The coal business of the Antrim Iron Ore Co. Ltd., was taken over at the end of the 1920s along with the old coaster **Glenaan** 332/84 which they had been using for that part of their trade. As the name suggests the company was originally formed to mine iron ore.

111.

Above: **Spray** *leaving Methil with a coal cargo about 1960.*

Right and below: **Arundel** *on her last coal carrying voyage for Stephenson Clarke in 1972 showing the view looking aft from the bridge and below, the view forward from the bridge on a summer morning in the North Sea!*

The main customers were the iron works of England and the company became shipowners to ship the ore out, particularly to the Tyne. The **Glenaan** was wrecked in 1932, but a secondhand coaster already renamed **Glendun** 633/15 continued the name of the old company until 1940 when she was wrecked while sheltering on a voyage from Garston to Belfast. She was not replaced.

Two new ships were ordered from Fullerton's yard at favourable prices, **Poplar** 343/27 and **Palm** 344/27. **Poplar** was wrecked off Harrington in October 1942, but **Palm** was to be the last steamer in the fleet when scrapped in 1963, a tribute to Fullerton's quality building. Further new ships were ordered from Scott & Sons of Bowling who had survived the slump while Fullerton's had closed down at the end of the 1920s. The new vessels were very similar to the old vessels though they were fitted with triple expansion machinery 11.25", 20", 32"- 24" working on superheated steam at 205 lbs. The dimensions were very similar (142.2' x 23.6' x 10.5') with a draft of 11'8" so the improved machinery gave a comfortable 10 knots. Ballast capacity was improved and an aft peak tank fitted holding 35 tons. The fore peak tank held 54 tons. Trade was generally improving and new vessels joined the fleet steadily. However some losses occurred, notably **Pine** 328/07 which was run down by her sistership **Olive** 328/07 while lying in Carlingford Lough, the difficult stretch of water lying between Newry and the sea. **Pine** was later salvaged and returned to the Irish trade as **Second**.

The company lost four ships during the Second World War, two of which may have been the result of the war. Though the company had the motor vessel **Karri** 354/38, two steamers were ordered at the end of the war, **Balsa** 405/47 and the appropriately named **Ebony** 405/47. They were basically similar to the pre-war series though the breadth was increased giving the dimensions 142.5' x 24.6' x 10.4'. The vessels continued to carry coal from Ayr and Irvine in Scotland, Whitehaven and the Mersey, mainly Garston, as well as South Wales and sometimes east coast ports. During the 1950s the fleet was rapidly reduced, but a new motor ship, the **Oak** 709/53, which was much larger than usual at 182 feet and a similar size Dutch coaster were purchased in 1955 which was named **Walnut** 539/55. The Frontier Town S.S. Co., ceased to operate in 1956 when **Balsa** was transferred and the Newry and Kilkeel company ended with the sale of **Palm**, the other two remaining vessels being under J. Fisher & Sons Ltd. Joseph Fisher became part of Cawood Holdings in 1966.

There were several smaller merchants based on the north east coast of Ireland. South of Newry at Dundalk there was Samuel Lockington & Co., who had the **John Irwin** 303/97 and later had **Shellie** 358/05 and **Carlingford** 345/08 built for them by the Dublin Dockyard. In 1921 they took delivery of **Margaret Lockington** 460/21, which was to serve them until the late 1950s. A similar vessel, **Whin** 466/20, was owned by Robert Neill & Sons of Bangor, Co. Down, and operated into the late 1950s. **Whin**, apart from carrying coal for Bangor also had other contracts and was the largest vessel to visit the Point of Ayr Colliery. Both these vessels were sisterships of a series of vessels built for R. R. Clark of Liverpool and may have originally been ordered by him. Neill's had purchased **Rhanbuoy** 273/93 from a company of the same name managed by Alexanders of Glasgow the same year she was built and renamed her **Rosabelle**. Unusually the hull was painted maroon rather than black. She was sold in 1906 after **Helen** 322/04 had been delivered. They also owned **Briar** 411/21 in the 1930s.

A very early supporter of steam was the East Downshire S.S. Co., which was formed in 1871 with the help of Lord Downshire, owner of the local estate around Dundrum. The company purchased the steamer **Lady Alice Kenlis** 214/68. She was a handy steamer with the dimensions 123.3' x 19.6' x 9.8'. A large steamer **Lady Downshire** 241/73 was built for the company in 1873. The ships were employed in bringing in coal and other supplies. Further vessels were added from time to time but the fleet never became large. The first **Downshire** 315/98 was sunk by submarine off the Isle of Man in Febuary 1915. The **Dunsford** 368/05 was purchased and renamed **Downshire** but she was torpedoed when bound for Dublin from Glasgow. The coasters used to have to go in over Dundrum bar to reach the company's quay and this required good steering and judgement on a fine day but in rough weather it was particularly difficult and in the old days after battening down all ventilators, doors and skylights they would come over the bar with surf breaking on to the ship. Deliveries were expected to be made in those days and Mr. E. J. Hennessy, the manager, was a typical hard-driving Victorian employer who also looked after his men should they fall ill. The work could be hard at the turn of the century, the labourer getting 17 shillings per week and a shilling extra if **Downshire** managed three cargoes in the week. After the loss of the second **Downshire** the company purchased the smaller coaster **Mountcharles** 286/10. As in many out of the way places, one or two deck passengers were taken by coasters making short passages and **Mountcharles** and vessels before her would carry a few passengers to Ayr, which was a popular short run for coal.

When prices had settled down after the war a new **Downshire** 398/25 was delivered from Scott & Sons, Bowling and **Mountcharles** sold. The ship was always smartly kept with the casing and bridge panelled out and grained, and woodwork varnished. Coal cargoes were the main activity. Dundrum Quay had direct rail access and in the days of the Belfast and County Down Railway over 100 cargoes of coal were discharged yearly. Cargoes of potatoes were also shipped out in season. In addition the company's boats carried cattle slung into the vessel by crane and taken over to Whitehaven. Under Captain Henry McCartney, during the Second World War, **Downshire** carried arms and equipment from Southampton and Manchester to the Normandy beaches, where she discharged into amphibious vehicles. She served the company until the late 1950s (front endpapers) by which time the old steamer was in need of extensive boiler and other repairs and so it was decided to sell her for scrap (see front endpaper).

Western Scotland

Much of the coal carried to Northern Ireland came from Scottish ports which shipped coal from the Midland Valley coal fields east of Glasgow, Ardrossan and Ayr. The main shipments were made from Ayr and steadily rose from 385,000 tons to over one million tons. There were no significant local collier fleets and much of the coal was collected by those from Glasgow or the many Irish based fleets, especially Kelly's. In the early 1940s **Stramore** 266/25 was nearly always on the run from Ayr to the cement works at Maghermore in Larne Lough as the Mate, Mr. R. C. March recalls: "The kiln coal was always very dusty and was tipped from wagons hoisted over the ship. When the wagon arrived under the crane the shore man would jam a wooden chock between the buffer and the bottom corner of the end door. Then he would knock open the catch on the door so that the weight of the coal inside came against the chock through which was a length of rope. When all was ready he would strike the buffers with his hammer and the ringing sound signalled the crane man to hoist the wagon into a tipping position at about 45° over the hold. The rope was then pulled and the chock came out to hang by a short chain from the buffer, the end door of the wagon opened and the contents fell into the hold,. Sometimes we had a welcome change from kiln to boiler coal. This was washed, almost dust free and usually loaded at a conveyor known as the 'yo-yo'.

The passage from Ayr to Larne was only about seven hours so we did not keep the usual watches; instead one watch took her as far as Corsewall Point, which was about half way and the other watch took her from there. Some weeks we managed five cargoes and were often short of sleep as all we got was part of our three and a half hours below on passage. We often went for weeks without a night in port and once logged Ailsa Craig three times in a day. We left Ayr shortly before midnight, passed Ailsa Craig about 1 a.m., discharged at Magheramore in time to get back to Ayr, load and get to sea again an hour or two earlier than the previous night and so pass Ailsa Craig for the third time. Loading at Ayr started at 6 a.m. and went on till 10 p.m., presumably two eight hour shifts, but we sailors of course had to be operational all the time."

Ayr harbour was served by the Glasgow and South Western Railway which came under the control of the L.M.S. Railway. Coal loading was originally by coaling crane, but in later years a coal conveyor was installed in the wet dock. Troon rivalled Ayr in the 19th century but coal shipments fell away and had ended by the 1940s. At the turn of the century about 182,000 tons were being shipped coastwise. Six 30-ton capacity steam cranes were in use, each capable of loading 150-200 tons per hour.

Glasgow shipments were around 380,000 tons in the 1880s and reached about 823,000 tons coastwise 'with over 3,327,000 tons being exported overseas. By 1948 coastwise shipments had fallen to 258,000. Much of the local trade was handled by 'puffers' which were introduced in the 1850s on the Forth & Clyde canal. They were soon made more seaworthy by fitting bulwarks and began venturing down the Firth of Clyde to the Western Isles and even Northern Ireland. Some were owned by local coal merchants. One of the early firms to enter the trade was William Robertson of Glasgow who had two steam scows (puffers) built in the mid-1860s but he did not develop this trade and concentrated on sail until 1878 when his first coaster **Agate** 184/78 was delivered. He went on to develop a large coasting fleet which was prominent in the coal trade, but was primarily a general coasting fleet as were those of Glasgow owners generally. Ross & Marshall and J. & J. Hay developed the local trades with fleets of puffers and both fleets moved large quantities of coal, handling supplies to distilleries and gas works. In 1958 Hay's fleet were carrying about 2,000 tons per week, particularly around the Firth of Clyde. Important customers were gas works at Millport on the Isle of Great Cumbrae and Rothesay on the Isle of Bute.

Coal was supplied at General Terminus Quay using five coaling cranes in 1911 which were operated by the Caledonian Railway and used for loading and bunkering. The Queen's and Prince's Docks were principally used for large ships. The main coal loading dock was Rothesay Dock which had four electric coaling hoists in use at the peak time between the First World War and the Second World War. The first coal hoist had been installed in the Prince's Dock as late as 1903. Regular visitors prior to the First World War were coasters of William Robertson, John Hay and T. Heiton & Co., whose fleet was managed from Glasgow although founded in Dublin. They were generally arriving with limestone from North Wales and leaving with coal for Dublin or other ports handy for a return cargo of limestone. Puffers of Ross & Marshall were regulars taking coal to Larne even in the winter months.

One of the coaster owners most closely involved with the coal trade was Mann, MacNeal & Co. Ltd., who managed the Ford Shipping Co. Beginning around the turn of the century they built up a sizable fleet. By 1908 they had **Ashford** 427/92, **Belford** 352/04, **Clifford** 359/04, **Dunsford** 368/05, **Earlford** 383/83, **Fairford** 367/91, **Glassford** 311/00, **Latchford** 458/97 and **Slateford** 355/03. Some were new vessels and some were secondhand, but all were active in the Irish coal trade. The company formed a Cardiff off-shoot in 1920, Mann, MacNeal & Carr Ltd., coal exporters, which was eventually taken over by Cory. The main company ceased operations about 1926. By this time Kelly's colliers dominated the coal shipments from Rothesay Dock. For example in January 1925 his vessels loaded 27 cargoes of coal while the vessels of all other owners only loaded 10 cargoes. This domination continued throughout the 1930s and 1940s, though one owner to make small inroads into it was Robert Cameron, who was also a coal merchant. He operated the old **Doon Glen** 128/93 in the 1920s, but in the latter part of the 1930s expanded so that by 1936 he had **Kyle Rhea** 323/21, **Kyle Rona** 307/10 and **Kyle Skye** 311/22, but the fleet was dispersed at the beginning of the 1940s. Coal was also shipped from Campbelltown which came from the nearby Macrohanish Colliery.

6.

*114. **Niewland** loading at Grange Dock hoists circa 1930. She belonged to the Shipping and Coal Company's Dutch parent company.*

The East Coast of Scotland

The Lanarkshire coalfield stretches from Glasgow through the Midland Valley of Scotland to the Firth of Forth and then along the northern side of the Firth as the Fife coalfield. On the southern bank there is the Lothian coalfield south east of Edinburgh. Westernmost of the ports was Alloa which shipped small amounts of coal up until the Second World War, cargoes often coming from the adjacent Alloa Coal Company. The colliers were loaded by coaling crane. These powerful cranes were capable of picking up a loaded coal truck of about 25 tons or so (114), and swinging it over the ship where one end was lifted and the contents shot directly into the hold via the end door of the truck. These steam cranes could be surprisingly fast and efficient. They were also installed at Dundee, Granton and Kirkcaldy. Considerable quantities of coal were shipped from the Lanarkshire coalfield via Grangemouth and Bo'ness, which was originally known as Borrowstoness. This old port was the main loading port in the 1860s when about 125,000 tons was shipped. By the 1880s this had fallen, but later revived and by 1914 four coal hoists were in use and shipments continued until the 1940s. The port was home to Love & Stewart, whose vessels were in the Baltic trade, as were Walker & Bain who owned the **Balmaha** 1428/24 and the coaster **Balfron** 362/20 in the 1920s and 1930s. Oldest of the companies was J. Denholm, established in 1851 and active in the Baltic trade.

114.
***The President** of J. Hay & Co., loading coal at Alloa about to receive another truckful.*

The adjacent port of Grangemouth was a later development. The original or old dock was opened in 1843, followed by the Junction Dock in 1859. Coal shipments were small and even by the 1880s were only a little over 10,000 tons. The Carron Dock had been opened in 1882 and coal traffic became important with the opening of the Grange Dock in 1906, which was equipped with four hoists (114). By 1914 some 103,000 tons was being shipped coastwise and there were some seven coal hoists in use. During the 1920s and 1930s shipments continued to rise with 541,000 tons being loaded in 1938. Hay's coasting fleet were active in the coal trade from the Forth ports generally and they had a branch office to handle this business at Grangemouth. By 1948 the tonnage was down to 53,000 tons.

Coal from the Lothians coalfield was handled by Leith and Granton. Shipments from Leith had only reached 72,000 tons by 1914 but were 226,000 tons in the late 1930s when there were three hoists in the Imperial Dock and three in the Edinburgh Dock in use. Considerable quantities were exported to Sweden and Finland particularly via James Cormack's ships which were active in this trade. He had originally begun business in 1872 with the steamer **Ella** 693/70, which he used in the timber trade particularly from Riga. The outward cargo was coal from Leith or other Forth ports. This trade proved very successful and by the 1900s seven ships were employed. The Company continued in the trade until the 1930s, by which time the voyages were more general, but still based on coal out to the Baltic and timber home. Granton did not spring to prominence until the turn of the century although the harbour had been constructed under the Earl of Dalkeith over 50 years earlier. At the beginnning of the First World War shipments were a little under a quarter of a million tons. This was loaded by three 25-ton capacity coal cranes. Shipments continued to rise and in the 1930s were 500,000 to 700,000 tons annually, but were below 10,000 tons by the 1950s.

The main developments were taking place in the Fife coalfield. Kirkcaldy had been used to ship this coal out throughout the early part of the steam era but never in particularly significant quantities and a single 25-ton crane was in use at the turn of the century. Burntisland was the first port to be developed and the West Dock was opened in 1876 by the Burntisland Harbour Commission for the coal trade. Three hydraulic hoists were used, but after a few years these proved insufficient and the East Dock was opened in 1901 with a further three hoists to cater for the increasing coal exports. About 25,000 tons were being shipped coastwise in 1914, with considerable quantities going overseas. Burntisland was acquired by the North British Railway in 1922 and almost immediately came under the London & North Eastern Railway.

However this port had already been overtaken by Methil, which went on to become the most important shipping port for coal in Scotland, the coal coming from the nearby East Fife coalfield. The first or No.1 dock was opened in 1887 with three hydraulic coal hoists and able to accept large sea-going vessels as well as coasters. The traffic was handled by the North British Railway and they soon found it necessary to construct a second dock (No.2), completed in 1897. This was fitted with three improved type hydraulic hoists and backed up by an auxiliary coaling crane. All the hoists were equipped with ramps down which the empty wagons could run by gravity to the sidings. Working flat out 60 wagons an hour could be tipped by one hoist, or about 500,000 tons per year.

Trade continued to increase and by the turn of the century more capacity was needed, and in 1907 Parliamentary powers were obtained to construct the No.3 dock. This much larger dock was provided with a separate entrance and nine coal hoists from Sir W. G. Armstrong-Whitworth, and all were fitted with anti-breakage devices to reduce damage to large coal. Much of the coal went for export but by 1914 about 103,000 tons was going coastwise. The new port attracted several firms to set up as ship-brokers and coal exporters. Among these was Matthew Taylor who opened for business in 1900 and became a shipowner in 1906 when he purchased the **Wans Fell** 300/82. She was a 24 year old iron steamer and was soon put to use in the local coal trade to the northern Scottish ports. The fleet expanded considerably during the First World War so that in 1918 it consisted of **Cairnie** 250/91, **Golfer** 377/91, **Leelite** 404/82, **Rayford** 471/94 and the original **Wans Fell** 300/82. In the 1920s

115.
Letchworth of Newcastle at the coal conveyor in Carron Dock, Grangemouth in 1933.

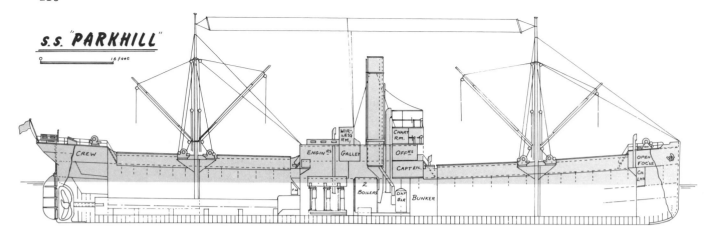

S.S. "PARKHILL"

16 feet

CREW

WIR-LESS RM.

ENGINᴿˢ

GALLEY

CHART RM.

OFFᴿˢ

CAPT ETC.

2 BOILERS

DKᴿ BLR

BUNKER

OPEN FOCLE

CH. LKR

116. Parkhill built in 1923 for Matthew Taylor of Methil.

he acquired larger coasters such as **Plyades** 705/03 which also traded to the south coast and tramp steamers suitable for the Mediterranean trade with coal out and esparto grass home. The company were Admiralty coal agents and often supplied coal to the naval bases at Malta and Gibraltar and so it was logical to have suitable ships. Only occasional voyages were made to the Baltic. The first vessel on the trade was **Aberhill** 1516/15. A new ship was ordered for this trade which was delivered by C. Rennoldson & Co., of South Shields as **Parkhill** 1823/23. She had a deadweight of 2,460 tons on a draft of 17' 1.5" and a light draft of 6' 7.5". The layout was typical for the 1920s, with the crew accommodation aft in the poop and the after hatches on the raised quarterdeck (116). Stowage was generous, offering about 49 cubic feet per ton deadweight. Two further vessels, **Maindy Hill** 1902/11 and **Methil Hill** 1978/17 were acquired. The **Maindy Hill**'s sides had several longitudinal corrugations, a patent design of the period. Thus Matt Taylor had a considerable fleet by 1927 as none of the vessels had been sold, though **Leelite** had been lost by collision with a trawler off the Humber the previous year. The fleet were being kept fully occupied by coal shipments from Methil, which were some half million tons during the 1930s. A look at the harbourmaster's log gives a picture of the fleet's operations. **Golfer, Aberhill** and **Rayford** are trading elsewhere. **Wans Fell** is active in the coal trade from Methil to Wick but on two occasions calls for bunkers while carrying other cargoes. The most regular visitor is **Cairnie** which, in the three month period, makes five voyages to Aberdeen and one each to Peterhead, Burghead and Inverness, also fitting in other local cargoes. **Plyades** is running to the south coast with coal. **Methil Hill** arrives from Grangemouth on two occasions and loads for Oran and later Algiers. **Maindy Hill** arrives from Bona with esparto and loads coal for Algiers. The **Parkhill** is running regularly with coal to London. The fall in trade at the beginning of the 1930s led Matt Taylor to offer his ships for sale and the **Parkhill** was purchased by J. Duncan of Cardiff and became the **Maywood** and so continued in the coal trade. The other large ships had all been lost in various ways by 1941, but further coasters were acquired in the late 1930s to replace losses and sales, though by the end of the Second World War the company was down to three ships. **Methilhill** 648/14, acquired in 1938, was sold for scrap in 1954, leaving **Moorlands** 420/20 and the company's last vessel **Sojourner** 435/20, sold at the end of the 1950s.

Whereas Methil was the Scottish port shipping the most coal out, Aberdeen was the biggest importer, though much of this coal was shipped out again in the form of bunker coal in the Aberdeen-based trawlers. Aberdeen had long been a centre of trade even before the steam age, based on the prosperous farming land in the area. The main harbour was constructed beginning in 1829 and followed by the Victoria Dock which was opened by Queen Victoria in 1848. The Aberdeen Lime Company were already bringing in lime for local farms and they also became active in the coal trade, as did the Aberdeen Commercial Company. The first Aberdeen coal merchants to own their own steamers were the brothers James and Alexander Davidson, who established their business in 1865 as coal, grain and granite merchants. Beginning with sail, they commissioned their first steamer in 1871 from local builder Hall, Russell & Co. She was appropriately named **Bon Accord**, which is the motto of the City of Aberdeen. Her dimensions were 170' x 26' x 14.8' and gross tonnage 469. Her dimensions would make her large enough for the Baltic trade in which the company had already established their sailing vessels, and was probably employed on voyages there as well as bringing in coal for Aberdeen. The general increase in Baltic and Mediterranean trade preoccupied the brothers for the next 20 years. Their fleet grew rapidly with as many as three new vessels a year. This was to continue until the shipping slump at the beginning of the 1880s, which became widespread by 1883. Many owners found themselves unable to operate on the much reduced freight rates and it seems likely as the slump dragged on that the Davidsons decided to sell their ocean fleet and concentrate on their increasing coal business. Steam trawlers were beginning to appear and the general industrialisation and prosperity pushed up coal demand. The company had a yard conveniently placed on Blaikie's Quay and so in 1887 six of the ocean vessels were passed to the Grampian S.S. Co., of Aberdeen and by 1888 the fleet was reduced to two vessels, **Bon Accord** 469/71 and the larger **Ballochbuie** 677/80, also a product of Hall, Russell's yard. The fleet was further reduced on the 6th of November when **Bon Accord** was wrecked off Sunderland.

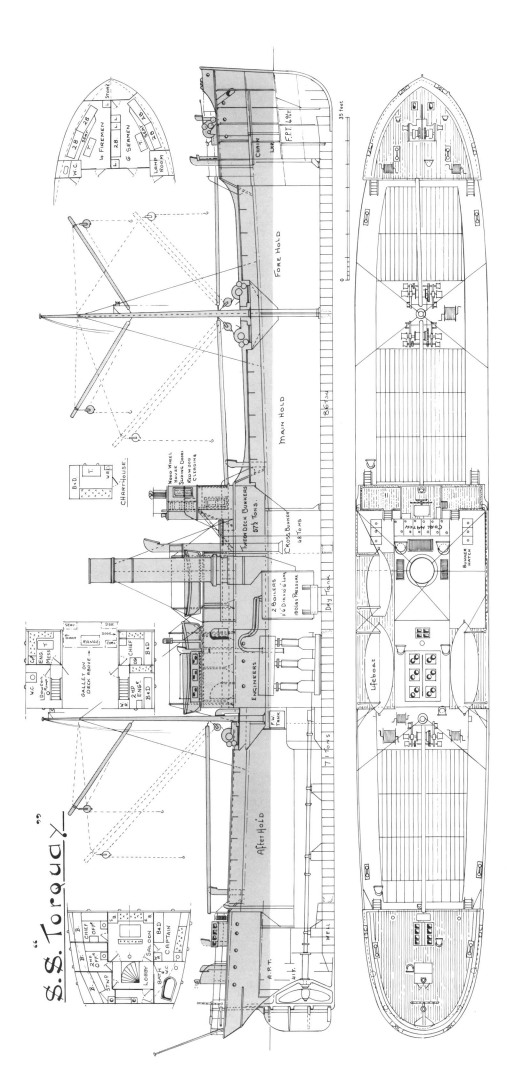

117

117. The **Torquay** had been built for the south of England bunkering trade of Renwick, Wilton & Co., Dartmouth by J. Crown & Sons in 1914. They sold her in the boom at the end of the war to the Turner S.N. Co., Cardiff in 1919 who resold her almost immediately to Manor Line (London) Ltd., who were also Cardiff based. When the slump hit the Cardiff trade, she was sold to J. & A. Davidson of Aberdeen in 1923. The accommodation was rather unusual with the captain, officers and steward in a generous size poop which was at upper deck level rather than on the raised quarter deck. The space below the bridge was used for bunkers. The hatches were a good size for working coal and this is probably why she lasted so long.　　　　Courtesy P.N. Thomas

*118. Coal being discharged on to the Upper Quay, Aberdeen around the turn of the century.
The coal was first loaded into tubs which were then hoisted on deck using the ship's winches.
Once on deck it was transferred to sacks to be carted away. A very labour intensive process
as can be seen from the number of men employed. The old collier dates from around 1870.*

The Company also faced competition in the coal trade from one of their previous employees for
John Ellis set up his own coal business in 1879 and was later joined by Charles McHardy in the
venture. The partnership of Ellis and McHardy had progressed sufficiently by 1881 to take the
steamer **Glassalt** on time charter. In 1887 the partnership decided to purchase **Spray** 606/72. She had
engines amidships and Ellis would have had experience of similar vessels when working for J. & A.
Davidson. She had been built for the coal trade of Pyman, Watson & Co., Cardiff. She was to prove a
very good purchase, serving them until 1932 when the name was perpetuated by a new **Spray** (111).

Adam & Co., whose fleet had paralleled Davidsons' in growth, were later primarily involved in
the Baltic and Mediterranean trades but were also coal merchants in Aberdeen. They began in a
similar way, though beginning earlier with steam. **Hayle** 353/67 was registered in Aberdeen in 1868
and in the early 1870s **Hayle** together with **Courier** 372/50 and the small iron steamer **Richmond**
191/71 had all loaded at Northumberland dock for Aberdeen. They were registered in the name
of J. B. Adam, except for **Courier** which was in the name of Thomas Adam. The big steamer **Thomas
Adam** 767/70, which was registered in the name of J. B. Adam, loaded coal for Dundee on at least
one occasion in 1872. They rapidly developed their ocean interests as the Adam S.S. Co., and later
moved their operations south, though the coal business was continued as Adam Bros., and **Altyre**
1003/78 ran coal regularly to Aberdeen. The Aberdeen Lime Co., continued to develop the coal side
of their business and had **Lady Cathcart** 648/82 built. When she was lost in 1889 she was replaced by
Duchess of Fife 670/90. They also owned smaller steamers for working into smaller harbours. The
Aberdeen coal trade was considerable, with over 431,000 tons being unloaded there in 1888.

A newcomer to the coal trade at the turn of the century was the Aberdeen Coal Co., which was
registered in December 1900. The company was set up by leading trawler owners in Aberdeen who
felt they were being overcharged for bunkers. John Brown of the Aberdeen Steam Trawling and
Fishing Co. became chairman. A yard was acquired on Albert Quay and a collier was ordered from
Mackie and Thompson, this was **Redhall** 841/02, a typical engine-amidships design. The venture prospered and by the end of the First World War the company had two large almost new colliers, **Redhall**
1093/17 and **Ferryhill** 1086/19. In 1920 the company changed its name to the Aberdeen Coal &
Shipping Co., as in the summer the vessels ranged further afield when not so much coal was needed in
Aberdeen. The company's operations were very profitable for the times and in the period 1919-
26 dividends never fell below 10% and in two years were over 20%. It was usual for the ships
to make two voyages a week from the Tyne but on one occasion nearly four voyages were achieved,
even though grab dicharge was not used. The pattern remained unchanged for the next 20 years but
was finally broken by the loss of **Ferryhill** which struck a mine off the Tyne in January 1940. The
Redhall continued until 1959 when with the high costs of operating steamers and falling demand for
coal she was sold for scrap and replaced by a smaller motor coaster **Ferryhill** 567/46.

Next to arrive on the scene was the Northern Co-operative Co. Ltd. whose coal department took
delivery of **Thrift** 506/04 from Hall, Russell. She had the dimensions 168.6' x 26.1' x 10.5' and was

very similar in style to Davidsons' much older **Spray**, as can be seen from the plan (120). The hatches are surprisingly small and loading and discharge could not have been very efficient and it would seem they were influenced in choice of design by the colliers of other local coal merchants rather than the engines-aft vessels used in the trade by the local coaster owners. However, the design had one advantage for them as during the First World War this type of ship was generally not requisitioned and so she was left to ply back and forth to Aberdeen with coal until 1931 when, with prices at a low ebb, a new collier was ordered from Hall, Russell.

The last coal merchant to take up shipowning was C. R. Davidson, who ordered two raised quarter-deck colliers in quick succession from Hall, Russell, **Firth** 406/08 and **Ferryhill** 411/09. **Firth** was torpedoed off the Suffolk coast in 1915 and her sister was sold in 1917. The **Whinhill** which had been built for them just before the war was sold in 1918 and the company ceased shipowning.

Adam Bros., and the Aberdeen Lime Company only just survived the First World War as shipowners and the latter did not replace **Portlethen** 146/08 when she was wrecked off Peterhead in 1923. The self-trimming collier **Ballochbuie** 921/05, which was built for the company, had already gone. J. & A. Davidson operated various old ships and were probably feeling the pressure of marine losses and the increased competition from the other merchants who moved into shipowning around the turn of the century. In 1923, with falling prices, they took the opportunity to replace the ageing **Brixham** 501/85 with the newer and larger **Torquay** 870/14. The company had been forced to purchase various ships at short notice over the previous 20 years as they had several marine casualties; **Violante** 863/83 was wrecked in 1899 on a voyage from Aberdeen to Sunderland and the replacement **Loch Leven** 851/78 was wrecked in 1902 on the Farne Islands. A replacement for this vessel was obtained in the form of **Advent** in 1905 and this vessel plus two purchased as replacements were all lost in the First World War. However, their luck changed with **Torquay** 870/14 (117) which served Davidsons for the next 37 years. Their main coal supplies came from the Londonderry collieries, but coal from Bedlington and Cooper & Cowpen was also taken. Bunker coal was still important throughout the 1920s and 1930s but total shipments of coal were slowly falling and the number of coal burning trawlers fell rapidly following the Second World War, and so the old **Torquay** had less coal to carry and as she was 46 years old, she was scrapped and replaced by a smaller motor ship in 1960, but the name **Torquay** was retained as it had become so closely connected with J. & A. Davidson.

Ellis & McHardy were more fortunate, to handle their increasing trade they purchased **Firsby** (ex **Denaby**) 1150/91 which had been built for the Denaby Main Colliery Company. She was registered at Aberdeen in 1904 and soon became locally known as 'big Spray' as she was quite a bit larger than **Spray** 632/72, which continued in service. The 'big Spray' was torpedoed during the First World War. **Test** 466/90 became the replacement. She had been built by Murray Bros., Dumbarton, for W. A. Granger of Belfast as **Number Twelve**, a most unusual name for a rather attractive coaster as the plan below shows. The whale-back stern was a feature of the period as was the narrow engine casing. The hull had rather fine lines and although this led to a good speed with low fuel consumption, the forward hold could probably not be filled completely with coal, so the smaller forward

119. Test.

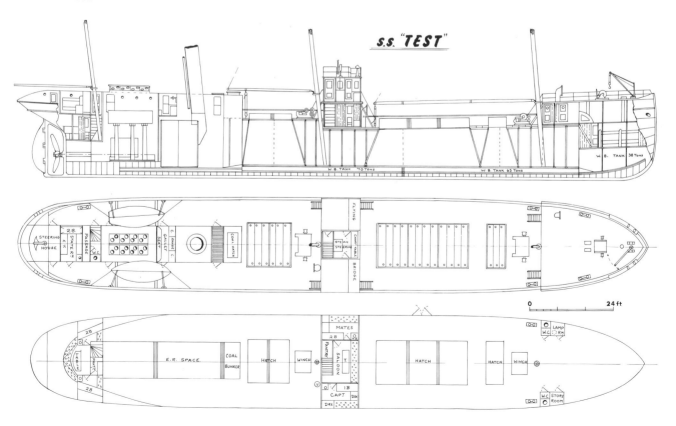

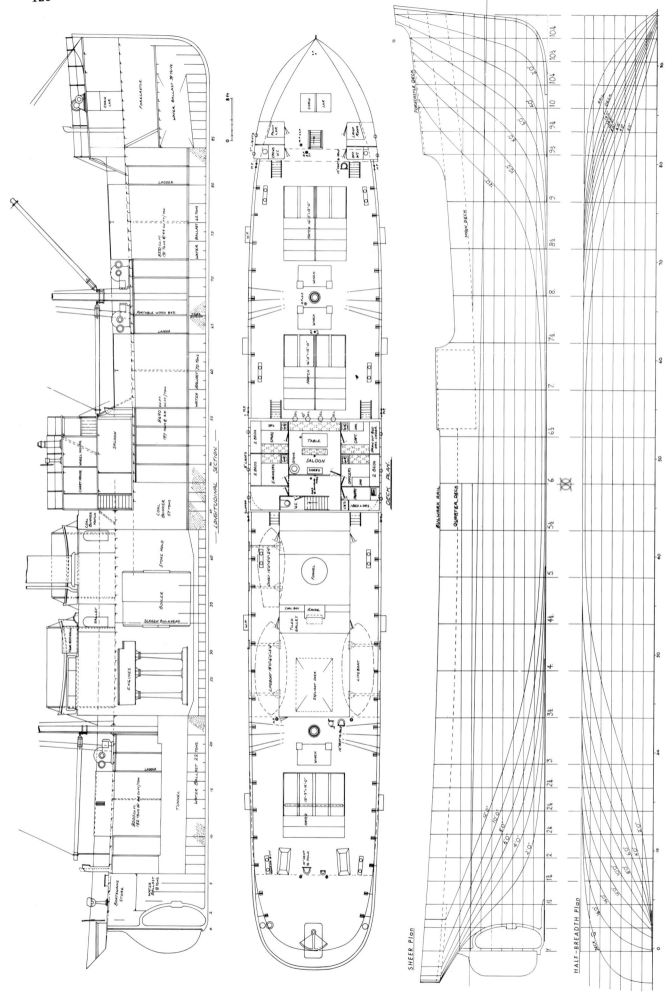

LONGITUDINAL SECTION

DECK PLAN

SHEER Plan

HALF-BREADTH Plan

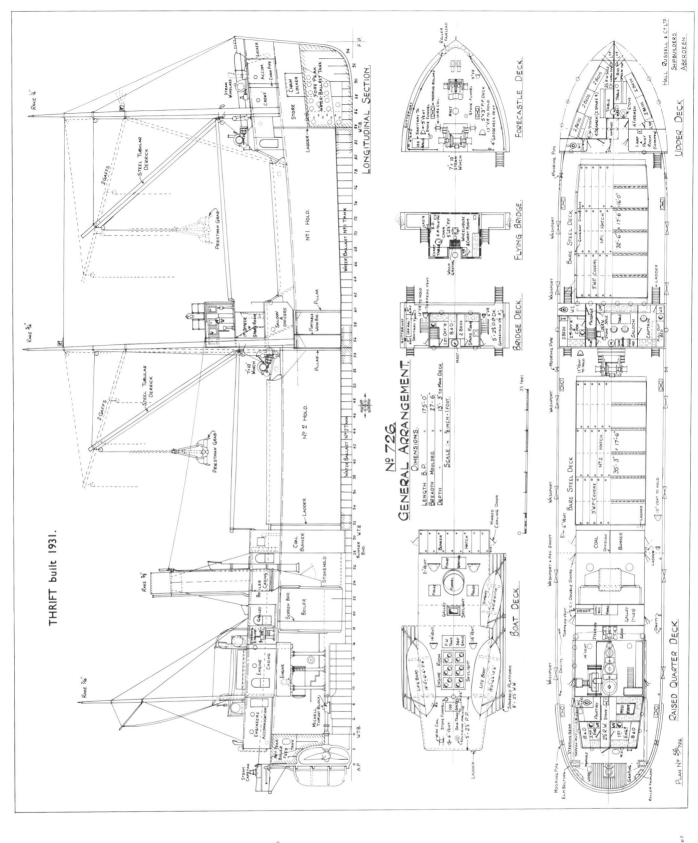

THRIFT built 1931.

RAKE 1/4"

RAKE 5/16"

RAKE 5/16"

RAKE 5/16"

STEAM WINDLASS
2 GAFFS
STEEL TUBULAR DERRICK
ACCOM.
CREWS
LOCKER
CHAIN PIPE
STORE
CHAIN LOCKER
FORE PEAK
WATER BALLAST TANK
LADDER
PREESTMAN GRAB
WATER BALLAST No 1 TANK
No 1 HOLD.
W.T.B.

F.P.

LONGITUDINAL SECTION.

2 GAFFS
STEEL TUBULAR DERRICK
WHEEL
SPARK ROOM
STORE ROOM
SALOON OFFICERS
PILLAR
PORTABLE WOOD BHD
PILLAR
7'-10" WINCH
PREESTMAN GRAB
WATER BALLAST No 2 TANK
No 2 HOLD.
W.T.B.

RAKE 5/16"

ENGINEERS ACCOMMODATION
ENGINE CASING
ENGINE
MICHELL THRUST BLOCK
AFT PEAK BOILER FEED TANK
STEAM CAPSTAN
A.P.

COAL BUNKER
BOILER CASING
GALLEY
STOKEHOLD
BOILER
SCREEN BHD
ENGINE
BUNKER BHD
W.T.B.

No 726.
GENERAL ARRANGEMENT.
DIMENSIONS.
LENGTH B.P. = 175'-0"
BREADTH MOULDED = 27'-6"
DEPTH = 13'-3" TO MAIN DECK
SCALE := 1/8 INCH = 1 FOOT.

35 feet

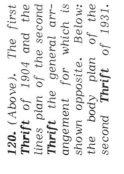

FORECASTLE DECK.
FLYING BRIDGE.
BRIDGE DECK.
BOAT DECK.

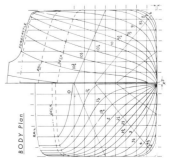

UPPER DECK.
BARE STEEL DECK
No 1. HATCH 32'-6" x 17'-6" x 16'-0"
3 W.P. COVERS
LADDER
BARE STEEL DECK
No 2. HATCH 35'-3" x 17'-6"
3 W.P. COVERS
COAL DIVISION
BUNKER
LADDER
GALLEY (TILED)
DRESSER
RAISED QUARTER DECK.

HALL RUSSELL & CO LTD
SHIPBUILDERS
ABERDEEN

PLAN No 56/726.

120. (Above). The first *Thrift* of 1904 and the lines plan of the second *Thrift* the general arrangement for which is shown opposite. Below: the body plan of the second *Thrift* of 1931.

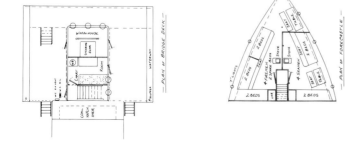

PLAN OF BRIDGE DECK.
PLAN OF FORECASTLE.

BODY Plan

25 feet

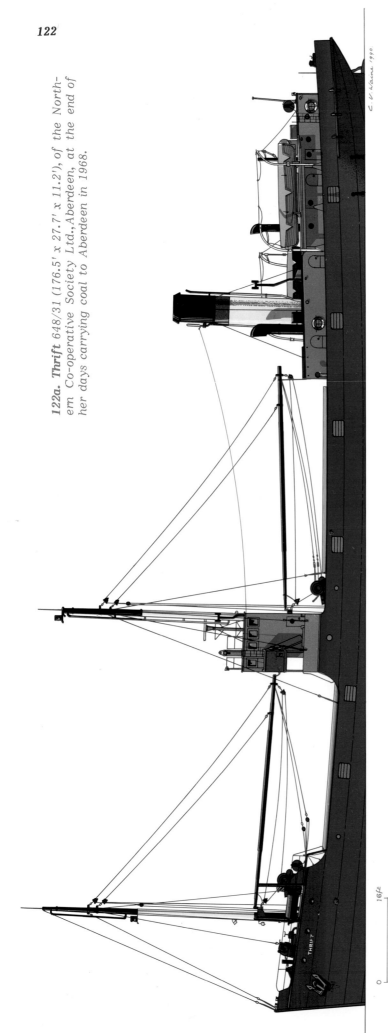

122a. Thrift 648/31 (176.5' x 27.7' x 11.2'), of the Northern Co-operative Society Ltd.,Aberdeen, at the end of her days carrying coal to Aberdeen in 1968.

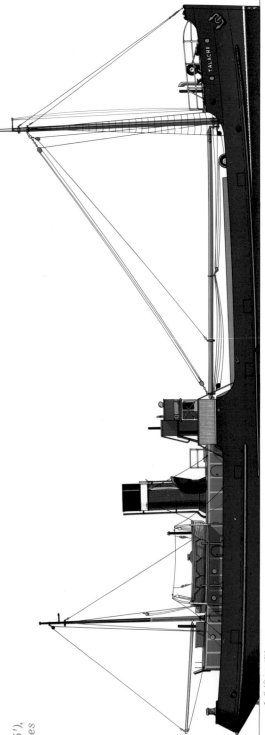

122b. Talacre 301/17 (130.5' x 23.2' x 9.5'), Point of Ayr Collieries, Ltd., North Wales in later years with the flying bridge.

hatch was used to adjust the trim. The forecastle was particularly long and the space was not well used forward compared with later designs. **Spray** 632/72 and **Test** 466/90 continud to serve the company until 1932 when a single larger coaster was built for them named **Spray** 963/32. She was a neat engines-aft vessel, (111). Although there had been some fall in bunker coal requirements it was still a very important part of Ellis & McHardy's business and so **Spray** was a regular visitor to Sunderland and often took cargoes from Lambton drops. She survived the war and continued to carry coal to Aberdeen where it was now at last discharged by grab. She was replaced by another new **Spray** in 1962 built by Hall, Russell of similar capacity but now a long raised quarterdeck motor coaster of all aft design.

Ellis & McHardy were not the first to order a new steam collier in the 1930s as the Northern Co-operative Society Ltd., as they had become, received their vessel a year earlier from Hall, Russell. The new vessel incorporated the most up to date design features then appearing on steam coasters (121), though one interesting retention from the past was a mizzen mast which was removed during the Second World War to make way for an anti-aircraft gun. The hatches were as large as was practical and the steel derricks were arranged to work Priestman grabs so that the new **Thrift** 648/31 could discharge herself. However the old method of discharge using gaffs and gin-blocks was also provided. They were used when the coal was shovelled into tubs in the hold and hoisted up by winch and taken ashore (see 118). The plan shows gaffs with three blocks allowing several gangs to work each hold. Two gaffs were initially fitted to each mast. To make the hatches as long as possible the foremast was placed well forward on the forecastle while the main was trunked into the back of the bridge structure. Accommodation and equipment was to a high standard with separate W.Cs being provided for the engineers, officers and crew. The **Thrift** survived the Second World War and became an institution on the Aberdeen coal run though she had a narrow escape when she grounded in fog at Robin Hood's Bay in 1957. She discharged her last cargo of coal, which was from Methil, on the 5th of September 1968 and four days later departed for Blyth to be broken up by Hughes Bocklow, the last of the Aberdeen steam colliers. However she was not the last to be built, for this was the smaller **Mount Battock** 396/39 which was built for the "Dodds" Steam Fishing Co., of which Lewis' were managers. She had a single long hatch for easy loading and discharge of bunker coal. Freight rates had been rising in the latter part of the 1930s and as the company had a large fleet of steam trawlers they probably decided it was cheaper to have their own collier. She was discharged at Lewis' own wharf by grab into their coal yard adjacent to their shipyard. She continued in the trade after coming under North Eastern Fisheries in 1958 and was eventually scrapped in 1968 a few months before **Thrift** (122).

Dundee also had a few colliers, perhaps best remembered of which were those of Robert Taylor & Sons of Dundee who began business as coal merchants in 1872. The steamer **Rose** was acquired in 1881 as the company now had branches at Aberdeen and Montrose. Expansion continued and **Thistle** 401/83 was built for the company but was lost soon after delivery on a voyage from Sunderland to Montrose. The company then purchased various secondhand ships and entered the Baltic trade. Among the vessels purchased was the old Dublin steamer **Arbutus** 356/54. At the turn of the century **Alice Taylor** 648/91 was in the coastal coal trade and **Nellie** 1447/76 was tramping. The latter was sold in 1902 and the **Alice Taylor** was wrecked in 1918 leaving the company without ships until the coaster **Inchbrayock** 363/09 was purchased in 1927 and after five years sold to Osborn & Wallis (see page 89). The old Aberdeen collier **Thrift** 506/04 had been purchased the previous year and renamed **Berryden**. She survived the war and was not sold until 1946, when she passed to Maltese owners. A replacement, **Brightside** 476/30, had been acquired in 1945 but was wrecked in September 1949. The company had by this time already invested in a motor vessel, **Mount Blair** 553/49, which served until 1961 when the company gave up shipowning, which was to be the pattern followed by other Scottish coal merchants in the years to come.

7.

124. *Isle of Dursey* 963/83, Captain Robert Coxon, from a drawing by his son F. C. Coxon.
Courtesy Sea Breezes

East Coast Colliers

Newcastle

The 1870s were years of great expansion for the Newcastle fleet and the coal trade. The home market, primarily London, was increasing slowly but much of this coal was carried by the colliers of the London merchants or the railways and so most of the vessels were built to carry Newcastle coal to the Continent, Baltic and Mediterranean. The trade was also helped by the need for pit props and timber generally, so there was always a likely return cargo for ships carrying coal to the Baltic. Similarly the high grade iron ore from Spain was much in demand by the steel makers of the area and this was the usual return cargo in the Bay trade, while grain was brought home from the Black Sea. There were no defined home trade limits and the ships made very varied voyages and these fleets are more properly considered as the beginning of the ocean steam tramps.

After the expansion of the 1870s and early 1880s the ensuing slump drastically reduced local fleets. The effects were most strongly felt in the Baltic, Bay and Mediterranean trades. Building costs had tended to fall and ships had become more efficient so that as the fleets overtook the available trade owners were able to stand some drop in freight rates, but as the number of cargoes available failed to rise sufficiently to absorb ships still arriving from the shipyards the situation became serious and companies could not carry on, often because under the old 64ths system shareholders in a ship were responsible for trading debts incurred by their ship. Consequently they were soon pressing managers to sell their ships and avoid further personal losses. Some of the ships went to Scandinavian owners and often these ships were regular visitors to their former home ports, as there had always been close ties between shippers and Scandinavian merchants. The lower operating costs of Scandinavian owners were taken advantage of by British owners who sometimes set up flag of convenience companies. Those companies who had begun to expand beyond the intermediate trade continued to do so, establishing themselves in ocean tramping. The decline in coastal and short sea colliers belonging to Newcastle, and to a lesser extent Sunderland owners was also encouraged by the expansion of the London collier fleets.

The change is well illustrated by Dixon, Robson & Co., and Culliford & Clarke. Dixon, Robson & Co., were building vessels aimed at the Bay trade and established their fleet in the early 1880s which in 1883 consisted of **Isle of Elba** 1006/83, **Isle of Arran** 679/81, **Isle of Bute** 1117/82, **Isle of Cyprus** 1061/83 and **Isle of Dursey** 963/83. The **Isle of Bute** was wrecked at Bilbao on the 10th of December, but was almost immediately replaced by the **Isle of France** 1048/83. They carried coal out to Spain, returning with iron-ore, but they also carried coal to London. The **Isle of Dursey** was a typical vessel of the period with engines amidships, square rigged on the foremast, and fore and aft rigged on the mainmast. She was slightly smaller than the average new building, measuring 210.1' x 31.3' x 14.1' with a bridge deck amidships and further aft a raised quarterdeck. The masts were placed at the fore end of each hold (124), though the hull followed the usual pattern, the main engine, built by the Wallsend Slipway, was a triple expansion of unusual pattern in which the high pressure was arranged above the intermediate pressure cylinder so that only about the same length of engine room was needed as that for a two cylinder compound commonly fitted. The arrangement meant that a single crank and connecting rod was used for both cylinders with the piston rod extended up through the top of the lower cylinder. The dimensions were 15.75", 22" and 44" with a stroke of 33" with steam supplied at 150 lbs per square inch from a single scotch boiler (125). This allowed

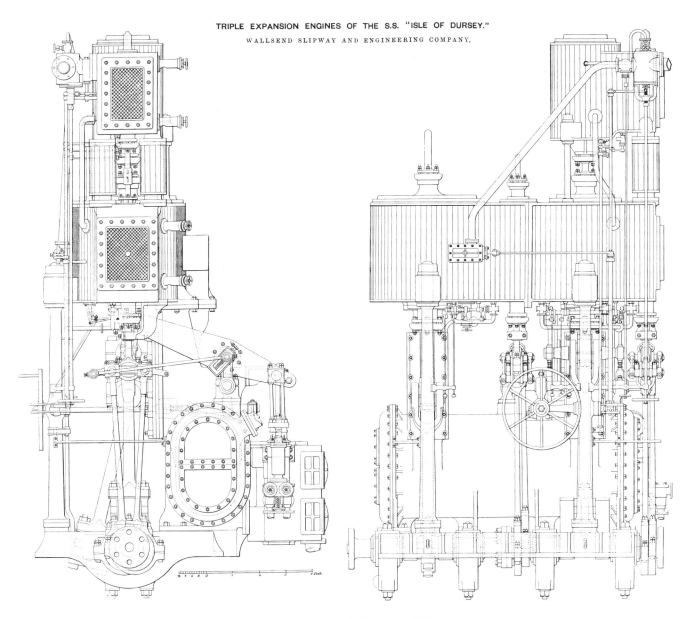

125. *The unusual triple expansion machinery of the* **Isle of Dursey.** Courtesy E. W. Paget-Tomlinson

the same amount of hold space to be retained but gave about a 20% economy in coal consumption and so allowed more cargo to be carried. The machinery was designed by Mr. Alexander Taylor of Newcastle. The steam yacht **Isa**, built in 1878 was fitted with similar machinery so some experience had already been gained. The machinery attracted some interest in 'Recent Practice in Marine Engineering'. Careful trials were carried out by the machinery builders, Wallsend Slipway Co. Ltd., Newcastle, and a set of indicator diagrams (how the steam pressure was converted into motion) were taken during a voyage from Middlesbrough to London. Under normal voyage conditions a speed of 9 knots was maintained with the engines developing 500 indicated horsepower at 72 r.p.m. and pressure of 143 lbs/sq.in. The boiler was fired by quick-burning north country coal, as usually used in coasters, and required just under 8 tons/day which worked out at about 1.5 lbs per i.h.p. per hour. Steam jackets were fitted to the high and intermediate pressure cylinders. The machinery proved economical. **Isle of Dursey** 1000/83 and her slightly larger sister **Isle of Iona** 1139/89 were often employed in the Goole coal trade which was opening up at the time. The voyages were to French, Belgian and Dutch ports, but the trading pattern was quite general with voyages to Spain and as far as Africa. During the 1890s the vessels were sold off to Norwegian, Dutch, Swedish and Italian owners in almost every case and the company went in for fewer large ocean tramps. The Isles Steam Shipping Co. Ltd., which owned the ships managed by Dixon, Robson carried a most unusual funnel mark, that of a white lighthouse showing a red light standing on a green base on the black funnel.

Culliford & Clarke, who were Sunderland based originally, had a fleet of 13 vessels by 1884 but by 1904 the fleet was reduced to two of the larger vessels, **Douro** 1644/79 and **Charrington** 1770/81 which were over 20 years old. The company dropped out of shipowning in 1906 but continued as agents and coal shippers. They returned to ship management in the 1930s based in London and had a number of ships during the Second World War, all old secondhand steamers such as **Glen Tilt** 871/20. They also took over management of the High Hook S.S. Co., owners of **Highwear** 1173/36 and **Highwood** 1177/36 which had been originally managed by the Springwell Shipping Co. when built. The ships were rapidly sold at the end of the war and management of the High Hook ships passed to E. R. Newbigin. Adam Brothers & Co., managed the colliers **Charles Mitchell** 776/65 and **Rouen** 751/76 but later went in for larger ships.

Edward Eccles managed to keep his old steamers running for many years in the coal trade and he had the same fleet: **Kingmoor** 844/72, **Kingscote** 1003/83, **Kingsley** 679/81 and **Edward Eccles** 797/72 in 1907 as he had twenty three years earlier. Popular runs were to London and Hamburg. Some coal cargoes carried in 1904 were 17 August 1904, **Kingmoor** Tyne to Rendserg, 20 July 1904, **Kingsley**, Tyne to Fechamp and **Edward Eccles** on the same day, coal to Brunsbittell at 3/9d per ton. The vessels ranged in length from 180 to 220 feet with engines amidships and most had raised quarterdecks. Their size made them useful where there were size restrictions or where merchants could not accept larger cargoes. Trading conditions began to improve slowly and with the demise of the collier brig and schooner, the engines-aft coaster came into service for the smaller harbours and coal cargoes. Steam coal was now needed in the more prosperous country districts as steam traction engines were in general use for threshing and some ploughing. One of the first owners was T. Thompson & Sons, who had begun with small sailing vessels and by 1904 had five vessels, including the new **Coaster** 269/03 (126). The company soon after came under the management of Robinson, Brown as 'T' Steam Coasters Ltd., which was formed in 1906. There was steady expansion with new vessels joining the fleet most years up to the First World War, many with names ending in 'er' such as **Quaysider** 595/13 which had the good deadweight capacity of 700 tons on a draft of 12'9" aft while most coasters of this capacity required nearer 14 feet, so she was always busy taking larger consignments of coal to the smaller harbours. The vessels were by no means confined to the coal trade although very acive in it and this was the case with most owners except for the few vessels belonging to coal companies. **Harton** 530/72 belonged to the Harton Coal Co., and was managed for many years by W. H. Parkes & Son of Newcastle. Unlike many of her contemporaries she had engines aft. When sold at the turn of the century she was purchased by the Hetton Coal Company for whom T. W. Jacques of Sunderland acted as managers. W. Swanston & Sons managed the old **Carbon** 459/55 for coal owner M. J. Hedley and went on to own a few colliers themselves. The fleet at the end of the 1890s consisted of **Boldon** 1109/89, **Dalton** 1275/77, **Colstrup** 482/74 and **Holmside** 842/93. The latter vessel came to London and was given the number 125 by the Coal Factors Society as soon as she went into service in 1893. There was little change in the fleet until the 1920s when a new company was formed, by which time **Dalton** was almost 50 years old. William Milburn of London and Newcastle (who are probably better remembered as one of the constituents of Port Line) acted as managers for the Ashington Coal Co., who had **Ashington** 885/92 and **Woodhorn** 1283/94 for a number of years around the turn of the century.

Though this was the age of the steam collier the weather could play a considerable part, as this report by the Tyneside correspondent of the Shipping Record for the 24th of January 1912 illustrates: "Such a severe south easterly gale as that which visited our shores last week is fortunately seldom experienced. The storm lasted unabated for three days and nights and played havoc with shipping. The story of the loss of **Wistow Hall** (3314/90) with 53 lives on the iron-bound Aberdeenshire coast makes pathetic reading as does that of the loss of the old Tyne collier **Frederick Snowdon** (725/66) with all hands. Besides these and other total losses there is a long list of casualties and shipping was completely dislocated. Steamers only commenced to arrive in the port on Friday and Saturday having in many cases been sheltering in Bridlington Bay or Portland. For three days not a single vessel was able to make for Blyth, Sunderland or Seaham as entry was impossible. The Tyne, however, once more proved its value as a harbour of refuge. Coal traffic was suspended for several days and collieries were laid idle by want of ships and coal was offered cheaply on the market and subsequently the scarcity of colliers for prompt loading led to a sharp advance in freights especially in the coasting trade." This sort of fluctuation in freight rates was a regular winter feature of the coal trade.

Not all Newcastle owners abandoned the Baltic and continental trade and one company to grow during the 1890s and 1900s was John Ridley, Son & Tully who, in 1884, had just the two ships **Lurline** 1033/71 and the larger **Storm Queen** 2129/80, lost on a voyage from Sevastopol to Rotterdam in 1888. They steadily purchased secondhand tonnage, which had often seen quite a few years service, under the guiding hand of James E. Tully. By 1904 he had seven vessels, largest of which was **Eleanor**

126. Coaster was managed for many years by Robinson, Brown of Newcastle. World Ship Society

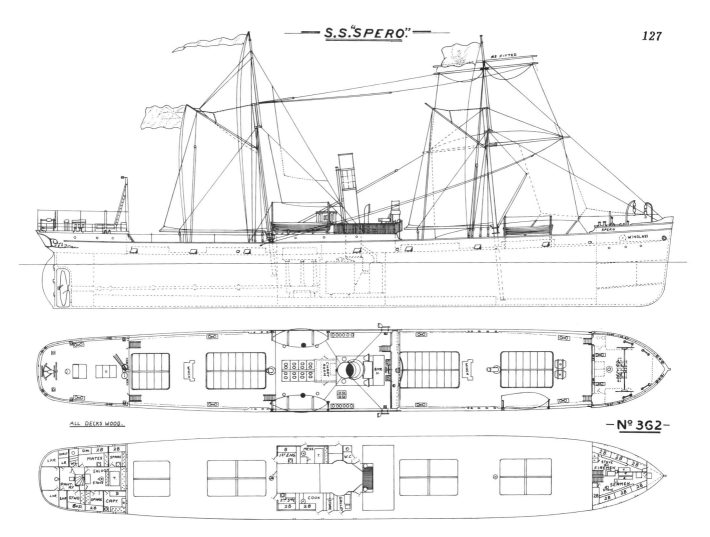

127. *The* **Spero** *of 1878. Supports for a canvas poop awning indicate Bay/Mediterranean trades. Note prominent pole compass on poop. The after winch placed between the hatches suggests discharge using gaffs, see photo 118.*
Courtesy Tyne & Wear Museums

1980/88 and was to remain in the fleet until after the First World War. Most were smaller vessels built in the 1860s and 70s, such as **Constantine** 753/66. Apart from these vessels he also managed the Tyneside Line Ltd., which had seven similar vessels including Stephenson Clarke's old collier **Gracie** 1275/79 which was purchased in 1900, (50). This company had one new ship **Greenwood** 1117/03 which joined the fleet the previous year.

Further new tonnage was added and the company expanded into the ocean trade during the next 20 years. They also managed the Screw Collier Co. Ltd., which was formed about 1908 and took delivery of **Constantine** 1459/09. This collier was put into the London coal trade and was given the number 69 by the Coal Factors Society. The vessels were running on the east coast during the First World War. The captain of **Eglantine** 1312/78 ran aground on Filey Brig in April 1915 while steering an erratic course evading a submarine, on the basis of a sighting of what was believed to be a periscope. The vessel was a total loss and it was accepted as a war risk loss. The company took delivery of further new vessels of a similar size and passed out of existence as shipowners about 1920 when **West Quarter** 1548/10 was transferred to the Tyneside Line (1920) Ltd. This company was formed in 1920 by the Tully family and had a paid up capital of £297,536. They sold their smaller colliers and went into ocean trading although they remained coal shippers until the firm sold up in 1940. J. E. Tully also controlled the Aydon S.S. Co. Ltd., which had been formed in April 1914 to own the first **Aydon** 1735/14. She was replaced by a new vessel **Aydon** 1928/23 and put on the London trade where she was allotted collier No. 52 while **Shildon** 2159/22 received No. 13, but this vessel was placed under the ownership of the Tyneside Line. They were both sold in the mid-1930s.

Another company to grow considerably during the period was the Pelton S.S. Co. Ltd. It was registered in May 1899 but the firm's predecessors had been trading for over 30 years. The original partners were R. B. Fenwick & J. Reay who were based at the Pelton Colliery Offices. They began shipowning in the boom of the mid-1870s. **Pelton** 761/76 was delivered by C. Mitchell with the dimensions 217.9' x 29.2' x 16.4' in 1876 and carried a fairly extensive sail plan (143). The layout was typical of the period with a single continuous deck as up to this time the raised quarterdeck steamer had not been perfected. The ship had McIntyre tanks in the holds but no other ballast. The crew were forward below the open forecastle, officers and captain aft in the poop with the engines amidships. The hatches were much larger than those fitted in **Hugh Taylor** built 8 years previously (18) A prominent feature of the bridge was the pole compass, placed there to reduce the effect of the magnetic iron hull. By the time **Spero** 871/78 was delivered two years later various changes had been made, the bridge deck was fully extended out to the sides of the ship and aft to the end of the engine-room skylight (127). The pole compass was also moved aft and had a prominent ladder for those wishing to inspect it and a conventional binnacle for the helmsman amidships. He also had to be careful if the vessel was shifting in port with the bunker hatch open as there was little room between it and the ships wheel. Interestingly the hatches were somewhat smaller on the later vessel possibly due to strength problems or to make the vessel more suitable for deck cargoes such as timber. Significantly, the McIntyre tanks (double bottom), had been extended under the boiler room and raised aft to plate over the awkward 'v' shaped area in the stern on either side of the propellor shaft. Additional ballast was provided by the fitting of an aft peak tank. Larger and improved versions of these vessel were developed leading to the four hatch tramp which became the backbone of Newcastle fleets.

Pelton was lost after only a few years service on a voyage from Cardiff to Le Havre with coal. **Spero** 871/78 served the company for 21 years until lost in collision off Scarborough in August 1899. She was later raised and broken up for scrap. The fleet built up steadily and in 1885 consisted of **Spero** 871/78, **Presto** 910/79, **Tempo** 1062/81, **Vivo** 1169/83 and one secondhand ship, **Great Yarmouth** 790/66 which had been built for the Great Eastern Railway. She stranded in the Baltic on the 28th of September 1887 and was eventually abandoned as a total loss the following month. The company was by now using names of musical terms ending in 'o'.

The company tended to maintain its fleet by purchasing new and secondhand vessels mostly to replace losses. During the 1880s vessels came from local builders such as T. & W. Smith, but **Brio** 1108/91 came from the Campbelltown Shipbuilding Co. In 1899 H. S. Gardiner took over the Fenwick interest and the new partnership of Gardiner and Reay registered themselves as the Pelton S.S. Company and moved to offices in Lombard Street, Newcastle. By this time the fleet consisted of **Presto** 910/79, **Tempo** 1062/81, **Moto** 1397/85, **Sinloo** 1086/82, **Rondo** 1155/89, **Brio** 1108/91, **Primo** 1372/98 and the newly delivered **Spero** 1199/99, the earlier **Spero** 760/78 having just been lost in collision. The company had steadily prospered while others had cut back or gone out of business. The Pelton S.S. Co., continued to grow in the better trading conditions prior to the First World War adding almost one vessel annually to their fleet. The vessels were all built to a high standard and well equipped as the contemporary press noted when **Tempo** 1379/11 was delivered which had a service speed of 10.5 knots. She was taken up as an ammunition carrier throughout the First World War by the Admiralty.

The ships worked in the coal trade on the coast and to the continent ranging as far as the Mediterranean. The colliers were fully occupied during the First World War and to replace losses and expand the fleet, vessels were purchased almost new from other owners. One of the vessels to join the fleet in this way was **Presto** which had been built as **Dunelm** 964/16 a few months previously. She was one of the smallest ships they owned, for most of the fleet were larger 4-hatch types with engines amidships. They were probably attracted by the large self-trimming hatches and good cargo gear (87). She was allotted collier No. 136 by the Coal Factors Society in 1919 and was sold to Stone & Rolfe in 1934.

By 1918 the fleet had risen to 16 vessels ranging in size from **Presto** 964/16 to **Zelo** 2339/17. Just under half the fleet had collier numbers for the coal trade to the Thames and in the 1920s it was the vessels which had collier numbers which tended to be retained in the fleet. One of these was **Lesto** 1893/18 which was allotted No. 140 in August 1919. She was almost identical with **Lightfoot** and her sisters (135), built for Witherington & Everett. The main differences were the bunker hatch placed in front of the bridge and folding masts. Several wartime features such as rearranged poop accommodation to house three gunners were incorporated (128). Their main gun would have been on the poop above. In such a position it was considered a defensive weapon under the Geneva convention. The other major feature was the fitting of a radio ('Marconi House') with accommodation for two radio operators. The remainder of the accommodation was on fairly conventional lines, the crew

128. Lesto: *Accommodation*
Courtesy P. N. Thomas

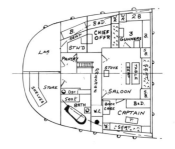

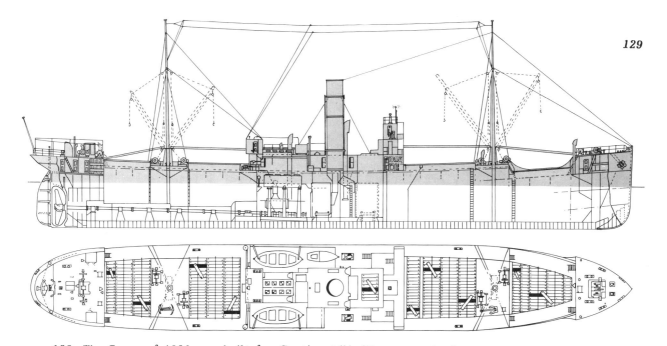

129. *The* **Spero** *of 1920 was built for Continent/Mediterranean trades.*   Courtesy P.N.Thomas

forward had mess rooms separate from their bunks, which was better than usual, while amidships the engineers also have comfortable accommodation which they shared with the second officer. Surprisingly the captain was aft but he would have the use of the chartroom below the bridge which had a bed, chart table and stove. She could load a full deadweight of 2,800 tons including 148 tons of bunkers on an even keel without much difficulty, stowing at about 47 cubic feet per ton. For the run to London and back only the cross bunker was needed, the extra capacity under the bridge was available for more distant voyages. Her registered dimensions were 268.0' x 37.9' x 17.6' with a draft of 19'9" which was about the maximum for the Northumberland dock on the Tyne. She was constructed by J. Crown & Sons who built colliers in some numbers for Newcastle owners. The hatches were large and she was self-trimming and this is probably why she lasted on the coal trade (see page 213) until the summer of 1954 when she was delivered to Rosyth for breaking up.

Somewhat larger vessels were built for the continental trade in the 1920s, smallest of which was **Spero** 1960/20 which had the dimensions 269.9' x 40.2' x 17.4'. Thus she was essentially the same length as **Lesto** and **Lightfoot** but over 2 feet greater in beam (129). **Spero** also had the raised quarterdeck extended much further forward with accommodation amidships. Note the awning aft to keep the poop cool in the Mediterranean. Murdoch and Murray also delivered a larger version to the company, **Moto** 2693/20, who was allotted collier No. 105 in April 1920, and so even these larger ships did some coal to London. Two single deck sisters **Stesso** 2290/22 and **Zelo** 2294/21 were delivered by Austin's and **Zelo** undertook a most unusual task when she assisted in raising the submarine H.M.S. Thetis.

At 0930 on Thursday the 1st of June 1939, H.M.S. Thetis left the Birkenhead Yard of her builders, Messrs Cammell Laird Ltd., for diving trials in Liverpool Bay. She had on board beside her normal complement of 5 officers and 48 ratings, 9 other submarine officers, 7 Admiralty civilian staff, and a number of employees from Cammell Laird. There were also staff from a Liverpool catering firm supplying the lunches and of course a Mersey Pilot. In all there were 103 persons on board. She seemed to take a long time to dive once she had reached the pre-arranged diving position, and when at last she did so, some onlookers on the attendant tug Grebe Cock remarked that all did not seem well, as the final dive did not seem controlled. When, after the agreed three hours of the test dive, she did not surface, their worst fears were realised. At 0740 hrs on the 2nd of June her stern reappeared above water which was spotted by H.M.S. Brazen, one of the searching destroyers. Hopes were raised that it might be possible to rescue the trapped men by burning holes in the exposed stern plating, even though it was realised that there could be little hope of finding all alive after such a long time submerged and no fresh air supply. She had on board more than double the number she was designed to accommodate, and consequently the available air would be soon polluted. Four of the trapped men were able to get out by using the Davies Submarine Escape Apparatus, including Captain Oram, with details of further escape plans. They were rescued between 0800 hrs and 1000 hrs on the 3rd and that afternoon, as the tide turned, Thetis swung round in the wires attempting to keep her stern on the surface, the wire parted and she plunged back on to the floor of the sea. All hope of rescuing the remaining 99 men in Thetis had to be abandoned, but salvage plans were formulated. The one finally adopted was novel and involved the use of a surface ship of about the same dimensions and deadweight as the ill-fated submarine, and of shallow draught in ballast conditions. A quick but thorough search about the country revealed that **Zelo**, one of the Pelton fleet of colliers, was lying at Cardiff under Admiralty Charter, which was revoked within hours and the vessel placed at the disposal of the salvage contractors. Details of the operation are described in 'The Admiralty regrets' by C. E. T. Warren and James Benson. She was steamed to Birkenhead and equipped for the task ahead of her. This involved building of extra temporary accommodation for some of the salvage crews and the rigging of eight huge beams, built up from long baulks, projecting about five feet at each side. Wires were passed under the Thetis and secured over the beams so that as the tide rose **Zelo** would gently lift Thetis off the bottom and be towed slowly and carefully towards the shallower waters of Moelfre Bay. A course had been carefully plotted to ensure a safe passage.

Bad weather intervened and **Zelo** had to return to Birkenhead for attention and repairs. On her return to the scene of operations things went fairly smoothly. On each succeeding tide **Zelo** lifted the Thetis and moved her a little nearer the safety of Moelfre Bay, where on Sunday 3rd September 1939 she finally grounded, and **Zelo's** task was done. She returned to Birkenhead to have the temporary equipment removed and then returned to normal duties. A plaque commemorating her achievement was presented to her. Thetis was re-built and renamed, and as H.M.S. Thunderbolt served with distinction until she was destroyed off the coast of Sicily by the Italian sloop "Cicogna" on March 14th 1943, all of her crew perishing. The **Zelo** was fortunate to be on charter to the Admiralty for the consumption of coal by the Navy had fallen from almost 2,500,000 tons in 1918 to 180,000 tons.

The Pelton Colliery and associated Pelton S.S. Company were major shareholders in Sir R.S. Gardiner's Rodney S.S. Co. Ltd., registered in December 1915. The first ship, which had already been delivered by Austin's, was **Alice Marie** 2210/15 and she was soon joined by a sister, **Rose Marie** 2220/16. Both were torpedoed within a few weeks of each other, **Rose Marie** in December 1917 and **Alice Marie** in January 1918. **Ashtree**, which had been purchased from Cardiff owners in 1919 by the Pelton S.S. Co. and renamed **Spero** was transferred as a replacement and became **Rose Marie** 1579/09. A new **Alice Marie** (130) was delivered from Austin's in 1920 and although having the same dimensions as her earlier sister, 280.0' x 40.5' x 18.4' she had the raised quarterdeck continued further forward and no bridge deck amidships. The ships were run alongside those of the Pelton S.S. Co. Both were placed on the London coal trade in the 1920s, being given Nos. 83 and 96 by the Coal Factors Society, though **Rose Marie** hardly had time to use hers as the number was issued on 31st of October and she was sunk in collision with **Livorno** which suffered a damaged stern on the 11th of December 1923. The crew were rescued by **Livorno**. A third vessel, **Belle Marie** 2168/24 was given No. 56 on completion. She was transferred to the Granger S.S. Co., before being purchased by the Consett Iron Company who had a number of mines, but the vessel was renamed **Garesfield** after one of the company's brickworks. So by 1938 the Rodney S.S. Co., had just **Alice Marie** which struck a mine in Barrow Deep two years later, and no further ships were purchased. The Pelton S.S. Co., was down to six larger vessels. The Rodney S.S. Co., had a fairly conventional funnel and houseflag which consisted of green and white horizontal stripes on which was superimposed a black 'G'. The Pelton S.S. however had a much more interesting design. The black funnel had three adjacent rows of red and black squares arranged in a chequer pattern, while the red flag had a yellow phoenix rising up from a similarly coloured fire.

A little later on the scene in Newcastle was the John George Hill Steam Shipping Company Ltd., in 1903, and again this company was based on earlier enterprises. This new company was formed when the Hill company came under the management of Witherington & Everett of Newcastle. Witherington & Everett had begun in 1899, though the new partnership had the benefit of Mr. Harry Everett's 21 years of experience in the office of J. J. & C. M. Foster who were shipbrokers and coal exporters with the old steamers **Mercator** 1055/71 and **Nereus** 891/65. Both vessels came from Westoll's fleet though **Nereus** came from Norwegian owners who had bought her in 1895. She had originally been **United Service**, built for William Gray and equipped with a lifting propellor to make better speed under sail. The Hill family had a much longer history as established shipowners, for J. G. Hill the founder of the company had begun investing in local steamers over 30 years before and in 1884 owned all the shares in **Bromsgrove** 667/68, **G. N. Wilkinson** 691/69 and **Vectis** 950/77 (42). These steamers were still in the fleet when management passed to Witherington & Everett, as well as the newer vessels **Gemini** 938/88, **Quickstep** 936/89, **Sprightly** 823/94 and **Swiftsure** 823/94. These latter vessels began a naming style which were all associated with speed and agility, suggesting

*130. The **Alice Marie** was built in 1920 for the Rodney S.S. Co. Ltd of Newcastle.*

that Hill thought much of his vessels' abilities or had a particular sense of humour, as their speed was similar to that of other colliers. The voyage accounts of **Quickstep** 909/89, which loaded about 1125 tons, for the period 1903 to 1909 (when a new vessel of the same name was delivered) show coal was loaded as follows: Tyne (often Tyne Dock) 37, Blyth 28, Sunderland 16, Hartlepool 5 and Amble 2, and from South Wales 24 (Cardiff 8, Barry 8, Swansea 6, Penarth 5, Port Talbot 3). Destinations were London 26, Bologne 10, Le Havre 14, Rouen 12, St. Malo 3, Terneuzen 10, Rotterdam 4, Amsterdam 2, Plymouth 11, Portland 4, Rochester 3, and Sheerness 7 (all from Cardiff). There were also 3 cargoes to Cork and 2 for Aberdeen.

The combined companies began building new tonnage and Witherington & Everett took delivery of their first new ship when **Tyne** 1097/03 was delivered in 1903 by Austin's. Building continued up to the outbreak of the First World War with one or two new ships being added each year, and followed a similar pattern of cargoes. The first **Skipjack** 1120/05 was wrecked in 1909 but was replaced the following year by a vessel of the same size, also from Crown's, which became **Skipjack** 1167/10 (132).

Few vessels were built for the company during the war, and several were sold. When prices fell in the mid-1920s the fleet was renewed with larger vessels, with several vessels being delivered in a year. So by 1926 the fleets consisted of a group of smaller older vessels, **Quickstep** 1446/09, **Spanker** 1875/17, and **Wear** 1164/12 under Witherington & Everett with **Bromsgrove** 1445/09, **Fleetwing** 1351/07, **Vectis** 1152/13 and **Swiftsure** 1414/20 under the Hill S.S. Co. Ltd. The **Swiftsure** (ex Jomaas, ex Moland) was purchased from continental owners when still almost new. She had been built by Brown's of Greenock to a typically continental design (132). The new vessels of the 1920s were of three sizes, with several vessels of each size. Three 2,880 deadweight vessels, **Lightfoot** 1894/22, **Sprightly** 1899/23 and **Speedfast** 1898/24, all raised quarterdeckers, were from Crown's yard. There was also a very similar single decker **Pegaway** 1826/24 from Smith's Dock which had the same cubic capacity 131,000 cubic feet but less deadweight at 2,850 tons. All four were built for the Hill S.S. Co. Ltd. The largest size were three 4,600 deadweight vessels, **Chevychase** 2719/26 and **Quickstep** 2722/28, which were delivered to the Hill S.S. Co. Ltd., while **Granta** 2719/27 was delivered to Witherington & Everett, who also had two intermediate size vessels **Alacrity** 2383/24 and **Crackshot** 2379/24 of 3,850 tons deadweight. All the larger vessels came from Smith's Dock.

Although **Bromsgrove** 1445/09 was allotted No. 80 by the Coal Factors Society she did very few voyages to London with coal prior to the First World War, suggesting that the number was requested so that it would be available if needed (133). Also the number board and appropriate coloured lamps could be made and put aboard. Her maiden voyage was from Blyth where she arrived on the 13th of November 1909 and sailed for Antwerp the following day with 2,002 tons of coal, receiving a freight rate of 5/3d per ton. The bunkers for the voyage cost 8/6d per ton. **Bromsgrove** sailed in ballast for Walker (Tyne) on the 18th arriving there on the 19th, from where she sailed on the following day for Cork. The cargo was made up of 1,275 tons of coal at a rate of 5/-d and a further 700 tons at 4/3d. She arrived at Cork on the 26th and sailed two days later for Port Talbot, where she arrived on the 29th to load for London. She sailed on the 30th with 1,999 tons on which the freight was 5/-d per ton and arrived in London on the 5th where discharging was slow and demurrage of £26-17-6d had to be paid to the ship for the delay. The next voyages were Tyne (Heworth) to Dublin, 2,005 tons at 4/4d per ton, Barry to London 1,978 tons at 5/3d per ton and Tyne Dock to Antwerp 2,009 tons at 4/9d.

As might be expected many of the coal cargoes were loaded on the Tyne, often at Tyne Dock. The destination was often Antwerp or Rouen, with quite a few going to Dublin and some to Cork. When Dublin or Cork was the destination, coal was often loaded at South Wales ports, usually Cardiff for a Channel port so the ship was well placed for a return in ballast to the Tyne, although a number of coal cargoes were loaded at Hartlepool and Blyth, but only the odd cargo from Sunderland. Apart from Rouen, cargoes were also taken to Dieppe, Le Havre, Calais, Nantes, Brest and St. Servan. Other continental ports visited occasionally were Hamburg and Rotterdam. This general round of coal cargoes came to an end completely on 13th of October 1914 when **Bromsgrove** was taken on time charter by the Admiralty. When **Bromsgrove** came off Admiralty charter she returned to a similar pattern of trade though by the end of the 1920s cargoes were not being taken to Ireland and the South Wales ports most often loaded at were now Newport and Penarth. The main destinations were Portsmouth and London, with Chatham and Portland also important, and less so Dartmouth and Devonport. The most common loading port was Howden Dock on the Tyne, closely followed by Blyth and Hartlepool. Coal was also being loaded at Burntisland and occasionally Leith and Methil. Rouen was still an important destination with odd cargoes to other French ports.

A sequence of voyages from 1928 illustrates the pattern:

22.6.28 Burntisland to Dagenham (London) (arrived 25.6.28) 1,797 tons at 2/9d per ton.
26.6.28 Dagenham to Howden (Tyne) (arrived 18.6.28)
28.6.28 Howden to Portsmouth (arrived 1.7.28) 1,347 tons coal at 3/3d, 502 tons coke at 5/3d.
 5.7.28 Portsmouth to Newport (arrived 7.7.28)
10.7.28 Newport to Le Havre (arrived 12.7.28) 1,964 tons at 4/-d per ton.
16.7.28 Le Havre to Lambton Staiths, Sunderland (arrived 18.7.28)
22.7.28 Lambton Staiths to Hamburg (for H. Stinnes) (arrived 22.7.28) 1,938 tons at 4/3d.
24.7.28 Hamburg to Hartlepool (arrived 26.7.28)

132. *Swiftsure 1414/20 was purchased when almost new from A/S Rundtur of Arendal and was photographed awaiting discharge off Erith. She was sold to Harries Bros., of Swansea in 1938.*

Photo: MacRae collection

27.7.28 Hartlepool to Dartmouth (for Dartmouth Coaling Co.) (arr.30.7.28) 1,965 tons at 3/3d.
1.8.28 Dartmouth to Tyne for orders: sent to Methil (arrived 4.8.28)
7.8.28 Methil to Portsmouth (arrived 11.8.28) 1.958 tons at 3/10d.

The voyages continued in this pattern until the 16th of October 1928 when **Bromsgrove** had to put in to Sunderland after a collision with the coaster **Dinorwic**. The slump began to have its effect and the vessel was laid up for much of the time from the beginninng of March 1931 until September 1931. In 1935 **Bromsgrove** was sold to Estonian owners and renamed **Alev**. More favourable freight rates were available in 1909 as compared with 1928 but by then the capital value of the ship had long been recovered, though it meant owners were not eager to place orders for new ships.

The **Vectis** 1152/13 on completion followed a similar pattern of trade until taken up on time charter by the Admiralty. She loaded around 1,500 tons. It is interesting to see how the freight rates changed. In January 1914 she obtained 3/9d for Blyth to Boulogne but in March 1921 obtained 10/6d for Blyth to Cowes. She had been on this run from 1919 for Stephenson Clarke. The rates soon dropped, and even for a November cargo from Blyth to Plymouth in 1924 the rate was just 4/3d. But the rates obtained in the war period were very high and **Lightfoot** 1875/16, on her first voyage on the 23rd of October 1916 from Lambton Drops, Sunderland to Purfleet carried 2,655 tons at a rate of 12/-d per ton for Cory's. After deduction of voyage costs the ship had earned £966, but this was small compared with earnings the next month when 26/6d per ton was obtained for a voyage from Hartlepool to Rouen and the ship earned £2,635 and was subsequently time chartered to Messrs. Faroult at £5,700 per month to continue the run. The arrangement was only to last a few months before the ship was torpedoed. A new **Lightfoot** 1894/22 was commissioned as part of the building programme in the 1920s. She was similar to the earlier **Lightfoot** and retained the poop accommodation for captain and officers which was, by now becoming somewhat old-fashioned, but it did allow the space below the bridge to be used for additional bunkers (135). Her deadweight capacity at 2,880 tons was about 100 tons greater, but earnings per voyage were at least ten times less on cargoes to Rouen. The pattern of trade for **Lightfoot** and her sisters was similar to the pattern which the earlier ships had been following, though Hamburg became a more important destination and **Lightfoot** made almost three times more voyages there than to London. The main loading points were Dunston (Tyne), Tyne Dock itself, Blyth and Hartlepool. Other important destinations were Harburg, Antwerp, Ghent, Dunkirk, Rouen and London. In August 1922 the rate for Tyne Dock to Harburg was 6 shillings and

132. Skipjack .
Courtesy Neill Hill

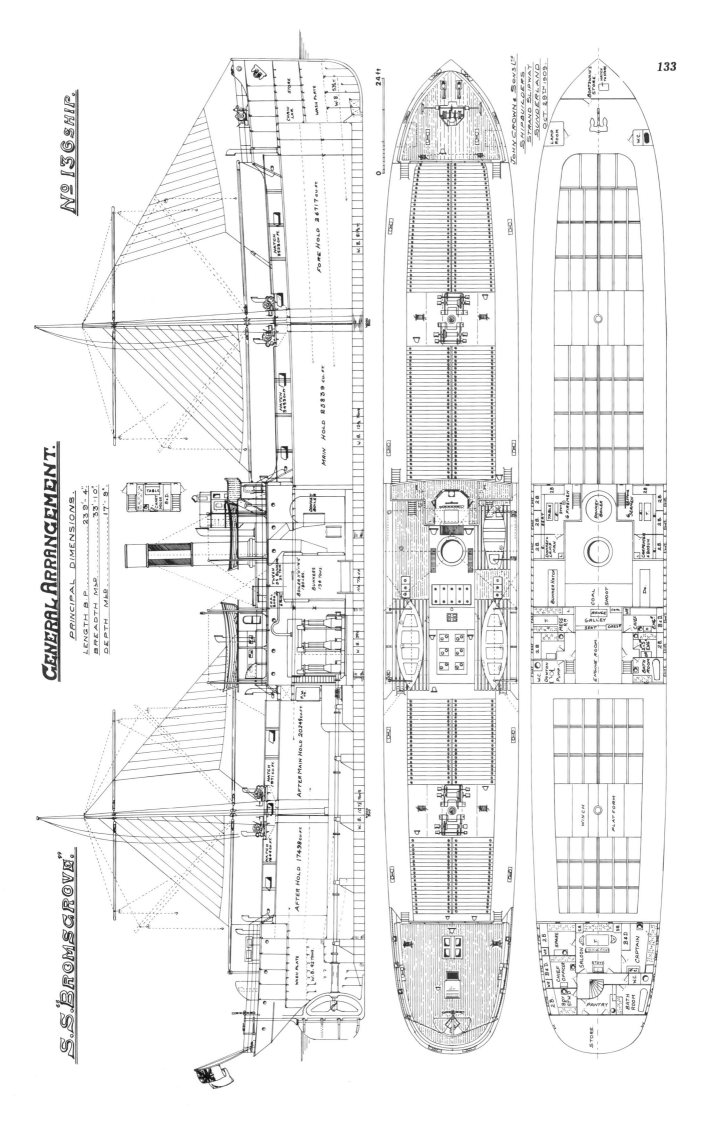

S.S. "BROMSGROVE."

GENERAL ARRANGEMENT.

PRINCIPAL DIMENSIONS.

LENGTH B.P. .... 239'-4"
BREADTH MLD .... 33'-10"
DEPTH MLD .... 17'-9"

No. 136 SHIP.

John Crown & Sons Ltd
Shipbuilders
Strand Slipway
Sunderland
Oct. 29th 1909.

FORE HOLD 26717 CU.FT.

MAIN HOLD 25859 CU.FT.

AFTER MAIN HOLD 20249 CU.FT.

AFTER HOLD 17498 CU.FT.

13 years later the same rate was accepted though the loading was further up river at Derwenthough. The ship earned almost the same amount after deduction of expenses. By the mid-1930s continental voyages were reduced with London the most important destination and south coast bunkering ports Dartmouth, Devonport, Portland and Portsmouth also taking a considerable number of cargoes. **Pegaway** 1826/24 was following a similar pattern though differing in the particular continental ports visited, and more distant voyages were made by both vessels, **Pegaway** going to Gibraltar. In the 1930s cargoes for electricity and gas companies became more important and **Pegaway,** from the 26th of June to the 16th of October 1929 made 15 consecutive voyages from Harton to East Greenwich for the South Metropolitan Gas Company at a rate of 3/4d per ton. Cargoes from South Wales tended to be less frequent but were replaced to some extent by Methil.

As might be expected, the largest of the fleet such as **Granta** 2719/27 (4,600 deadweight) made more distant voyages to the Baltic and occasionally the Mediterranean. About half her coal was loaded at Hartlepool and a quarter each at Tyne Dock and Lambton Drops, Sunderland. Over half went to Hamburg or Harburg (on the opposite bank of the Elbe) with some cargoes to Denmark (Aalborg) and Sweden. Many of the London cargoes were taken in the winter, often to Beckton Gas Works or for Stephenson Clarke, who paid around 2/6d to 2/9d per ton. Some voyages were also made to Antwerp, Amsterdam, Rotterdam and Rouen. This pattern continued until the outbreak of war.

E. R. Newbigin, who was to operate a few colliers in the 1920s and 1930s had previously acted as manager for several companies which they controlled in varying in degrees. They began in 1896 with **Temon** 795/73, which was wrecked the following year. They then acquired **Ancient Briton** 1003/82. In October 1907 the Newbigin S.S. Co., was formed and **Ancient Briton** 1003/82, **Lindisfarne** 1189/70 and **Heworth** 1043/00 were transferred from their single ship companies to the new company which also received its first newbuilding, **Greenbatt** 1407/08 from J. Priestman the following year and began the use of names beginning 'Gr'. Greenbatt was the name of Mr. Newbigin's house. **Gripfast** 1109/10 was followed by other newbuildings in the war years. The fleet was modernised under E. R. Newbigin who held almost half the shares before the capital was increased in the latter part of the 1920s, by which time the fleet consisted of **Greenbatt** 1407/08, **Gripfast** 1109/10, **Greatend** 1495/20, **Greyfriars** 1145/20 and the new **Greathope** 2297/26, all of which except **Greathope** had collier numbers for the London coal trade. The old **Greenbatt** was disposed of but otherwise the fleet remained much the same in the 1930s.

The Sharp family had long been involved in the Newcastle shipping scene and Robert Sharp held 8 shares in **Euclid** 432/66. These shares passed to his heirs for R. Sharp junior, J. G. Sharp and T. W. Sharp were joint owners of the shares by 1884 and also owned 18 shares jointly in the **Elemore** 997/81. They were managing four vessels by 1888 and had one more by the turn of the century suitable for the continental coal trade. Names beginning with 'E' were often used. The company followed a similar pattern of development to that of Witherington & Everett and began building new tonnage after the turn of the century. **Elleray** was completed at Blyth in 1905 for the "Elleray" S.S. Co. Ltd. (T. W. Sharp manager) and was followed by the slightly larger **Elvet**, completed in April 1912 by W. Dobson & Co., Newcastle for the newly formed Sharp S.S. Co., registered the previous month and managed by Sharp & Co. (136). She was typical of the colliers being built at the time, a raised quarterdeck vessel with the dimensions 140.0' x 33.5' x 15.4'. Her cargo gear included two derricks per hatch and cargo gaffs for ports where coal was discharged by shovelling into sacks and hoisting them up to the top of the hatches by hand using the blocks on the gaffs. They were then carried to waiting coal lorries which were still horse-drawn in many places. The section at frame 112 illustrates why the narrow space between the shaft tunnel and the side of the ship was sometimes plated over. She was sold to Cardiff in the mid-1920s, see page 79. By 1918 they had the steamers **Elford** 1739/15, **Elleray** 1201/05, **Elvet** 1289/12 and **Elsdon** 1522/14 (lost on a voyage from Hull to Odense with coal in 1925) and **Elwick** 1717/17. Ten years later only **Elwick** remained in the fleet but four new ships had been built. The sisters **Sandysike** 1694/22 and **Rotha** 1699/23 were most suited to the east coast and near continental trade and **Sandysike** was allotted collier No. 55. Two larger sisters were then added, **Stelling** 2136/24 and **Elterwater** 2162/25. The company then concentrated on larger ships, building the **Glanton** 2822/29 and **Kyloe** 2820/30 and all the smaller vessels were sold by 1935.

The Burnett S.S. Co., was registered in 1900 and managed by Burnett & Co., who had been in business for some years. A new fleet was rapidly delivered from Wood, Skinners, who were also shareholders in the company, so that by 1904 the fleet consisted of **Bentinck** 1148/03, **Birtley** 1029/00 **Hartley** 1150/03, **Hebburn** 1032/00, **Heworth** 1043/00 and **Tynemouth** 1038/02 which were all raised quarterdeckers with engines amidships. There was also the single decker **Marsden** 929/01. The ships were employed in the London and continental trade. These early ships were soon sold and replaced by larger versions from Wood, Skinner's yard, such as **Hebburn** 1938/08 (272.0' x 40' x 17.8') and **Towneley** 2476/10 (305.5' x 42.2' x 18.6'), both raised quarter-deckers with engines amidships. The company continued to build ships during the First World War and in 1919 the vessels were allotted collier numbers for the London trade, they were **Burnhope** 2683/17 (No.59), **Horden** 2677/14 (No.62) and **Tynemouth** 2684/17 (No.70). They were all raised quarter deckers from Wood, Skinner with the dimensions 321' x 43.2' x 19.5' and so among the largest vessels to have collier numbers at that time. Larger vessels were added in the 1920s from Wood, Skinner's yard suitable for general tramping and the smaller vessels sold and this trend continued in the 1930s.

The increasing coal shipments from Newcastle in the early 1920s led to the establishment of

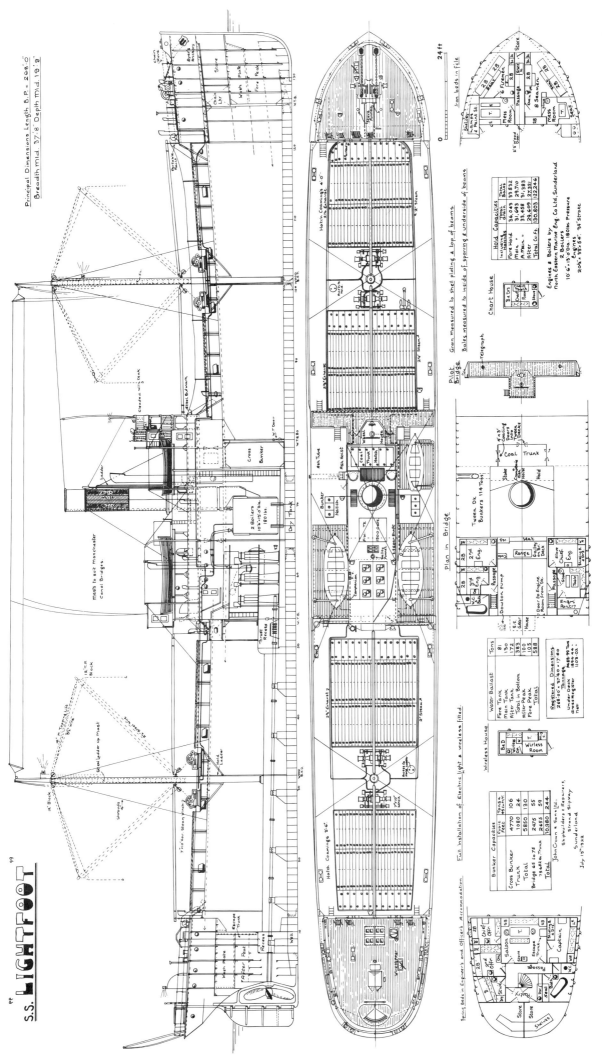

S.S. LIGHTFOOT

Principal Dimensions Length B.P. = 208' 0"
Breadth mld. 37' 8" Depth mld. 19' 9"

Masts to suit Manchester Canal Bridges.

Girth measured to shell plating at top of beams
Bales measured to inside of sparring & underside of beams.

Full installation of Electric Light & Wireless fitted.

Spring Beds in Engineer's and Officers' Accommodation.

Plan in Bridge

Chart House

Pilot Bridge

Wireless House

Hold Capacities

Including Spaces	Grain	Bale	Total Bale
Fore Hold	36,043	33,832	
Main "	31,693	29,710	
A. Main "	33,458	31,983	
After	29,609	27,332	
Total Cu.Ft.	130,803	122,244	

Engines & Boilers by
North Eastern Marine Eng. Co. Ltd, Sunderland
2 Boilers. 180lbs Pressure
10'6" x 13'0" Dia.
Engines
20½" x 33" x 54". 36" Stroke

Bunker Capacities

	Cubic Feet	Tons
Cross Bunker	4770	106
Trunk	1080	24
Total	5850	130
Bridge 65 to 75	2475	55
75 aft to Trunk	2655	59
Total	10,980	244

Water Ballast

	Tons
Fore Tank	81
Main Tank	130
After Tank	172
Total in Bottom	383
After Peak	100
Fore Peak	105
Total	588

Registered Dimensions.
28 00' x 37' 90' x 17' 60

Under Deck Tonnage	2488-99 Tons
Gross Register	1894-44 "
net	1103-02 "

John Crown & Sons Ltd,
Shipbuilders & Repairers,
Strand Slipway,
Sunderland
July 15th 1922.

24 ft

Iron beds in file

2 Boilers
10'6"x13'0" Dia.
180 lbs.

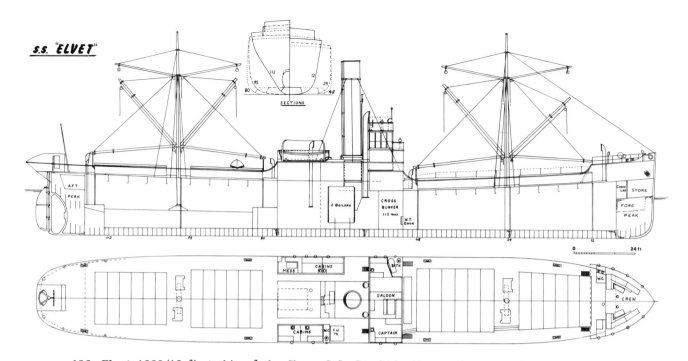

S.S. "ELVET"

136. Elvet *1289/12 first ship of the Sharp S.S. Co. Ltd., Newcastle.*   Courtesy P. N. Thomas

several new collier owners. One such was the Monkseaton S.S. Co. Ltd., registered in May 1922, which was managed by E. L. Anderson. One of the main shareholders was Major H. S. Streatfield who had considerable local colliery interests. The company took delivery of two new colliers in 1923, **Marjorie S.** 1742/23 and **Murie S.** 1701/23, which were named after the Major's daughters. They were allotted collier numbers the following May for the London trade, becoming No.146 and No. 143 respectively. They were both single deckers built by Swan, Hunter. **Marjorie S.** was seven feet longer, having the dimensions 253.0' x 37.2' x 22.0', and in loaded trim they carried about 3,000 tons on a draught of 19 feet although the mean draft was about 17'11". They were designed to load in Northumberland Dock and this was about the maximum draft the dock could accept conveniently. Soon after completion **Murie S.** was fixed on a six month charter carrying coal to Hamburg. As they were built for the near continental trade they only carried about 90 tons of bunkers, enough for about 10 days steaming in good weather. As the trade declined somewhat in the latter part of the 1920s both were sold. **Murie S.** was purchased by Arthur Stott who was a Newcastle coal and coke exporter and like many other coal shippers and exporters in Newcastle, had the odd ship from time to time. William Dickinson, who were previously involved in the Spanish iron ore trade also exported coal and coke. In 1935 the company became part of Harrison's (London) Ltd., and the coal side of the business was further developed. A number of vessels were managed and some of these were put on the London trade during the war (one survivor of which was **Garesfield** 2168/24 which belonged to the Consett Iron Co. Ltd.)

Antony and Bainbridge managed a number of vessels over the years beginning in the 1920s. They were mostly coasters though their subsidiary the Derwent Shipping Co., registered in 1926, owned **Hillfern** 1535/20 in the 1930s (79). Other coaster owners with a considerable interest in the coal trade were Gillie & Blair, who had a separate coal exporting department. They handled considerable amounts of coal and **Deemount** 569/33 was built for the Aberdeen coal trade on long term charter. Robinson, Brown continued to manage 'T' Steam Coasters but in the boom after the First World War Mr. T. E. Brown formed the Brown Shipping Co. (Newcastle) Ltd., in December 1920 and provided £58,000 of the £150,000 capital. The new enterprise purchased 9 'Kil' class naval patrol vessels at a price rather less than coasters were fetching of a similar size. A considerable number of these vessels were sold off by the navy almost as they were completed in 1918. Many were launched by Smith's Dock. The original design was intended to confuse enemy submarines and was made to appear symmetrical. G. A. Connell and G. W. Grace were fellow directors and subscribed £35,000 each to the venture, but they also purchased **Kildavin** for their Side Shipping Co. Ltd., which they managed. The vessel was converted for them by J. Samuel White of Cowes and was named **Leaside** 634/18. She carried a deadweight of 650 tons which gave a generous stowage rate around 48 cubic feet per ton. Because of their draft of 14'6" they could not compete with the ordinary coaster of the same deadweight and in addition their fine lines meant that they could not lie aground loaded satisfactorily and so were only suitable for larger harbours. Conversion was a matter of removing the interior accommodation, armament and one of the boilers, which reduced the speed from 13 knots to about 11. In practice some proved difficult to steam on the single boiler and as freight rates fell their inability to compete in the coasting trade soon became apparent and they were sold during the latter part of the 1920s, **Leaside** passing to Italian owners in 1928. Joplin & Hall of Newcastle also had several under their management but they had sold up by the mid-1920s. The Side Shipping Co., had been formed in December 1914 with a capital of £45,000 equally held by G. A. Connell and G. W. Grace, except for £1,000 subscribed by T. E. Brown, and this association also extended to the partners' other shipowning company, Quayside Shipping Co. Ltd., registered in June 1919, which in the 1920s owned **Akenside** 1894/23 which was collier No.72 on the London trade. They also operated large ships in the Latvian trade in the 1930s. They had no ships after 1947 and eventually closed down as the coal export trade ended. However G. W. Grace & Co. Ltd., operated a few larger steam coasters from the end of the Second World War until the early 1950s from London. B. E. Common of Common Bros. (who had much larger ships) formed Home Line Ltd. at the beginning of the 1920s and operated several 'Kil' conversions, including **Tynehome** 628/19 and **Wearhome** 625/18. In the 1930s they were replaced by **Cedartree** 1557/28 which was given No.63 for the London trade in 1933. The vessel had been purchased from Howard·Jones Ltd., (Tree S.S.), Cardiff.

The engines aft collier began to appear slowly in the 1920s although most Newcastle owners still preferred the traditional engines amidships design which they had been using for over 60 years. Errington S. Dunford & Co., set up the Dunford S.S. Co. Ltd., in May 1922 and ordered engines aft colliers. First to be delivered was **Emile Dunford** 961/22 which arrived from the Coaster Construction Company of Montrose the same month the company was registered. It was a most unusual flush deck vessel with just a 30 ft. forecastle, but **Enid Dunford** 869/22 was a conventional large coaster design. Among the shareholders were Soc. Commerciale d'Affretements de Commission of Paris, the Ashington Coal Company and Swan, Hunter & Wigham Richardson Ltd., Wallsend, and they built two larger engines aft colliers for the company, the sister ships **Errington Dunford** 1196/23 and **James Dunford** 1196/24. They were well-designed all-aft self-trimming colliers (139) of 1,790 deadweight. The positioning of the bridge aft as well simplified steering gear and reduced the chance of the bridge being damaged during grab discharge, though it was not particularly popular with captains for it made judging where the bow was during docking more difficult. The hatches were made as large and also as long as possible by offsetting the steam winches. The aft accommodation was well arranged and a serving hatch was placed between the engineers mess and galley and so avoided one sprint along a wet heaving deck, but this was still necessary to reach the officers accomodation below the bridge. The machinery was conventional except for the steam dome in the form of a miniature boiler placed on the upper part of the main boilers. In heavy seas the strong movements of the stern could cause the water to surge back and forth in the boilers and any water splashing up into the main steam pipe could cause priming and damage to the main engine. The steam accumulator prevented this problem. The engines aft design also made life in bad weather more difficult for engineers as the engine governor had to be particularly effective to prevent the engine racing when he propellor lifted out of the water. The vessels ran to Thames power stations for a time but were sold in the mid-1930s, Dunford's continuing as coal shippers. The Dunford name had long been associated with Newcastle shipping, firstly as Elliott, Lowry and Dunford who built up a considerable fleet in the 1870s and early 1880s which was engaged in the continental trade. But with the end of the boom they did not fare so well and in the 1890s as Dunford and Elliott the fleet slowly dwindled as ships were sold off and not replaced so that by 1904 only **Caffila** 1348/82, **Cilurnum** 1370/81, **Cydonia** 1029/76 and **Monkseaton** 1776/82 remained and were soon sold.

Another owner to build engines-aft colliers in the mid-1920s was R. S. Dalgliesh and R. I. James who were coal shippers and operated from Hull also. They already had ocean tramps and two smaller tramps **Whitworth** 1400/19 and **Plawsworth** 1489/20 on the coast and near continental coal trade of the traditional design, both owned by the Robert Stanley S.S. Co. Ltd. First of the new vessels was **Letchworth** 1317/24, delivered to another Dalgliesh managed company, the Watergate S.S. Co. Ltd. **Letchworth** was allotted collier No.67 in 1925 for the London trade (115). S. P. Austin delivered a near sister **Tamworth** 1332/24 to the Robert Stanley S.S. Co. Ltd., but their most interesting delivery was **Queenworth** 2047/25 with dimensions 275.0' x 39.9' x 18.1' and was thus similar to the colliers the Admiralty had been chartering a decade earlier. They continued in the trade post-war with **Letchworth** 2873/42 and **Queenworth** 2066/43, which was scrapped in 1960. Other tramp owners to have a few vessels in the coastal and continental trades were B. J. Sutherland and W. A. Souter, who were also shareholders in the Northern S.S. Co. Ltd. This company had the midship-engined colliers **Ashington** 2189/21, **Bedlington** 1600/24 and **Cramlington** 1500/24, all purchased secondhand in the mid-1920s. They were managed by Gjemre & Co. Ltd. who were coal exporters and remained so after the ships were sold in the 1930s. Swan, Hunter, the builders of **Cramlington** (ex Forestash) were also shareholders, possibly because they took shares as part payment.

Even in the mid-1920s the high volume of coal shipments and the falling prices for new tonnage was still attracting new owners and one such was the Hartley S.S. Co. Ltd., registered in February 1924 by Richley, Halvorsen & Sample with a capital of £30,000. Two new single deck engines-amidships colliers were built for the company by Smith's Dock at a price of just over £41,300 each. Named **Horsley** 2143/25 and **Hamsterley** 2160/25 they were allotted the numbers 177 and 179 for the London coal trade. A third vessel, **Hartley** 2147/24, also from Smith's Dock, foundered in a severe gale in mid-channel on the 27th of December 1924. The vessels were sold in the mid-1930s. **Horsley** retaining her collier number as she was purchased by William Cory for £26,000 and renamed **Cordale** in 1937. There were generally close links between Newcastle owners and London merchants who often chartered the ships. One such link was between the Tyne & Wear Shipping Co. Ltd., which was set up in late 1926 by J. E. and F. Dawson and E. Edwards. It was managed by Dawson's. The vessels were run in association with E. Foster & Co., the London coal factors, and **Efos** 1245/24 was named after the company's telegraphic address. A second vessel, **Regfos** 1548/10, got its name in a similar way derived from Mr. Reginald Foster, senior partner. The vessel had been the **West Quarter** of J. Ridley, Son & Tully which the new company purchased in the late 1920s and was given the collier number 129 in November 1929 for the London trade. An account for Voyage 207 of the **Regfos** in June 1934 shows clearly the varied and numerous expenses involved in carrying a cargo from Seaham to London. The voyage was made for E. Foster & Co., under a charter dated 2nd October 1933. The loading brokers were France, Fenwick Tyne & Wear Co. Ltd. The vessel arrived at Seaham on Saturday June 16 at 7.30 p.m. ready to load, but loading did not commence until Tuesday at 5.00 p.m. and was not completed until Wednesday morning at 9.15 a.m. Total cargo loaded was 2,016 tons and bunkers were an additional 69 tons 18 cwt. The various costs at Seaham are seen on the bill sent to the owners by France Fenwick for disbursement: (Cargo) Transires 1/-d, Trinity Dues & Life-boat 2/8d, Dock Dues etc. £38-15-7d, Telegrams, postage etc. 10/9d, Agency (fee) £4-4-0, Trimming (cargo and bunkers) £13-8-8, Pilotage £6-18-11, Water 5/-. **Regfos** sailed at 9.45 a.m. for London and arrived ready to discharge at Albert Dock Hoists at 7 p.m. on Thursday and was off the discharging berth at 7.30 p.m. and began discharging at 8 p.m. Discharging was completed at 6.45 p.m. on Friday, rather longer than usual because part of the cargo was for Dudman's Dock. The cargo was made up of three different consignments, each at a different freight: 747.25 tons at 2/4.5d, 500 tons at 2/7.5d and 768.75 tons at 2/9d. The total was £260-9-8d but as the charterers, E. Foster & Co., also acted as ship's agents in London they deducted the ship's London expenses as follows: Entries at Gravesend & London (Coal Factors Society) 3/6d, Tonnage duty & Entry £3-13-6d, Trinity dues, Lights & Entry £6-12-1d, Pilotage (per R. Stubbs) £4-6-6d, Watermen (E. A. Lynch for mooring work in Thames etc.) £3-10-0d, Telegrams 5/-d and Agency £4-4-0d. This left £237-6-8d.

By the time **Regfos** reached Seaham again a week had gone by and it was time to pay the wages: Captain Swinbanks £8-0-0, Mate £4-7-9, 2nd Mate £3-16-6, Bosun £3-1-0, Steward £3-2-6, Mess Steward £1-17-6, Chief Engineer £5-8-0, 2nd Engineer £4-10-0, Three A.B's (each) £2-16-0, Two Ordinary Seamen (each) £2-0-3, Donkeyman £3-1-0, Four Firemen (each) £2-16-0. Total £60-16-9d. There was also Donkeyman's overtime at Seaham loading, shifting ship and pumping ballast and in London pumping ballast and steam on deck which came to 20 hours (£1-5-0). An Able Seaman was also paid overtime as nightwatchman in Seaham 14/8d. Additionally the Captain had paid for gratuities, telephone, telegrams, pilot's food and national insurance contributions for the crew, total £4-4-0. Thus the owners were left with £106-18-8 from which to pay for bunkers, repairs, insurance of the ship and office expenses, and so probably made only a few pounds profit on the voyage. **Regfos** survived the Second World War under the command of Captain Swinbanks, who had been in the ship with the previous owners. He took part, with his ship, in the Normandy landings. She was damaged on the beach and remained aground for a month until successfully refloated and repaired. She served the company for a number of years after the war.

Sunderland

There was considerable interchange between Newcastle and Sunderland and the **Regfos** was actually registered there although managed from Newcastle. Far fewer companies were based in Sunderland where large colliery controlled fleets dominated the scene such as the Lambton, Morton association, especially before the turn of the century. One man to rise to particular prominence who was not a coal owner was James Westoll. During the latter part of the 1870s and 1880s he purchased and built ships suitable for the Mediterranean trade so that his vessels became known as the 'Black Sea Yachts'. There was a strong connection with Short Brothers yard on the Wear which built over 40 ships for the fleet. The usual round was coal or patent fuel to Italy and Egypt and then to the Black Sea to load grain. This large fleet was taken over by James Westoll junior in 1895 on the death of his father and the Adamson family continued to be major investors in the enterprise and had sold the last of their wooden sailing vessels. They had been shipbuilders, but did not make the change to iron. The home and near continental coal trade was not neglected and the smaller vessels were regularly employed in this way. The fleet grew particularly rapidly during the 1870s and 1880s so that by 1884 it numbered 22 vessels. Unlike most owners his fleet continued to grow in the 1890s as he built larger vessels aimed at the Mediterranean trade but he did not sell his smaller ships which progressively moved into the continental coal trade, so that around 1908 there were some 32 vessels in the fleet. The vessels over about 2,200 gross tons were mostly making voyages to the Mediterranean or Spain with occasional large cargoes to the continent from South Wales in some cases. James Westoll liked to have his ships on a trade, probably on charter so that they quite often repeated voyage after voyage with slow variations appearing over the years as the pattern of demand changed and cargo sizes increased beyond the vessels' capacity. Of the smaller vessels **Birch** 1611/82, **Consent** 1431/79, **Lucent** 1422/79 were on the coastal trade, the latter often running from Swansea, while **Ambient** 1470/04 was carrying Welsh and Scottish coal, mostly coasting. The slightly larger vessels ran to the continent: **Beneficent** 1963/81 had been working to Amsterdam and Rotterdam but was now coasting. In 1907 **Brittania** 944/77 was running from Bo'ness to London and then made more varied coastal runs, occasionally going to France. **Cogent** 2051/83 was mainly making continental voyages to Hamburg, Bordeaux and sometimes down to Spain. **Diligent** 2184/88 was working to the near continent and Mediterranean, as was **James Westoll** 1990/84, **Lizzie Westoll** 2858/95, **Magnus Mail** 2317/89, **William Adamson** 1986/84, **William Middleton** 2539/93 and **F. D. Lambert** 2214/92. **George Allen** 2309/90 was mainly running to Spain but from 1910 was fixed Tyne to Rotterdam. **James Cameron** 1807/82 was on charter running Cardiff/Tyne to Zeebrugge and later

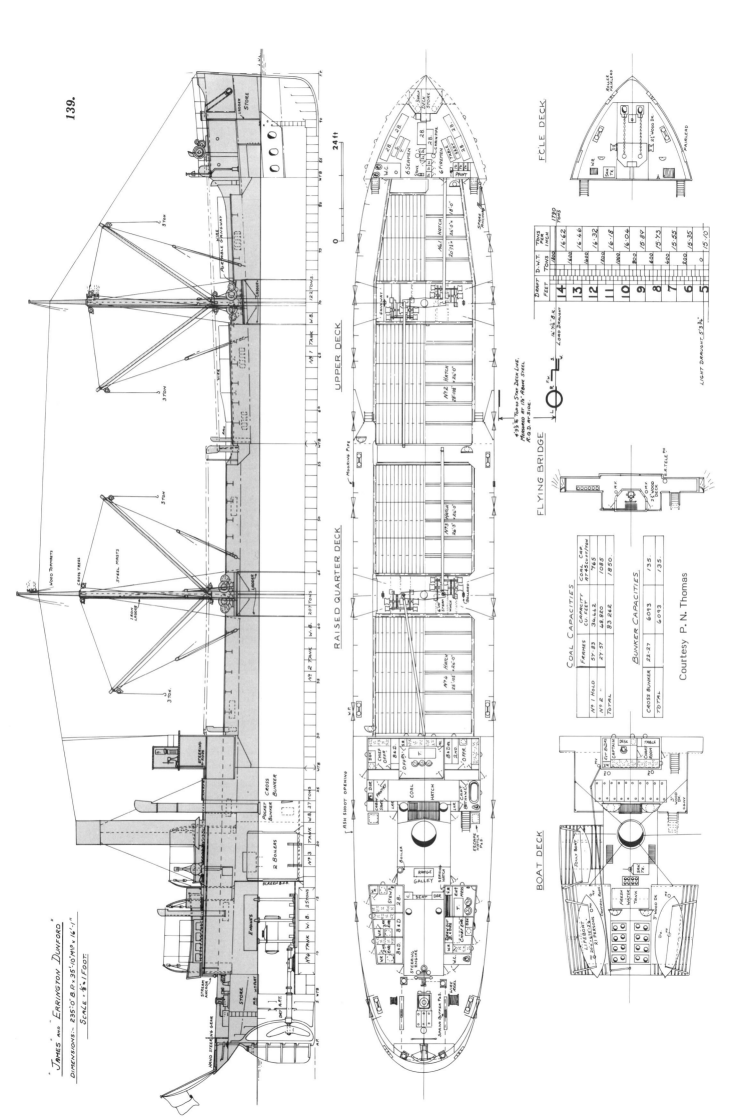

"JAMES AND ERRINGTON DUNFORD"

DIMENSIONS:— 235'-0" B.P. × 35'-10" MLD × 16'-1"

SCALE = 1/8" = 1 FOOT:

139.

UPPER DECK

RAISED QUARTER DECK

F'CLE DECK.

FLYING BRIDGE

BOAT DECK

24ft

DRAFT FEET	D.W.T. TONS	TONS PER INCH
14	1800	16·62
13	1600	16·46
12	1400	16·32
11	1200	16·18
10	1000	16·04
9	800	15·89
8	600	15·73
7	400	15·55
6	200	15·35
5		15·10

1790 TONS

LOAD DRAUGHT

LIGHT DRAUGHT 5'13¾"

COAL CAPACITIES

	FRAMES	CAPACITY CU. FEET	COAL CAP AT 45 CU.FT/TON
N°1 HOLD	5Y-83	34,442	765
N°2 "	2Y-57	48,820	1085
TOTAL		83,262	1850

BUNKER CAPACITIES

	FRAMES	CAPACITY CU. FEET	COAL CAP AT 45 CU.FT/TON
CROSS BUNKER	22-27	6093	135.
TOTAL		6093	135.

Courtesy P. N. Thomas

from Methil on charter. The vessel was lost in 1910 returning from Rouen to the Tyne. **President** 1894/07, the newest member of the fleet, was fixed from Hull or North East Coast to Hamburg. The trend was now to replace the smaller ageing ships in order to remain in the coasting and continental coal trade. The sisterships **Sir Walter Scott** 1465/08 and **May Scott** 1465/09 were purchased from J. O. Scott of Newcastle and some further new buildings delivered, smallest of which was **Rudmore** 969/11. If there were no particular members of the family, shareholders or charterers to be commemorated the ships were often given names ending 'ent', but this was soon to be changed to names beginning 'West' with the formation of the Westwick S.S. Co. Ltd., in August 1916. The first steamers were large ocean going tramps. A number of ships were lost during the First World War, but 23 ships remained in the fleet in mid-1918 although some were 40 years old. Many were sold at the end of the war and the company was down to 9 ships by 1922. **Barmoor** 2225/09 was purchased the following year from the Burnett S.S. Co., and was initially employed to Hamburg and Harburg mostly, loading at Methil, Leith and Immingham, and then Tyne to London in the winter with more cargoes from Sunderland by the beginning of 1924. A similar pattern was followed in 1925 and 1926 with more varied voyages including Stettin and other Baltic ports in 1926. The pattern was similar with more Tyne-London voyages in the winters of 1927 and 1928. French ports such as Nantes and Rouen were now visited and the 1929 winter included some Antwerp and Ghent cargoes, as did those of 1930 and 1931. **Barmoor** was laid up from April to October 1932. The vessel was owned by the Westwick S.S. Co. Ltd., as were the next two purchases, the sisterships **Andelle** 1832/22 and **Lys** 1830/20, which were built by Austin's for the Normandy Shipping Co. (Stephenson Clarke managers) and provided the company with two modern engines-aft raised quarterdeck colliers. Both were regularly employed on the Tyne, Blyth or Sunderland coal run to London. **Andelle** was allotted No.41 by the Coal Factors Society and in the latter part of the 1920s was making quite a number of voyages from Grangemouth to London. In summer the Baltic and German ports of Hamburg, Stettin and near continent such as Antwerp and Rotterdam were visited with cargoes from as far afield as Swansea. A similar pattern continued in the 1930s. **Lys** was sold in 1935 and **Andelle** to the Admiralty in 1940.

James Westoll Ltd. was formed in 1929 when James Westoll the second died, just as new ships arrived from Austin's for management by the company. **Westburn** 2842/29 and **Westavon** 2842/29, owned by the Westwick S.S. Co. Ltd., followed the traditional engines amidships three island layout and measured 312.0' x 45.2' x 21.0'. They went straight on to the London trade. **Westburn**'s maiden voyage on the 23rd of November 1929 was from South Dock, Sunderland to Beckton Gas Works, 4,244 tons at 2/7.5d, and the income from the freight after deduction of ship's expenses was just £153. The next run from the Tyne to Beckton left a surplus of £226. Winter 1930 was spent solely on this run but in summer, when the need for gas was less, the ship made voyages to Hamburg. In winter 1931 the voyages to Beckton were from Hartlepool and Sunderland for Stephenson Clarke. In the spring of 1932, after a voyage from Methil to Bordeaux, 3,925 tons at 5/-d, which made a surplus of only £89 among others, the vessel was laid up for the summer and autumn, but then returned to the Beckton winter run. This became the established pattern with various other voyages in summer as well as Beckton, and in the latter part of the 1930s to Barking also. In the late 1930s and during the war the ship ran from the Tyne and Hartlepool to Beckton and this continued until the 1950s. **Westavon** followed a similar trading pattern. The steamer **Westcove** 2734/12 (ex **Corcove**) of Cory's, of almost identical dimensions to the new steamers, had been purchased in 1927 and was given collier No.39. She was put on the Tyne to Hamburg trade and also made voyages from Sunderland to Amsterdam and Stockholm. In the winter she ran on the London coal trade from the Tyne mostly, but by the early 1930s was more often running from Sunderland to London. She was taken over by the Admiralty and used as a block ship in 1940. **Beneficent** 2944/31, a slightly larger engines-aft raised quarterdecker from Pickersgill struck a mine off Southend in 1940. Thus the fleet was down to just the **Westburn** and **Westavon**. **Westavon** was finally sold in 1959, by which time it was owned by the Vedra Shipping Co., which had been formed by Mr. J. W. Adamson, who had been a Westoll director.

Among James Westoll's contemporaries in the 1880s was Robert Wetherley, who acted as manager for **Euclid** 686/66, **Southwick** 614/61 and **Waldridge** 662/68, in which Robert Sharp, who was agent

140. Westburn *2842/29, of the Westwick S.S. Co. (J. Westoll Ltd., managers).* Photo: Alex Duncan

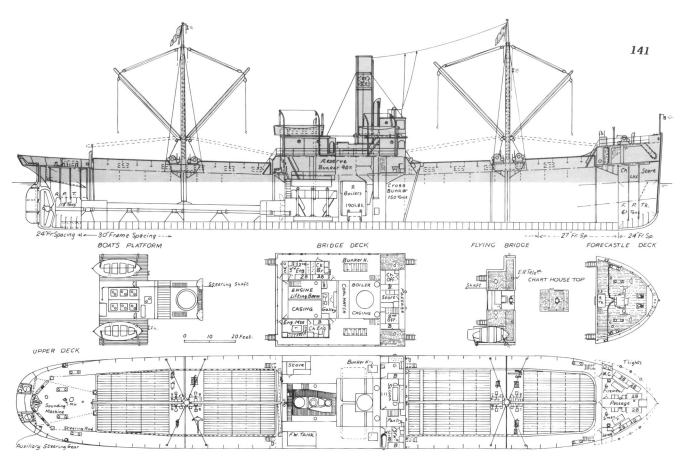

141. Coquetdale 1597/23. *Note closer frame spacing at the ends of the ship to reduce the risk of bottom damage in ballast in heavy seas.*   Shipbuilding & Shipping Record 20 September 1923

for the Hetton Coal Company, held an interest. Freer & Dix also had a few colliers beginning around the 1880s. They had **Ella Constance** 638/58 in which they each had 16 shares and managed larger steamers in which they had a few shares. They subsequently purchased **Waldridge** 662/68 which was lost in January 1895 on a voyage from the Tyne to Bologne with coal and bricks, and **Allerwash** 381/61 which often loaded coal at Goole. They managed the Freer & Dix S.S. Co. Ltd, which in 1904 had four steamers, the larger of which were employed on more distant voyages, but the old **Allerwash** was employed on the coast until the 1920s when the Freer & Dix S.S. Co., which had not owned any ships for a number of years, acquired **Guardian** 381/96. They also managed the Sunderland S.S. Co., which owned **Camberway** 782/19 and **Waterway** 723/21 for a time between the wars. Speeding, Marshall & Co., and post-war in the 1920s Septimus Marshall, managed a few steamers. **Brinkburn** 1598/24 was owned by the Brinkburn S.S. Co. Ltd., and almost half the shares were held by Sir John Priestman the builders who had coal interests too. Builders sometimes built for their own account if no orders were to hand and a number of shipbuilders became owners in this way. Sir John Priestman was also associated with the Enfield S.S. Co. Ltd., which had been formed as early as May 1898. In the 1920s it had the old steamer **Enterprise** 1114/05 which had been built by J. Crown & Sons and had been owned by coal merchant J. L. Hill of Sunderland and **Coquetdale** 1597/23, of about 2,550 tons deadweight, a sistership to **Brinkburn**, and was a single deck steamer rather than a raised quarterdecker. She had large hatches which made her a good self-trimming design (142), suitable for coal and timber (note the derricks placed well up the masts to clear a timber deck cargo). The layout was typical of the period with a well arranged cross-bunker sufficient for voyages to the Baltic with space available for coal under the bridge deck for longer voyages, and the determined owner could stow cargo there for the return voyage. Especially in the German trade, colliers generally had a cable shackle between windlass and hawsepipe so that when the vessels were returning in ballast and met heavy weather the anchor cable could be secured, the shackle knocked out, and the anchor cable then run out through the mooring pipes on to the bottom. Sufficient was then paid out to stop the drift and keep the ship head to sea, and so it acted as a sea anchor. All the steamers were disposed of in the 1930s. Thomas Rose managed a number of coasters throughout the period which often did local coal runs and was also involved in coal exporting and continued to operate until after the Second World War. One of the companies which he managed was the Wear S.S. Co. (1917) Ltd., in which C. M. Tate had a shareholding, but one of the biggest shareholders was the United Methodist Church which held £35,000 of the £82,050 capital. The Weardale S.S. Co. Ltd, was an entirely separate enterprise which was the shipping arm of the Laing family, perhaps best remembered for their shipyard in Sunderland under James, later Sir James Laing. James Laing often retained shares in the ships he built, generally electing to subscribe for 8 of the 64 shares, though he did own **Tynedale** 408/68 initially, but sold it in the early 1870s. By the mid-1880s he was managing five ships and the shipping side continued to expand and the family had ten steamers, all with names ending in 'dale' by 1904. The smallest was **Borrowdale** 1093/91 but most were larger and best suited to the more distant continental trade. In the 1920s the company put two colliers on the London trade. They were the **Dore** 1975/27 and **Ramshope** 1896/27 which were allotted collier numbers 165

*142. Copsewood of 1925
on sea trials.*

and 223 by the Coal Factors Society. They were both sold in the 1930s.

The Hartlepools and Middlesbrough

Initially Hartlepool and West Hartlepool had a number of fleets with smaller vessels suitable for the near continental trade such as E. Cook & Co., F. Haskind, George Pyman & Co., and the West Hartlepool S. N. Co., but in general they developed their interests in more distant trades to such an extent there were virtually no owners operating in the London trade around the turn of the century and much of the trade was later handled by Newcastle based fleets. However for a time the situation was completely changed by Furness, Withy when Sir Christopher Furness decided to build a fleet of colliers to carry the bunker coal needed by his own fleet and others in London and elsewhere. Orders were placed with a number of yards and between 1905 and 1908 numerous colliers were built. First to be delivered were some smaller vessels around 235-240 feet in length, followed by a group some 276-280 feet in length. Among the smaller group were **Ryhope** 1334/07 (collier No.173), **Dagenham** 1456/07, **Whorlton** 1469/07, **Easington** 1387/07, **Thornley** 1327/07 (collier No.110) and **Collingwood** 1278/05 (collier No.114). They came from a number of different yards and differed in some details. Most had a 36' beam but **Collingwood**, one of the first to be built, had a beam of only 33.8' and a single boiler (144). This allowed her bunkers to be arranged in the bridge deck above the boiler and alongside it so no forward hold space was given up to a cross bunker as it was in the twin boilered **Thornley** (147) and so she offered 95,200 cubic feet as against the **Thornley's** 87,890 cubic feet, though the latter had a hull depth (moulded) of 5" less. The deadweight of both vessels was about 1,870 tons. All the stern behind the aftermost hold watertight bulkhead was given over to water ballast. This allowed over 75 tons to be carried to help keep the screw immersed for the voyage north in ballast. The larger series included **Thimbleby** 1865/07, **Grantley** 1869/08, **Cramlington** 1824/07 and **Rouen** 1968/09 (collier No.99). By the early 1920s the fleet was managed from Newcastle, having been managed from London for a time previously, and was considerably reduced in numbers with just **Ryhope** 1334/07, **Collingwood** 1278/05, **Thornley** 1327/07, **Rouen** 1968/09, **Croxdale** 1296/06, **Ludworth** 1301/07 and the smallest, the appropriately named **Peter Pan** 938/09. They worked regularly in the Goole trade and were about the largest vessels which could easily navigate the river up to Goole docks. To these were added the new steamer **Eldon** 1867/23 built by the Furness Shipbuilding Co. Ltd. with the dimensions 307.0' x 45.1' x 22.1'. A raised quarterdecker, she was given collier No.84 on completion. The vessel was sold to German owners in 1929 when Furness, Withy gave up collier owning.

Middlesbrough was the base for several companies which operated vessels in the coal trade. Perhaps best remembered are Constantines. Joseph Constantine was apprenticed to Warley, Pickering & Co., who were well established ships' chandlers. Joseph Constantine and Warley Pickering junior, the son of the firm, began to invest in sailing vessels which were often run under the Norwegian flag. The first steamer of the partnership was **Toftwood** 1060/72, which was bought in 1891 and also run under the Norwegian flag. Several more ships were added and continued to run in the Baltic trade under the Norwegian flag. The firm became Constantine & Pickering in 1897. The first British registered steamer was **Riftswood** 1832/90 which was used in the more distant continental trade. Though the Constantine & Pickering S. S. Co., was formed in 1901 the ships continued to be owned on the 64 share system. To cater for the coasting trade R. A. Constantine and T. H. Donking was formed, Mr. Donking was Warley Pickering's cousin and they acted as managers for the Meteor S.S. Co., set up in 1907. The first steamer was **Cedarwood** 654/07 and this side of the business slowly developed although the main interest was ocean tramps. Further coasters were added, which were employed in the general cargo trade. The Joseph Constantine S. S. Line was registered, with J. Constantine subscribing £711,224 of the £779,900 capital in 1920, and with his death two years later his sons R. A. Constantine and W. W. Constantine took over the helm. T. H. Donking left the partnership with R. A. Constantine and **Ardshean** was transferred to Constantine's as **Edenwood** 804/20. The coasters

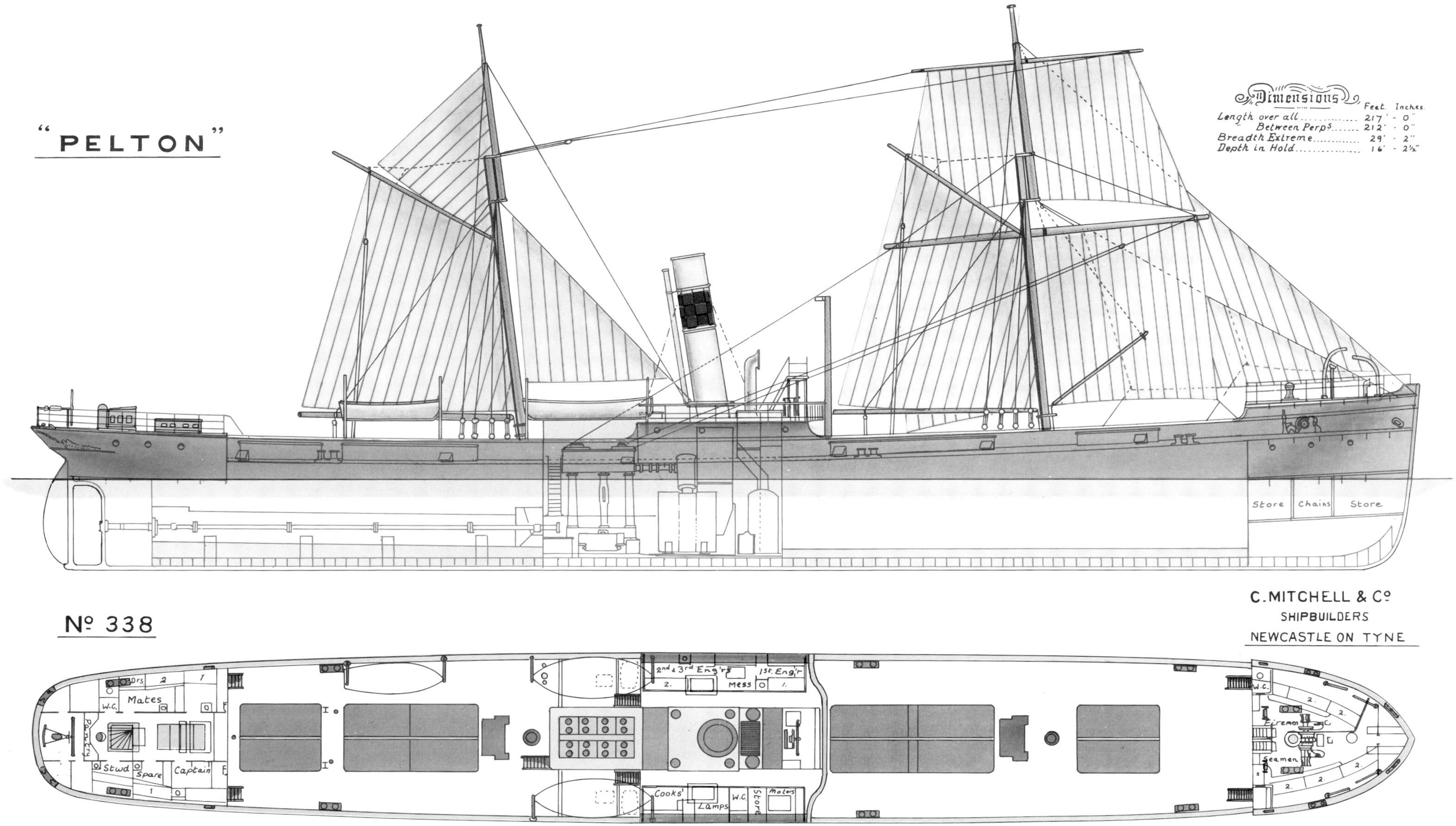

"PELTON"

Dimensions	Feet	Inches
Length over all	217'	0"
Between Perps.	212'	0"
Breadth Extreme	29'	2"
Depth in Hold	16'	2½"

Store Chains Store

Store

C. MITCHELL & Cº
SHIPBUILDERS
NEWCASTLE ON TYNE

Nº 338

1st Eng'r

Mess

2nd 3rd Eng'r

Mates

W.C.

Store

Cooks'

Lamps

Seamen

W.C.

W.C.

Mates

Captain

Spare

Stew'd

Pantry

143. Pelton 761/76 built by C. Mitchell, Newcastle

Courtesy Tyne & Wear Museums

now operated in the East Coast coal trade and the collier **Levenwood** 803/24 was first to be delivered followed by the sisters **Larchwood** 914/24 and **Copsewood** 969/25 (143). The ships often carried coal to the cement works of Associated Portland Cement Manufacturing (A.P.C.M.) at Swanscombe and Greenhithe on the Thames, returning northwards with cement. Considerable care was taken with design and the hulls were tank tested for later vessels. The machinery used superheated steam and 'poppet' valves on the H.P. cylinder rather than slide valves, to increase efficiency. First to be delivered was **Linwood** 992/32, followed by **Parkwood** 1049/33, **Cedarwood** 899/33, **Avonwood** 1056/34 and **Westwood** 1040/35. **Parkwood**'s first cargo was coal from Harton & Heworth staithes (Tyne) to A.P.C.M. (Thames), arriving on the 10th of May 1937 after carrying out loaded trials. The sequence of coal carrying voyages then was Wear to Thames (for A.P.C.M.), Seaham to Ipswich (for Londonderry collieries), Wear to Thames (for A.P.C.M.), Tyne to Portsmouth (for John Hudson), and Goole to Ipswich (for Evesons). The freight for the latter was 2/9d per ton and 1,140 tons were loaded. The voyage was delayed at Blacktoft for almost 10 hours and so the profit on the voyage was £2-8-6d. The next coal cargo was Sunderland to Thames (A.P.C.M.) followed by Tyne to Portsmouth, Methil to Thames and Tyne to Dieppe, which was the last voyage for June. **Cedarwood** followed a similar pattern of trade averaging about 55 voyages a year. So the company had an impressive fleet of smaller coastal colliers by the end of the 1930s, consisting of **Avonwood** 1056/34, **Cedarwood** 899/33, **Copsewood** 969/25, **Homewood** 870/27, **Levenwood** 803/24, **Linwood** 992/32, **Northwood** 1146/36, **Parkwood** 1049/33, **Southwood** 1149/37, **Westwood** 1040/35 and the new motor collier **Edenwood** 1167/38, which attracted considerable interest when she began running from the Tyne. In addition the company managed the four ships of the North West Shipping Company on the death of Mr. Williamson of Workington who operated in the East Coast coal trade. Coombes (Middlesbrough) Ltd., was registered in August 1918 with James Coombe contributing £7,450 of the capital of £7,800. Mr. A. Marshall subscribed £7,000 and the vessels were managed by Coombes, Marshall & Co. Ltd. A few coasters such as **Bilton** 746/20 and **Eskburn** 422/17 and the larger **Norburn** 2028/08 were owned in the 1920s.

Goole, Hull, Immingham, Grimsby and Ipswich

The next port south to have regular colliers was Goole. William France, originally based there, had moved to London but his vessels regularly carried coal from the port, as did those of Stephenson Clarke. Alexander Meek managed the Yorkshire Coal & Shipping Co., and his vessels mostly ran in the Hamburg trade, carrying general cargo also. They sold out to the Goole S.S. Co., in 1895 and went into ocean tramping. The growth in the coal trade meant that the Railway and Extension docks were packed with ships waiting to load. One of the companies to concentrate on colliers was Hunter & Ezard, who managed the steamers **Lisette** 899/99, **Nell Jess** 496/96 and **Wreathier** 855/97 around 1900 which were owned by the Goole & West Riding S.S.Co. Ltd., **Edie** 1035/03 was soon added, a raised quarterdeck steamer having the dimensions 220.0' x 34.1' x 12.5' so that they had a very modern fleet. The firm later became H. W. Ezard and eventually H. W. & C. M. Ezard. They became managers of the Yorkshire Coal and S.S. Co. Ltd., to which vessels were transferred including **Edwin Hunter** 1337/14. She had been built for the Goole and West Riding S.S. Co., which made a profit of £17,479 in 1915 and paid a dividend of 12% tax free, despite the fact that **Edwin Hunter** had been interned in Germany. The company paid wages to the crew's dependents and so incurred a further loss in the early part of the war. The company continued in to the early 1920s and re-named its two remaining ships. **Edwin Hunter** became **Abbeville** and **Edie** became **Merville**.

Also active at the same time was John H. Wetherall & Co. Ltd., and the Wetherall S.S. Co., which was registered in 1900, though he had the steamer **Pearl** 677/98 and sailing vessels before the formation of the owning company. Trade was good and by 1908 the company had six modern steamers **Pioneer** 121/01, **Rescue** 711/00, **Knottingley** 824/07, **Airmyn** 852/03, **Hessle** 952/07 and a new **Pearl** 613/04. The earlier vessels, such as **Knottingley** had engines aft but larger vessels such as **Blacktoft** 1109/10 had engines amidships because in the engines-aft design with full bunkers the vessel would have to be drawing more water aft when sailing from Goole in order to arrive on an even keel. Vessels down by the head are difficult to steer. With engines and bunkers amidships the vessel could leave on a much more even keel and so could be of larger capacity for a given draught. The Wetherall S.S. Co., went into voluntary liquidation in 1917 by which time only **Laxton** 1017/05 remained. Wetherall's continued through the 1920s with **Airmyn** and **Blacktoft** but the boom years were over for them. Some of their competition came from G. B. Wadsworth who made the changeover from sail to steam in the late 1890s and by 1904 had **Lizzie** 631/00, **Eastham** 569/91 and **Cornhill** 900/91, all with engines amidships. His fleet similarly grew in the boom years prior to the First World War. In the early 1920s it was down to **Argus** 704/06 and **Eurus** 825/13 and subsequently gave up operating separately from the Goole & Hull Steam Towing Co. Ltd., which the family controlled. This company had tugs with seagoing barges and had been established as early as December 1868 as a limited company. They owned a number of small steamers such as **Dickey** 507/01 and **Knowle Grove** 370/09, which they operated for many years. They also managed the Hook S.S. Co. from the mid-1920s which had **Kalua** 722/08 and **Lulonga** 821/07. The latter had been built as Wetherall's **Knottingley**, while **Kalua** had engines amidships. The fleet was augmented in the 1930s by **Aruba** 1159/16, a Dutch built steamer.

Several new companies set up in the 1920s and one of these was Calvert's. Alfred Calvert ended the war with **Essex** 297/96 and **The Mermaid** 194/91, but he and John S. Calvert set about acquiring ships in the early 1920s. Alfred Calvert managed the six ships of Alfred Calvert (Shipping) Ltd.,

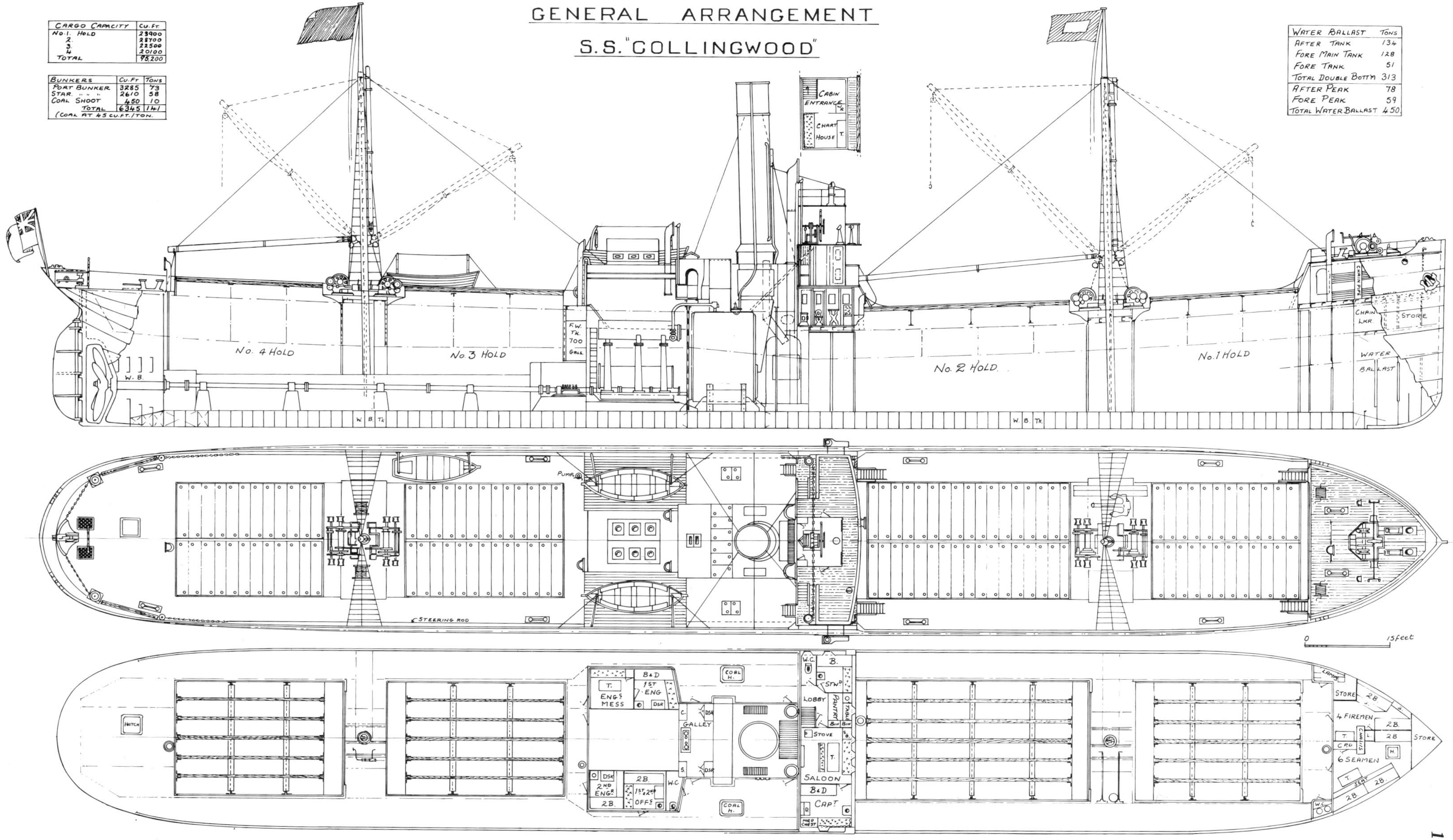

GENERAL ARRANGEMENT
S.S. "COLLINGWOOD"

WATER BALLAST	Tons
After Tank	134
Fore Main Tank	128
Fore Tank	51
Total Double Bottom 3/3	
After Peak	78
Fore Peak	59
Total Water Ballast	450

CARGO CAPACITY	Cu Ft.
No.1. Hold	23900
2	21700
3	23500
4	20000
Total	78200

BUNKERS	Cu Ft.	Tons
Port Bunker	3285	73
Star.	2645	58
Coal Shoot	450	10
Total	6345	141

(Coal at 45 Cu.Ft./Ton.)

No.1 HOLD

No.2 HOLD

No.3 HOLD

No.4 HOLD

CHAIN LKR.

STOKE

WATER BALLAST

CHAIN PIPE

CABIN ENTRANCE

CHART HOUSE

F.W. TK FOR GALL.

W.B.

0   15 Feet

STEERING ROD

PUMP

STOKE

4 FIREMEN

6 SEAMEN

CREW'S

STORE

W.C.

SALOON

CAPT.

PANTRY

LOBBY

STOVE

GALLEY

ENG'S MESS

1ST ENG.

2ND ENG.

OFF.

COAL H.

146.
Ralph Creyke, built in 1879.
Captain Atkinson's first ship.

ranging from **Lilias Calvert** 804/88 to **Alfred Calvert** 2788/03, which was too large for Goole. John S. Calvert, also operating from Adam Street, managed the Calvert S.S. Co. Ltd., which had eight ships ranging from **Glenville** 1074/00 to **S. E. Calvert** 4642/06. The largest single share-holder was Captain B. Larssen of Hull, who held £7,500 of the £32,000 capital of the company, which was registered in June 1921. Most of the vessels were over 2,000 tons and suitable for the Baltic trade from Hull. Calvert Colliers (1923) Ltd., was registered in September 1923 to own **Dernes** 880/24, which had a deadweight of about 1,350 tons. John S. Calvert was the largest shareholder with £6,650 of the capital of £13,600. By 1926 Alfred Calvert had sold off his fleet completely and J. S. Calvert was managing the **Dernes** and three vessels for the Calvert S.S. Co. Ltd., **Glenville** 1074/00, **John S. Calvert** 1151/07 and **S. E. Calvert** 1485/17, which were all sold during the slump. Another new venture from the 1920s was Buck S.S. & Coal Exports Ltd., which was registered with a capital of £10,000 in April 1923 and took delivery of the **Cyrille Danneels** 1585/24. This vessel was specially built to be the largest collier which could trade from Goole and so gave the captain some anxious times getting away on occasions. She was built by the Goole Shipbuilding & Repairing Co., and had the dimensions 250.8' x 38.0' x 14.5' with a draft of 15'6". She was a raised quarter-decker with engines amidships and could load about 2,200 tons of coal. Though named after a Belgian customer, the vessel also ran to London. She had collier No.228 from February 1926 and was sold in 1932 to George Gibson of Leith and subsequently sunk during the war. Prior to the delivery of the new ship T. H. Buck had purchased **Therese** 1299/09, followed by her sister **Fernande** 1311/09 from F. Bouet of Caen who had them in the South Wales trade. They were given collier numbers 230 and 229 respectively for the London trade in February 1926. **Fernande** passed to Italian owners and **Therese** to the Limerick S.S. Co., in the latter part of the 1930s.

The only one of the collier companies to survive the Second World War was that of the Atkinson family. The business was begun by Captain E. P. Atkinson who had been in command of the Goole S.S. Co.'s steamer **Frankfort** engaged in the Baltic trades. He retired from the company's service at the age of 68, but finding the inactivity not to his liking purchased the old **Ralph Creyke** 730/79 from the Goole S.S. Co., in June 1909. She had been built by Short Bros. and had later been lengthened. The vessel was wrecked off Flushing in 1912. Captain Atkinson and his son A. W. Atkinson registered the Ouse S.S. Co., in May 1916 and the first ship for the company was **Faxfleet** 843/16, but on delivery she was requisitioned by the Admiralty for collier duties at Scapa Flow. When returned at the end of the war she entered the Yorkshire house-coal trade to Antwerp, Bruges, Ghent and Rouen for a time at the beginning of the 1920s. She had a deadweight of about 1,000 tons and this suited Bel-gian merchants. In 1919 **Belge** was purchased and re-named **Swynfleet** 1168/14 and continued the use of local names ending in 'fleet'. The vessel had been built for the Danube grain trade which required a shallow draft, which also made her suitable for the Ouse to Goole (147). The good size hatches made her self-trimming as a collier. The layout followed the usual practice for the period with the engineers on the port side and the officers on the starboard side of the bridge deck (below the life-boats). There was accommodation for the captain and steward off the saloon below the bridge as well as a W.C. and bath. The vessel had a single main boiler and so there was room for coal bunkers on each side of it. Deadweight capacity was 1,620 tons on a draft of 13'5". She managed the continually shifting shoals of the river well. A particular problem area was where Ouse and Trent met at Trent Falls. Here the sandbanks could be shifted in a matter of hours if one or other of the rivers had received a heavy thunderstorm. Groundings often occurred and on one occasion **Swynfleet**'s bow kept catching on the bottom and the vessel would swing round. Eventually the captain made the last of the passage going stern-first. A further owning company was created in February 1924, the Ebor S.S. Co., with a capital of £6,000 which purchased **Broomfleet**. The vessels settled down to a round of coal cargoes on the coast, particularly in the winter, sometimes on charter to France, Fenwick with Baltic voyages in summer. In the slump at the beginning of the 1930s the vessels were laid up for long periods. Most of the coal cargoes had been loaded at Goole up to this time, but for some years prior to the war the vessels carried more coal cargoes from north east ports. Discharge was always by shore cranes and tubs or later grabs. The ships all had derricks and winches but were rarely used. **Broomfleet** was lost on a voyage to Ipswich from Goole but the remaining vessels **Faxfleet** 832/16, **Swynfleet** 1168/14 and **Yokefleet** 822/10 were trading at the beginning of the war.

Hull was never a base for collier fleets, although Hull owners carried coal from the port brought by the Hull & Barnsley railway to Alexandra dock. Massey & Sawyer were shipowners, coal fitters and merchants. Their ships ran regularly to ports in the Baltic and Mediterranean and so offered a liner service. Coal shipments were often taken from the port by Newcastle colliers which also loaded at Immingham and Grimsby, where the main destination was the bunkers of the many trawlers and drifters. **George Frusher** 662/01 and **Mons** 641/19 were acquired by the Consolidated Fisheries of Grimsby in 1927 and 1929 for a specific purpose. They ran a shuttle service between Blyth and Yarmouth to supply fishing vessels with bunkers. One crew operated both ships, sailing the loaded

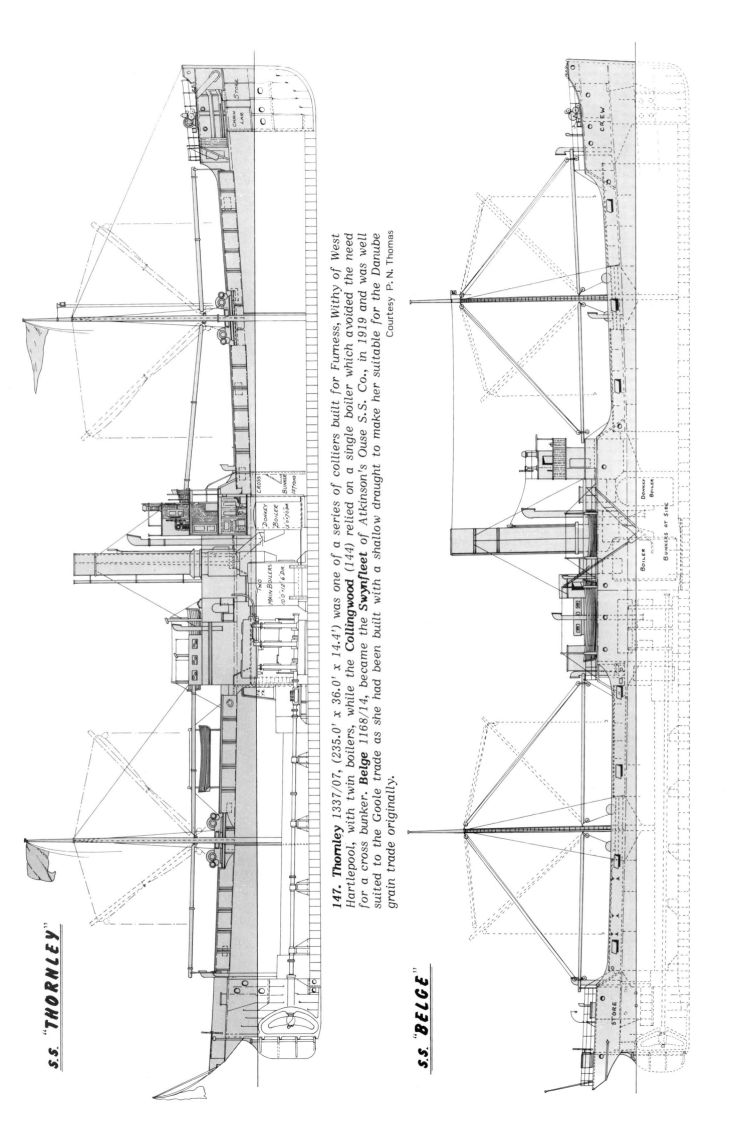

S.S. "THORNLEY"

STORE

CHAIN LKR.

CROSS BUNKER 127 TONS

DONKEY BOILER 26'-7"x10'-2"

TWO MAIN BOILERS 10'-0"x12'-6"DIA

147. **Thornley** 1337/07, (235.0' x 36.0' x 14.4') was one of a series of colliers built for Furness, Withy of West Hartlepool, with twin boilers, while the **Collingwood** (144) relied on a single boiler which avoided the need for a cross bunker. **Belge** 1168/14, became the **Swynfleet** of Atkinson's Ouse S.S. Co., in 1919 and was well suited to the Goole trade as she had been built with a shallow draught to make her suitable for the Danube grain trade originally.

Courtesy P. N. Thomas

S.S. "BELGE"

CREW

DONKEY BOILER

BOILER

BUNKERS AT SIDE

STORE

Mons, *880 dwt.*
Shipbuilding & shipping Record
1st September 1921

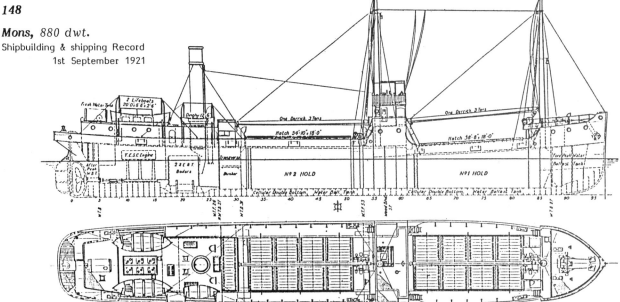

ship from Blyth and leaving the light ship to be loaded and shifted by the trimmers. She was usually left in the import dock, under a watchman only.

When the other ship was discharged, she returned to Blyth, and the crew simply left her and went down to the Import Dock and took the loaded one away. This arrangement suited the crew very well indeed, for they took their watch ashore at the discharging end, and were thus able to spend more time with their families and friends than would have been possible under any other arrangement. The arrangement came to an end with the outbreak of the Second World War, and both ships were disposed of in 1939.

George Frusher, built in 1901 and lengthened in 1905 was 38 years old and **Mons** was a youngster of 20 when she was sold to Charles Strubin of London after 10 years service with Consolidated. **Mons** was a typical steam coaster (148) and had been built in the boom after the end of the First World War by Dibles (1918) Ltd., of Southampton. She was fitted with a triple expansion engine and twin scotch boilers. The extra expense of twin boilers was not general in coasters with a length of 178 feet. She was fitted with reconditioned machinery which had been made in 1891 by J. Penn & Sons Ltd., London. She was built as **Lorient** to the order of Morgan & Cadogan of Cardiff but they soon sold her in the boom which affected Cardiff, particularly at the beginning of the 1920s, and she passed through several hands before being sold to Consolidated Fisheries. Sisterships included **Afon Towy** (W. Coombs & Sons, Llanelly), **Avanville** and a second **Lorient** 685/21 for Morgan & Cadogan.

Further south some of the smaller merchants and exporters had a few ships, as for example Mellonie & Goulder of Ipswich. They purchased several coasters at the beginning of the 1920s and in 1922 had **Isabel** 234/98, **Millwater** 365/21 and **Rosie** 115/07. They also signed an agreement with John Chambers Ltd., of Lowestoft on March 11th, 1920 for the building of **Marjorie Mellonie** 717/21 at a price of £52,210 which was delivered in November 1921. The **Millwater** was renamed **Elise Mellonie**. The ships were soon sold when trade fell away and last to be disposed of was **Marjorie Mellonie** in 1928, by which time she was managed from London and the company had become part of William Cory & Son. The company had a somewhat unusual discharging installation at their yard. It was a discharging crane with a fixed horizontal jib, with a heavy 'H' section girder along its length bearing the grab carrier. The crane ran on elevated rails between the quay and the inner extremes of the yard. It could swing right round (below) and was able to reach over the far side of a ship to load a barge, deposit coal anywhere in the yard, or load road and rail wagons. It was scrapped in 1974 when the yard was modernised.

*148. Mellonie & Goulder's coal wharf at Ipswich showing their transporter crane and the collier **Marjorie Mellonie** alongside in the 1920s.* MacRae collection

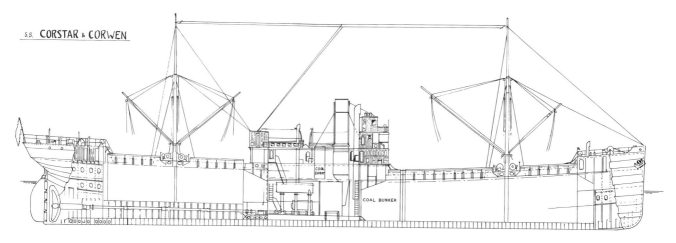

149. Profile of the D-Type standard steamers **War Dart** *and* **War Dagger.**

8. Southern Fleets between the Wars

The First World War completely changed the work of the collier fleets and all the larger vessels were taken over by the Navy. Cory's depot at Rochester was used by the army, in addition staff were encouraged to volunteer for service and a complete battalion of the East Kent Regiment was raised from Cory personnel by October 1916. The regiment was known as the Buffs and this is why **Corland** was originally named **Buffs** 3431/17. The company was then fully stretched supplying coal to essential war users, but the expansion of the business continued with the establishment of a French subsidiary and developments at Rouen. In 1918 the coal and tug business of R. & H. J. Rea Ltd., was purchased. The tug and barge operations remained under the Rea name, but Rea's colliers used carrying coal to bunkering facilities at Bristol and Southampton were integrated with the Cory fleet. The four colliers formerly owned by Rea Shipping were taken over in 1918, though **Tregarth**, which had been requisitioned by the Admiralty as a naval collier, was not released until 1920.

Cory's fleet suffered considerable losses. At the beginning of the war they had 28 vessels, and three more were built during the war. All were placed under a subsidiary company, Cory Colliers Ltd. in March 1916. Of this total of 30 vessels, only 12 remained. Seven vessels were added, including three German colliers built for Hugo Stinnes and surrendered to Britain as war reparations in 1919. They were purchased from the Shipping Controller in 1920 and became **Corstream** 1755/12 **Cordale** 1656/11 and **Corpath** 1820/12. The 'Cor' prefix had first been seen on **Corton** 3405/13 but it was not applied to the whole fleet until 1920. Two D-type standard steamers **War Dart** and **War Dagger** were also purchased from the Shipping Controller and renamed **Corstar** 2337/18 and **Corwen** 2337/19. These vessels had the dimensions 285' x 42' x 18.9' and a draft just under 19'6". The layout was that fairly often used in midship-engined colliers (149) though the crew were accommodated in the poop with the officers and engineers amidships. The large hatches and general layout suited the coal trade and they were to be part of the Cory fleet for many years. Two similar vessels were ordered from Swan Hunter & Wigham Richardson which became **Corduff** 2345/23 and **Cordene** 2345/24. Cory's continued to expand and the Mercantile Lighterage Company was taken over in 1920 and the Falmouth Coaling Co., was set up. Mellonie & Goulder were taken over in 1928 but the name continued to be used. Businesses were also started overseas.

Further vessels were ordered from Austin's in the late 1920s and a turning point was reached with **Corbridge** 1703/28 and **Corminster** 1703/28, for they were the last of what had become the traditional engines-amidships design. The **Corminster** however was the first ship to load coal at Dover from the Kent coalfield. Cory's then went to a completely new builder for their first modern engine-saft colliers, the Cowpen Drydock & Shipbulding Co. Ltd., of Blyth, who delivered **Corglen** 2822/29 (4,310 tons deadweight) and the smaller **Corbrook** 1729/29 (2,500 tons deadweight). So at the end of 1929 the fleet consisted of the two engines-aft colliers plus the engines amidships colliers, which divided into three main groups on length:

240-270 feet.   Corbrae 1926/12, Corbank 1933/13, Corness 1553/09, Corbeach 1569/13, Cormount 2240/18, Corstream 1755/12, Cordale 1656/11, Corpath 1820/12, Corbridge 1703/28, Corminster 1703/28.

275-285 feet.   Corfell 2098/08, Corcliff 1968/12, Corcrest 2373/18, Corstar 2337/18, Corwen 2337/19, Corduff 2345/23, Cordene 2345/24, Corchester 2374/27.

Over 310 feet.   Corland 3431/17, Corsea 2764/21.

The largest vessels were used in the Bay and Mediterranean trade in summer and to Beckton in the winter, as were the slightly smaller group which also carried industrial and household coal to Cory's three wharves at Albert Dock, Erith, and Rochester. It was for this trade that **Corhampton** 2495/33 was built (151). She was the first engines-aft collier from the company's usual builders, S. P. Austin & Son. Considerable care was taken with the design and a model of the proposed hull form was tested in the water tank at the National Physical Laboratory, Teddington. The tests were used to ensure the required service speed of 9.75 knots would be reached on the minimum power and fuel consumption. Subsequent trials of the ship showed a service consumption of just over 13 tons of bunkers per day when carrying 3,800 tons on a mean draught of 19'3". One other new feature was the adoption of a cruiser stern in place of the old counter stern. Although four holds might have been expected the aftermost hold was divided up so that five grades of coal could be carried. The whaleback protecting the steering gear and providing a lamp and paint locker was similar to that found on vessels built before the turn of the century. The dimensions were 292' x 42.5' x 21.3'. The crew were still accommodated in the forecastle. The vessel was sunk while on passage from Blyth to London when attacked by German aircraft in November 1941. Also delivered in the same year was the smallest vessel built for the Cory fleet between the wars, **Corhaven** 991/33, with the dimensions 208.0' x 34.0' x 12.7' and so well suited to Goole and smaller southern harbours. Company expansions continued in the 1930s and a joint venture with Charrington's, the Deptford Wharfage and Discharging Co., was set up and Coal Distributors (South Wales) Ltd., was established to market Welsh coal.

In 1934 the Chairman, Sir Arthur Cory-Wright, was able to report to the annual general meeting that the 22 colliers owned by Cory Colliers Ltd., had all been fully employed during the previous year in the trade of William Cory & Son at rates of freight which in aggregate were profitable. This was assisted by the sale of older inefficient ships leaving the new more economical ships to run profitably so modernisation of the fleet continued throughout the 1930s. A series of smaller colliers with the dimensions 257.0' x 9.5' x 18.9' were built by Austin's and the Burntisland Shipbuilding Company. Grab discharge was used for unloading and the small engines-amidships type had too many obstructions and were not very handy. However they were good in ballast returning northwards as the slow revolutions of their engines (65 to 69 r.p.m.) and the inertia of the long shaft meant that the screw did not race, as by the time it began to speed up it was going back into the water again. In the engines-aft replacements the governor was too slow and would cut the steam just as the screw was going in again and so they would lose way. The answer was for the engineer to operate the hand throttle which was made the more difficult as the stern, and consequently the engine room, could get rather lively.

The accommodation was well arranged with all the crew aft, though the second engineer had a walk round the deck to reach his cabin from the engineers mess. The hatches were as large as practical and the space not easily reached by grab below the bridge was used for a ballast tank (153). The vessels were supplying all the customers on the Thames and elsewhere with the smaller wharves and storage areas. They were particularly occupied supplying the cement works of Cliff, Northfleet, Greenhithe and Swanscombe. Tunnel Cement used to take one of the smaller ships about once a week. They usually used poorer quality coal which was loaded at Seaham. The smaller colliers also carried coal to Woolwich Arsenal, Greenwich Power Station and Bowater's paper mill. The coal from Methil was mostly used by power stations and the ships carried this. So Cory's small colliers soon proved their worth and repeat orders were placed so that 10 of the 'F' class of about 2,700 deadweight had been built with the delivery of **Corfen** 1867/44 by which time **Corfen** 1848/40 had already struck a mine and been sunk. The others were **Corfirth** 1803/34, **Corfleet** 1803/34, **Corfell** 1802/34, **Corbrae** 1788/35, **Corburn** 1786/36, **Corfield** 1791/37, **Corferry** 1788/37 and **Corfoss** 1849/42. The first three vessels had masts and derricks while the remainder had masts for navigation lights only and no derricks or attendant winches. Bunker coal for Cunard at Southampton and P. & O., was also carried, although P. & O. had their own two colliers, **Easton** 1587/19 (155) and **Redcar** 1558/20 which were given collier numbers 102 and 107 respectively in 1920 for the Thames. They were always well kept and were easily recognised by their blue lifeboats. It is interesting that these two colliers should run separately as the P. & O., had taken a controlling interest in Cory's in 1917. So though there was less demand in the summer this was offset by the ships going into drydock for their annual overhaul. **Corfen** 1848/40 was the only one of the series to be built by J. Crown & Sons and was fitted with steel hatch covers which were just being introduced on colliers and were similarly fitted to her replacement.

The hatches on all the colliers built in the latter part of the 1920s had to incorporate various Board of Trade recommendations. There would seem to be little scope for variation in the traditional method of wooden hatch boards and canvas tarpaulins in battening down the hatchways of colliers. It had been in use for hundreds of years and, done properly, was satisfactory. The canvas used was always of the best quality, and the weather hatches of every ship carried at least two good canvasses, with an older but undamaged one on top, to take the stains and oil from the straps of steel, wire rope, or the chafing of manilla sometimes used as lashings. These lashings were one of the results of the then Board of Trade improvements consequent upon serious losses due to hatch covers being stove in during the winters of 1923 and 1924. In the newer ships (post 1925) the hatches were almost always laid fore and aft in the beams so that they could be more efficiently secured by the lashings. The older system of laying them thwartships to a centre beam lost favour. With this type all the hatchboards often had to be removed when loading which was not very popular with the seamen, for all the boards had to be laid on the deck alongside the hatchway, see **Collingwood** (145).

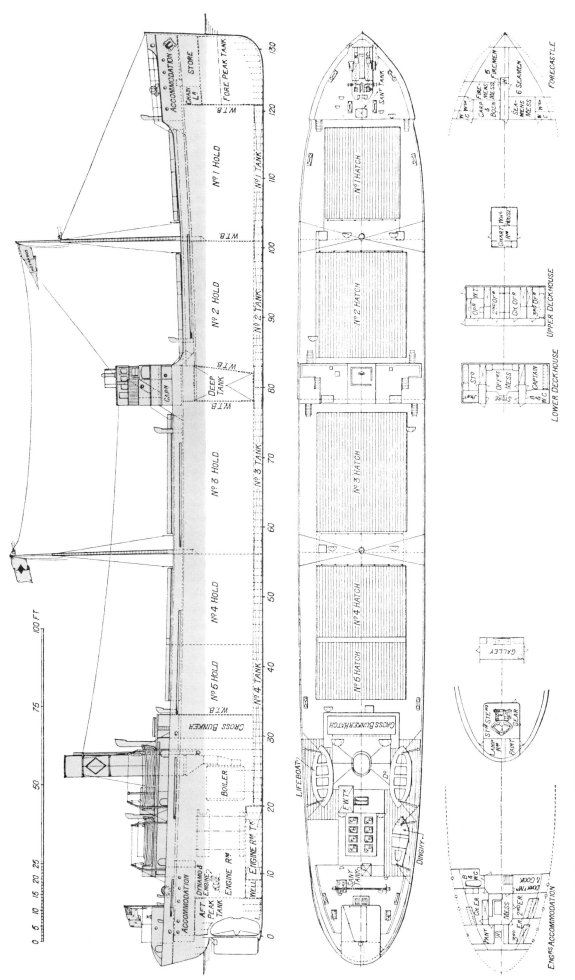

151. Corhampton of 3,800 tons deadweight was built by S. P. Austin & Son Ltd., for William Cory & Son Ltd., London. The large engines-aft colliers were being built in some numbers for London fleets from the beginning of the 1930s, but it was still usual to have derricks so they could operate outside the London coal trade should the need arise. An unusual feature of the accommodation was that of the engineers in the stern rather than as seen in the **Corfirth** (153).

Shipbuilding & Shipping Record 16 November 1933

There were many different ideas about the stripping of the hathways prior to loading, all aimed at making the opening and closing of the holds operations that could be carried out by the Watch Aboard (usually of two and, at the most, three men). Cory's, like most collier owners, signed crews in the north and so as many as possible of the crew went ashore. Those remaining aboard went ashore the following trip. It must be remembered that few of the later colliers had any sort of lifting gear or derricks ready rigged. In fact quite a few, notably the flatirons, had not even proper masts. All they had were two steel poles upon which, to comply with international Regulations, lights and shapes could be displayed, and between which the radio aerial could be stretched in later years. Those with deck gear, when engaged for lengthy charters carrying coal to the utility companies in the South of England, usually removed all derricks. They either stowed them away on board or put them ashore in the care of their usual repairer, to be re-installed if it became necessary to do so. Rarely, if ever, were they ever used again!

As by far and away the greater proportion of the coal burned by the Electricity and Gas producers was small and washed duffs, it never became necessary to use the Anti-Coal Breakage devices to be found at all the coal ports around Britain. Thus none of the beams were unshipped at the loading end and preparing for loading became a simple operation. The wooden wedges securing the tarpaulins under the long steel battens were knocked out along one side and both ends. The tarpaulins were then folded neatly back along the length of the closed side, one on top of the other, the hatchboards then piled on top and that hold was ready for loading (152). Also shown is one of the hatch hooks that made the handling of the up to 600 hatchboards easier.

As each section of the hold was filled the watch aboard swept the landing edges of the beams clear of coal and spread the hatchboards in that section. When the hold was filled they first shifted the ship to the next hold to be loaded, then battened down the completed hold, securing the tarpaulins with long steel battens held firmly in place by the wooden wedges driven home with the maul. The safety straps were then put in place and secured with a nut and bolt.

The beams on which the hatchboards rested differed from ship to ship. Some were deep webbed, whilst others were comparatively shallow but more substantial, with wide flanges ensuring they would remain upright when unshipped. Many ingenious devices were introduced in efforts to reduce both time and labour expended in preparing the ships for loading or discharging. One of the least popular was the rolling beam system. In this the beams lay on a sort of shelf along the inside of each side of the coaming, prevented from shifting by the raised edge of the coaming plate itself. When they were required to be shifted for discharging, a sort of trolley at each end of the beam lifted them and they were rolled along to one end of the hatchway, where they were secured by hefty bolts, the trolleys being used for each beam in succession.

Neither the crews of the ships nor the coal gangs at the Power Stations were very fond of them, none trusting the allegedly safe bolts. Conseqently they were almost always unshipped by the crane and either stowed on deck at either side of the hatchway or put ashore out of everyone's way. They were, of course, replaced as each hold was emptied and before the crane moved on to the next hold. They were not liked at all, for they could, and often did, jam tight against the coaming plate, making hard work of a job that should have been fairly easy and simple.

Then came the steel hatches. Although strictly speaking, they were not new, they were a vast improvement on the originals, used in the big French colliers of the P.L.M. line. These were mostly of one piece, corrugated transversely for extra strength, but were the very devil to handle because of their excessive height and great weight. They needed high fairleads for the lifting wires, though later variations were hinged in the middle. They were difficult to make and keep watertight, and after a series of damaging and sometimes fatal explosions they were abandoned. The explosions were caused by lack of ventilation allowing gas leaking from pockets in the broken coal to accumulate below the steel hatch covers.

New steel hatches were designed and made by J. MacGregor of Whitley Bay, Northumberland, and were readily accepted by both the shipowner and seamen and were a vast improvement on the

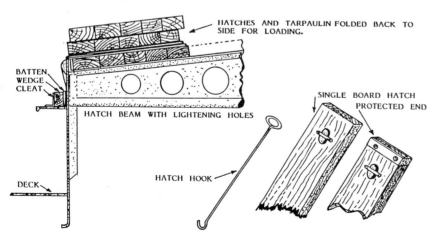

HATCHES AND TARPAULIN FOLDED BACK TO SIDE FOR LOADING.

BATTEN
WEDGE
CLEAT

HATCH BEAM WITH LIGHTENING HOLES

SINGLE BOARD HATCH
PROTECTED END

HATCH HOOK

DECK

152. Section through the hatchway of a collier prepared for loading, See also photo, page 21.
Drawing: Captain J. A. MacRae

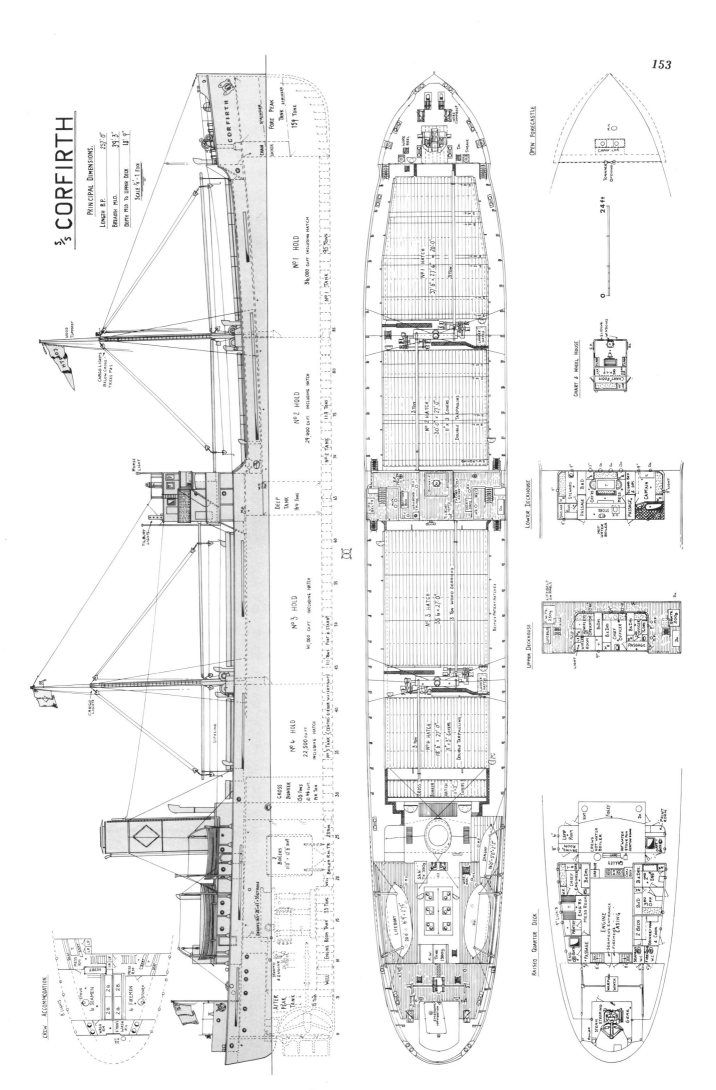

S/S CORFIRTH

PRINCIPAL DIMENSIONS.

LENGTH B.P. 257'-0"
BREADTH MLD. 39'-3"
DEPTH MLD TO UPPER DECK 18'-9"

Scale ⅛" = 1 Foot

CREW ACCOMMODATION

OPEN FORECASTLE

CHART & WHEEL HOUSE

LOWER DECKHOUSE

UPPER DECKHOUSE

RAISED QUARTER DECK

old system. Though at first each hatch had to be handled separately, very soon the single pull system was produced after the Second World War. In this the lids were all lifted to the rolling position, and the winch wire secured to the end one. The wire was rove through a guide block and pulley so that all the lids moved together towards the stowed position. As they approached the end of the coaming, a trip plate engaged a small wheel on the after end of each side and tilted the lid, the following one pushing it forward towards its correct position, to be tripped and pushed in its turn until all the hatches or lids, as they came to be known, were stowed in the minimum of space in an upright position. They were secured in the stowed position by safety chains. They were sometimes damaged by swinging grabs but later they were stowed under a winch table to prevent this.

Attempts at 'containerisation' were not successful with coal. Some containers of coal were once loaded at Garston on the Mersey, but for several reasons the idea was abandoned. There was a question of returning the empty containers, stowing them whilst the remainder of the cargo was discharged, and loading them back into the holds of the ship, making them secure. Then again, should a return cargo be available it could not be taken.

Decks of colliers also came in for a fair amount of wear and damage from coal and seawater. There were many types of deck paints on the market but few would last long. The usual colour was black as they were often tar or pitch based. The Texas Oil Company brought out 'Texacoat' which was similar to tar in both smell and texture. It looked well when applied, but failed to stand up to the weather. Monroe Brothers of Liverpool tried this unsuccessfully in the 1930s and began using a mixture of pitch and Trinidad asphalt. The drums were heated to remove the mixture which was boiled upon the galley stove. The boiling liquid was then poured on to the well chipped dry deck and spread with a trowel as evenly as possible. As it set quickly in contact with the cold deck it could not be spread thinner than about a quarter of an inch. It used to last very well until the seawater got under it eventually and it began to peel off in sheets.

The boat deck was generally painted red-oxide except around the coal bunker hatch, which was painted black when it was on this deck. The moulding along the outside of the boat platform was often painted white. The after part of the boat deck was usually over the engineers accommodation and it was a Board of Trade regulation that all steel decks over accommodation were sheathed with 3" planking. This wood area of the boat deck was caulked with pitch and the excess scraped off. The wooden deck was scrubbed and a mixture of creosote and raw linseed oil applied. After a time this gave the wood a deep mahogany colour. Eventually it was painted over, generally with red oxide. The bridge deck was also wood. It was scraped, scrubbed and generally treated with several coats of raw linseed oil tinted with red lead after which it was given several coats of varnish, similar treatment was given to the bridge where it was wooden. The forecastle head, when it was wood, was cleaned and treated with a mixture of creosote, Stockholm tar and raw oil. This soaked into the wood and resulted in a black colour. It was often later painted with a red lead mixture to keep out the leaks. The exact treatment would depend on the master's or mate's ideas. Another popular mixture was 'black varnish' which could be purchased very cheaply and was often used on ships bottoms and some would make their own version by purchasing coal tar, creosote and naptha from the local gasworks very cheaply, though most of the larger owners generally specified paint via the marine superintendent.

Crewing the colliers on the London trade was generally considered a good berth, particularly by firemen who would probably only work two watches down and two watches back for a week's pay as the round trip usually took four to six days. However when trade was bad in the early 1930s crews were signed off over the weekend to reduce costs and signed on again on Monday for sailing.

Wm. France, Fenwick & Co. Ltd., were slightly more fortunate during the First World War. They entered the war with 20 ships, six were running between London and Goole and the remainder in the east coast coal trade to London. They suffered five losses, all of their modern vessels serving with the Royal Fleet Auxiliary. However they were able to sell some vessels profitably as they were shipowners rather than merchants. In all, three vessels were sold including **Sherwood** 1353/04 for £50,000 to the Gas Light & Coke Co. Ltd. They ended the war with 12 vessels, but only three were under 10 years old. The prospects for trade seemed bright and the company took over two three-island type colliers which had been ordered by the Shipping Controller, somewhat reluctantly as the specification was not very good. They had the dimensions 268.0' x 37.9' x 17,6' and so were rather larger than the C5 type, carrying about 2,900 tons. They had a raised quarterdeck and although the vessels, which became **Whitwood** 1926/19 and **Deerwood** 1914/19, cost £82,500 they proved successful in service and served until the Second World War. Vessels which had been seized by the Germans, mostly in Hamburg at the beginning of the war, were returned to their British owners or to the War Risks Association if the owners had accepted compensation. These vessels were sold at public auction and the company purchased **Garesfield** for £72,000 which became **Bearwood** 1757/11 and **Leversons** for £67,000 which became **Braywood** 1774/09 and they proved successful, serving the company for over 20 years. The vessels were well suited to the London and near-continental trade, particularly the Bordeaux-Copenhagen range where cargoes were usually of between 2,700 and 3,300 tons. The company's most expensive purchase was **Dalewood** 2902/21, ordered in 1920 from Eltringham's Ltd., at a cost of £162,000. Though she was a raised quarterdeck steamer with good-sized hatches, her capacity of 4,450 tons proved too big for the London or near-continental trades available to the company and bunker capacity was not adequate for longer voyages. To make matters worse the hull had to be strengthened after only a few voyages. There was no option but to sell to German owners

155. *The P. & O. coastal collier* **Eston** *at sea circa 1935. Top: A heavy sea breaks over the bow. Centre: The officers dining in the saloon. Bottom Right: The engineer looks on as the donkey-man oils the piston gear on the main engine. The main steam valve control is just in front of the engineer while the engine-room telegraph is on the white pillar. Below: A stoker at work.*

Courtesy Topham Picture Source

who offered £44,500 in 1923. Bernard Blumfeld then used her to carry coal to Hamburg from the north east coast.

Towards the end of 1922 shipbuilding prices had fallen sharply as owners, seeing the low freights to be had, held off ordering, but like Cory's, France, Fenwick needed to replace war losses and the fleet was getting older. The company put out a specification asking for a quotation for colliers of 2,900 tons deadweight and 3,300 deadweight, to be raised quarterdeckers, and that the after holds should have the tank-top level with the top of the shaft tunnel to try and eliminate the continual grab damage to the shaft tunnel. Some 30 builders were invited to tender and after some deliberation Sir James Laing & Sons were given an order for two 3,300 ton vessels and two 2,900 ton vessels. Two further 3,300 ton vessels were ordered from Vickers Ltd., of Barrow-in-Furness, who had been forced to tender for vessels such as colliers by the lack of Naval work for which the yard was designed. They built **Helmwood** 2156/23 and **Dashwood** 2154/24 at a cost of £41,500 each. The arrangement of the deep tanks specified by the owners can be seen on the plan (157). These deep tanks improved the ballast capacity to 942 tons but problems were immediately noticed when the ship loaded coal and captains reported the vessels were extremely 'tender'. Obviously something had to be done to correct this lack of stability caused by raising the centre of gravity of the cargo. Neither France, Fenwick nor the builder had carried out any calculations prior to construction. There was no wood sheathing, so the bottom of the hold was made of half inch thick plating to withstand grab damage. This plating and attendant supporting stiffeners had to be removed from No.3 hold, an expensive operation. It also improved the cubic capacity which was not considered too good even though it was 47 cubic feet per ton initially. They were powered by a triple expansion engine with cylinders 20", 33" and 39" stroke developing 1,050 indicated horsepower, driving a four-bladed cast iron propellor. Steam was supplied at 180 lbs per square inch by two single ended boilers. The engine exhausted to a separate condenser. The accommodation was laid out with internal passageways for the engineers and officers, while the crew were housed in the poop. The cross bunker held about 135 tons and the side bunkers and shoot a further 119 tons so this was available for more distant voyages. The modifications were confined to the four larger ships of the Helmwood class as the two smaller vessels **Fernwood** 1892/23 and **Moorwood** 1892/24 were not built with a deep tank in No.3 hold. The larger ships were mostly used carrying washed coal from the Humber to near continental ports. After the initial problems the vessels served in the fleet for many years.

Developments had also been taking place in other directions for in June 1923 the Washington Coal Company was taken over, followed in November 1923 by a controlling interest in the Denaby and Cadeby Main Collieries Ltd., in a joint venture with the Constructive Finance Co. Ltd. The collieries were near Doncaster and had a fleet of larger colliers ranging from **Sampan** 1730/98 to **Winterton** 3868/13, which were engaged in more distant trading. The ships were owned by the Denaby Shipping and Commercial Co. Ltd., which had been formed in 1920 with London offices. At the turn of the century the fleet of four vessels was managed by T. R. Nicholas from offices in Doncaster and the vessels traded from Hull.

By 1927 France, Fenwick were thinking about the need to replace the older vessels, even though some were laid up. This had been partly caused by the boom in construction when building prices fell rapidly in the early part of the 1920s and the more modern ships tended to take what trade there was. Having had the recent problems with the engines-amidships colliers, they began to consider the practicality of building large engines-aft colliers as these eliminated the problem of the shaft tunnel continually suffering grab damage and also increased the cargo capacity by eliminating the weight and space taken up by the shaft. This was of particular interest, as the larger ships carrying washed coal were not able to take full cargoes and were often sailing 200 to 300 tons light even though they had quite good stowage rates around 47 cubic feet per ton. The company's technical advisors felt that the problems of trim, distribution of water-ballast and hull strength would be too difficult to tackle for vessels of 4,000 tons deadweight or over but the board were eventually convinced by Mr. Kenneth Pelly that a vessel should be built and evaluated so that when there was an upturn in trade they would be in a position to order the right vessels. Unlike previously, a detailed specification was worked out and a price agreed with Austin's without going out to tender and so the **Chelwood** 2742/28 joined the fleet. She had a deadweight of 4,190 tons and 310 tons bunker capacity. Assuming half full bunkers she could take a full load of coal stowing at a little over 49 cubic feet per ton and immediately proved so successful on the washed coal trade that a sister-ship **Chatwood** 2768/29 was ordered. To improve cubic capacity a little further the hatch coaming was raised 9 inches and the sides and ends were sloped off which also improved trimming. This feature was incorporated in all subsequent vessels built during the 1930s. A smaller version, **Bushwood** 2314/30, was built by Austin's for £39,500 for the continental trade where there was still a strong demand for vessels around her deadweight of 3,540 tons. When the company went back to Austin's for a third vessel of the larger class, the yard could not offer the required delivery date and so the vessel **Kirkwood** 2780/30 was built by Hawthorn, Leslie & Co. to plans supplied by Austin's. But she had a very short life as she was sunk on her third voyage while lying at anchor in the Elbe by an American liner. Further engines-aft colliers were built to take advantage of the improving trade and **Dalewood** 2774/31 was the first to use superheated steam and so improve economy still further. The fleet, by the end of the 1930s, was 25 vessels, many of which were modern engines-aft types. The fleet included two motor coasters which were built for time-charter, though the arrangement did not work out well and the vessels were sold after three years. The **Phylwood** 1013/35 was also built for a 10 year time charter to the Shoreham Shipping & Coal Co. Ltd., as was **Betswood** 1067/36. The

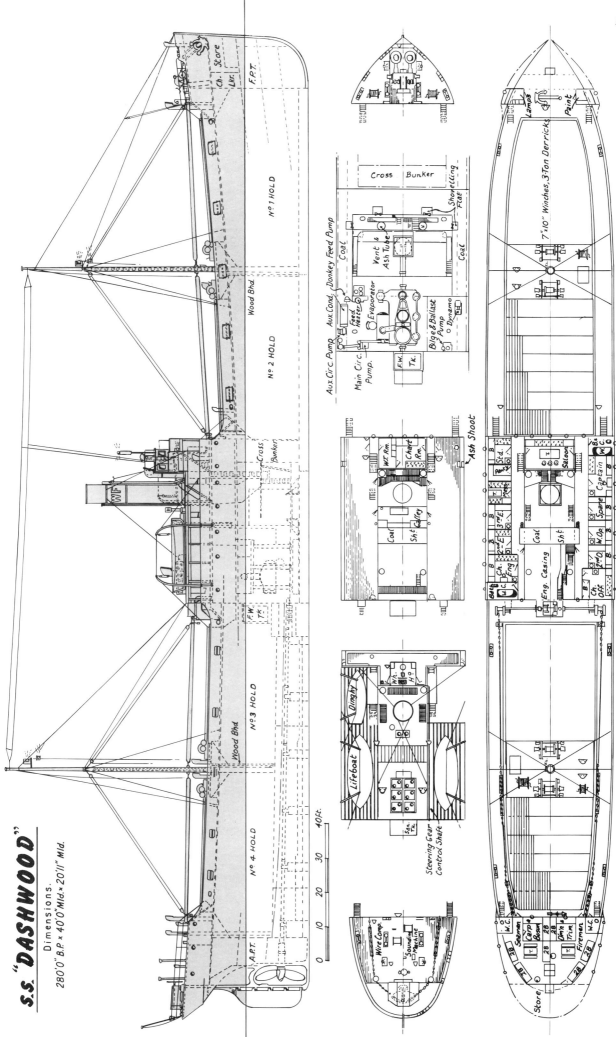

S.S. "DASHWOOD"

Dimensions.
280'0" B.P × 40'0" Mld.× 20'11" Mld.

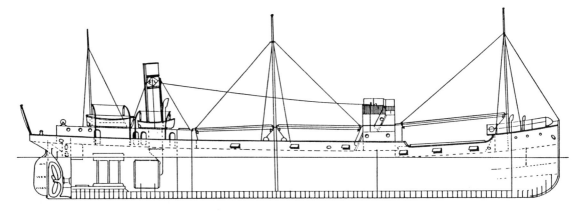

*158. E. T. Lindley's **Balcombe** (200.1' x 30.8' x 12.7'), built by John Lewis, Aberdeen in 1925.*

Yorkshire collieries the company owned contributed little in the way of profits, but secured a certain amount of coal shipping business for the fleet. In 1933 the company carried about 2,000,000 tons of coal despite the fact that delays and repairs amounted to 40 days per ship. The French trade was steadily lost as the French Government progressively restricted foreign vessels carrying coal to French customers. The Spanish Civil War caused France, Fenwick to drop out of the coal and ore trade from North Spanish ports in 1936, but their collieries began to make profits in the general trade upturn.

Though the fleet was largely expanded with new vessels the opportunity was taken in the slump of the early 1930s to acquire some secondhand vessels at very low prices from H. Harrison (Shipping) Ltd. They were **Seaton** 1530/24 purchased for £5,600 in 1932, which became **Sherwood**, and **Taunton** 1551/24 purchased for £7,300 in 1933 which became **Eastwood**. Bearing in mind that the **Seaton** had cost £35,000 when built, they were bargain prices and although not engines-aft types they soon recovered their purchase pice. Harold Harrison registered his company in September 1920, having sold most of the John Harrison Line to Leopold Walford in that year and subscribed most of the £1,000,000 capital. He already had some vessels under his own name, first of which was **Ralph Harrison** 959/18, and set about acquiring more so that by 1922 he had four vessels which were built to his order and seven secondhand, oldest of which appropriately was **Stonehenge** 732/76. He concentrated on coasting and the coal trade, but most were sold during the mid-1920s as new vessels were delivered from a variety of yards. The initial vessels were named after members of the family but all the later vessels had names ending in 'on' so that by 1927 the fleet consisted of **Alfred Harrison** 518/20, **Alfriston** 763/19, **Kempton** 597/25, **Surbiton** 649/26, **Torrington** 691/26 and **Westerham** 531/12. These were typical coasters with engines-aft, while **Atherton** 1534/23, **Clapton** 2001/11, **Dunston** 2010/24, **Farnham** 1599/21, **Paddington** 1545/24, **Seaton** 1530/24, **Taunton** 1551/24 and **Ralph Harrison** 959/18 had engines-amidships. The latter had Thames collier number 121 and **Islington** 1494/24 which was sunk in collision in 1926, No.48. The numbers were regisered with the Coal Factors Society for Harold Harrison by Temple, Thompson & Clarke, London shipbrokers who specialised in the coastal trade. **Torrington** 691/26 was sold in 1929 to Robertson of Glasgow for £12,000 and **Polmanter** 700/21 purchased and renamed **Torrington**. The vessel was regularly employed running east coast coal, usually from Blyth to Portsmouth and Hamble, but in the slump of the early 1930s all the steamers were sold, though **Mayrix** was purchased in 1934 and became **Kempton** 794/20 but was sold in 1937 as new motor coasters were delivered, but all these were sold by 1940.

Harrisons (London) Ltd., was an entirely different operation and was a subsidiary of J. & C. Harrison who had sold their coastal colliers to Cory's. They were involved in the ocean trade and were also bunkering contractors. They returned to owning coastal colliers just before the First World War and by 1918 had **Harden** 1686/12, **Harlow** 1785/15 and **Harlech** 1081/14. The latter was lost on a voyage from Hull to Brixham in 1924 by which time she was under Harrison's (London) Colliers Ltd., which had been formed in 1919. The fleet remained small in the 1920s and were sold by the early 1940s.

Harold Harrison's partner in John Harrison Line had been E. T. Lindley and he also invested in colliers after the sale of their business, retaining the same address as H. Harrison (Shipping) and John Harrison, 3 East India Avenue, London, for a time. Like Harrison he purchased a number of ships at the beginning of the 1920s which he sold and replaced with new vessels so that by 1927 he had **Balcombe** 929/25, **Brynmor** 2582/21, **Copthorne** 1450/23 (Collier No.126), **Gatwick** 1379/24, **Hookwood** 1537/23 (Collier No.145), **Horley** 929/26, **Outwood** 648/26 and **Timberham** 1546/24. As can be seen they ranged from big coasters like **Balcombe** (158) to colliers and more distant traders. His ships were often used to carry cargoes to the Thames for the Shipping & Coal Co. Ltd., who did not become significant owners until the 1930s. The partners formed a joint venture in November 1923, the Striver Shipping Co. Ltd., which owned **Plodder** 519/18 and was managed by H. Harrison (Shipping) Ltd. The arrangement lasted a short time before the vessel joined H. Harrison as **Ralph Harrison**. E. T. Lindley sold the remainder of his coasting fleet in the slump of the 1930s and purchased three colliers from the South Metropolitan Gas Board, **Lowfield** 1536/17 in 1928, **Waypark** 1543/18, both of which were sold in the mid-1930s, but retained **Nutfield** (ex-Bermondsey) 1561/19 and used her in the London coal trade (Collier No.35) and the vessels were quite often chartered by the Shipping & Coal Co. Ltd., for their cargoes to Dagenham and elsewhere on the Thames. **Nutfield** remained

159. Dagenham *the only Hudson collier to survive the Second World War.*   Photo: G.A.Osbon

under his management, although following a collision carrying coal from the Tyne to London in December 1942 she was sold to the Ministry of War Transport and became **Empire Nutfield.** Mr. Lindley dropped out of shipping when his ship was laid up and then eventually used to dispose of a cargo of chemical ammunition by being scuttled in the Atlantic in 1946.

Another company to go in for small motor coasters for the coal trade to coal depots in the centre of London which required navigation under the low fixed bridges was Q. M. Camroux & Co. Ltd., (D. G. Harris manager) which is perhaps better known as the Newcastle Coal & Shipping Co. Ltd. They began in the mid-1930s and were still operating at Rosebank Wharf in the 1950s. Their first ships were **Camroux I** 324/34 and **Camroux II** 324/25 built by Pollock, but **Camroux III** 409/35 came from Smith's Dock and **Camroux IV** 590/38 from Holland. They delivered coal cheaper than either the railways or dumb barges could into the heart of London, discharging just below Hammersmith Bridge.

The First World War caused John Hudson & Co. Ltd., to become collier owners. Prior to the war, coal from Northumberland and Durham and Fife coal from Methil had always been brought to Dagenham in chartered ships, but chartering of ships became so difficult and expensive that the John Hudson Coal Company began to acquire their own ships. First to be delivered was **Oxshott** 1241/15 which had a deadweight of 2,124 tons. She was built by the Campbeltown Shipbuilding Company, but further ships were all built by Osborne, Graham & Co. Ltd., they were **Hornchurch** 2159/16 and **Upminster** 2176/17. **Hornchurch** was lost by enemy action in 1918 and was replaced by a slightly larger vessel of 3,310 tons deadweight, **Hornchurch** 2162/19 and followed by a sistership **Dagenham** 2178/19, (159). The slightly smaller **Lulworth** 1969/20 was the last of the new fleet to be delivered.

Hudson's had been in the London coal trade from 1842 and became associated with Samuel Williams from about 1900. Samuel Williams was originally a lighterman and began his own lighterage business in 1855. He became involved in dredging and contracting, including work on the Thames Embankment, however he is probably best known for his works at Dagenham dock. Several attempts had been made to build a dock there and Samuel Williams acquired the property in 1887 when the latest of those attempting to build a dock failed. He filled in the marsh with spoil his lighters carried away from the tunnels being constructed for London's Underground Railway system and he soon established what was to become a large industrial estate. By 1894 the east and west jetties had been completed for handling the spoil barges and the existing wooden pier purchased in 1887 had been extended and an eastern arm added. This was immediately put to use discharging colliers which could come alongside at any state of the tide. They were discharged by four one and a half ton capacity hydraulic cranes equipped with large tubs into which the coal had to be shovelled in the ship's hold. The pier had a rail connection and the coal was distributed locally by rail. The docks and coal handling facilities were expanded steadily and by 1900 there were grab cranes in use for rapid discharge to rail or barges. By 1903 a reinforced concrete jetty (No.4) was complete. Though hydraulic cranes (using high pressure water) were the smoothest in operation Arthur Williams decided on electric transporter cranes as the severe winters had caused hydraulic cranes to freeze at a number of locations on the Thames in the particularly cold winters of the period. They were extremely efficient, the power being supplied from the dock's own generating station. They had a particularly long reach and could load barges on the inside of the jetty or railway wagons on the jetty itself. There were eight of these great structures on the quay and the drivers became really skilled at manipulating them, so that no time was lost in clearing ship after ship of their cargoes. They gave excellent service from the time they were built in 1903 until they were demolished in 1939 to make way for even faster electric cranes. They had discharged countless millions of tons of coal into barges and trucks (164).

Samuel Williams had earlier built a fleet of iron barges to take the strain of grab discharge and in 1905 Samuel Williams secured a controlling interest in John Hudson (London) Ltd. which had recently been formed to handle the London end of Charles Hudson, Pearson & Fearney of Newcastle.

The latter became J. Hudson (Tyne & Wear) Ltd., and was not involved in the take-over. The company had been formed soon after the death of John Hudson. The take-over brought even more coal business to Dagenham and the No. 4 jetty was lengthened to cope.

In April 1920 the Hudson S.S. Co. Ltd., was formed to take over the ships which up to that time were operated by J. Hudson & Co. The capital was £320,000 with A. E. Williams as Chairman. The fleet continued in the east coast coal trade and no changes were made as the trade prospects seemed rather uncertain. **Upminster** was lost in collision in 1928 and no replacement was undertaken until 1934. This became **Upminster** 1013/34, a much smaller vessel of 1,400 tons deadweight built for the London house-coal trade. She soon proved such a success that a sistership **Brasted** 1076/38 was built.

A new jetty was built to the west of the Thunderer Jetty in 1938 and was equipped with powerful electric cranes by Messrs. Stothert and Pitt, and carrying huge seven and a half ton grabs made in the workshops by Williams. Earlier, in 1935, an important agreement was signed with the then London Power Company Ltd. for the storage of coal at Dagenham, for use in an emergency, when the supplies of coal were interrupted by severe weather, war or other reasons. For the supply of coal to the capital had to be maintained at any cost, and the clouds of war were gathering for all but the blindest to see. Hundreds of thousands of tons of coal were stock-piled at Dagenham before, during and immediately after the war. Eventually the coal stocks at the Dagenham Docks disappeared, their places being taken by the gleaming oil tanks.

Though Charrington, Gardner, Lockett & Co. Ltd., had extensive coal business in the London area, nearly all their requirements were met by chartered vessels though their **Camden** 1425/11 was joined by **John Charrington** 1586/29. She could do 10.5 knots and once managed to reach Blyth from Gravesend in a little over 25 hours. She was unusual among colliers in having white bridge paintwork and was known as the 'North Sea Phantom' or 'Blyth Express' among the collier crews.

Perhaps the most unusual coal carrying vessels in use in the 1920s were the ferro-concrete barges built at the end of the First World War belonging to the Crete Shipping Co. Ltd., which was managed by Stelp & Leighton Ltd. The barges and a dozen tugs were all ordered by the Shipping Controller and the Admiralty in an effort to save steel. The sea-going tugs were of fairly conventional design except that the hulls were constructed in concrete and they had towing winches. The barges, of about 700 tons gross, had dimensions of about 180' x 32' x 17'. Towed by the tugs they carried coal both coastwise from east coast ports and to the continent. The barges had three holds and had a donkey boiler for raising the anchor. There was a cabin aft for a small crew and the captain had an open bridge from which to steer the barge. In heavy weather the tugs on occasion got into difficulties when the barges started to take charge of the tugs. The tugs and barges were slowly disposed of during the 1920s and replaced by more conventional colliers which all had names ending in 'stone', such as **Bluestone** 1367/23, while the concrete vessels all had names beginning 'crete'. All were sold in the slump of the 1930s. **Coralstone** 1371/24 and **Dewstone** 1371/24 were sold to Australian owners for the Newcastle/Sydney coal run, and so remained colliers.

Members of the Constant faily had been active in shipping on the Thames for many years and Martin Constant had a few coasters such as **Curraghour** 393/12 which he engaged in the South Wales coal trade. This led to the setting up in the mid-1920s of Constants (France) Ltd., which had the steamers **Ightham** 1777/09 and **Wrotham** 1757/11 which were emloyed in the Bay trade from offices in Cardiff. The company became Constants (South Wales) Ltd., about 1929, but the head office remained in London. Further secondhand additions were made to the fleet and the use of names ending 'inge' became usual such as **Beltinge** 1736/16. The ships were regularly used to carry coal to Bremen, Bordeaux and Bilbao, returning from the latter with iron ore. There were eight ships on the trade in 1938 and considerable quantities of esparto grass were being carried as return cargoes as the company moved into general tramping. Enriques, Fletcher & Co. Ltd, were managers of the Aldershot S.S. Co. Ltd., which was established in July 1915, and by 1922 the fleet consisted of **Chaldon** 1492/19 and **Sherburn** 1317/20. Among the shareholders was G. R. Cawood of Harrogate who was prominent in the coal trade from Leeds. All the vessels were sold in the slump of the 1930s.

Gordon & Stamp of Sunderland built up a considerable fleet in the 1880s and in the 1890s moved to London from where they were operating a fleet of 22 ships by the turn of the century in the north east coal trade to near and more distant continental ports under the title of the Gordon S.S. Co. Ltd. The London trade was also served and among the vessels owned was **Gordonia** 2338/81 and the name was perpetuated by J. S. Gordon & Co., of Newcastle in the 1930s with **Gordonia** 1687/22 which was given Thames collier No. 44. James Gibson and Sons owned the odd collier and managed the Mid-Surrey Shipping & Trading Co. Ltd. This company had the **Clearlight** 878/05 and subsequently purchased **Yewmount** which they renamed **Jim** 833/08, (161). The vessel had belonged to John Stewart & Co., of Glasgow who often engaged his fleet of large coasters in the London coal trade and so the vessel would have been a regular visitor to the Thames. She had been built for the Southampton trade of D. H. Willey, Southampton and was designed as a collier with large hatches and a ballast tank under the bridge. She was later under Hill (Southampton) Ltd., as J. H. Hill had become, the vessel retaining her original name of **Hampshire**. There were considerable sales of coal on the south coast and some of the local merchants had ships from time to time, especially those who supplied bunkers. G. Player of Teignmouth had the steamer **G. Player** 667/04 built in 1904. Whiteway & Ball had

GENERAL ARRANGEMENT.

S.S. "YEWMOUNT."

Principal Dimensions

Length B.Perps --- 195·0
Breadth Mid --- 32·6
Depth Mid --- 13·9

Scale ⅛ = 1 Foot

Hold Capacities

Hold	Including Hold	Hatch	Total
Fore Hold	10445	889	11334
Main Hold	15412	1908	17320
After Hold	19867	693	21560
Totals	45724	4490	50214
Cubic Feet			

Bunkers

	Tons
Cross Bunker	65¾
Coal Hatch	15¾
Totals	81½

at 45 Cubic Feet per Ton

Water Ballast

	Tons
Fore Tank	67
Main Tank	95
After Tank	60
Total in Bottom	222
Fore Peak	57
After Peak	18
Deep Tank	80
Total Ballast	377

Registered Dimensions

195·00 x 32·65 x 11·90
Under Deck Tonnage 595
Gross 833
Net 393

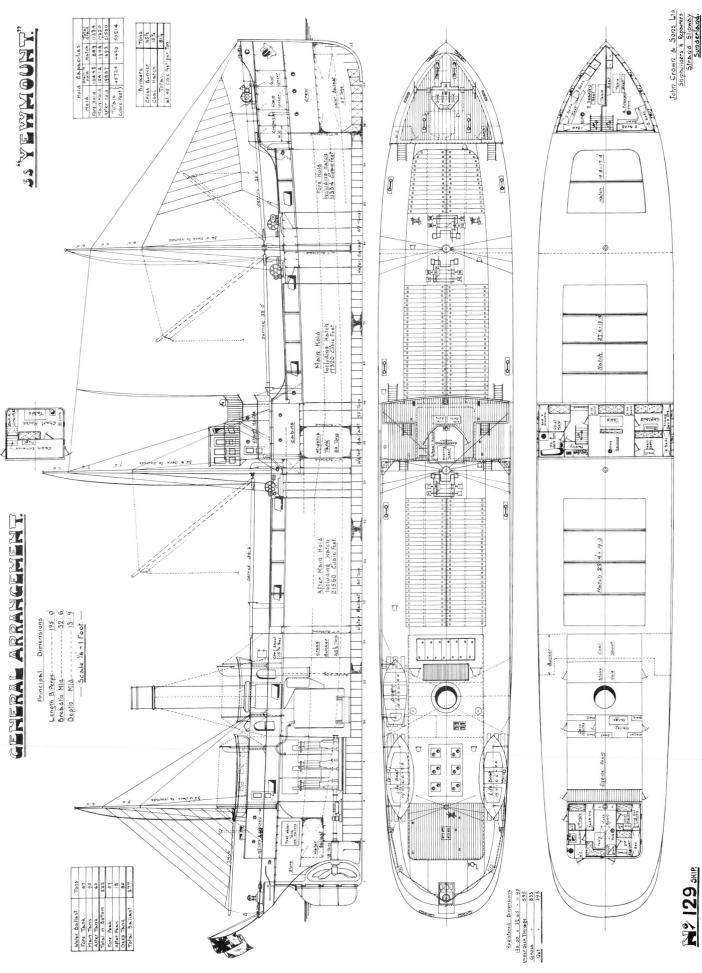

John Crown & Sons Ltd
Shipbuilders & Repairers
Strand Slipway
Sunderland

N.º 129 SHIP.

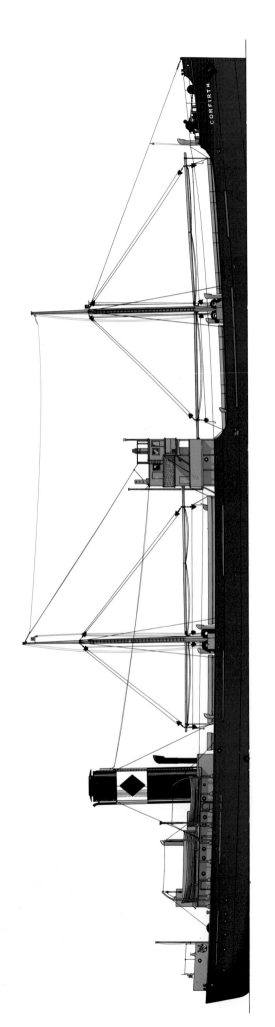

162. Dashwood 2154/24 (281.2' x 40.2' x 18.8'), was one of the last engines-amidships colliers built for London owners France, Fenwick & Co. Ltd., and operated in the Thames and near continental trades. **Corfirth** 1803/34 was one of a series of smaller engines-aft colliers built in the 1930s with the dimensions 257.0' x 39.5' x 16.7' to join Cory's fleet.

four vessels in 1904 including **Torquay** 726/90. They traded to the Baltic in summer and **Belliver** 755/03 foundered there on a return voyage to Plymouth in 1911. The firm later became W. Ball & Son and their colliers were regular visitors to Goole in the coal trade. They lost the **Dartmeet** 886/16 soon after completion and dropped out of shipowning.

Dartmouth and Torquay were the southern bases for Renwick, Wilton & Co., who also had offices in Newcastle and were connected with the Channel Coaling Co., who supplied large quantities of bunkers there. The partnership had been set up in the 1880s when T. Wilton had moved to Dartmouth from Tyneside. In the 1890s they acquired the old London collier **Vanessa** 1166/72 from John Fenwick & Son and later, from the same fleet, **Mazeppa** 1164/72 which served the company until being wrecked at Flamborough Head in May 1908 on a voyage from the Tyne to Dartmouth with coal. A new ship, **Kingswear** 1457/09, was then built, a single deck engines-aft design. The fleet was augmented by **Torquay** 870/14 with engines amidships (117). They sold their ships in the boom years of 1919, but Wiltons' in the form of T. & C. Wilton of London, continued in the coal trade from London in the 1920s and 1930s using place names from around Dartmouth for their colliers. **Haytor** 1189/25 was completed for the company and received collier No. 75. The much larger **Newton Abbot** 2689/28 (collier No. 110) was completed by J. Crown & Son in 1928 and finally **Bovey Tracey** 1212/30 (collier No. 60). The by this time old-fashioned engines amidships design with no raised quarterdeck was used (164). The layout follows the usual pattern though the crew were housed aft above a large aft peak tank and the forecastle was fitted with a tonnage opening to reduce tonnage. **Bovey Tracey** was bombed and sunk off Southwold in November 1941. The company managed a few ships for the Ministry of War Transport after the loss of their own ships, the **Haytor** having struck a mine in July 1940.

Hawksfield & Son Ltd. of Dover became coastal collier owners in 1929 through **Hookwood** 1537/23 which was owned by the Hookwood S.S. Co., in which they held a 50% stake. During the 1930s they acquired further second-hand vessels (**Kenneth Hawksfield** 1546/24 and **Peter Hawksfield** 959/18) and the four year old Kelly collier **Rosapenna** which was renamed **Kathleen Hawksfield** 900/33 (106). The company operated ships until the mid-1940s. R. H. Penney & Sons was registered in 1895 with offices in Brighton but had a long history dating back into the sailing ship era when they had vessels in the New Zealand trade and later steamers in the continental and Black Sea trades. After the turn of the century they purchased some large coasters which were used in the coal trade to nearby Shoreham; **Algeiba** 555/02, **Algethi** 548/02 and **Algores** 342/99, which was the most frequent visitor to Shoreham. Furher coasters were added, all with names beginning 'Alg-' and there were 5 vessels in the fleet in 1918, some of which regularly loaded coal at Goole. **Algardi** 759/04 was allotted Thames collier No. 135 in 1922 but by the mid-1920s all the old coasters had been replaced by **Algol** 1566/24 (163) which served the company until sold to Monroe Bros. in 1941. The company continued operating steamers until the 1950s when the **Algeiba** 869/23 was sold.

Also active in Shoreham, but particularly in the 1930s, were the Shoreham Shipping & Coal Co. Ltd. As the Shoreham Shipping Co. Ltd., they had the collier **Seagull** 658/02 built in 1902 and she regularly carried coal to Shoreham for many years, but in the 1920s and 1930s their coal was carried in chartered vessels, often belonging to Rix of Hull and later Atkinson's **Yokefleet** 822/10 was on time charter. The company then entered into a long time charter arrangement with Wm. France, Fenwick & Co. Ltd., for two sisterships **Phylwood** 1013/35 and **Betswood** 1067/36 with a purchase option. This was exercised on **Phylwood** in 1939 when it was sold at a good profit to Stephenson Clarke, immediately becoming **Broadhurst**. Because of the war and the fact that **Betswood** was requisitioned by the Government to maintain supplies to Shoreham, the company were not able to exercise their purchase option until 1946 when she was registered in the name of the company who sold her the next year to Stephenson Clarke.

The vessels were of particular interest to Stephenson Clarke as they had their own regular trade into Shoreham for which they were designed. In 1936 they had been appointed to manage the two colliers belonging to Brighton Corporation used to supply the corporation's power station and so would have vessels available to take extra coal needed in winter and to some other south coast customers, prominent among which were gas and electricity undertakings. Considerable changes had been taking place in the company, which still had its headquarters in London in St. Dunstan's Alley, a short distance from the Coal Exchange. During the 1914-18 war there had been little change to the fleet though two small steamers were acquired to served Shoreham, **J. B. Paddon** 570/14 purchased in 1916 and **Hove** 435/13 purchased in 1917. There was probably little scope for expansion of their own

163. Algol *of R. H. Penney & Sons, Brighton off Bristol Docks.*
Photo: E. N. Taylor

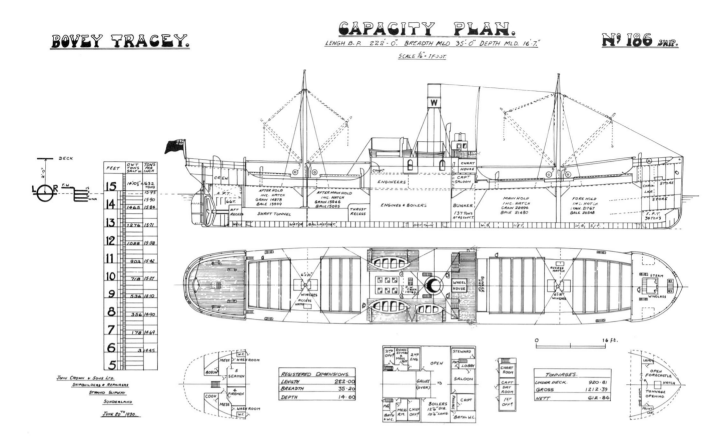

CAPACITY PLAN.

LENGH B.P. 222'-0". BREADTH MLD 35'-0" DEPTH MLD. 16'-7".

SCALE 1/16" = 1 FOOT.

N⁰ 186 SHIP.

164. One of the few small engines amidships colliers to be built for southern owners after the turn of the century, **Bovey Tracey** was delivered in 1930 to T. & C. Wilton of London.

Courtesy P. N. Thomas

164. Dagenham Dock. The electric transporter cranes on No.4 jetty used for coal discharge from 1903 until the late 1930s. The photo shows the first four of the eight transporter cranes which were eventually installed on the jetty.

MacRae collection

fleet as one of the company's biggest customers was rapidly acquiring ships which were placed under Stephenson Clarke management and at the end of the war 16 ships were being managed for the Gas Light & Coke Company. A separate company, the Normandy Shipping Co. Ltd., was formed in 1915 in a joint venture with the Powell Duffryn Steam Coal Co. Ltd., under Stephenson Clarke management to export coal from South Wales to France. The new venture took delivery of two large engines-aft colliers **Aube** 1837/16 and **Somme** 1828/16 with the dimensions 260.0' x 37.5' x 17.5' feet. Both were lost within a year to enemy action on voyages to France. To replace these losses, five steamers were acquired from the Shamrock Shipping Co. Ltd., whose vessels were in a similar trade. They were **Trostan** 1624/83, **Moyle** 1761/07, **Beltoy** 1544/15, **Glynn** 1106/99 and **Gransha** 1192/01. New engines-aft replacements, sisters of the earlier vessels, were ordered from Austin's and as **Vaux** 1830/20, **Lys** 1830/20, **Andelle** 1832/22 and **Nivelle** 1830/23 were delivered and the Shamrock ships were sold, all except **Trostan** returning to the Shamrock fleet. The vessels were usually employed carrying duff coal from Newport to Powell Duffryn's Patent Fuel works at Rouen and Rochefort where the coal was manufactured into briquettes popular on the continent. Occasional voyages were also made to Nantes and Bordeaux. However, the French trade did not develop as expected and the Normandy fleet was sold in 1925, two of the vessels passing to French collier owners F. Bouet of Caen. Stephenson Clarke could claim to have brought the big engines-aft collier a step nearer for the London trade for **Andelle** was purchased by Westoll and ran to London regularly though their own **Combe** 2030/12, built by Wood, Skinner, had been larger with the dimensions 275.2' x 39.0' x 18.6'. The vessel was lost on a voyage for the Russian Government to Archangel in October 1915. **Keynes** 1706/15 was the last engines-amidships collier built for the company and was slightly smaller than **Combe**.

Stephenson Clarke became a limited company in 1922, and a new company the Maris Export & Trading Co. Ltd., was formed with Powell, Duffryn to combine the South Wales export business of the latter with the North East coal exports of the former and generally act as export shipbrokers. The company had **Ilse** 2844/29 built which was transferred to Stephenson Clarke after a few years. With the retirement of Colonel Stephenson Clarke in 1928 the company was liquidated and a new company, Stephenson Clarke & Associated Companies was formed with Sir Stephenson Kent as chairman, who had been a partner in the earlier firm. The whole of the ordinary share capital was acquired by the Powell Duffryn Steam Coal Co. Ltd., though the directors remained unchanged and the Clarke name was represented by Mr. R. S. Clarke. A replacement for **Combe** arrived in the form of **Borde** 2014/21 and in 1924 **Ashley** 1323/24 and **Matching** 1321/24 were delivered. The former from Wood, Skinner and the latter from J. Crown & Sons. They were built for the company's coal trade to Dudman's Dock on the Thames. An unusual purchase was the **Ravonia** which had been converted into an up-river collier. She was re-named **Lancing** 703/08 and was used to supply gas works above the fixed bridges. The flatiron **William Cash** 1186/29 was built with this trade in mind (166), but was mainly used carrying coal to the Bournemouth Gas & Water Company at Poole and the company's Pitwines works was commemorated and served by **Pitwines** 932/23 which was the name given to **Wandle**, purchased in 1931. The year also saw the delivery of **Flathouse** 1546/31, named after the Portsmouth gas works which was regularly served by the ship for the next 30 years, although other destinations, particularly the Thames were visited (165). There was a general increase in business and so the demand for gas and electricity rose during the 1930s. To meet this the company had a steady building programme throughout the 1930s and Sir Russell Bancroft, chairman of the Southampton Gas Light & Coke Co., was commemorated by **Sir Russell** 1548/33, built to supply the works. There then followed a series of smaller vessels to serve Shoreham, Portsmouth, Southampton and Poole with up to 3 vessels joining the fleet each year so that by 1939 the fleet had reached 19 vessels including **Eleanor Brooke** 1037/38 and her two sisters just delivered.

A later arrival which took some trade with their ships was the Shipping & Coal Co. Ltd., set up by Scheepvaarts en Steenkolen Maats of Rotterdam, which owned a fleet of colliers under the Dutch flag, mostly with names ending in '-land'. The parent company imported large quantities of Northumberland coal to Holland and contracted to buy the entire output of various mines on an annual basis. Though this gave the company coal at favourable prices they were left with small steam coal and slack below about one inch in size which was difficult to sell in Holland. However, such coal was used in both cement making and power stations alongside the Thames and so a British office was set up to reach these customers. Contracts were traditionally fixed in January while electricity

165. *Flathouse   1546/30 of   Stephenson   Clarke, London.* Photo Alex Duncan

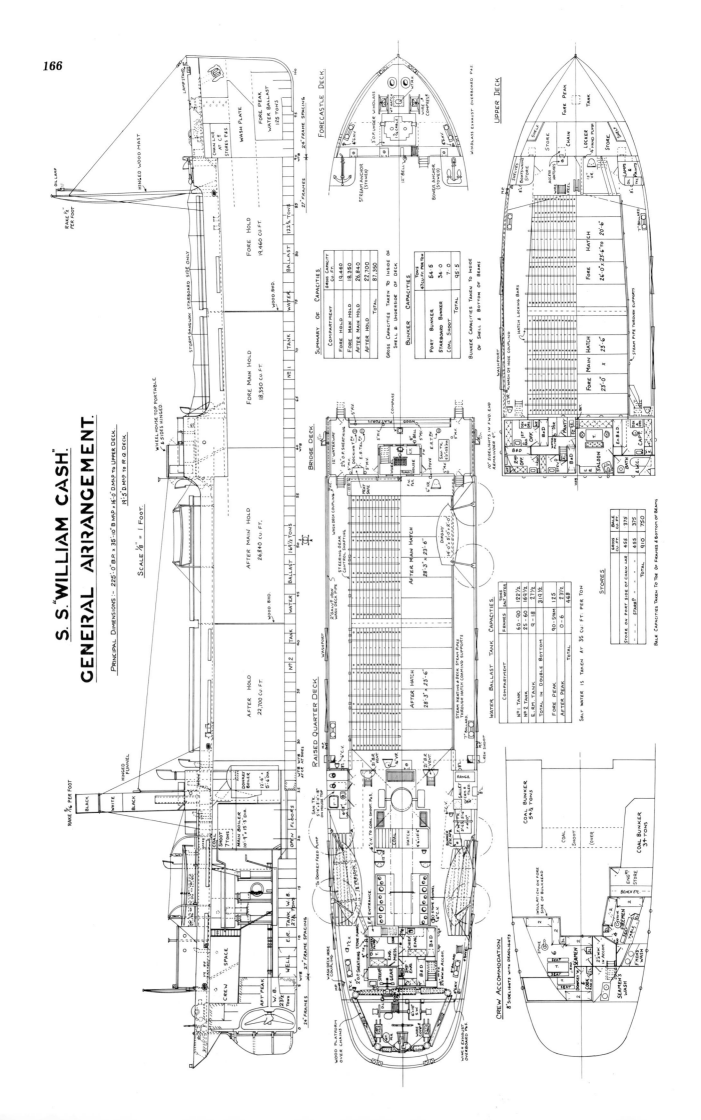

S.S. "WILLIAM CASH."

GENERAL ARRANGEMENT.

PRINCIPAL DIMENSIONS :- 225'-0" B.P x 35'-10" B MLD x 16'-0" D.MLD TO UPPER DECK.

19'-5" D.MLD TO R.Q. DECK

SCALE 1/8" = 1 FOOT.

FORECASTLE DECK.

UPPER DECK.

BRIDGE DECK.

RAISED QUARTER DECK.

CREW ACCOMMODATION.

SUMMARY OF CAPACITIES.

COMPARTMENT	GROSS CAPACITY CU. FT.
FORE HOLD	19,460
FORE MAIN HOLD	18,350
AFTER MAIN HOLD	26,840
AFTER HOLD	22,700
TOTAL	87,350

GROSS CAPACITIES TAKEN TO INSIDE OF SHELL & UNDERSIDE OF DECK.

BUNKER CAPACITIES.

	TONS 47CU.FT. PER TON
PORT BUNKER	54.5
STARBOARD BUNKER	34.0
COAL SHOOT	7.0
TOTAL	95.5

BUNKER CAPACITIES TAKEN TO INSIDE OF SHELL & BOTTOM OF BEAMS

WATER BALLAST TANK CAPACITIES.

COMPARTMENT	FRAMES	TONS SALT WATER
Nº1 TANK.	60 - 90	122½
Nº 2 TANK.	25 - 60	169½
E. RM TANK.	9 - 18	27½
TOTAL IN DOUBLE BOTTOM		319½
FORE PEAK	90-STEM	125
AFTER PEAK	0 - 6	23½
TOTAL		468

SALT WATER IS TAKEN AT 35 CU. FT. PER TON

STORES

	GROSS CU. FT.	BALE CU. FT.
STORE ON PORT SIDE OF CHAIN LKR	455	375
STAR BD	455	375
TOTAL	910	750

BALE CAPACITIES TAKEN TO TOE OF FRAMES & BOTTOM OF BEAMS.

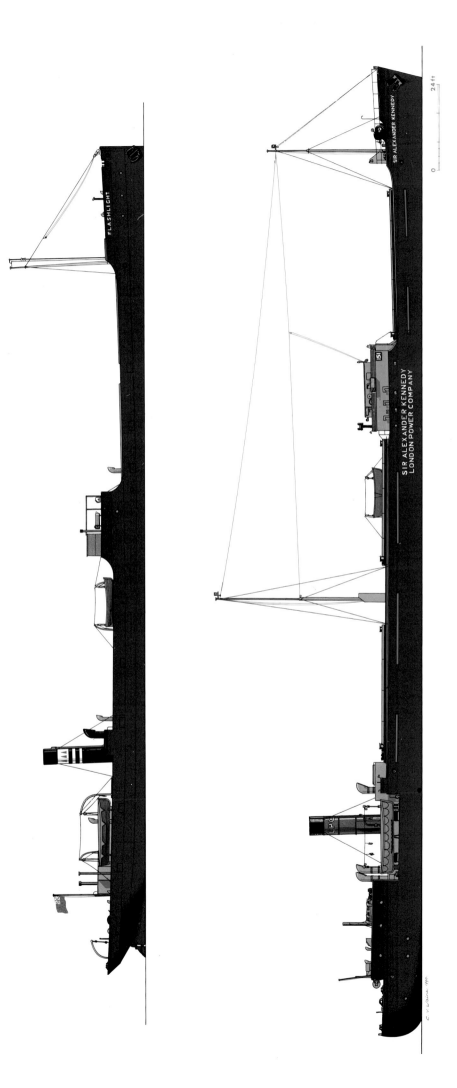

167. Flashlight 934/20 (216.5' x 32.0' x 13.4'), was built by Austin's yard for the Gas Light & Coke Company and was one of several up-river colliers or flatirons built to navigate under the low fixed bridges of the Thames to serve their Nine Elms Gas Works. **Sir Alexander Kennedy** 1714/46 (260.0' x 39.6' x 16.6') illustrates how the size of flat-irons had increased by the end of the Second World War. She was the last collier to be built for the company before Nationalisation and was intended to serve Battersea Power Station.

companies usually settled their annual requirements in April so there was always a period in the spring wondering if all the coal purchased would be successfully sold, but fortunately it always was. No ships were placed under the British flag initially, but with prices favourable in the mid-1920s **Foreland** 522/27 was built. The company had some 20 vessels under the Dutch flag and as trade picked up in the 1930s some of these colliers were transferred to the British flag operation so that in 1938 **Queensland** (ex-Beijerland) 1617/28, **Foreland** (ex-Dirksland) 1817/15 and **Waterland** (ex-Gaasterland) 1107/15 (Thames collier No.82) were all bringing small coal and slack to the Thames. **Lowland** (ex-Noord Holland) 974/11, though under the British flag, mostly ran from Goole to the continent. An important customer was West Ham Power Station, supplied by barge from Dagenham Dock. Samuel Williams were always keen to get colliers to use their facilities and relations became so good between the company and Williams' own Hudson S.S. Co. Ltd., that cargoes were swapped to each other's ships to keep deliveries on time, or one hold might be made available to carry a part cargo. Another power station supplied was Croydon via Deadman's Dock. Commercial customers included Associated Portland Cement Manufacturing Co., Tate & Lyle, Unilever and Watney Coombe & Reid, the big brewers. Another important customer was London Transport's power station which was also supplied post-war. Extra tonnage was chartered from E. T. Lindley and, occasionally, Richard Hughes. The latter's **Maurice Rose** 1600/30 was time-chartered for 3 months and caused consternation when it was found that they would only do 8.5 knots rather than their own company's 10 knots and so kept missing turns at Dagenham causing expensive delays, she was not chartered again. The charters were arranged by Temple, Thompson & Clarke, the coastal shipbrokers.

The numerous London collier arrivals were still handled by Tilbury Hailing Station as radio had yet to come to most colliers and was not general until after the Second World War. The hailing station had a long history and had been set up by the Coal Factors Society. About 1850 a list of ships for admission to the Pool of London was issued. Colliers on this list could not proceed above Gravesend without receiving from the Harbour Master written authority to do so. Each was allotted a temporary number which had to be written in a conspicuous manner on either side of the bow. The numbers had to be of not less than one foot in height and of reasonable width, and had to be maintained in legible condition until each vessel was discharged.

Part of the Harbour Master's duties at that time was to provide as many berths as possible in the Pool and Lower Pool, that is between London Bridge and Irongate Stairs, at which colliers could be discharged, generally into lighters, at the same time keeping a passage clear for through traffic. There were no less than 10 collier tiers in this short stretch of the Thames, but the number of moorings available gradually reduced as the need for them disappeared with the advent of the large steam colliers, and the provision of safe discharging quays which either served directly the actual consumers, or the stock yards of the factors and merchants. Turns at these buoys were allocated as the ships passed Tilbury and Gravesend, being communicated to them by Tilbury Hailing Station, manned by staff of the Coal Factors Society. It is uncertain where this was actually situated prior to 1867, though there is strong presumptive evidence that it was on the pier at Tilbury then in existence, of dummy barges connected by gangways. A move to re-site the station on the Gravesend side was stopped by the great steam collier firms, for the north side of the river was by far the most convenient and safest, all incoming vessels having to keep to the starboard hand, or north side. A new office was opened by the World's End public house, on the old causeway, but it proved to be unsatisfactory. Its shortcomings were partially corrected and the station continued in use until 1923 when the last structure, a disused concrete 'pill box' constructed as a gun position in the First World War, was taken over and a wooden house built on top. It had a pronounced list, which it retained.

The primary object of the hailing station was to keep all interested parties informed of the movement of vessels, especially colliers, as they passed in or out of the Thames. Their identities were established, when names were rusted away or illegible, by their Tilbury number by day, exhibited on a large board on top of the wheelhouse on the starboard side, and by night using a combination of coloured lights either vertically or horizontally, which enabled the operator to establish their names by referring to the code book. In addition many vessels had their names in large letters below the bridge amidships and sometimes the name of the owner when a gas or electricity company. For instance **Hackney** of the Central Electricity Generating Board, had as its day number 223 exhibited on a large hinged board on the wheelhouse top. (It had to be hinged so that it could be laid flat when transiting the bridges up to Battersea and Fulham power stations). The night signal consisted of horizontal coloured lights, reading from forward to aft, White, Blue, White, Red. **Jet Black** can be seen displaying her number in the photo on page 66. Vertical lights were generally used by the down-river colliers where height was not a problem. The short post just above the number carried blue over red over blue over red, (the light code for 73) at night. This system of identification was apparently in operation prior to 1865. The advent of V.H.F. radio, by which all ships reported their positions and E.T.As (estimated time of arrival) rendered these signals unnecessary and they were rarely used during the last few years of the hailing station's life. Prior to this the orders for the colliers were shouted across the water to the captain by megaphone.

Up to the beginning of the Second World War, the station passed news of arrivals and sailings of ships solely to the Coal Exchange, who in turn passed it to the interested parties, Electricity Generating Stations, Gas Works, Factors, etc. After the war the operators communicated directly with the firms concerned and mainly acted as a link between owners, agents, merchants, pilots, boatmen and others in the river, and the masters of the ships, passing any messages and instructions that would help them to avoid delay and facilitate the rapid turn round at the allotted berth.

More than colliers latterly made full use of the Hailing Station and its facilities. For it was manned day and night, 24 hours a day, by first class conscientious operators who used every endeavour to obtain the desired information from whatever source they could and they rarely failed. The inward passage was considered by many colliers to end at the Ovens Buoy (169) about a mile further down the river from the Hailing Station and would enter 'end of passage' in their logs or 'full away' on passage when outward bound. It would be the point at which it could reasonably be expected that no further engine manoeuvres would be necessary and the engineers could settle down to their sea routine and the engines set to the required revolutions for a sea speed to reach the destination at a set time, taking advantage of the tide as much as possible and setting up the engines to run as economically as possible.

169. The Ovens Buoy from a photograph (below, right). MacRae collection

Tilbury Collier Signals: The card issued to colliers using the service which was placed on the bridge in a prominent position. This particular card was carried by the flatiron ***Hackney*** *of which Jim MacRae was captain.* MacRae collection

TILBURY COLLIER SIGNALS.

S.S. ___"H A C K N E Y"___ DAY NUMBER ___223.___

NIGHT LIGHTS—HORIZONTAL.

LIGHTS AS BELOW WHEN PROCEEDING **UP** RIVER.

AFT.

Please read Signals from FORE. *of S/S.*

AFT LIGHT. FORE LIGHT.

IMPORTANT—In order to enable your vessel to be made out as soon as possible at the Signal Station you are particularly requested, during daylight, to place the NUMBER on the FRONT of UPPER BRIDGE *before* entering Gravesend Reach and to see that the figures are large and distinct.

At night care must be taken to display the signal lights correctly until either ANCHORING or PASSING, and again when getting UNDER-WEIGH.

COAL FACTORS' SOCIETY. *COAL EXCHANGE, LONDON.*

9.

*170. **Fulham** discharging at Fulham Power Station.*
Courtesy E. N. Taylor

Utilities,
Flatirons & War Again

Having seen the benefits of controlling their own fleet, the Gas Light & Coke Co. ordered and purchased a number of ships at the end of the war so that they could have a more purpose-built fleet. They had suffered some of the heaviest losses, losing 11 of the 18 ships acquired just before and during the First World War, also some of the vessels remaining such as **Horseferry** 1812/03 had been designed for the general cargo trade, while **Ignifer** 1451/07 was built to trade on the Canadian Lakes. These vessels had been serving the Beckton Works or Regents Canal Dock where coal was discharged into lighters for despatch to the smaller works nearby. Although the company had the engines-aft colliers **Flamma** and **Lucient** (270.6' x 38.2' x q18.0') built at the end of the war, only **Chartered** 2021/21 was of a similar design. The name may appear out of place where the theme running through them is one of coal and fire, but the company had received a Royal Charter as early as 1812 and was often referred to as the chartered company to distinguish it from later companies with similar titles. The largest ship for the new fleet was **Halo** 2365/19 from the Dublin Dockyard Co. She was a raised quarterdecker with the dimensions 284.4' x 41.9' x 19.0' able to carry 3,350 tons deadweight on a draught of 19'3", and had been ordered by the controller of shipping during the war, as had **Jetblack** 1560/20 which was of the standard C5 design (66), also from the Dublin dockyard. The trio of engines amidships colliers was completed by **Gaslight** 1696/20 a raised quarterdecker from Wood, Skinner. The latter vessel usually took about three tides to reach Charlton Buoys, her usual first stop latterly. Captain Jones recalls that she had a habit of parting steering chains and they needed frequent adjusment though the gear was fitted with a Dunston brake to reduce stress on the chains.

On the south side of the river the South Metropolitan Gas Co., had taken delivery of four further colliers from the Dublin Dockyard of the C5 type which had been laid down for the shipping controller at the end of the war, although based on their own earlier ships, and the fleet had seven of the type when the last, **Brockley** 1559/20 was delivered, though the C5 type did not have the raised quarterdeck. In addition there was the slightly smaller **Effra** 1325/10 and **Redriff** 1256/17. The latter was sold when the purpose built **Camberwell** 1568/24 was delivered. She was a slightly larger version of **Dulwich** design (65) including a raised quarterdeck and the plating over of the shaft tunnel in No.3 hold. A sister **Redriff** 1577/25 was also built, followed by **Brixton** 1551/27, in which the deep tank was extended the entire length of the shaft tunnel to give a level bottom to the after hold. As the new ships arrived some of the Dublin built ships were sold, both the flush deck ships and the raised quarterdeckers. The fleet then remained unchanged, apart from war losses, until after the Second World War.

The Commercial Gas Company's shipping operation also continued after the First World War, in which they were fortunate not to lose any ships. The company's up-river colliers were sold in 1926 as they were having increasing difficulties reaching Poplar and could not berth, because of silting, with full cargoes on neap tides. William Cory successfully tendered to deliver coal cheaper by barge, transhipping it from their much larger colliers down river. Wapping was still served by **Mile End** 859/11 which at 165.6' registered length was the smallest engines-amidships collier trading on the Thames. **Stepney** 808/16 was a conventional coaster design (60), and was the last vessel in the fleet in 1944 when sold. The agreement reached with the South Metropolitan Gas Company in 1930 meant that the latter's fleet was then used to supply coal via lighters loaded at the South Metropolitan jetty at the East Greenwich Gas Works.

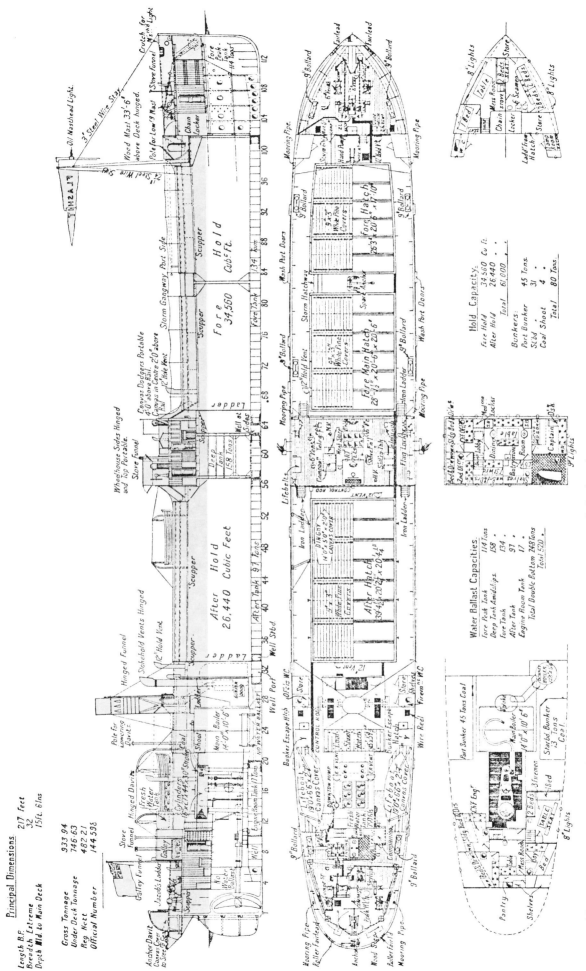

171. **Flashlight** *was built for the Gas Light & Coke Company by S. P. Austin & Son Ltd., in 1920.*

Shipbuilding & Shipping Record 5 August 1920

The only major additions in the 1930s to the down-river fleets of the Gas companies was that made by the Gas Light & Coke Co., in 1936. This vessel was **Mr. Therm** 2974/36 and a sistership **Gasfire** 2972/36, with the dimensions 318.4' x 45.7' x 20.0', a truly impressive vessel able to carry 4,610 tons of which up to 150 tons was bunkers. The design allowed about 50 cubic feet per ton stowage necessary for carrying a full cargo of the lighter Durham gas coals to the works at Beckton. The usual range for loading was Tyne/Hartlepool. The design had conventional hatches with wood hatch covers and 3-ton derricks in case they were needed for outside trading (214). They were later removed as the vessel was fully occupied running to the Beckton Works. The cruiser stern was generally being fitted to colliers at this time, but the bow was similar to that used on the Maierform hull design which was being promoted in the 1930s. To facilitate discharge hopper side tanks were fitted along the sides of the holds giving them a partial 'v' shape so that the coal slid down within reach of the grabs for easy discharge. Some of the more inaccessible space below the bridge was also made over to water ballast. The crew accommodation was of a very high standard for the time with the firemen and seamen having mess rooms. A nice touch was the fitting of glass panels looking into the engine room as no portholes were possible. The plan shows the vessel as fitted after the war, complete with radar scanner on the bridge. The name derives from a small man-like figure shaped to resemble a dancing flame, used in the company's advertising. A large bronze plate depicting this figure was placed on each side of the lower bridge. A rather smaller vessel suitable for the Regents Canal Dock, the **Icemaid** 1964/36 was also delivered, the unusual name relating to refrigerators which were gas operated.

The design was later to be used as the basis for a standard collier type during the war years later (see page 191). Early experiments with up-river colliers had been made over 35 years previously by the Commercial Gas Company and had proved successful, now the Gas Light & Coke Company decided to follow their example and supply their up-river plants in the same way. The first 'flat-irons', beginning with **Flashlight** 934/20, were built to serve the Nine Elms Works and had the dimensions 216.5' x 32.0' x 13.4'. The layout, (plans 167, 171), followed that which had been used for larger three hatch coasters from about the turn of the century with the well deck and fore hold larger than the after hold so that there were two hatches forward of the bridge. To reduce air-draught as much as possible mast, funnel, davits, ventilators and even the upper part of the wheelhouse was designed to fold away to pass under the bridges. The six seamen and donkeymen were accommodated in the low half-height forecastle and must have been difficult to enter even in moderate seas. The three firemen were accommodated aft and had to stoke about 8.75 tons of coal per day to maintain the service speed of 9.25 knots. On trials a speed approaching 10 knots was obtained with the engine developing 620 i.h.p. from steam at 180 lbs per square inch. The 114 tons of fore peak ballast was augmented by a 185 ton capacity tank below the bridge accommodation to keep the ship low enough in the water to transit the bridges safely in ballast. In later vessels all the crew were accommodated aft and the raised quarterdeck extended further forward. The stern anchor was also arranged for immediate use rather than having to be hoisted over the side and recovered by davit.

In order to meet delivery dates the other vessels in the series, **Afterglow** 936/20, **Ethylene** 936/21 and two extra vessels, **Suntrap** 939/29 and **Horseferry** 951/30 were all built by different builders. The gasworks at Nine Elms had vertical retorts for which the most suitable coal was washed 'nuts' which were generally loaded at Goole. The company then ordered five flatirons with the dimensions 225.0' x 36.0' x 15.3' to serve the Fulham Gas Works further up-stream where the jetty was able to accept slightly larger vessels. Again the lead vessel **Fireglow** 1261/25 came from Austin's yard who also built **Homefire** 1262/25 and **Lady Olga** 1266/27. Readhead's built **Sir David** 1275/27 which was named after Sir David Milne-Watson, Lady Olga's husband, who was Governor of the Company. Last of the series, **Torchbearer** 1267/29, came from John Crown & Son, Sunderland. Management of all the vessels was placed with Stephenson Clarke, who also managed **Brook** 1436/06 for the Brentford Gas Company which the company purchased from Stephenson Clarke in 1919 and so became ship-owners. The next year they purchased **Cranford** 1710/19, probably in an effort to get some control over the high rates being asked for vessels chartered. When the Gas Light & Coke Co. took over the company in 1926 the remaining vessel **Cranford** was sold, but the lighters which had been used to take the coal up to Brentford were retained in association with Stephenson Clarke as the River Lighterage Company which now collected coal from the Beckton Works for Brentford.

The Wandsworth, Wimbledon and Epsom District Gas Company were early pioneers of the 'flat-iron' and were probably forced by the high prices at the end of the First World War to purchase some secondhand tonnage. The conventional coasters **Ewell** 1011/06 which had been purchased in 1915 and **Ravonia** 703/08 purchased in 1919 were converted in that year to flatirons and joined the purpose-built **Mitcham** 1125/13. In addition there were the conventional vessels **Limehouse** 562/03 which was purchased in 1919 and sold back to the Commercial Gas Co., in 1923, and **Avonwood** 864/15 acquired in 1920 and converted into a 'flat-iron'. She was sold in 1924 to become **Broomfleet** of Atkinson's Ebor S.S. Co., Goole, and converted back to a coaster. The first new flatiron was **Wandle** 889/23 and was almost immediately followed by **Woodcote** 1242/24, a considerable jump in size. The Burntisland Shipbuilding Company prepared the design (173). The seamen and firemen were accommodated aft in this vessel as the forecastle was completely occupied by the chain locker and a large ballast tank to keep the bow low enough to pass under the bridges. The superstructure was also kept low, the funnel folded aft and the mast for navigation lights was telescopic

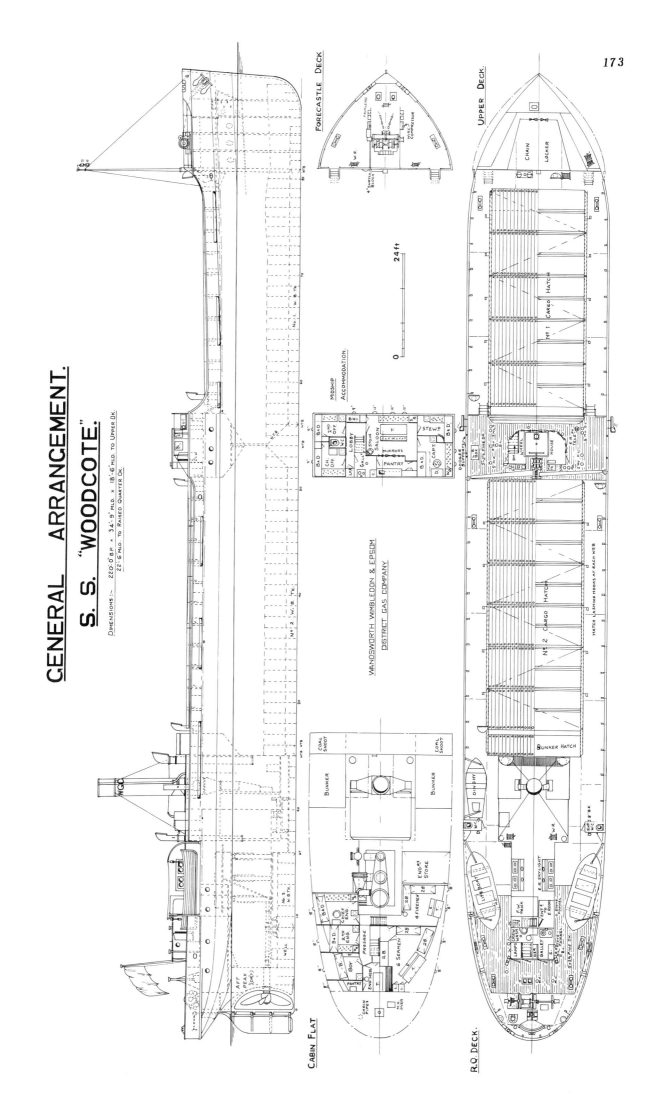

GENERAL ARRANGEMENT.

S. S. "WOODCOTE."

DIMENSIONS :— 220'-0" B.P. × 34'-9" MLD. × 18'-6" MLD. TO UPPER DK.
22'-6" MLD. TO RAISED QUARTER DK.

WANDSWORTH WIMBLEDON & EPSOM
DISTRICT GAS COMPANY

FORECASTLE DECK

MIDSHIP ACCOMMODATION.

UPPER DECK.

CABIN FLAT

R.Q. DECK.

and lowered into the hold. In order to get the wheelhouse low enough the midship accommodation had to be below the level of the fore-deck. Unusually a small galley was provided amidships next to the pantry which certainly made the stewards life much easier in bad weather, a second small galley was provided aft for the remainder of the crew. The work-boat (dinghy) was squeezed in alongside the engine room casing rather than beside the after-hatch where it was placed in the Gas Light & Coke vessels. For ease of discharge, sloping tank sides were fitted. The vessel served the company for 10 years and was then sold to Stephenson Clarke who renamed her **Cerne** and traded her for a further 21 years until she was scrapped in 1955. The early vessels were soon sold in the 1920s and were progressively replaced by larger ones as operating experience was gained, working closely with the Burntisland Shipbuilding Company. **Woodcote** had the dimensions 220.7' x 34.9' x 16.4' but **Wimbledon** 1598/37 measured 259.3' x 39.6' x 16.6' and had a deadweight of 2,375 tons, an increase of 650 tons over **Woodcote**. The improvements were largely the result of Colonel Croft, the company's manager. Though it was not until 1934 that a jetty was built for modern grab discharge which could be accomplished in about 5 hours allowing the vessel to catch the next tide. Prior to this a pontoon with two one and a half ton cranes had discharged the colliers to barges in mid-river.

Jobs aboard the company's 'flat-irons' were much favoured by crews as many facilities such as boilersuits were provided. Captains were expected to do at least 46 trips a year and with the new facilities Captain Tickler in the **Wandle** managed 72 cargoes. A bonus was paid for all extra cargoes over 46 and the company had a good pension scheme for officers long before most owners.

By the 1930s the growing use of electricity in the South led to the building of new large power stations which needed coal in considerable quantities. Several of the electricity companies decided to become owners to ensure regular supplies. Demand for elecricity had been stimulated by the First World War and the shortcomings of the small local companies had become apparent and the need for a fully integrated network able to supply the whole of London was strongly advocated by Francis Fladgate, who became chairman of the project in January 1920 with the formation of the London Electricity Joint Committee (1920) Ltd. However the largest undertaking, the County of London Electricity Supply Co. Ltd., did not join. The company followed a policy of chartering tonnage from the leading collier owners to supply Littlebrook and its other power stations. Prominent among those chartering to the company were Stephenson Clarke, William Cory and France, Fenwick. The new company was incorporated by Act of Parliament in 1925 as the London Power Company and power was to be provided from the new power stations at Battersea and Deptford. The latter site was already occupied by a power station built in the 1890s and designed by Ferranti for the London Electric Supply Corporation. The station became Deptford West, but the major part of the new company's needs were to be met by Battersea Power Station, the largest built anywhere in the world when it came into operation in the 1930s. Sir Leonard Pearce, the company's engineer-in-chief, would have had ample opportunity to study the operations of the up-river colliers bringing coal to the nearby Nine Elms Gas Works and so it was not surprising that when a fleet of flatirons was ordered to serve the new power station that Stephenson Clarke & Associated companies should be asked to manage them as they not only managed the flatirons serving the gas works but also were suppliers of coal to many of the electricity undertakings. The order for the initial series was split between Austin's and the Burntisland Shipbuilding Company who had produced successful vessels to serve the gas works at Wandsworth.

The order was placed in 1931 and the first to be launched was **Alexander Kennedy** 1313/32 at the Burntisland Shipyard (175), which was completed in September along with **Tyndall** 1314/32 from Austin's yard. **John Hopkinson** 1314/32 and **Ferranti** 1317/32 then followed before the end of the year. **Alexander Kennedy** had the dimensions 227.0' x 36.4' x 15.4' and so was rather larger than the 'flat-irons' serving the Nine Elms Gas Works. The layout of **Alexander Kennedy**, which was named after the L.P.C's First Engineer, shows how they were arranged. A wedge-shaped deep tank below the bridge amidships was fitted to avoid coal trimming though hopper sides to the holds was not considered necessary for grab discharge. Grab crane drivers usually managed to get this coal out by letting the grab swing in under the hatch coaming! The funnel was elongated sideways to make it fold aft as flat as possible for passing under bridges as shown on the top left of the plan. A further vessel **Colonel Crompton** 1495/33 was added to the fleet and incorporated experience gained with the operation of earlier vessels. The dimensions were increased to 237.0' x 38.2' x 15.9'. Perhaps the greatest change the crew would have noticed was that the steam steering gear had been moved on to the stern in a separate house of its own (177). In **Alexander Kennedy** it was tucked in by the engineers' cabins and over the crew quarters below. No doubt the engineers kept it particularly well oiled and greased to try and reduce the continual rattle of the steering chains. To simplify trimming the deep tank below the bridge was increased in size. The increase in breadth meant the ship tapered towards the bow for three-quarters of the forward hold length. The basic design of the early series was similar to **William Cash** which had been built some two years earlier, the main difference was that Stephenson Clarke's own vessel had four holds instead of two, so that different grades or consignments of coal could be carried, and no deep tank was fitted below the bridge. The L.P.C's up-river fleet was further augmented to meet the increasing needs of Battersea with the delivery of **Charles Parsons** 1554/36, **George Balfour** 1570/37, **Leonard Pearce** 1571/38 and **Joseph Swan** 1571/38, all from Austin's yard. They were an enlarged and improved version of the **Colonel Crompton** with the dimensions 239.0' x 38.7' x 16.2'. In the 1930s the vessels were mainly occupied carrying steam coal from South Wales but this was progressively replaced by coal from the North East coast in

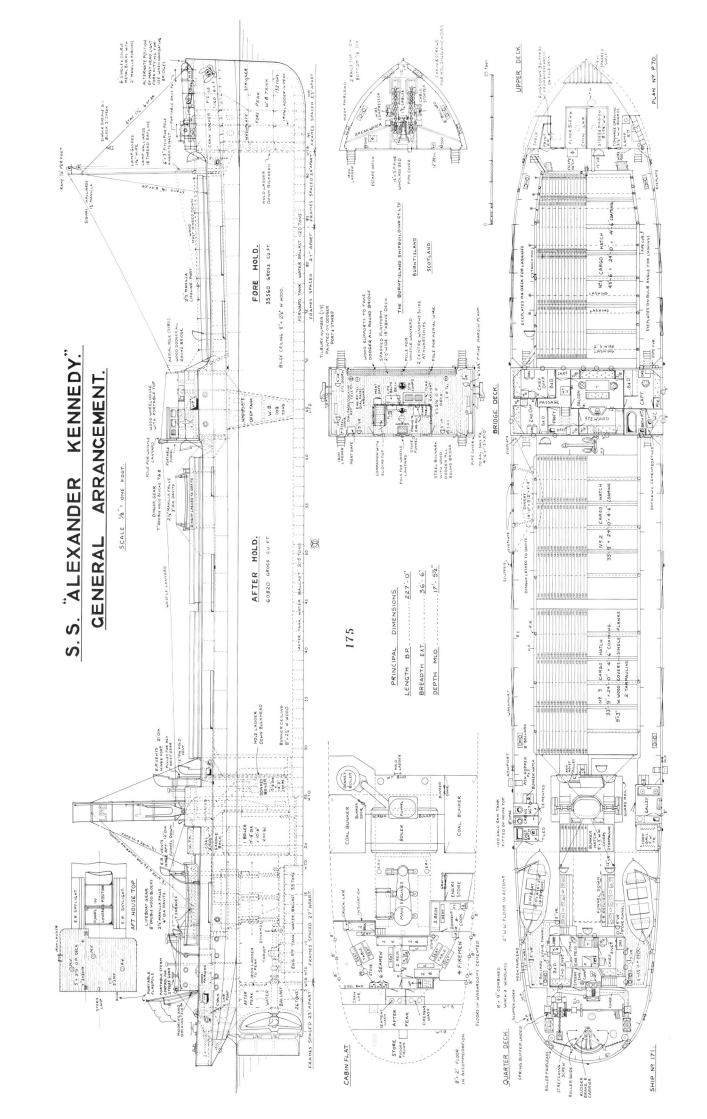

S.S. "ALEXANDER KENNEDY."
GENERAL ARRANGEMENT.

SCALE ⅛" = ONE FOOT.

PRINCIPAL DIMENSIONS.

LENGTH B.P.	227'-0"
BREADTH EXT.	36'-6"
DEPTH MLD.	17'-5½"

THE BURNTISLAND SHIPBUILDING Co. LTD.
BURNTISLAND.
SCOTLAND.

PLAN No. P70.

SHIP No. 171.

UPPER DECK.

BRIDGE DECK.

QUARTER DECK.

FORE HOLD.
35560 GROSS CU. FT.

AFTER HOLD.
60820 GROSS CU. FT.

CABIN FLAT.

175

later years. The **Francis Fladgate** 2268/33 was the lone conventional collier in the fleet, built to serve Deptford West.

While Battersea Power Station was on the south bank, Fulham Borough Council were pursuing a similar project on the north side of the river. Their site had been occupied by a power station since 1897. The new station was to be one of the large power stations which contributed to the national grid. Construction was begun in 1931 and in 1934 tenders were invited to supply the station for a period of 20 years. They followed the example of the London Power Company and ordered three up-river colliers from the Burntisland Shipbuilding Co. **Fulham** 1599/36 was delivered in February some months before the new power station officially opened, followed by **Fulham II** 1596/36 and **Fulham III** 1594/37. The design was similar to those built for L.P.C. and had registered dimensions which were almost identical at 238.1' x 38.3' x 16.5'. The steam steering gear was better arranged, separate from the accommodation, but sufficiently clear from the stern so that it was easy to move around the stern with mooring lines, but as with the L.P.C. ships a stern anchor was fitted so they could anchor at any time and there would be no danger of the vessel swinging when the tide turned. The holds were also slightly differently arranged with sloping slides to the holds as in **Woodcote** and a much smaller ballast tank below the bridge. The mast required for navigation in all these later vessels was telescopic, housed into a vertical guide, while in **Alexander Kennedy** and **William Cash** it folded down on to the fore hatches. Experience with the first three vessels soon showed that slightly larger vessels could be used and **Fulham IV** 1584/39 and **Fulham V** 1562/39 were delivered in 1939 with the dimensions 247.0' x 39.6' x 16.5'. Whereas the earlier **Fulhams** had followed the traditional format for colliers of counter stern and vertical or near vertical stem, the two new vessels incorporated the revolution which swept through shipyard design departments in the 1930s. This was the change to a raked stem and cruiser stern (177). The change to a cruiser stern which was more elliptical increased the length somewhat. In the bows the fore peak was reduced a little in capacity, mainly because the chain locker was placed lower. The first three vessels had a dead-weight of about 2,350 tons and bunker capacity of 105 tons. The new vessels carried another 50 tons, though bunkers were reduced to 101 tons. They had to carry a second navigation light as they now exceeded 250 feet in overall length and although the proposed plan shows it behind the wheel-house at the fore end of the hold, in the final design it was placed at the after end of the hold. The new proposal also brought in the much more easily trimmed cross-bunker even though it did reduce cargo space. The ship's timing for the run up river was important and it was necessary to pass Gravesend at the time of low water at London Bridge, so allowing five hours to reach Fulham or Battersea. Discharge was done so that the collier could sail on the next tide as soon as the vessel was afloat. Discharge time was thus important and so the power stations had the most modern equipment then available. The vessels had to be strongly built as they had to lie aground fully laden for discharge.

Though Messrs. Priestman Brothers of Hull produced their first mechanical grabs in 1875, some firms were reluctant to invest in the new technique, and used the old-fashioned tubs on cranes or even basket and whip rigs into the 20th century. For example, Messrs. Hawksfield & Sons of Dover installed a 5-ton electric crane as late as 1923, the first of three, which enabled the use of a grab for discharging their coal cargoes. Though the grabs that became so common at the discharging berths of colliers were almost always of the same basic design the cranes differed as the years went by and new techniques evolved. Slewing cranes at the older berths had separate hoppers at the side or rear. Battersea, Deptford and Fulham power stations had this arrangement. Though the hoppers at Battersea were big enough to allow two cranes to work into each, this was very rarely done except in an emergency. Those at Deptford were smaller. Provided all were mobile and could travel the whole length of the jetty, if one became unserviceable another could take its place. The hoppers weighed the coal and recorded the weights electrically in the foreman's office. Later installations did away with the individual weighing machinery and it was done by one huge scale in the main transmission belting system. The coal was passed to the main belt system by an undercrane belt, and then deposited wherever it was required, in either the bunkers or stockpile. Nearly all modern cranes at the newer post-war Electricity Generating Stations and the Gas producing works were of the Kangaroo type, that is they dropped their loads into a hopper which was an integral part of the crane itself, built into the front of it. As the crane did not have to slew that 90 degrees to a hopper at its side, much time was saved. In all the hoppers there was a substantial grid over the outlet at the bottom. Its purpose was to trap any scrap metal, wood or other junk brought up by the grab, and which could possibly damage the costly rubber belting. Powerful electro-magnets were additional safeguards, usually fitted at the mouth of the chute where it discharged on to the main belt. Railway truck buffers were often found, which was not surprising when one considers the extremely rough treatment the trucks received when being jolted to discharge the fine wet coal stuck in the corners. The Norfolk Spade was introduced with the intention of shifting this coal with greater ease and less danger. Though this was used without fail if the quantity of coal stuck up was considerable, for lesser quantities a quick shake could work wonders. As a consequence there were many ships whose engine room bell was made from a truck buffer which at some time had come from the end of one of Partridge Jones and John Paton's trucks.

Some of these great conveyor belts were more than a mile in length, and a tear was a costly thing to repair, not only in the expense of the new section, but in the loss of production of sorely needed power. Continuous production processes, interrupted for perhaps only minutes, were difficult

177

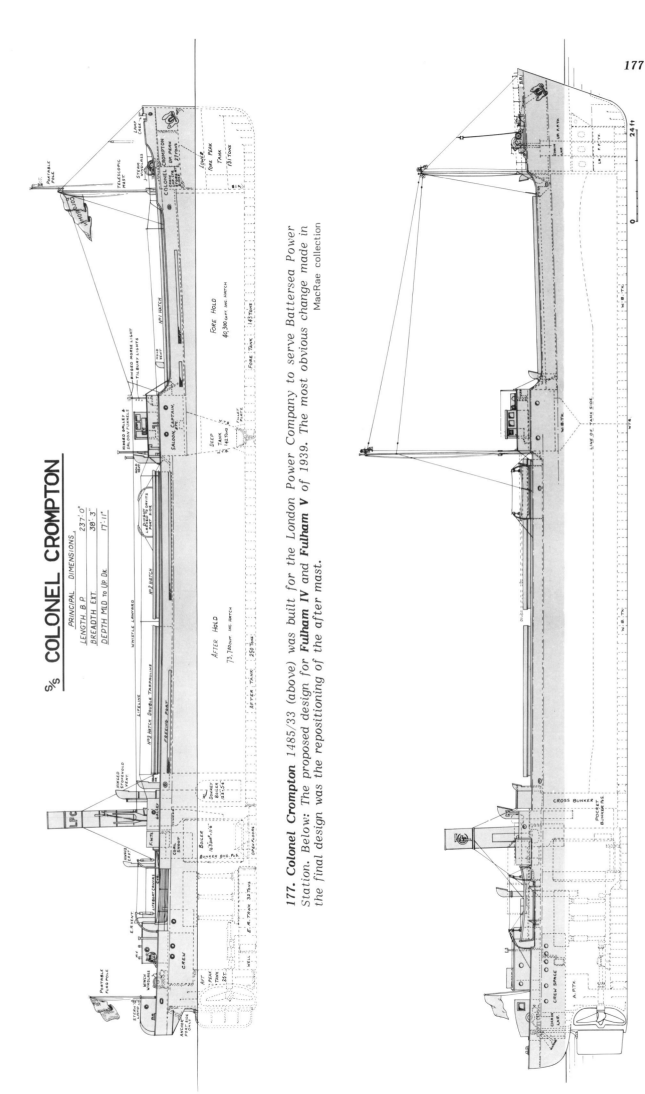

177. *Colonel Crompton* 1485/33 (above) was built for the London Power Company to serve Battersea Power Station. Below: The proposed design for **Fulham IV** and **Fulham V** of 1939. The most obvious change made in the final design was the repositioning of the after mast.

MacRae collection

to get started again, and plant could suffer damage. At Woolwich Power Station, where on the 4th of November 1964 one of the jetty cranes overbalanced and fell into No.1 hatchway of **Greenland,** a temporary replacement crane from the Woolwich Arsenal coal jetty was installed. It was old and slow and could pick up only a laughably small load. Days were needed to discharge one of the flatirons, and in the process the ships had to be turned round in the berth.

Naturally everyone was intrigued when, suddenly, new construction was started on the mysterious deep beams supporting ordinary rails that had been laid the length of the jetty, a permanent replacement was to be built. Rumour had it that the new installation would be the last word in efficiency, and completely automatic, depending for its operation upon electronic circuitry. Apparently the only time it would need the touch of human hand was when it was shifting from hold to hold. It was the brainchild of one of the Board's engineers, an extremely clever technician who, unfortunately, died before the crane he designed was completed.

However, the Ellis Colski Unloader (205) was not successful, simply because there were many imponderables to be taken into account. The first and, perhaps, the most important, was the movement of the ship in what was then an extremely busy tideway. No mooring can ever prevent a ship moving when large, fast and deep-draughted traffic is passing each way continuously. Wire compressors were never intended to hold a ship rigid for they have huge springs inside the heavy steel boxes which form the base sections to prevent sudden loads breaking mooring lines. Thus the grab, full of coal, and just leaving the heap in the hold, might be given a thrust in any direction, and swing wildly about as it began its swift journey to the guide section of the unloader. This was unfortunate, for the grab, in its ascent, was to operate some trip switches. These were to first bring into position below the grab a hydraulically activated shoot which would receive the load of coal from the grab as it tripped the second switch which caused it to open and release its load.

Frequently, the ascending grab did not stop in time and yet more damage was done to the crane head, which had to be repaired on many occasions during its short life. It was designed to discharge a bulk cargo at the rate of 360 tons per hour using a 3 ton grab, but in practice much less was actually achieved. The Ellis Colski was experimentally operated for about nine months, but as there were no observable economical advantages over conventional unloading equipment it was abandoned after that time and finally scrapped in 1974. The station was then shut down for most of the time, and what fuel was needed was supplied from Deptford and other riverside stations where there were efficient cranes. It might have stood a chance if it had been erected to supply a station such as Brighton 'B' where there is no rise or fall of tide, though even here passing traffic restricted to three knots can be disruptive. Not all the discharging installations were cranes in the accepted sense of the word. There were many transporters around the coast and provided everything worked well could be very fast indeed when the operator was experienced and skilled. At Shoreham, for instance, the two transporters could quite easily discharge the 4,000 ton ships of the **Captain J. M. Donaldson** class in a tide, provided there were no hold-ups in the belt system due to weather or condition of the coal.

On the original London Power Company up-river colliers or flatties as they were ultimately known, the wheelhouses were constructed to fold down, at about half height, after the top, made in three sections for ease of handling, had been removed. This left not only the helmsman exposed to any inclement weather, but also the chart table, drawers, and the other navigational instruments. Then two interesting facts were observed. The continual passage of deeply laden ships through the same arches of each bridge was causing a scouring effect, deepening the channel and allowing an earlier move to be made both going up to the berths and coming down again. Moreover it was seen that when the windlass brake handle was screwed up as tightly as possible, it was in an upright position and very much higher than the top of the wheelhouse.

Trial trips were made and though there were some heart stopping near misses with the wheelhouses up, there were very few contacts made that caused damage. With the outbreak of the Second World War in 1939 it became vitally necessary to protect the bridge personnel against aerial attacks. Bags of sand were tried but the idea was abandoned when it was found that the wooden decks of some older ships were being distorted and made unsafe. Eventually a form of plastic armour, mainly consisting of granite chippings and asphalt, was devised, making it possible to bolt each 'tray' of the stuff to a wooden framework surrounding the wheelhouse and confining the extra weight - by no means as much as sandbags - to the original beams and stiffeners. It made a much neater job and gave more room outside. It was a very real protection against a heavy 'rain' storm of shrapnel! Wheelhouses protected in this manner were not as unpopular as those where large and heavy concrete slabs standing on edge and so built up to the necessary height, were allegedly securely held in a wooden framework. Experience had shown that a near miss or a hit on another part of the ship had the effect of causing the slabs to collapse like a pack of cards, perhaps trapping inside the wheelhouse the men it was meant to protect.

Convoys and the Second World War.

When war broke out, the coastal convoy system was re-introduced at once, for there remained on record and in the memories of many individuals, accounts of the enormous losses suffered by the Mercantile Marine on the east coast during the 1914-18 war. Such a system became even more essential when low-flying aircraft and the fast motor torpedo boats (later to become known as

'E'-boats) put at risk the supplies of fuel to the London and south coast areas. It was here that the great concentrations of industry had grown between the wars, and huge electricity and gas generating stations had been sited. These alone demanded immense quantities of fuel in regular supply and when the factories went on 24 hours a day working, the resultant increase in power and heat requirements meant that more and more coal had to be supplied.

Though at the beginning of the war there was only one type of convoy, it soon became apparent that a different system would have to be devised, for the speed of a convoy is the speed of the slowest ship, and this, in the case of some older colliers, was very slow indeed. Independent sailings were tried, but losses started to mount alarmingly, and this concept, except in the case of extremely slow and shallow drafted ships, was abandoned. So two classes of convoy were organised, fast and slow. Fast would be of ships capable of maintaining a speed of ten knots or more, and consisted of the bigger ocean going ships, with perhaps some of the newer colliers and more modern coasters.

The slow convoys were to consist of ships able to steam continuously at 8 knots. Even slower ships were to be allowed to sail independently, keeping close to the shore for safety and protection. There were not many colliers able to maintain the ten knots demanded for fast convoys, though at first there were a few who claimed they could, basing such claims on the trial speed figures arrived at when they were young and full of vigour. There were always fast ships in the slow convoys, prepared to suffer the frustrations of a slow crawl for a few days, rather than wait for the next fast convoy. Most of the colliers on the east coast sailed in the slow convoys. Eight knots were asked for, a speed quite beyond the capabilities of some of the Lake boats, brought over from the Great Lakes of North America to make good the losses suffered amongst the regular colliers. Such a one was the **Chemong**, managed on behalf of the Ministry of War Transport (M.O.W.T.) by Messrs. Witherington & Everett (below).

Chemong 1902/24 along with her sisters such as **Anticosti** 1925/20, **Granby** 2051/22, **Wellandoc** 1926/27, **Coity Castle** 2767/19 and **Covalt** 2450/19, to name a few, crawled round the coasts of Britain at speeds varying from 6 to 8 knots, usually independently but sometimes in the slow convoys, where they easily out-did the flatirons in unpopularity. These were bad enough, their scanty freeboards and lack of top hamper making them difficult to see, but they could be, and usually were, steered with reasonable accuracy. The Lake boats having nothing forward of the wheelhouse right at the fore end of the ship, by which the movement of the ships head could be judged, coupled in some cases with two huge rudders, made them most unreliable bedmates. They were involved in numerous collisions, though that was only to be expected in such conditions. In fact there were few regulars in the coastal convoys who had not acquired 'convoy stems' by the end of hostilities in Europe. **Chemong** was one of the few Lake boats to survive the war years in European waters and return to her peace-time occupation on the Great Lakes.

Captain J. B. Roberts recalls an early convoy in 1939: "The Germans soon mined the coastal route between Blyth and Tyne and the customs launch told us in **Polgrange** 804/20 to steer 80° true well out to sea from Blyth to avoid mines and then turn south to pick up the convoys off the Tyne. We then steamed to Hull roads where the convoy anchored for the night outside Spurn Point. One hour before daylight we heaved the anchor in short ready for the 'off' when the naval control boat cancelled the sailing orders. It was the occasion of the first air-raid on the roads and after two to three days food began to run out, so the mate and steward were taken ashore by naval launches to get food, the mate returned and said they were sweeping with chains and wires in an effort to find out what had been dropped. This was about December 1939 when it was dark by 4.30 p.m. so we could just reach the Nore and thence to Southend in daylight at eight and a half knots, but many coasters could not maintain speed when cleaning fires and would start falling behind after about 8 hours or so, and **Galacum** 585/15 was always getting left behind. After a few months we were issued with a rifle! By spring 1940 coasters and colliers began to have machine guns fitted. On arrival at Southend we had to anchor in an allotted square on the chart and fly a certain signal. **Polglen** 795/15 said you go first to us in the **Polgrange** (223) and I will follow you. We anchored off the Nore and he came up behind and anchored too close. The strong eddy tide sheered him into us, we both had our life-boats swung out and his fouled our forestay. We decided it was best if we moved so we changed our signal and moved on to a better anchorage at Southend. We were both bound for Portsmouth and when the launch came out all the onward bound ships and our company's other ship all got their orders but we did not. After waiting a few hours we decided to lower the

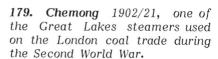

179. *Chemong* 1902/21, one of the Great Lakes steamers used on the London coal trade during the Second World War.

MacRae collection

boat and go to Naval control on Southend Pier to find out the reason for the delay. On enquiring, the Controller looked at his chart and said but you are not THERE, pointing to his chart. I assured him that the ship did exist and suggested he stepped outside to see for himself. Then he said 'how did you get here?' - I said 'our own dinghy'. 'That's against regulations' he said, but we eventually sailed in the next convoy. Dover convoys were very tough. Eleven of us sailed from Southend and as we rounded Dover the shelling began, but the shells fell mostly astern of the ships though we did not know what it was at that time. Then the dive-bombers came and the mate sprinted to the machine gun but as he arrived he looked aft to see a bomb go straight through the engine room skylight of **Polgrange** and jumped overboard, not waiting for the explosion! The ship sank stern first and fortunately there were soon motor launches picking us up. One of Everard's loaded with cement was hit producing clouds of cement dust and they beached her between Dover and Folkestone. I could see clouds of smoke and flames from the Wilson line ship ahead of us, **Leo** I believe. Seven ships were sunk in this first attack and between Dungeness and Beachy Head E-boats got two more, just two got through. After that naval control told us; 'no more convoys round Dover', but the order was soon changed and Dover sailings resumed. Though two destroyers came out of Dover when the convoy was attacked, there was little they could do.

D.E.M.S (Defensively Equipped Merchant Ships) began convoys without escorts initially but from spring 1940 about one destroyer escort was used. The usual routine was assemble about 4 a.m. outside Tyne piers for convoy. Arrive Spurn anchorage before dark, leave 5 - 6 a.m. next day and arrive Southend. Next morning leave at crack of dawn to have daylight around Dover. Only necessary crew were on watch, remainder had orders to lie flat on deck with helmets on facing France! Outside Barrow Deep (Shipwash) we formed into two columns, and Harwich ships joined here. There were no north bound convoys round Dover, we steamed back independently. Ships bound for Shoreham had to go to St. Helens Roads in convoy and then back to Shoreham, having passed it once. There was a good naval officer in charge at Blyth who used to give us a night in port even if we were loaded. We loaded in Blyth one Saturday and shifted to await the convoy but a German plane flew up and down the river machine-gunning us and dropped a mine in the middle of the harbour. No vessels were allowed to move until the mine was located and this was eventually done by hauling a barge with electric coils on it to trigger the magnetic mine. Ships with dynamos were degaussed, (demagnetized), which was denoted by a white or yellow cross, while others were 'wiped' periodically by steaming over a series of electric cables, they were indicated by having a white bar painted on the side.'

Captain MacRae continues: The east coast convoy (southbound) usually originated at Methil, Fife, on the Firth of Forth, and was joined at various points as it made its way south towards the Thames. Additional ships came from Amble, Blyth, Tyne, Wear, Seaham, Hartlepool, the Tees and Humber. The formation was of two lines abreast, the columns being two cables apart, with one cable separating each ship from the one ahead of it. That was the theory, but the realities brought grey hairs to the heads of Commodores, Senior Officers of the escorts, and many others. The Commodore and his staff were always aboard the largest ship possible, where there were plenty of spare cabins, and a catering staff to cope with the extra work involved for a few days. More often than not **Scottish Fusilier**, a passenger cargo steamer, would be designated, or another of her breed having plenty of speed if necessary. She set the pace from Methil, passing set points at set times, in strict accordance with a prearranged timetable. As the convoy arrived at the joining positions, newcomers would fall in behind the last ship in each column, taking up positions according to their given numbers, odd or even, in port or starboard columns.

As progress was made towards the south and more and more ships joined the convoy, it became a long straggling procession of ships, most of them belching out clouds of thick black smoke, the result of burning north east bunkers. There were few oil burners, and even fewer motor ships amongst them, for in those days bunker coal was plentiful and comparatively cheap. Nearing E-boat alley, frantic signals from the Commodore and escorts, commanding and imperious at first, but finally pleading, that less smoke be made fluttered from the yards of the protecting ships. They were seemingly ignored, for at that time none of the ships had been fitted with the smoke consuming device which, in later years, enable them to conform with the various Clean Air Acts.

E-boat alley, generally understood to refer to that part of the passage that lies between the Sheringham buoy and the Shipwash lightvessel was, as its name implies, a favourite hunting ground for the fast and heavily armed motor torpedo boats built by the enemy for the harrassment of coastal shipping. The normal peacetime route for all traffic between the Thames and the north passed to the south of the Haisbro' Lightvessel, then close north of the North East Cross Sands buoy thence to a position close to the Cross Sand lightvessel and so straight down to the Shipwash lightvessel. Life could be a little trying at times near the Cross Sand buoy, where collisions were frequent even in peace time. So that if two passing convoys, using the same swept channel on reciprocal courses, were attacked and the order 'Scatter' given to both, sheer hell would break loose, and casualties mount alarmingly.

So the naval authorities provided two swept routes between the Shipwash and Sheringham buoy. One was through the Would, the normal route, whilst the other was via Hearty Knoll, well outside the normal route, and as a result, cordially hated by everyone. The different convoys used either route, and it was frequently changed overnight. Both routes were more or less continuously swept by the ubiquitous minesweepers, for the enemy made almost nightly forays against our shipping, laying hundreds of mines on the routes our ships had to take through the narrow waters. These mines gradually became more and more sophisticated; there were contact, magnetic, pressure, acoustic and proximity mines, sometimes with delayed action devices which made the task of sweeping them ever more difficult and hazardous.

Because of mines the convoy routes were moved, the route buoys being periodically moved further and further out from the coast. The route buoys were controlled by radio, being switched on as the convoy approached, and off as the last ship had passed in safety. It was a dangerous proceeding and resulted in many errors in navigation, sometimes with disastrous results. On the night of the 6th of August 1941 about a dozen ships were led on to the Haisbro' Sands by an escort, **Agate**, six of them never getting off again. Many valuable lives were lost on that terrible night, but even greater losses were averted when following collier captains spotted the error of navigation and led the remainder of the convoy to safety. Had the escort heeded the signals earlier the disaster would have been averted.

It was a hateful area, E-boat alley. Everyone was tensed up and suspicious of the slightest unusual circumstance. The enemy would tie their boats up to the route buoys, and lie there waiting in the dark, quite invisible to the radars on the few naval craft fitted with them. Screaming through the passing convoy, with guns blazing and firing torpedoes, the E-boats often went down between the two lines of ships so it was difficult to fire back because of hitting the ships opposite. The enemy could inflict inordinately heavy damage within seconds, and be well out of harms way in a few more. All hands were pleased and relieved when their ships had passed safely through the 'Alley', for they were able to grab a few hours of sleep before going on watch again. But for those in the south bound convoys their troubles were only then about to start in real earnest, the Masters being the greatest sufferers.

Position became of the greatest importance. The big ocean going ships in the van of the convoy were usually compulsorily piloted into the Thames. Consequently when they stopped to pick up pilots, because of the danger of acoustic mines being detonated by the combined noises of two ships, no one was allowed to pass another vessel in the narrow waters of the Thames Channels. As a result all had to stop and mill around. It was here that most of the convoy stems were acquired. End on collisions became so frequent and commonplace that repairs ultimately consisted of cropping out the damaged bow plates vertically from deck to keel bar, and replacing them with a single vertical plate, making future repairs less costly in both time and money. Damage to the stern usually involved the steering gear, and repairs were often prolonged and costly, for lengthy searches all over the country were made for the spare parts. As the months went by those parts became even scarcer and more and more expensive.

As the ships of the south bound convoy neared the Shipwash lightvessel, the Commodore was at the receiving end of innumerable requests to be allowed to proceed independently. All sorts of reasons were put forward but they were invariably refused, and a stretch that would normally take about seven hours to cover, sometimes took as long as twenty four hours of nailbiting frustration with tempers become more and more frayed. It must be remembered that most of the ships were on the feed yourself system, whereby each man made his own arrangements for food and drink on the passage, arrangements that were, at times, very sketchy indeed, and intended to be augmented at the nearest public house selling pies and similar dainties. The consequence of any undue delay meant that men's stomachs began to complain, often quite audibly, at the lack of nourishment.

Plentiful supplies of fresh meat and dry stores were usually available at the convoy centres. One of them, on Southend pier, was extremely popular with the crews, for additional luxuries such as chocolates and sweets, together with a fairly generous supply of cigarettes and tobacco, could be obtained from the N.A.A.F.I. Such a haphazard arrangement as the 'feed yourself system' could not be tolerated for long, and eventually a more satisfactory method of ensuring adequate meals for all hands was devised. Each man paid a fixed sum to the Chief Steward, and in return was provided with hot meals. The new system was open to abuse of course, but it was better than the old hit or miss arrangements, and meant the end of the old style feed yourself system. But it was not until 1971 that all the shipowners agreed to provide all food without deducting any proportion from the seaman's wages.

To return to our inward bound convoy. The pilots boarded the compulsory ships in the Barrow/Nore area, instead of the normal peacetime Sunk lightship area, and by the time they were all aboard and the ships steaming at increasing speeds towards their berths in the rivers and docks, the colliers were free to go their own ways. The sky above the Thames Estuary became ever blacker with the dense clouds of smoke emitted by every ship, all in a tearing hurry to get tied up before dark and the almost inevitable nightly air raids.

The northbound convoys assembled at Southend-on-Sea. The convoy conference was held in one of the buildings on the end of the pier, and it was most interesting to get to know the men and women who were to control our destinies for the next few days or weeks, depending on how far one had to go. The Masters of all the ships had to attend these conferences together with their Second Officers. The Chief Stewards of ships requiring provisions, and one of the crew who would shop for the rest of the crowd, would be allowed to accompany him. The conference took place 24 hours before the convoy was due to sail. At it the Masters received their secret instructions with regard to rendezvous in the event of separation with any special routing instructions. The Second Officer was given the list of amendments to the Chartlets of his route. He had been asked to obtain cigarettes and tobacco for his brother officers, whilst the Chief Steward wangled what extra meat and stores he could out of a generous N.A.A.F.I. staff. The crewman who had come ashore with them completed his shopping as soon as possible and then retired to the ever open bar, there to await the return boat.

Sailings of the convoy were always arranged so that under normal circumstances of weather and visibility, it would be passing through E-boat alley during the hours of darkness, making a ship a difficult target for low-flying aircraft, but ideal for the very fast E-boats. All ships were allocated a number, indicating the order in which they would pass through the gate in single file, the formation that would last until the whole convoy had cleared the Shipwash, and the Commodore had signalled to form two columns. The stations were adhered to, more or less, until approaching Flamborough Head - the Geordie Cape Horn.

Here some, if not all, of the colliers edged further and further ahead, nearer the front of the convoy. To do this without risk of collision, the two vertical columns became one long horizontal line stretching from the Yorkshire coast on the one hand to the distant horizons on the other, no one daring to pass the Commodore until the S.O.E. had made that longed-for signal 'Proceed independently to your destinations'. Immediately huge columns of black smoke rose from every funnel, as the firemen shovelled more and more coal into furnaces. In a matter of hours the whole convoy was spread out over the waters near the coast, and a great pall of black smoke indicated to any lurking enemy that here, indeed, were rich pickings!

The defensive armament ranged from 4" anti-submarine guns right aft, and firing a 30 lb shell, to the noisy 12-pounder with its vicious bark, and the fantastic Oerlikons and Bofors guns mounted in any place with a good field of fire. There were small arms such as Lewis, both mounted and strip, and the twin Colt automatics firing shells about an inch in diameter, armour piercing, plain, explosive and incendiary following each other in rapid succession, a very fine weapon. One of the 'flatties', **Tyndall** 1314/32 had a pair of Colt machine guns mounted on either side of the bridge, and a somewhat bizarre accident happened one day. Because of the necessity of keeping an efficient lookout for the other ships in the convoy, small lookout cabs had been built at each end of the bridge walkway, usually over the engine room telegraph. These were of wood, for they were intended as protection against the weather only. They were all removed after the war, much to the disgust of the navigating officers. who had found them to be a bit of a boon in bad weather. However, to clean these magnificent guns the training stops had to be temporarily removed, enabling the guns to be swung inboard, allowing the gunners easy access to the barrels. During one such cleaning session, on a fine bright day, a sudden alert came over the air. Without hesitation the gunners hurriedly clipped a magazine into each gun, and slipped into the harness, and cocked the triggers, ready for action. The Master took up his position on the front platform and searched the skies for signs of the approaching enemy planes. Suddenly he gave a yell and excitedly pointed to port and low down, where two fast planes were screaming in just above the wave tops and well below mast height. The gunner on the port mount held his fire until he was sure his round would do damage and then let go with both guns, following the plane as it raced in towards the fore end of the ship. The stream of bullets went through the wooden shelter like a rip saw and the top disintegrated into minute fragments of dust. The Old Man simply stood there, white faced and rigid. As his colour returned he said, quite firmly "Make sure the training stop is never again removed Mr. Mate" and stalked off to his room.

The strip Lewis and that awful Marlin, an American design, were abominations cordially hated by everyone who came into contact with them. The strip Lewis, having no cooling system and intended for short bursts of fire, sometimes continued firing until the magazine was emptied, whilst the Marlin had to be cocked and fired three times at least to be absolutely sure it was emptied. When operational the Marlin had three rounds in the 'pipe', and no one really trusted the damned thing, no matter how many times it was cocked and fired.

There were one or two other slightly hazardous innovations, such as the P.A.C. (parachute and cable), the Holman Projector and the Schermuly bomb, all claimed to be deterrents against low-flying bombing attacks. That they were deterrents is not to be doubted, for no airman is going to risk flying at high speed low over a convoy of ships when he knows that the air immediately above that convoy is thick with hundreds of lengths of extremely tough piano wire hanging between small and almost invisible parachutes about 100 feet apart. The P.A.C. consisted of a fixed mounting on top of the wheelhouse, loaded with a Schermuly rocket which was fired by means of a percussion charge. The rocket was fitted with a stirrup at the bottom, to which was attached the actual piano wire, the first five feet being covered with asbestos as protection against the fierce heat of the rocket blast. The remainder of the wire was stowed in figure of eight coils, together with the bottom parachute, in a very substantial steel box, the heavy lid being kept on as a protection against the weather. As can be imagined it took remarkably steady nerves to refrain from operating the trigger until the attacking aircraft was within effective range, for the premature discharge was a waste of material, and there were not too many replacements available at times.

When the rocket reached its maximum height the parachute containers at top and bottom of the

183. Hetton *of the Hudson S.S. Co., painted grey during the Second World War. Note the life rafts ready for launch secured to the stays of both masts and the gun ready for action on the poop.*
Photo courtesy National Maritime Museum

wire automatically fell off, and the 100 feet of extremely tough piano wire was supported between parachutes. An attacking plane, coming into contact with this wire at high speed, would be wrecked in theory. Unfortunately the trigger was operated by means of a set of cords made fast at strategic points about the bridge structure, all very similar to the whistle cord. Many a pilot has pulled one of these lines, asking "Is this your whistle, Captain?" They were informed of their mistake when the heavy steel lid flew past their heads - or clouted them! Steel helmets became THE headwear.

The Holman projector was another deterrent to low-flying bombing attacks, this time from right aft, a favourite approach of heavy bombers. It was in effect a mortar, but was unlike any of those used by the army. It consisted of a long steel tube about four inches in diameter, mounted vertically on the after housing. It was operated by either compressed air or steam, the latter being the more popular amongst the ships' gunners as it was more reliable. A Mills bomb, with the pin removed but the handle kept in position by means of an outer casing like an opened tin, was dropped down the tube, open end first. As it hit the bottom it triggered off a jet of compressed air (or steam) which projected the missile about 250 feet into the air and path of the approaching attacker. As it cleared the tube the outer casing separated and fell off, releasing the handle and activating the fuse. When the bomb reached maximum height it exploded, showering the immediate vicinity with shrapnel.

The mortar was quite conspicuous and on one occasion excited the curiosity of the Commanding Officer of one of the escorts, who steamed alongside and sought an explanation. His reception of the verbal explanation, a slightly dubious 'Oh', produced the offer of demonstration. There being no practice bombs left (there never were), it was decided to use a live round, as it would be quite safe, the debris dropping well astern of the ships as the escort was on the port quarter out of harms way. Unfortunately, as the live round was dropped into the Holman, the ship gave a violent roll towards the escort. All hands watched, fascinated and tongue-tied, about 40 pairs of eyes on the escort ships, following the course of the ascending bomb, which as it reached its maximum height above them, exploded with the violent crack characteristic of a Mills bomb. Only when bits and pieces started to fall about the spectators and into the adjacent waters was there any reaction at all. Within seconds, or so it seemed, the escort was about a mile astern, and across the water came the boom of a tannoy, the speaker making specific suggestions as to what to do with the Holman Projector. It was not fired again except in action against the enemy!

Yet another product of the practical joke department was the Schermuly Rocket Bomb. The Schermuly Line Throwing Apparatus was well known amongst seamen all over the world, and it was no surprise when they produced an adaptation intended as an additional deterrent against low-flying bombers. An ordinary line carrying rocket was adapted and fitted with a small but powerful bomb in its head, fused to explode so many seconds after being fired, when it had reached a height of about 250 feet, and scaring the pants off the pilot of the attacking plane and others!

To fly straight a rocket needs drag of some sort and this was provided by about ten feet of inch rope attached to the normal bridle, and suitably protected against the heat of the rocket blast by asbestos covering. The rope was coiled into a stout paper bag which was hung by a loop of string on the operator's wrist. As the rocket was fired, the rope tore its way out of the bag, which of course was left hanging empty on the wrist. There were nit-wits who made the rope itself fast to their wrists, and there were several nasty accidents attributed to this. The whole thing was awkward to handle and to fire, for the gunner had to watch both the approaching plane and the little spirit level in the handle of the launcher. The 'Old Man' was intrigued by the detailed instructions and determined to have a go himself. He loaded the gun with a real bomb, looped the paper bag holding the 'tail' on his right wrist and steadied himself against the bridge rail. He was wearing a brand new duffel coat and he had to bend forward to see the spirit level, causing the coat to bulge a little. Satisfied the bubble in the level was right in the middle of the glass he pressed the trigger - and stared with horror at the deep scorch mark on his new coat. He was startled out of his wits when the bomb exploded with quite a frightening bang almost overhead - and beat the writer by a short head into the shelter of the steel wheelhouse. It was locked away after that.

Other anti-aircraft devices which gave us a lot of amusement and even more frustration, were the balloons and later the kites, flown by all the ships in the convoys. Of the two, the kites were the worst to handle, for though the balloons were awkward, the kites were possessed of the devil. The balloons were generally brought off to the outgoing ships at Southend by the balloon craft, which with their cluster of captive balloons hovering above them reminded one of the door to door rag and bone men of our youth, barrows festooned about with gaily coloured balloons to exchange for rags and bottles etc.

At Southend it was almost certain to be brought off by the motor tug **Eileena**, perhaps the most famous of the balloon craft operating in the Thames. She and her consorts generally carried four to six fully inflated balloons straining at their tethers. Transfer to a ship's gear was simple, the clip hook of the flight wire being passed to the balloon craft and hooked on to the flying bridle of the balloon allotted to her. As the craft paid out her wire the ship took the strain until the whole weight was on her gear, when the craft's wire would be released. Simple? Was it hell! In dead calm weather it was moderately easy but just the suspicion of breeze and the wind took charge. The unfortunate who had been detailed to go up the mast to disconnect the craft wire, had his work cut out to avoid being swept off his perch or having a finger or even hand cut off. On the 'flatties' it was not quite so bad as the balloon winch was generally on the raised deck between the after hatches, but on those ships with masts and accompanying gear it was almost always at the head of the foremast, and in bad weather crew members were injured on occasions.

One vessel that shipped a balloon at Southend for the run to the Tyne, was issued one with rogue tendencies, which developed later. Off Robin Hood's Bay she asked for permission to proceed at her best speed to the nearest port which was Hartlepool, to land a seriously sick seaman. She was told to go at full speed up the middle of the convoy and then proceed independently. Unknown to her and the rest of the convoy, because it was almost dark with low cloud, her balloon was flying at an angle of about 45 degrees, acting like a scythe, and cutting adrift all the balloons of the ships in the port column as she passed them. No-one noticed what had happened until a broken wire whipped across the face of a man on the lookout of another ship. By then it was too late. The severed balloons drifted with the wind, rising higher and higher until they burst and fell as a crumpled silver coloured sheet far inland, and caused quite a furore amongst the locals who found them, as they could be mistaken for collapsed parachutes. During thunderstorms many were hit and set on fire by lightning, the tethering wires dissolving into a thin tenuous line of brown dust, whilst the wire remaining on the drum fused into a solid block.

It would be best to try and forget those awful kites, but in the interests of history they must be mentioned. They were introduced in an attempt to reduce the soaring costs of the balloon services in both balloons and hydrogen gas needed to inflate them, and to make good the losses through tears in the rubberised fabric. Kites were cheap to produce and repairs could usually be effected by the ships crew. Getting them into the air was another matter altogether. The ship had to be steaming of course, but if the wind was from the aft and at the rate of about 6 to 9 knots, then there was no chance of getting the contraption airborne. On the other hand with a strong head wind, then watch out! They had no tails, relying for drag on the exactness of the flying bridle, and on a short tether plunged all over the place, tempting the controller at the brake handle to let them soar quickly and out of the way. Fine if they did soar, but often they would plunge violently into the sea, smashing at least one stiffener, and making itself even more unpleasant to handle when brought back on board, soaking wet and sticking to everything. I do not think the enemy were deterred by a single kite, as it must have been fairly simple to judge the curve of the tethering wire and fly round it. But a mixed selection of kites and balloons flying from a convoy of 100 ships, that was a different matter.

The standard charts for the coast were divided into sections covering the routes between Southend and the Firth of Forth, and re-printed as small chartlets for easy handling. Each covered about 3 to 5 miles of the convoy route (185), and were contained in a varnished canvas envelope. They were a boon to the watchkeeper on the bridge during the hours of darkness particularly. They were issued at convoy conferences to those not already in possession of a set, whilst those who had were given a list of corrections instead. The charts used on coastal ships were the responsibility of the Second Officer, as were the corrections. Though it was the responsibility of the Master to see that the Notices to Mariners were kept up to date, if the Second Officer failed to remind him that one was overdue, then trouble could be expected.

Most of the big shipping companies left in Britain now send their folios of charts ashore to be corrected. The girls who do this job for the companies are provided with master transparencies covering the charts in question, to be sure of the exact position of the correction, unlike one incident during the war. The Second Officer was a temporary appointment, and had no certificates of competency, and the regular officers began to doubt that he had ever been to sea. On one of the charts he was correcting, No.1607, required the insertion of a new wreck buoy just outside the Nore gateway. Unfortunately, a previous user of the chart had leant over it with his sou'wester on, and the water resting on the turn-up had run on to the chart, wetting it very thoroughly in a huge patch covering the affected area. So to avoid this, he very carefully drew the symbol for a can buoy two miles north of the correct place - and left it, even though it meant that the buoy was firmly in the middle of the Maplin Sand! He left the ship at the next port. It was the Second Officer's task to correct the chartlets every voyage, and it meant checking every buoy, wreck, and

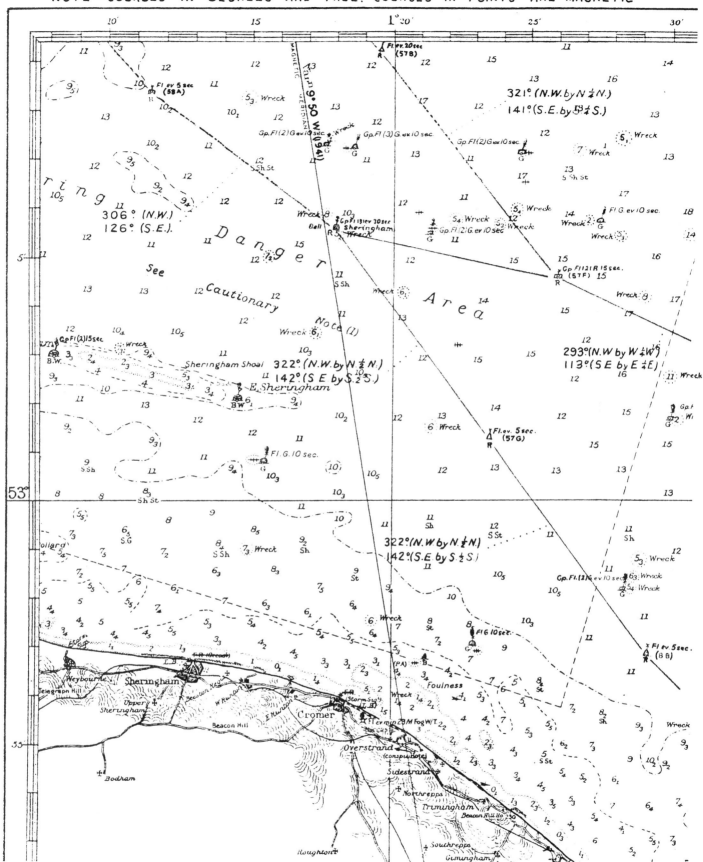

185. A chartlet (No.15) for the east coast convoy routes showing the area off Cromer. The route and bearings were superimposed in red on portions of the standard charts and there were 33 chartlets covering the coast from Southend to Methil in Scotland. Note the number of wrecks marked by the time this chart was issued in April, 1944. The chartlets were issued to navigating officers with extensive instructions giving details of all buoys and their positions, together with alternative emergency routes and general proceedures to be followed while in convoy and when leaving it.

MacRae collection

other navigational hazard every two or three days, a task not made easier by the steady proliferation of wrecks caused by enemy actions in the only channels into and out of the various ports, as well as attacks by aircraft and E-boats in the restricted waters of the convoy routes. Unfortunately the various wrecks were not at that time named, and as they increased in number more confusion was added to an already confused situation, especially if the new wreck was very close to, or over, one previously notified. Such a one was that near the Sheringham Buoy off Cromer (185). A ship had been mined and sunk there, and duly plotted on the chartlet. Within a week another had hit her and foundered in dense fog. Almost at once, a converted tanker/aircraft carrier stranded on the same two vessels and became a total loss. Incidentally one of the escorting ships went down between the two lines of the colliers in the first convoy to pass this notorious spot after this incident, warning all not to mention they had seen a wrecked aircraft carrier at Sheringham, when they went ashore next day. But the first thing asked after mooring at Deptford Power Station was "Did you see the aircraft carrier at Sheringham?" How they got to know, heaven alone knows, unless Lord Haw Haw (German propaganda) had announced it.

E-boat alley and the Thames Estuary were the more dangerous places and the chartlets gradually grew blacker as wrecks were marked in. In the Thames Estuary anti-aircraft gun platforms were built at strategic points in an effort to prevent the laying of mines, and attacks on the convoys as they left the anchorage at Southend. Some were concrete towers supporting a cast concrete platform bearing the guns and quarters for the gunners, whilst the others consisted of several stilt-like towers all inter-connected, with web like gangways. The Nore Tower, actually a collection of about seven towers on stilts, was hit by a ship in dense fog with some loss of life.

There was one thing that the convoy system showed with startling clarity, that it is possible to anchor almost anywhere in the North Sea. It is not advisable to drop the 'hook' in the Silver Pit or the Norwegian Trench, but practically anywhere else the anchor can be put down with confidence. Nowadays, of course, the charts are criss-crossed with pecked red lines denoting the presence of underwater gas pipe lines, and the warning printed on the title lines of the chart regarding the danger of fouling them.

When fog hit a convoy in otherwise fine weather the order to anchor was usually given. None of the merchant ships, and precious few of the escorts, were fitted with radar, so that it was impractical to proceed, though a fog buoy could delay or avoid this. It was a gadget towed by a ship which sent a fountain of water into the air as they moved through the water (187). They were all very well, provided the chap ahead, whose fog buoy you were following, had previously demonstrated skill in steering and station keeping. You could then be reasonably certain that by keeping his fog buoy close to the starboard side of your bridge, you were not only keeping the correct distance from him, but also from the ship on your port or starboard beam, depending upon which column you were in. It can be rather disconcerting to be staring out through what appears to be dense fog, straining your eyes trying to catch a glimpse of the other ship that should be there, only to find you are practically rubbing noses against the grey painted side of a ship actually in contact with your own. This happened once, though the two ships came apart without trouble or damage. One of the great hazards was the lack of efficient lookouts. By guess and by God was the guiding line of navigation during fog on the east coast. Those ships that had officers who had been many years on the coast were counted lucky, for they seemed to have acquired an instinct for position, perhaps recognising a quirk of tide or wind that told them a lot more than one could believe possible.

Colonel Crompton 1495/33 (177), a relatively modern up-river collier was to be my first permanent appointment with the then London Power Company. Captain Cyril Topson was master. Referred to as Toppy by everyone, including Mrs. Topson, Toppy had a well-developed sense of humour, though he could get rough at times with malcontents and troublemakers, he rarely lost his temper. I accompanied him to the Convoy Conference on Southend Pier on one voyage. Before the conference began we met the Commanding Officers of some of the big ships that were to accompany us to the Tyne. Each vied with the other in telling yarns until Toppy got his hearing. He complained bitterly "You simply cannot trust the engineers these days can you? We were approaching the Tyne the other day. Visibility was none too good and we were looking for some familiar landmark, when the chief pointed to Port and said 'there's Souter'. It wasn't, you know; it was Marsden. Just shows you, you cannot rely on engineers." There were raised eyebrows all round, and a distinct cooling in the atmosphere as Toppy wandered off towards the bar murmuring to himself something about 'that'll hold 'em'.

Toppy looked more like a schoolmaster than a ship's Master, though there was no one more efficient in running a ship than he. He had a great personality and he was able to get away with things that, in another, would have started a riot. On the way back to the ship one night, during the last days of the war, we called in for a final drink at the famous Noak's Ark in Deptford. Seated at a table just inside the black-out screen were two of the more famous ladies of the district. As Toppy, who knew them by repute, as did we all, passed their table he bent down and murmured "What are you drinking girls?" Scenting a free drink they chorused "Gin and tonic". Toppy picked up one of the glasses, took a sip and in a surprised tone of voice said "So it is", and ambled over to the bar to buy beers for three convulsed shipmates. Even the ladies had to laugh, and of course, eventually got their drinks.

The most hazardous convoy route remained that through the Dover Straits. The ships continued to face the additional hazard of shelling until the positions were overrun in 1944, as for a short distance they were within range of German heavy guns, although as they were at maximum range their accuracy was not that great. The main threat came from German aircraft which could reach them from France in a few minutes, and motor torpedo boats (E-boats) at night, as Mr. R. Hughes recalls on one of the later convoys. "The passages we did in wartime were not the same as peace time as regards navigation and we did not either keep an official or a scrap log of our movements. Masters got a routing from port to port from the Admiralty. There was a convoy about every four days. If we were coming from, for example, Hull or Sunderland and bound south for such places as Poole in Dorset, Portsmouth, etc. our route would take us first to Great Yarmouth and then down towards Felixstowe, then across towards North Foreland and inside the Goodwin Sands towards South Foreland. Now the shelling area could start from the South Foreland towards Dover Gate and bend towards Folkestone. Generally one would take about an hour and a half or more to clear the area.

It was a long time before the Admiralty and escorts of convoys got the right speed for the right convoys, as if the weather was bad or the signal came to proceed at your utmost speed etc., then a lot of us were left on our own to try and get through. To my mind the screeches of the shells were worse than bombing to many, which got on their nerves. I always felt the engineers and firemen down below had the toughest time, especially during the night as there were screens over every door and porthole, and they could not see what was going on. In convoys we would be following the dim blue stern light of the ship ahead and we rarely had our hands far from the engine room telegraph or the whistle lanyard. I know one old captain from **Kyle Bay** took a bag full of shrapnel to show the brokers in London what they were going through. We generally had to renew all our derrick falls, boat falls etc. as shrapnel was stuck in ropes everywhere. On one trip the shelling was very bad off Dover Gate. I think the Commodore's ship in the convoy was **Bovey Tracy** (164). He came very near alongside us with the escort destroyer and told us to get on at our utmost speed and the fireman shouted to him that we were the Birker Force and not the Air Force! We were lucky that trip not to be sorted out by dive bombers etc. which were always a danger, as I'm afraid we came through on our own. The other ships had gone clear and I believe the master was decorated for taking us through safely. **Birker Force** was well equipped as we had a machine gun on either side of the protected bridge. She was demagnetised as a protection against magnetic mines. The lifeboats were swung out at sea and secured by lashings. To keep the boats in position a 'puddening spar' was lashed between the davits at about half the depth of the boat which had round padding on it. There were also a selection of liferafts and we all had the latest lifejackets. Later in the war a 5-pounder gun was added aft and another gun on the monkey island over the wheelhouse.

Another time we were just south of Dover Gate when a shell burst and the bridge was covered with some sort of black oil. The Captain foolishly tried to rub it off on one of the wheelhouse windows and he got some sort of poisoning from it. He went to see the doctor in Portsmouth and he gave him some ointment but it took quite a few days to clear. We even took a cargo of coal to Dover itself during that time. I don't think there was a window intact in Dover. We discharged our cargo there with grabs, 1,200 tons in 8 hours, sometimes less. A thing that we had different from our voyages to London was if we were going south through Dover Straits and the shelling area we used to pick up about 8 or 12 soldiers and a sergeant. I never really knew what they were supposed to do with .303 rifles, probably from the First World War, only to try and shoot enemy planes down, or if we were attacked by E-boats. We picked them up where we loaded coal for the south. We had no special accommodation for them, so they just lay on the floor in their hammocks. The poor fellows were sick most of the time as they were soldiers and not seamen and as soon as we arrived at our discharging port they were ashore, probably to catch trains for the north so as to pick up other ships going south. I, like many more, am fortunate to have got away with it as there were many casualties and loss of life during that period."

To make good losses, the public utilities were given permission to order replacement 'flatties' and some larger ships. The Gas Light & Coke Co. had several of these, last of which was **Firelight**, completed in 1943 (189) by the Burntisland Shipbuilding Company; a slightly smaller version of **Mr. Therm** (214). With raw materials in short supply economies were made compared with the pre-war vessels in the size of the captain's cabin and saloon space. Various wartime additions are shown on the plan, most prominent of which are the gun positions on the bridge and aft. A small house was added on the boat deck for the gunners. Similar small deck houses were fitted to many vessels and were sometimes retained after the war. The funnel was as short as practical and had no outer casing to save top-weight and steel. No winches were fitted to save on cost and weight. One new and improved feature was the fitting of early type steel hatch covers. Like all war-built vessels there was a plate at the bottom of the stem for handling paravanes. To replace losses a series of nine Empire colliers of a similar size and at just over 4,100 tons deadweight were built by Gray's Yard at West Hartlepool between 1940 and 1941. Five were lost during the war and two of the four

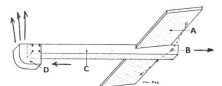

187. Sketch of the fog buoy towed by ships in Second World War convoys. The wooden body (C), was usually 3" x 3" timber. Surface A provided lift and the towing wire was shackled on at B. The scoop passing through the water surface at about 8 knots made a fountain 3 to 4 feet high of spray, easily discernible. MacRae collection

survivors joined collier fleets: **Granta** 2841/40 (Witherington & Everett) and **Rogate** 2849/46 (Stephenson Clarke).

By far the biggest series were the colliers of about 2,800 tons deadweight and similar to **Icemaid** which had been built for the Gas Light & Coke Co., in 1936. In all 17 were built and, beginning in 1941, two or three vessels were completed each year, mostly by the Grangemouth Dockyard Co. Ltd.,Grangemouth. **Empire Lagoon** 2013/41 was the second in the series (191). They were equipped with deck gear and had wooden hatch covers. **Empire Lagoon** was managed for the Ministry of War Transport by the Hudson Shipping Co., and they must have liked how she ran for they purchased her in 1946 and she traded for them as the **Hudson Bay** until scrapped at Blyth in 1964. They also purchased **Empire Pioneer** which became **Hudson Bank**, and most of the others were sold to collier owners after the war. As the war was drawing to a close three slightly larger versions were built, to compensate for the fitting of hopper side tanks. Two became **Arnewood** 2125/45 and **Dashwood** 2156/46 of France, Fenwick (190), while a third became **Corflow** 2159/46 in the Cory fleet. The accommodation was rearranged aft with the cabins placed flush with the sides of the ship forming a poop deck.

Perhaps the greatest single war action in which coasters and colliers took part was the Normandy landings, beginning on the 6th of June 1944. In the first week over 600 merchant ships were involved, many of which were coasters. Those colliers which could be spared were also used carrying supplies to the beachheads and a variety of other special tasks. **Mr. Therm** of the Gas Light & Coke Co., was requisitioned some months before the landings and directed to Blyth where more armaments and accommodation was added and the shipyard also cut away the lower part of the three bulkheads between the holds so vehicles could be driven through the holds. Her task was to carry Canadian commandos and a section of the Royal Engineers to Courcelles where she arrived safely and beached to discharge. This was happening to other ships around the country, as Mr. R. H. Hughes, mate of **Birker Force** recalls: we went to Birkenhead to carry a few cargoes of flour to Swansea when one day an American Commander, Clyde Washer, Marine Superintendent, U.S. Forces, came aboard asking for the master. I informed him that he was ashore at the broker's office. He then said he would go and see him as he liked the ship and she would suit his purpose. She was to be taken over and used by U.S. forces and he gave orders to the quay foreman to discharge the vessel as quickly as he could. The next day we proceeded to Plymouth and on arrival the master was told to give all hands leave for 48 hours as that would be the last leave we would get in the near future. We had no idea what we were going to do. Whether the master knew and had to keep it secret, we did not know. We were fitted out with many extras such as about 12 wooden toilets situated around the engine casing, two big iron coffee urns on the galley stoves and special arrangements for cooking. The holds were stowed with food, clothing and all manner of equipment and stores, tons of ropes with hooks attached to them for securing amphibious craft alongside which they would be working from a bay along the coast. They had a few large landing craft at Plymouth at the time and we got instructions to follow them out one day. I did not know where we were going, but the master did inform me that as we approached Torbay we headed towards the French coast, which the master did not like as the visibility was not very good. We were well astern of the leading landing craft when we suddenly heard them dropping their anchors. Before the master decided to anchor we heard a short burst of gunfire. Then one of them, seemingly nearest to us, signalled us to proceed towards Torquay at our utmost speed, which we did. On arrival at Torquay we were not told by the Americans there what had happened. After many years I recall either reading it in a newspaper or hearing it on radio that a certain German E-boat commander recalled how he sank three American landing craft and regretted that he could not wait around to pick up any survivors as he thought there were British destroyers in the vicinity. We remained at Torquay, just discharging and loading the same cargo. We had gangs of coloured Americans as well in Torquay. We would have them on different shifts and I think they were just timing them, to get the ships discharged faster every day. The coloured soldiers were very efficient at their job. We used to go on practice runs out to Slapton Beach nearby. Sometimes they worked by night discharging into amphibious D.U.K.W's and taking them ashore up the sand dunes. They used to take photographs of everything. We were not allowed to have a camera or a diary. I believe they made a few mistakes in and around the village of Slapton, but I have long forgotten the details of what happened. We were still with them when we got orders to proceed to West India Dock, London, through the Straits of Dover. We had a straight run with no trouble. It would take pages to try and make an inventory of our cargo; hundreds of tennis rackets and balls, cricket bats and balls, a few hundred wheelbarrows with a bag of cement in each; N.A.A.F.I. stores of all descriptions. After the holds were filled up and battened down, our deck cargo consisted of Bailey bridging, material to cross rivers. After loading was completed we went to Surrey Commercial Dock, London. We had no idea then where we were bound, but something was telling us that we were going somewhere special, as Surrey Docks were full of ships of all descriptions, loaded down to the scuppers. It was to wait for D-Day to go to the beaches at Arromanches in France. We then did countless runs with various cargoes from Southampton to the various beach heads. On arrival at Southampton the loading master used to come aboard. Ex-masters of ships recruited, as far as I was led to believe, acting as stevedores. The men used to call this particular gentleman 'Straight Ammo'.This was meant to mean as far as the crew were concerned not dangerous regardless of what was loaded, in case the men demanded danger money, seemingly they could claim if the full cargo was 1,200 tons, but it would be always about 50 to 100 tons short of that. We were loading one day and I noticed some dark powder coming out of the

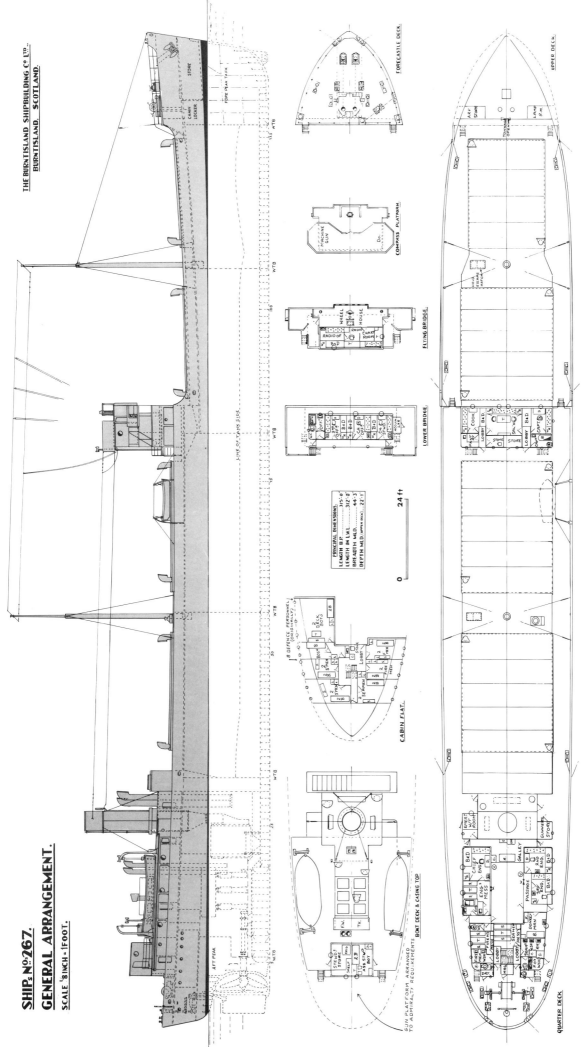

MacRae collection

THE BURNTISLAND SHIPBUILDING Cº Lᵀᴰ.
BURNTISLAND, SCOTLAND.

SHIP Nº 267.
GENERAL ARRANGEMENT.
SCALE '8INCH = 1FOOT.

FORECASTLE DECK.

COMPASS PLATFORM.

FLYING BRIDGE.

LOWER BRIDGE.

CABIN FLAT.

PRINCIPAL DIMENSIONS.	
LENGTH B.P.	315'-0
LENGTH ON L.W.L.	312'-0
BREADTH MLD.	44'-3
DEPTH MLD. (UPPER DECK)	22'-1

0   24 ft

GUN PLATFORM ARRANGED
TO ADMIRALTY REQUIREMENTS.

BOAT DECK & CASING TOP.

UPPER DECK.

QUARTER DECK.

189. *Firelight* 2841/43 was built to replace war losses. The dinghy stowed alongside No.3. hatch was placed on the lifeboat platform after the war. The platform was extended forwards to make room for it. Also the bosun and carpenter who had been in the gunners' house on the boat deck were moved, the bosun to a cabin which had been the gunners' mess while the adjacent cabin used for two deck boys had originally housed eight defence personnel. During the war ammunition was stored adjacent to the W.C.'s on the quarter deck. A second radio operator had been in the chief steward's cabin on the lower bridge.

Nº 217 SHIP

S.S. DASHWOOD
DIMENSIONS: 268'-0" B.P. × 40'-9" × 19'-6" MLD.

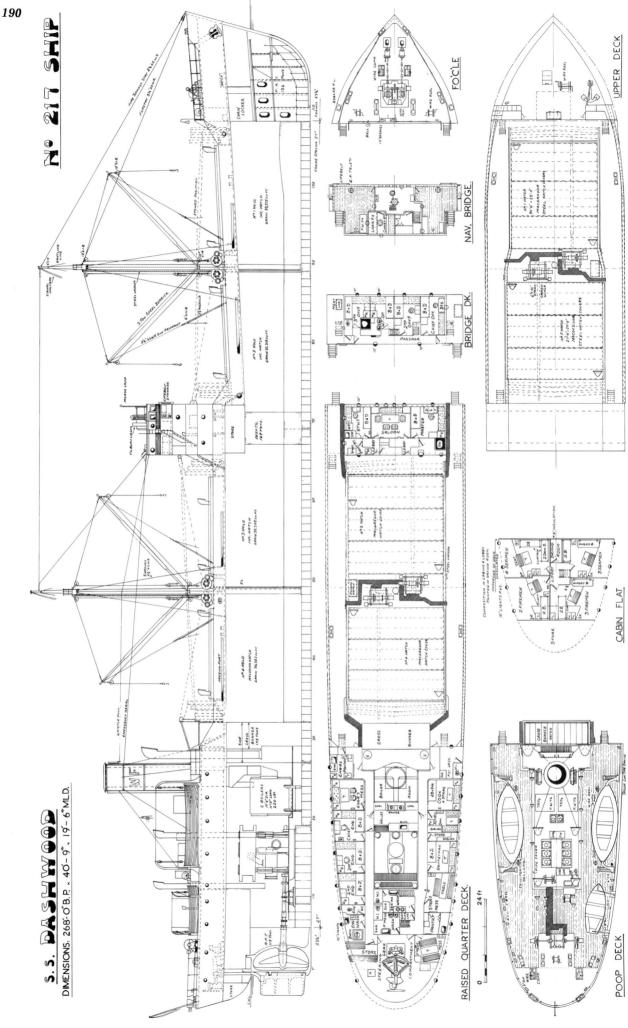

FOCLE

NAV. BRIDGE.

BRIDGE DK.

UPPER DECK

CABIN FLAT

RAISED QUARTER DECK.

POOP DECK

24 ft

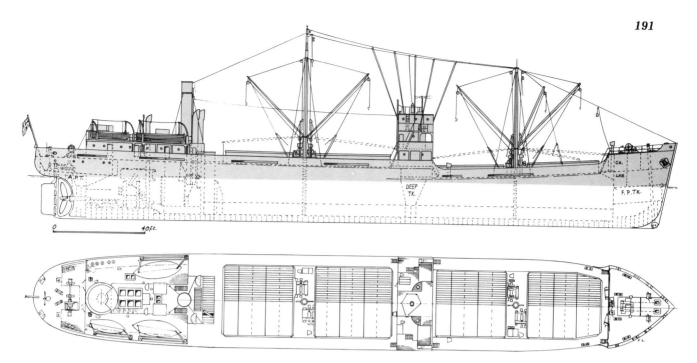

191. *Icemaid type standard collier* **Empire Lagoon.** Shipbuilding & Shipping Record 30 August 1945

cases as they were landed on top of one another. However, a high-ranking officer came aboard and told the dockers to go on the quay immediately as seemingly all of them were wearing hob-nailed boots. A long delay occurred, evenually they came back on board to complete loading, with some special sacking covering over their boots. This high ranking army man informed the master that not only we would have gone up in the sky but also a large part of Southampton Docks as well, as one spark off those nailed boots would have set it off.

On another voyage from Southampton we were waiting to load and I noticed the fire brigade men coming aboard, going towards the forecastle where our fore peak tank top was situated and were in the process of lifting off the cover. I asked them who gave them permission to do so as it had been filled with fresh water and a pump attached so that the troops could use it for drinking and washing purposes. Also naturally it would be difficult if not impossible only in very calm weather for a coaster to make a passage with no cargo if our ballast tanks were not full. The loading master had asked the fire people to do this so that he could get more cargo aboard! When I informed the master of what they were doing he quickly told them to re-fill the tank and seal it up again as it was before, and gave the loading master a bit of a lecture about the ballast tanks."

Courtesy R. H. Hughes

10. Nationalisation

192. Captain J. M. Donaldson
Photo: Philipson Studios

At the end of the war in 1945 the country was in a far worse position than after the First World War and so began a long re-building process, but not of the export markets as all the coal being produced was needed at home, particularly in the bad winter of 1947. Long overdue dry-dockings slowly began. The guns with their gun mountings were taken off and the 'plastic' armour was removed from around the wheelhouses. The wooden wheelhouse of one of the 'flatties', **Ferranti** 1317/32 was of teak, as were most of the pre-war ships, and when the war ended and the protecting armour removed, a sorry sight was revealed. The varnish that had last seen the light of day five years before, was hanging off in tatters, whilst everywhere there were inch holes drilled to accommodate bolts that secured the framework for the plastic slabs. The bolts, being of steel and virtually bare of a protective coat of paint, had rusted leaving rust stains below each hole.

It took over twelve months of scraping, sanding, bleaching, scraping, weathering, sanding, oiling and then varnishing and varnishing to remove the consequences of years of neglect, and the coats of dirt inevitable on a collier loading dusty coal. The same sort of thing happened on all ships that had survived the war and all had of necessity been neglected. Just about everything was in short supply, but the utilities continued to have priority and so were able to obtain newbuildings. The London Power Company had not received any additions to its fleet since **William Pearman** 1552/42. The large down-river collier **Oliver Bury** 2904/46 was delivered by the Burntisland Shipbuilding Company and there were two new 'flat-irons', **Sir Joseph Swan** 1554/45 and **Sir Alexander Kennedy** 1714/46, which was built by Austin's (167). This was the most advanced flat-iron so far constructed for the company with cruiser stern, raked stem and steel hatch covers. The cruiser stern had first been seen on **Charles Parsons** 1554/36, which was almost lost a few months after the delivery of **Sir Alexander Kennedy**. She had previously had a close escape during the war when she was attacked by enemy aircraft at 1830 hrs on Christmas Day 1941, in a position about nine miles from the port War Signal Station at the Heugh (Hartlepool). The main engines were put out of action and the bridge damaged. A slight leak was caused by a near miss on the 27th of December, but she got back into the port, was pumped out, and the leak stopped. Two of the crew were injured in the attack, as well as three of the gunners, but all recovered from their injuries. A lifeboat, unshipped in the attack, was later found washed ashore at Sandsend.

About six years later she was sunk in collision with **Cydonia**, about three miles W.S.W. from Southend Pier, whilst entering the Thames Estuary with coal from Barry Dock, in October 1947. Her position, when she finally settled on the bottom, was upright, approximately midway between No's 3 and 4 Sea Reach Buoys. Her masts and funnel were plainly visible at low water and her position was clearly marked by a wreck-marking vessel. But she was over-run by **Grelrosa**, deeply laden with timber and bound in for the Surrey Commercial Docks. **Charles Parsons** suffered further extensive damage, all her bridge and after housings being completely destroyed, and the hatch coamings flattened. Her cargo was discharged into lighters, not without difficulty because of weather and industrial action. She was eventually raised and taken to the Blackwall yard of Messrs. Green and Silley Weir for detailed examination, where it was decided to rebuild the ship completely. This was done and the ship re-classified with Lloyds after almost 12 months work.

Not long after re-entering service she was involved in another serious incident, when colliding with the dumb barge **Rocksand** which, laden with cable gear, was lying alongside **Lord Kelvin**, the cable steamer, at Enderbys Dolphins, East Greenwich, on June 3rd 1949. The Wharf was also considerably damaged, and although **Charles Parsons** was holed it was above the water line and she was able to make Deptford buoys. The ship had numerous other scrapes in her long life, which ended in the scrap yards at Antwerp on 10th April 1967 after 34 years of carrying coal to the London Power Stations.

The crews also had some lucky escapes as Captain MacRae also recalls: "**Tyndall** was for Deptford Power Station on this occasion, and had swung off the Power Station. Bill Johnson, the Chief Officer, was on the fo'c'sle head and dressed for the bitter weather in seaboots and oilskins, tried to reach a poorly thrown heaving line, and in doing so slipped and fell overboard into the icy Thames. He was a good swimmer and easily reached the wire mesh guards over the suction intakes. As the ship came alongside he was able to climb up the short ladder hastily thrown over the fore deck and dashed down to get his wet gear off, and changed ready for the evening meal. As he sat down old Davie grunted "Strange time to go bathing Mr. Johnson" and made no further comment then or ever again on what was a miraculous escape. David Pirie, the Master, was a dour Scot who ceaselessly sucked a foul old pipe, even, so it was believed, taking it to bed with him. His brother Alex Pirie was another well known master in the fleet.

Falling overboard was an ever-present risk for all seamen, but perhaps the most unusual incident was that involving **Sir Joseph Swan** in the 1960s. On this occasion the ship was tied up to the Jarrow East Tier. A German ship tied up alongside during the day, to await her turn for coal at the loading berth. As usual there were very few crew members aboard 'Jo Swan' for the ship would not be loading before the following Monday. Consequently all those who had homes in the north east, the majority of the crew, had gone ashore. The Master, Chief Steward, two of the sailors and the donkeyman, an Arab, lived on board, and usually stayed aboard whilst the ship was at the buoys. It was not a very pleasant prospect, having to climb a pilot ladder when the ship was light, and most of the ballast out of her. Late at night, about 23.30 hrs, when the dynamo was shut down (in those days there was no all-night lighting) the Master, who had turned in early, heard a bit of a thud and the sound of breaking glass, followed a few minutes later by soft moaning sounds seeming to come from his wardrobe, against the ship's side. There being nothing inside, he listened outside the Chief Steward's room in case the Steward was having a nightmare, but the door opened and the steward appeared. He also had heard the thump. Both went on deck and walked across to the starboard side. The sound of breaking glass was explained by a broken bottle on the after deck, but there appeared to be no reason for the moans until they looked over the side and to their horror were able to make out the body of a man jammed between the two ships, in a more or less upright position. On the Master's instructions the steward ran to the crew's accommodation and roused the Arab donkeyman and told him to get the diesel dynamo going again as quickly as possible. The Master himself switched on the radio transmitter and, calling Cullercoats Radio, asked him to get hold of the River Tyne Police and have them stop all traffic, even small motor boats, in the vicinity of Jarrow East Tier, explaining why. This was done immediately.

The nightwatchman on 'Jo Swan' had meanwhile called the remaining members of the crew and had brought a huge piece of timber midships. This lowered as far as possible down between the two ships, stopped any likelihood of the ships coming together and crushing this unknown man. Meanwhile a quick check on the German ship revealed that the Radio Officer was missing. One of the young men on the German volunteered to be lowered head first down beside the unconscious man, and pass a rope round him to prevent him falling farther down. This he was able to do and in a very short time both men were safely back on deck again. The Radio Officer was, surprisingly, quite conscious, but still very bemused. His injuries were astonishingly light, for he suffered only a slight abrasion to his chin and a small twist to his left ankle. It was a few hours before the mystery of how he got there was solved. He was at a party in the 2nd Officer's room and the schnapps flowed freely. When the last bottle was emptied, Sparks remembered that he had an unopened bottle in his radio room on the top bridge, and went to get it. There was one tot left in another bottle so he polished that off and threw the empty bottle over the side. He heard it crash on the deck of 'Jo Swan', and in his stupor, lolled against the bridge rail to see what damage he had done. Only he lolled too far and fell, passing out like a light as he dropped the 35 feet, and consequently suffering little or no damage to himself.

Crews varied a lot but **Ferranti** at the end of the war was the happiest ship in the fleet as far as I was concerned. W. R. (Bob) Wilson was Master when I was sent there, and that was the beginning of three very happy years until I was fool enough to strand her on the wreck of the **Fort Massac** at the entrance to the Thames in the Sunk Channel when fog closed in. There seemed to be a gay madness about everyone who served in her at this time, steadied only by the influence of Axel Johnson, the lamp trimmer/bosun, who was respected by all. He and his after gang kept the ship spotlessly clean, despite the fact that in those good (?) old days the crew fed themselves, buying and cooking their own food. He and two characters named Wally Howells and Johnny Gardner made up the forward watch and I shudder to think what would have happened had he not been there to dampen the other two.

Ferranti had six hundred wooden dominoes in the shape of hatch boards which had to be thrown up and placed after each discharge. Some were inclined to be a bit warped and Wally lifted one above his head and started revolving about his vertical axis, pretending to be Flying Officer 'Kite', a well known music hall character of the time. It would have been alright had he been down on the deck, but performing as he was on the edge of a thirty foot drop it was, to say the least, a little frightening. This same character stalked into the Officers' Saloon one lunch time dressed for all the world like the cowboy he pretended to be. Most of us had our backs to him and noticed nothing until we were startled by the booming Wilson laugh, and turned to see what was amusing him.

One of the Engineer Officers, who served for many years after the war, was named Arbus. Ferdie was an Estonian and like nearly all his countrymen who went in for engineering, a clever fitter and technician. He caused the heartiest Wilson laugh when, one morning at breakfast time he came midships, and standing in the saloon doorway, somewhat hesitantly announced "I am sorry Captain, I have put a hole in the bottom of your ship". It appeared that he was sounding the engine room bilge using a four foot sounding rod in the sounding tube, which also happened to be the bilge suction pipe. Ferdie had put the rod into the pipe and let it drop. To his surprise, the rod, all four feet of it, disappeared into what he knew to be only a two foot depth. So he investigated. Apparently the scouring action of the ashes and muck that tends to accumulate in the bilges of a coal burning ship had worn the plate so thin that it needed only a slight tap to penetrate it.

The weather was bad and deteriorating, so Captain Wilson had already decided to turn back to the Tyne for shelter. When we got back to the buoys a gang of workmen came aboard and fitted a new suction pipe into another well and filled the leaking one with concrete. The Chief Engineer was Freddie Anderson. One evening he returned to the ship after a most enjoyable session at the Bass Tap. The nightwatchman, a keen fisherman, had caught three large eels and to keep them alive had filled the hip bath in the engineers toilet with dock water. Freddie, seated on the throne beside the bath, suddenly realised that the phosphorescent glow in the water was caused by a living creature and dashed out of the toilet. "There's some bloody great snakes in there", and refusing to return until they had been removed. Fishing was always a popular pastime and in later years, as pay improved, more expensive fishing gear was invested in.

Then, as sometimes happened, a collier arrived off the port at which she was to load or discharge her cargo, too late on the tide to make her berth safely, she usually anchored outside. As soon as this decision was reached, the anglers on board, and every ship had them, made preparations for a couple of hours fishing. The cook was told to get ready his largest frying pan, whilst those whose duties kept them on the bridge, discussed loudly, and in the Master's hearing, the advantages of anchoring in selected spots. If he happened to be down below in his room, the conversation was carried on in somewhat heated tones by those concerned, apparently with their heads jammed down in the ventilator of his cabin!

A suitable anchorage having been arrived at by the Master, within a matter of minutes rods and hand-held lines were hanging over the sides and stern, the latter being the most favoured place, avidly sought by all. The most sheltered spot was usually bagged by one of the watch below, with all the latecomers keeping a wary eye open for signs that the occupier was becoming weary or bored, and about to vacate the prime spot for the comfort of his own room, or in later years the messroom.

Bait was always a bit of a problem, for that obtained from the local angling shop would not keep for ever, and became somewhat expensive to buy. Many were the alternative temptations offered; raw liver, bacon rind and even old black shoe laces were tried in place of more conventional baits. The first fish caught, if any, usually ended up back in the sea, impaled on several hooks of varying sizes. If a peeler crab was spotted as the line was reeled in great care was taken to land it on the deck, for peelers were highly esteemed both by the fish and anglers. Weird and wonderful were the rigs, ranging from the sophisticated rods with expensive reels, to a length of spun yarn with a short piece of half inched nylon bent on the end, with two or three hooks and weighted by a purloined nut from the engine room. It often made me raving mad to watch these Heath Robinson contraptions yanking in fish after fish, whilst my own two rods remained ignored and neglected.

One gentleman, perhaps the keenest of all where fishing was concerned, used a similar rig. Night or day, summer or winter, rain hail or snow, he would be there, hanging over the side or stern, fishing. During the Middle Watch and during the first two hours of the Morning Watch he would sit in the galley for warmth and light, holding in his right hand his line, the end hanging over the stern, waiting for the jag that would tell him a fish was showing interest. The rest of the crew learned that the safest way to cross the poop was with an arm held in front of one's face. The ultimate was reached one day when the ship was lying at Harton Buoys in the Tyne. Bill was standing in the midships toilet with his right arm extended out of the porthole, holding his line. In his left hand he held a book he was reading. The sight of that arm jerking at each 'bite' made by the bow waves of passing launches or tugs caused near hysterics among the returning watch ashore as they approached the duty boat.

A favourite spot for fishing was 'under the Head' when northwest or northerly gales threatened to bring the struggling north bound ships to a halt, all tried to make for the shelter provided by Flamborough Head, where, incidentally, was one of the last of the Lloyd's Signal Stations. It was never a comfortable anchorage for everybody was on tenterhooks and fidgety, thinking of the lost hours of the watch ashore, and imagining the owners and agents trying to fix quick cargos from nearer, but, to the crews, less convenient ports. However, the anglers got down to business straight away, and many fine catches were made off Bridlington. It was strange that although one anchored in exactly the same place a week or two afterwards, there was no guarantee that such a catch could be repeated. And when one says exactly, with radar such precision was perfectly possible.

If bound for Shoreham or any other of the channel ports, and the tide was going to be missed, long mackerel lines were trailed aft as the engines were put dead slow ahead. Perfect summer weather, calm smooth seas and unlimited visibility made trolling for the blue and silver fish a lazy pleasure, until strong yanks at the line told of many fish falling for the brilliantly coloured feathers at each hook. A lot of people will not eat mackerel because of its flesh colour, but it is really a tasty fish and very popular amongst seafarers. There are other fish of the same family, not quite so popular because of their green bones, but garfish make excellent eating too.

In the days of the convoys, when there were long delays at Southend, many a profitable hour was spent with the rod. Fishing was only possible for perhaps an hour or two either side of high or low water, for the rush of the incoming or outpouring tide was terrific. A hefty weight was needed to keep the end of the cast on or near the bottom during neap tides, whilst spring tides made it well nigh impossible to do so.

Ferranti was the only ship of the L.P.C. fleet ever to load at a port never considered a collier port. This was Boston in Lincolnshire and, much to his surprise, Bob Wilson was told to take his ship there to load. It was an experiment in the never ending search for ways and means of reducing the cost of fuel for the Power Station. Grimsby, Immingham - both inside the dock and at the berth on the river, at the Alexandra and King George Docks, Hull, as well as the riverside berth had all been used to a greater or less extent. We loaded to an even keel position and left the locks at about an hour to high water, so as to have plenty of water available over the bar at the entrance to the almost straight cut. All the way down there was an ominous sound of the keel dragging through the sand and gravel of the river bed. We managed to clear the River alright, but Bob Wilson strongly advised against a repetition.

Goole was used for a short time, but the coal was found unsuitable for the existing grates at the power stations designed to burn fuel from other regions. Going up the river to Goole was an experience never to be forgotten. There was always a strong flood tide running through the channel, and though, on a fine summer's day the banks were really beautiful with ripening crops to be seen on both sides, it could be a heart stopping business. At times you have to steer almost at right angles to the way you want to go, to stay in the channel, whilst nearly all the buoys and markers bore some signs of close contact in the past. The actual operation of loading at Goole was similar to that in South Wales, that was by means of tips. However the method of conveying the coal to the tips differed at some of them, as the coal was brought by canal from the collieries, in compartment boats containing up to 40 tons of coal. These were lifted up to an appropriate height, and the contents tipped into the chute and so into the holds. The later C.E.G.B. colliers that loaded in Goole never used these barge lifts as the coal from those particular collieries was not suitable at all. However the South Eastern Gas Board ships were often loaded there, with coal for gas making.

The channel in the river was always changing. So much so that the leading marks were on wheels to make it easier moving them to new positions as the channel altered. Slower ships could rarely get down the river in one tide and had to tie up at Blacktoft, to a special jetty built for the purpose. Many of the highly improbable tales told of raids on the local farmers hen houses may have had a grain of truth in them. But there is no doubt that the keeper of the local hostelry was glad to entertain the crews of vessels tied up there. Of course some exaggerated the dangers of the transit of the river. That it was dangerous there was no doubt, especially for the low powered ships, who had great difficulty in making headway against the strong tides of the Springs. But the horrifying tales told of capsized ships rolling over and over with all hands being lost were difficult to believe.

Flatiron working and Thames Pilotage.

The Fulham power stations fleet of flat-irons had also suffered some losses which had been made good with further deliveries from the Burntisland Shipbuilding Company. They were similar to **Fulham V**. The first of the series, **Fulham**, was the cause of more 'bunkeritis' than any other in the electricity fleets. Theoretically she could carry 104 tons of coal, this assumed that every inch of the bunker space was bunged up tight to the deckhead. Of course, this never happened and it was considered a good trim if between 80 and 85 tons were taken. In summertime a little extra could be taken with safety on top of the hatches, but in winter, when it was needed badly it was most unwise.

With a daily consumption at sea of about 14-15 tons, delay occasioned by stress of weather caused real anxiety amongst the officers, bringing on attacks of that awful 'bunkeritis'. This showed itself as a constant parade up and down the deck and frequent tappings of the barometer on the part of the Master and exact measurements of the remaining coal taken every few hours, on the part of the Chief Engineer. Bunkering facilities were few and far between and getting fewer as oil took over as fuel for merchant ships. So the phrase 'Dicing with death off the Longships' came to have a very real meaning to those who sailed the older ships, and especially **Fulham**, around to Barry to load in winter.

One Chief Engineer, an Irishman, did not give two hoots in hell for anyone but his wife and family. His ability as an engineer was undoubted, which was just as well for Mick was a bit of

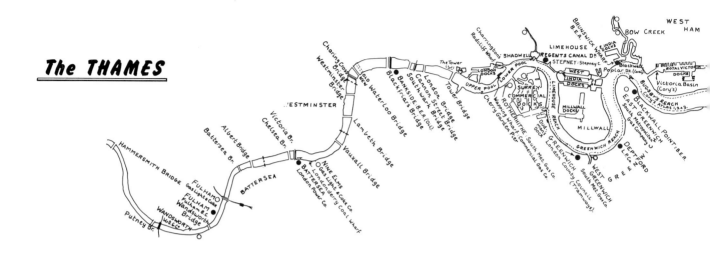

The THAMES

196. *Map of the River Thames showing the main destinations for coal cargoes.*

a wet hand in port. But he had 'confounded' the main engine on two occasions when, during periods of bad weather, violent racing had caused the tumbler blocks on the intermediate pressure crosshead to part and they were able to get the ship safely into port for repairs. For this, many of his 'crimes' were overlooked, not only by his shipmates who had a very real affection for Michael, but also by the Superintendent engineers who had to deal with him in service matters.

On one occasion one of them paid a visit to the ship at Barry Dock, at about 1300 hrs, and could find no one about at all, with the exception of the donkeyman, a 'Mussulman' who, of course, did not drink beer. He waited in fuming impatience for about an hour, and then went ashore, his temper gradually getting worse and worse, to make a few enquiries. On his way up the dock road, he encountered Michael weaving his somewhat erratic way back to the ship, with beer bottles sticking out of all his pockets. The Superintendent stopped his car, got out and proceeded to tear off an almighty strip at Michael. Mick listened to him with the grave courtesy of a drunken Irishman, and when he had finished said "Jesus Christ! Can a man not go ashore to confession now?!!" and stalked off in high dudgeon. Michael eventually had to go ashore with a stomach ulcer and, sadly, died soon after.

The bunker problems had not gone unnoticed and at the end of the war the first motor flat-irons were ordered. The oil engine needed less bunkers and of course no boiler, and so cargo capacity could be improved. **Fulham VIII** 1773/47 was the last collier to be delivered to the company as by the time **Fulham IX** and **X** were delivered the electricity companies had been nationalised. They were the first three motor ships owned by any of the electricity generating bodies and when they came into service they were undoubtedly the most outstanding ships in the coastal service. Air conditioned throughout the sumptuous accommodation, they were much sought after berths. **Fulham VIII** had an experimental engine system of intricate design and complexity, and over the years spent a considerable time undergoing either repairs or modifications. The other two, of more conventional design, rarely gave serious trouble.

Frank Montague and George Desforges were the two bridge 'pilots' for the Fulham Station. Monty, as he was known by everyone on the Thames, and he seemed to be known by everyone between Deptford and Fulham as all passing craft hailed him, retired in 1965 as his health was beginning to give him trouble. He then went aboard **Fulham X** late one night, to bring her down river. In his usual fashion he walked through the accommodation and banged heavily on the master's door, bawling out "Wot abart it, Mite?" The Master wandered out in his pyjamas, sleepily rubbing his blurred eyes, and complaining bitterly of the din. Monty said the water was there and he would go and make a start at singling up the moorings. The Master said he would follow as soon as he was dressed. When he appeared on the bridge he seemed a little distraught and worried, and Monty remarked on it. Eventually he was told that there was a woman in the old man's bunk, too drunk to get dressed and go ashore. Monty was shocked and dashed down below to do something about it, and so avoid the serious trouble that would have followed public disclosure of the facts.

Sure enough, there in the dim light of the Master's night light, was a figure lying under the bed clothes, one shapely leg hanging over the side of the bed. Monty grabbed the leg and yelling "come on young woman - out of it" yanked it hard, and found himself wildly waving a plaster and wax stocking display leg. Roaring like a bull he stormed up on to the bridge, intent on wrapping the leg round the old man's nut, only to find the culprit had taken refuge on top of the wheelhouse.

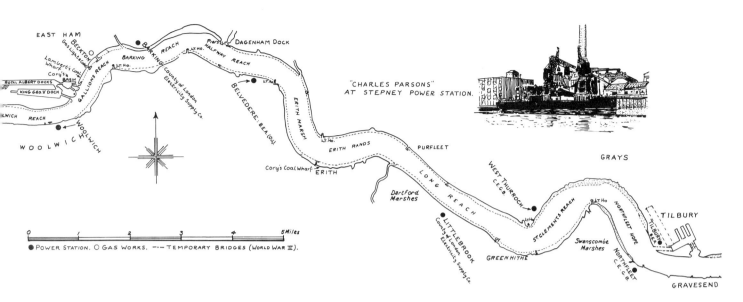

EAST HAM

BECKTON
Gas Lighters·

DAGENHAM DOCK

Lambert's Coal Wharf

Cory's BASIN

ROYAL ALBERT DOCKS

KING GEO.V DOCK

Pier

BARKING

BARKING REACH

HALFWAY REACH

BARKING County of London Electricity Supply Co.

WOOLWICH REACH

GALLIONS REACH

WOOLWICH

BELVEDERE BEACON (W)

ERITH MARSH

"CHARLES PARSONS" AT STEPNEY POWER STATION.

ERITH RANDS

PURFLEET

GRAYS

Cory's Coal Wharf ERITH

Dartford Marshes

LONG REACH

WEST THURROCK C.E.C.B

ST CLEMENTS REACH

NORTHFLEET HOPE

TILBURY

Tilbury

LITTLEBROOK County of London Electricity Supply Co.

GREENHITHE

Swanscombe Marshes

NORTHFLEET C.E.C.B

GRAVESEND

0   1   2   3   4   5Miles

● POWER STATION. ○ GAS WORKS. —·— TEMPORARY BRIDGES (WORLD WAR II).

Piloting the colliers up the Thames to their destination was an exacting business as recalled by Bob Holland and Dick Waterhouse. **Fulham IX** and **X** had Mirrlees engines on one shaft. They were nicely fitted below and even had a cafetaria for the crew. To go from ahead to astern the engine had to be stopped and re-started in reverse using compressed air. Most motor ships were direct drive like this, but not all of them. **Fulham VIII** was a pilots nightmare and gave much trouble with her two engines coupled to one shaft. If you were in trouble on her and wanted a double ring astern you'd get it alright, but when you wanted to go ahead again it took too long for the engineers to uncouple it. It took several seconds and it was vital that when the pilot wanted the ship to stop it did stop, otherwise damage could result.

Bridge pilots were previously watermen, though Bob Holland began as a lighterman in 1928 before becoming a waterman shortly before the war and worked mooring ships around Erith, Barking and Beckton. Initially it was the Gas companies who needed pilots. In the 1930s W. G. Lockey was the pilot for the Wandsworth & District Gas Co., and he would often take one of the ships down and bring another of the company's ships up on the same tide. The lighterage and barge traffic was heavy in those days, though things were being improved with the demolition of Chelsea Bridge. Waterloo Bridge was replaced by a new bridge during the war and officially opened in 1945. It was in a decrepit state for many years before and the centre two arches (No.4 and 5 from the south side) were shored up and they could not be used by river traffic. A tug was always in attendance to help lighters through. Coming down on the ebb tide to it there was a nasty set of currents and it was necessary to aim for the buttress of the No.2 arch from the north side so that the current would set the vessel over right into the centre of the arch. Traffic bound up-river used arch No.3 from the south side. The replacement bridge was built alongside the old bridge and traffic continued during the building and demolition, as it did when other bridges on the river were rebuilt.

Matters had been further complicated during the war by the construction of temporary bridges across the Thames. One was at Charing Cross and went over to just the upper side of Hungerford Bridge. For the pilots it meant that as soon as they came through Waterloo Bridge and entered Charing Cross Bridge they were on top of Hungerford Bridge and they were not in line. The other temporary bridges were at Lambeth and a third from Battersea Park over to Chelsea. A fourth temporary bridge was planned below Waterloo but was never completed. The temporary bridges were pulled down at the end of the war. Lionel Mutter took up **Sir Joseph Swan** and she touched bottom causing some damage even though there should have been plenty of water, so soundings were taken and it was found that there were still old parts of the bridge foundations sticking up at Battersea.

Many watermen would have liked to be bridge pilots but not all were able to tackle the job. A tug skipper might think because he could tow six lighters through a bridge then he could follow the same course with a ship, but this was not so because the string of lighters were flexible while a collier was rigid. Bob Holland obtained his experience by steering for other pilots as they did not like the idea of helmsmen off the ships especially with the added hazard of the temporary bridges during the war. Sometimes the ship's bosun would be on the wheel, but few seamen liked steering up through the bridges, even though the vessels had longer rudders than normally fitted, to improve the response. But it had to be remembered that the steam steering gear was slower to respond than the hydraulic gear of motor vessels. Tom How organised the bridge pilots and there was considerable competition from watermen to join this select band. Tom How contracted with the London Power

Company to provide pilots and had similar arrangements with Fulham ships which were all under Stephenson Clarke management. The Gas Companies had their own recognised pilots. The arrangement continued after nationalisation of the fleets. The river pilots worked from Limehouse, just below the pier, before the war during which the place was moved to Hanover Hole Tier. With the expansion of the power stations after the war, the flat-irons reached their peak with Battersea alone taking 650,000 tons a year with the completion of the 'B' station in 1955. Similar large quantities were taken by the other power stations and gas works. On average there would be about five ships going up on each tide. A considerable amount of coal also went up in barges.

The art of bridge-piloting was not underestimating the tugs for Bob Holland. "If I was working up river at Tower Bridge and saw a tow at London Bridge I would automatically pull her down to 'slow'. If I began to fall behind the tug I would go up to half speed, but if I was gaining I would put her on 'dead slow' and would blow the whistle hoping he would give way and go over towards Blackfriars. But a lot of tug skippers could not do this if they were towing six 200 to 300 ton barges with an old tug of low power. There was also the need to watch out for tugs dropping or picking up barges. This was made more difficult during the war as sidelights were screened and of reduced power and sometimes this led to near-misses. Things were much improved when V.H.F. radio was generally fitted so that intended movements could be reported and the positions of other vessels ascertained, especially in poor visibility.

There was a difference between handling steam colliers and motor colliers. With a steamer, say, going up to swing at Pimlico. You would stop the engine and blow five blasts for rounding. Nine times out of ten when you rang 'full astern' you would get a kick ahead first to break the vacuum in the engine which you did not want. With motor ships you got the movement wanted as soon as you rang down for them. Sometimes you got the wrong movement though, especially if, say, the third engineer was on duty and could not be bothered to look at the telegraph indicator. On one occasion the pilot aboard **Harry Richardson** 1198/50 got 'full ahead' instead and finished up under a jetty at Rotherhithe."

Unless the collier's captain was a regular trader and could get a dispensation in order to do his own pilotage below bridges, a Trinity House pilot would bring a loaded collier as far as Hanover Hole Tier, just below Cherry Garden Pier, which was within sight of Tower Bridge. Here the bridge pilot took over. It was usual practice for a bridge pilot to bring a light collier down river and transfer to a loaded ship at Hanover Hole Tier and take her up. There was a mark (a white disc) painted on the river wall by the upper (Surrey) entrance to Surrey Docks and when the water reached this mark there was enough water and headroom in the bridge-holes to take a ship up. Some pilots used to judge the water level by the piles of Cherry Garden Pier. The water could rise three feet in ten minutes and then stop. This was the sort of situation when radioed information from the tide gauge lower down the river relayed to the colliers by Tilbury Signal Station was useful. It all depended on the tide and the amount of land water coming down; this could increase rapidly with heavy rain. It was possible to go above Hammersmith Bridge and be neaped up there for a week.

While Hammersmith Bridge has the least headroom of any bridge, it did not concern the colliers, for Wandsworth Bridge was the last one they had to worry about. Only certain bridge arches have sufficient depth of water and at night these working arches were marked by two orange lights set horizontally. Taking a collier up, once you shaped up for London Bridge you had two further bridges to take into consideration, since they are so close to it. These were Cannon Street Railway Bridge and Southwark Bridge, so a course has to be steered which took the ship safely through all three or you could easily hit one of them. Waterloo Bridge, re-built at the end of the war, was easier to take a ship through than the original, whose alignment had made things difficult for the older pilots. The narrowest and shallowest bridge was Westminster.

With land-water it was a job coming down on the ebb with the tide rushing out. Instead of springing a collier's head off the quay automatically, the stern had to be sprung off, checked, let the head come off and then let go. It all had to be done in a hurry as they were big ships. The land-water gave pilots a difficult time especially when swinging them and backing them up because of all the extra engine movements. Going down river however, in these conditions with land-water plus flood tide it was possible to set off with the empty collier six hours before high water, change to the full one and berth four hours before high water, so it was as if the tide never went out. However, in order to keep the berths clear regular dredging was necessary at both Battersea and Fulham where the power station cooling water intake could silt up as well as the berths. The dredgers would lay out their mooring chains and there was always a danger of one of these chains getting round the ships propellor. Some of the dredgers' skippers would keep a look out for the colliers and move in-shore, but others kept dredging to the last moment. At Fulham there could be up to 14 feet of water under the ship at low water when dredged.

The pilot usually arrived five hours before high water to take the ship down and would let-go about four and a half hours before high-water. If, having left Fulham and on arrival at Battersea Bridge, he could see 5.5 courses of stones on the pier, and next Victoria Rail Bridge showed 4 courses of stones, the pilot had a comfortable margin. Then on reaching Westminster Bridge there was 5.5 or 6 courses of stones showing he could get down to London Bridge safely and transfer to the loaded collier and bring her back up. On the other hand, if it was 5 courses of stones at Battersea 3.5 at Victoria Rail and 5 at Westminster it would be essential to hurry back and keep the loaded collier head-up ready to go. The tide might be late but that could not be counted on. There was sufficient light at night to see the courses of stones on the bridge piers.

A tides work was usually three different colliers say, one down, one up and another down. Battersea needed a ship to berth every tide so there was a loaded ship on the buoys which could go alongside after the empty one left and about two hours before high water the loaded one left Pimlico Buoys and would berth at Battersea Power Station. The pilot would then return with the next loaded collier which would go to Pimlico Buoys. In this way if there was a fog there would always be a loaded ship ready to berth at Battersea. It was essential to check from bridge to bridge how fast the tide was rising, especially on the spring tides and when coming down from Fulham if only four courses of stones were showing it was too late to risk it, and the only thing for it was to make the ship fast at Pimlico Buoys off Battersea Power Station and wait for the next tide before taking her any further.

Flatirons sailed from up-river power stations as soon as the ship was afloat but the ship might have poor bunkers, reducing her speed, which could delay getting down-river. Tower Bridge was not lifted for a collier, but when going down, by which time it was half flood, if the bridge was open for other traffic it was possible for a flat-iron to navigate the south standing part of the bridge. It must be remembered how much other traffic there was on the River in those days. While the big ships went no further than the Upper Pool, there were small coasters working up to Brentford and Isleworth, tugs and lighters, sailing barges (with their gear lowered, drudging-up with their anchors). Then there were motor barges, both dry-cargo and fuel, which included petrol, water barges, and smaller craft. All competing for space in a narrowing river. It was essential to know what each one was likely to do. In fog the pilot had to think very carefully before getting under way as once under way he was committed, said Dick Whitehouse. There were so few places where a ship could be anchored if it suddenly shut in thick with fog. Pimlico, when bound up, was one of the first places where a collier could swing safely to her anchor, for some of the flatirons were as much as 270 feet in length.

The anchor was used to swing the ship head to tide for going alongside. On Spring tides it was necessary to swing the ship as soon as possible because modern stockless anchors can drag. With a neap tide you could leave it later. Once at the berth a boatman in attendance took the ship's lines ashore. The bridge pilot's services were paid per ship, the rate being the same whether light or loaded. The managers, Stephenson Clarke Ltd., handled the financial side of things for the power companies and later, after nationalisation.

Considering the collier traffic, both gas and electricity, the size of the ships and the prevalence of fog, until the Clean Air Acts reduced smoke pollution, accidents were remarkably few. On one occasion **Charles Parsons** was leaving, piloted by Albert Forrest. He always did complain about her steering qualities, although nobody else did, and while bound-up at 2 a.m. from Hanover Hole Tier he was shaping to come through Tower Bridge and she took a run and went head-first into the Southern abutment. The impact folded her stem around like the flap of an envelope. She was brought back to East Lane Tier, below the bridge, and the coal was discharged at a down-river power station. When she was dry-docked at Green & Silley Weir's, Blackwall, it was discovered that there was a piece of oily waste material inside her steering mechanism. It was thought to have been there since the war, when she had been badly damaged and then repaired. Most collisions were not too serious, causing little or no inconvenience to the thousands of Londoners who poured over the various bridges every day on their way to or from work, but on Saturday 18th of March 1950 a notice to the general public was published in the Times. The headlines read "Battersea Bridge closed to all traffic" and it was followed by "Scotland Yard announced today that Battersea Road Bridge would be closed to all traffic, except pedestrians, until further notice. Light traffic would be diverted via Albert Bridge, and heavy traffic via Chelsea or Wandsworth Bridges."

Ships that came into contact with any of the bridges, usually suffered far greater damage than they inflicted on the solid structure of the bridge, but an exception was in the case of **John Hopkinson** 1314/32. She had discharged her cargo of small coal at Fulham Power Station, and was on her way back to Barry Dock in South Wales to load another cargo for the Thames. She had actually cleared the Battersea Railway Bridge and was shaping up to 'shoot' the working arch of Battersea Road Bridge, always a difficult manoeuvre, when something prevented her from making a clean approach and she would not come to starboard enough. Though the engines were immediately rung and put full astern, this had no effect on either her speed through the water or her swing to starboard, and she came into violent contact with the bridge buttress, the port bow striking the North side of the working arch. The metal used in the construction of the bridge was cast steel, and the impact, coupled with the brittleness of the casting, caused huge chunks of the metal to go flying in all directions, one great 3 ton piece falling across the windlass and so badly damaging it that the port anchor ran out uncontrolled. The ship bounced off the buttress, and, being still underway, moved quickly over to the south side of the arch, where the galley housing, a substantial structure on the starboard side of the ship, came into contact with and badly damaged yet more of the girders supporting the arch. Of the seven curved, cast steel beams in the structure of the whole arch, five were broken off rendering the bridge unsafe for any but the lightest of traffic. It was immediately closed to all traffic, though after further surveys in daylight on the 18th-19th March, pedestrians, cycles and light motor cycles were allowed to use it. But it was closed to all other vehicular traffic including buses, for twelve months, while the damage was being repaired.

The machine used in making the parts for the original bridge had long since been scrapped, and a new one had to be built to cope with the huge steel castings needed in the reconstruction. The cost of this, added to the expense of the piling driven into the river bed about the damaged buttresses must have been considerable. The piling referred to, with the scaffolding built on top of it, seriously reduced the width of the working arch, the only one available to ships of any size. The ship suffered extensive damage. Immediately after the contact she beached herself on the south side of the river, where she remained for twelve hours, during which time the work of damage control was completed. The port anchor cable, most of which had run out uncontrolled as the ship ran aground, was disconnected at the nearest shackle, the end being buoyed for recovery later. The 'Hopkinson' was moved downstream the following tide, escorted by tugs, and moored at Pimlico Buoys off Battersea Power Station for a more detailed examination and assessment of damage. She could not be allowed to transit the bridges between Battersea and the Tower if there was even a remote chance of her foundering, and blocking what was then a most important navigational channel. She was judged to be quite safe to move, and it was decided to take her down to the Blackwall yard of Green & Silley Weir for temporary repairs for the return north for survey and permanent repairs.

In common with almost all the 'flatties', **John Hopkinson** had been designed to make a light ship transit of the Thames bridges fully ballasted, and her domestic and engine room fresh water tanks full. The fore peak top tank had been penetrated in the first contact with the Bridge at Battersea. To maintain as high a level as possible in the tank it was decided to keep the ballast pump going full belt, and the result was a spectacular cascade of water pouring continuously through the holes in the bow. It showed up in the press photographs, though the accompanying captions caused some amusement amongst those involved. 'The pumps on the S.S. **John Hopkinson** working furiously to prevent the ship sinking' was as far from the truth as it was possible to be. But no one would have believed that water was being pumped into the ship, rather than out of it, trying to ensure that her head was down low enough to clear Westminster Bridge with safety.

The damage to the ship proved to be far more extensive than was at first imagined. It affected important safety equipment as one of the lifeboats had been holed and distorted, and of course the hull had been penetrated in several places, both in the actual collision and in the subsequent grounding. The galley had been so crushed that it had to be totally rebuilt, and a new counterbalance shaft had to be made and fitted to the hinged funnel. So permanent repairs had to be completed before **John Hopkinson** could be allowed to leave. It took nine weeks to effect the necessary repairs. There were of course other collisions with the Thames bridges, though none were as serious as the **John Hopkinson** affair.

Perhaps the most famous of the contacts was that made by **Dulwich**, one of the 'Flatirons' belonging to the South Eastern Gas Board, which collided with Vauxhall Bridge on its way up to Wandsworth Gas Works, causing extensive damage to herself amidships, and to the metal work of the bridge. This was of malleable steel and though it was badly distorted, it did not break. **Dulwich** moored for examination at the Pimlico Buoys, and when she was found seaworthy she went up to her discharging berth the next day. On her way down the river after discharging she again hit the same bridge, but in another arch, inflicting further damage upon herself and the bridge! There were about 47 flatirons on the Thames in the early 1950s and so collisions were inevitable.

In March 1946 the County of London Electricity Supply Co., came a step nearer owning their own vessels with the formation of Coastwise Colliers Ltd., which was formed by Stephenson Clarke, William Cory and France, Fenwick to own vessels for long term charter to the company for the supply of Barking and Littlebrook power stations in particular. Initially the companies transferred vessels from their own fleets so **Balcombe** was re-named **Colwyn** 2760/43 from Stephenson Clarke, and similar names beginning with 'Col' were given to the vessels from Cory and France, Fenwick, so that in 1949 the fleet consisted of **Coldharbour** (ex Cormull) 1865/42, **Coldridge** 2883/42 (ex Cormain), **Coldstream** (ex Pinewood) 2853/45, **Collingbourne** (ex Wrenwood) 2847/43, **Colnbrook** (ex Sound Fisher) 2931/41, **Colwyn** (ex Balcombe) 2760/43 and two new vessels **Coleford** 2852/48 and **Colville** 2918/49. Vessels were also ordered, in particular a series of 10 smaller colliers to carry coal from Goole to power stations at Poole, Portishead and Prince Rock, Plymouth. The whole scheme came under review when the new British Electricity Authority was established on 1st of April 1948 as the result of nationalisation. The following year it was agreed to wind up the company and all the vessels were transferred back to the participating owners. Of the new vessels, **Colville** was sold to Stephenson Clarke and became **Heyshott**, while **Coleford** was purchased by France, Fenwick for £197,500 becoming **Bestwood**. The colliers had continued to serve the same power stations throughout. The British Electricity Authority continued to work closely with the collier owners but as coal mines were nationalised too the owners were purely carriers for the two nationalised industries. A winter and summer programme would be worked out with the Authority and a rate would be fixed for a six month period usually, which could then be extended. In all there were 13 power station wharves and Barking Power Station alone needed 7,000 tons of coal a day in winter.

The ten vessels on order were taken over by the British Electricity Authority and became the first new steamers to be delivered to the Authority beginning with **Poole Harbour** 1366/49 and followed by a further five vessels with 'Poole' names to serve that power station, and the series was completed by **Mendip** 1362/50, **Bodmin Moor** 1362/50 and **Brent Knoll** 1362/50. They were built by John Crown, William Pickersgill and Austin's. The vessels all had the dimensions 227.3' x 36.0' x 14.3' (213), and were a smaller version of **Pompey Power** 1428/49 and **Pompey Light** 1428/49 (201),

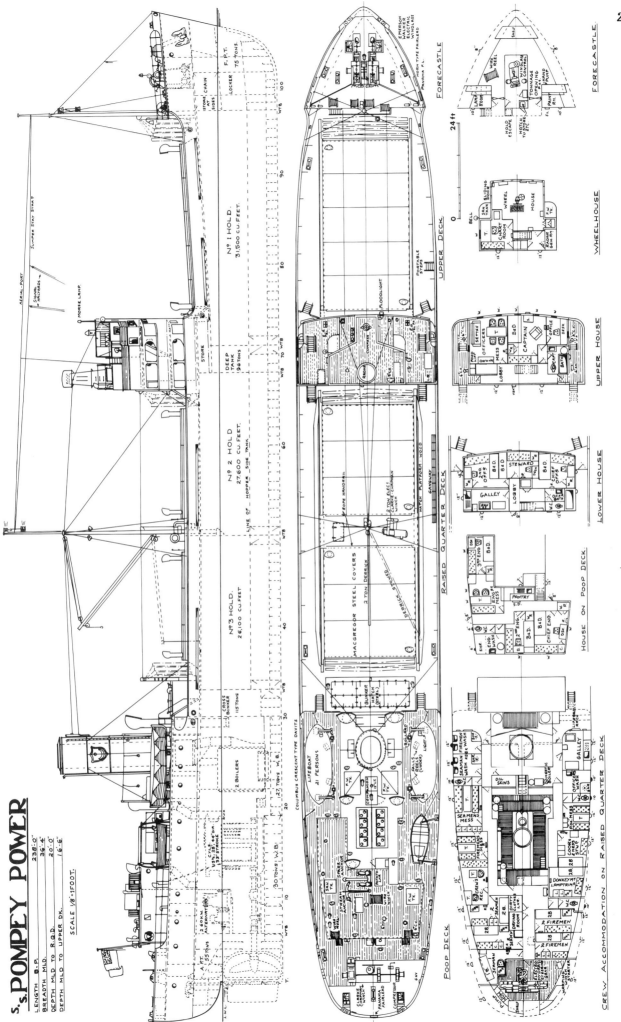

s.s. POMPEY POWER

LENGTH B.P. 238'-0"
BREADTH MLD. 36'-4"
DEPTH MLD TO R.Q.D. 20'-0"
DEPTH MLD TO UPPER DK. 16'-6"

SCALE 1/8"=1FOOT.

24 ft
0

FORECASTLE

WHEELHOUSE

UPPER HOUSE

LOWER HOUSE

HOUSE ON POOP DECK

CREW ACCOMMODATION ON RAISED QUARTER DECK

UPPER DECK

POOP DECK

RAISED QUARTER DECK

which measured 242.0' x 36.5' x 14.4' and had been built by Austin's to the order of Portsmouth Corporation. The Corporation, in an effort to ensure regular supplies for their power station, invited tenders and accepted that of £265,000 from Austin's yard. They were impressively equipped with radar, echo sounder, radio direction finding and gyro compass, while the deck machinery was all electric. In contrast the 'Poole' class only had echo sounders when delivered. By the time **Pompey Power** was delivered in January 1949 the power station had been nationalised for 9 months but she made her first voyage in the funnel mark of the Corporation, as shown on the plan (201). The accommodation was of a particularly high standard with single or twin berth cabins for all the crew, with separate mess and recreation rooms. To achieve this the engineers had their accommodation in a house on the poop deck. The cabins were similarly spacious for the officers on the bridge. The second ship **Pompey Light** was delivered in B.E.A. colours. All the vessels were managed by Stephenson Clarke so there was no change initially, but the 'Poole' class were managed for some years by Cory's. To supply the down-river power stations, the new Authority ordered a series of six large colliers of about 4,600 tons deadweight. The registered dimensions were 327.0' x 46.2' x 20.3', while the length between the perpendiculars was 320'7" and overall length 338'11". The seamen and firemen had single cabins and the officers accommodation was of a particularly high standard (203, 2). A characteristic feature of the ship was the large streamlined funnel which was not very effective at clearing smoke and the flue was later extended. The series were all built by William Pickersgill, beginning with **Cliff Quay** which was named after the power station at Ipswich, and ending with **W. J. H. Wood** 3357/51. Though wired for the fitting of radar, it was not installed until some time after the vessels were delivered. The hatch covers were of the latest MacGregor 'single-pull' design. There were four holds with hopper sides for rapid grab discharge. The engine of 1275 i.h.p. used superheated steam at 220 lbs/sq.in. and gave a service speed of 10.5 knots.

The series was almost immediately augmented by a further series of four vessels from Austin and Pickersgill to serve the newly extended Brighton power station. Breadth was reduced to 43'6" and and depth of hull by 2ft., decreasing the draught by the same amount to suit Shoreham, while the length was increased slightly giving the moulded dimensions 323.0' x 43.6' x 20.4'. As rather more powerful machinery of 1475 i.h.p. was fitted in the more streamlined hull they were able to maintain 11.25 knots. Because of the smaller hull, deadweight was reduced to 3,600 tons. At a late stage in the design they were given what was the latest style in streamlined superstructure and funnel. Incompletely scratched-out lines on the tracing reveals that open rails aft had initially been proposed, with a rather taller and narrower funnel, indicated by dotted lines on the plan (214). A funnel of this style had been fitted to **Borde** 3401/53, built by Austin's for Stephenson Clarke to the same basic hull design as **Cliff Quay** the previous year. First to be delivered was **Sir William Walker** 2901/54 and last **Charles H. Merz** 2947/55. **Sir Johnstone Wright** 3382/55 was a repeat of the **Cliff Quay** class, but with the streamlined superstructure style of the Brighton vessels. She was the last steam collier built for the authority and with its delivery gave them a fleet of 51 colliers. To augment their fleet further the British Electricity Authority invited the London companies which had traditionally chartered their colliers to London power stations to build further 4,600 deadweight colliers. Time charters were agreed and Stephenson Clarke, Cory's and France, Fenwick all added similar 4,600 ton steamers to their fleets. The names of the Authority's vessels were all prominent figures connected with the electricity industry and followed the style begun by the London Power Company. The choice of such long names must have added hours to the paperwork connected with the ships!

The up-river power stations were also being expanded and the final phase of Battersea power station in particular required more flatirons to serve it. The initial installation of the second phase was begun in 1944 and was to be completed in 1955. In all eight flatirons were ordered and first to be delivered were four motor vessels beginning with **Dame Caroline Haslett** 1777/50 and ending with **Blackwall Point** 1776/51. Surprisingly they were followed by four steamers **Brimsdown** 1837/51, **Brunswick Wharf** 1782/51, **Deptford** 1782/51 and **Hackney** 1782/51 (204). They could carry about 2,690 tons on a draught of 17'1.5", while the motor ships carried about 60 tons more. The vessels all had identical moulded dimensions of 270.6' (overall) x 39.6' x 18.6'. The steamers ran regularly from South Wales until the supplies of coal ran out and had their annual overhauls at the Penarth Pontoon and Engineering Company's works at Penarth for many years. They were closely similar to **Sir Alexander Kennedy**, built for the London Power Company just prior to nationalisation, except that single berth cabins were provided for all the crew by extending the accommodation forward on either side of the engine.

The gas companies similarly began to replace their war losses and increase their capacity. The Nine Elms works was expanded and berthing was provided for flatirons up to 270 feet in length capable of carrying about 2,500 tons. Five new motor vessels were ordered but only **Adams Beck** 1773/49 was delivered before the gas industry was nationalised under the Labour Government. The only real change was that the fleet now belonged to the North Thames Gas Board as from the 1st of May 1949, and even the funnel mark remained the same. The new Board took delivery of the remaining four flatirons in the series and ordered a further two vessels. The last to be delivered was **Thomas Livesey** 1779/53. The Great Beckton works was not forgotten. To supply the 5,000 tons or so needed each day a series of five large steam colliers beginning with **Frederick John Evans** 3337/54 and ending with **Thomas Goulden** 3332/55 were delivered from three different yards, the lead ship from Austin's with three from Hall, Russell and one from Pickersgill's yard. They were all similar (206) with the dimensions 325.0' x 46.2' x 20.1' approximately, though **John Orwell Phillips** 3391/55

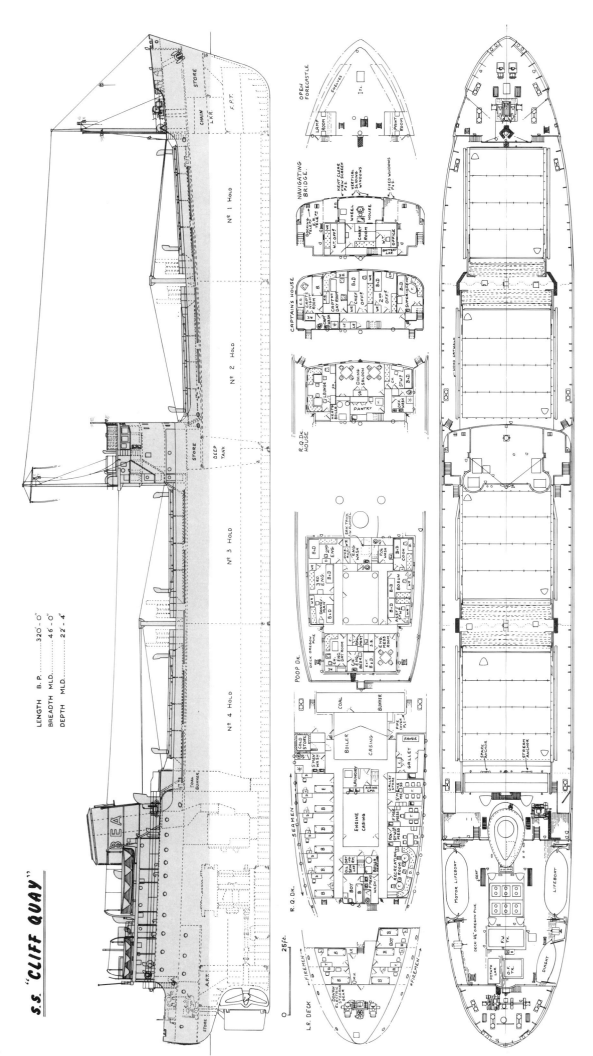

S.S. "CLIFF QUAY"

LENGTH B.P. ....320'-0"
BREADTH MLD. ....46'-0"
DEPTH MLD. ....22'-4"

203. **Cliff Quay**, delivered by William Pickersgill in June 1950, was the first ship in a series of similar vessels built for the British Electricity Authority who also invited London collier owners to build similar vessels for charter to them. The North Thames Gas Board also used the basic design for their vessels.

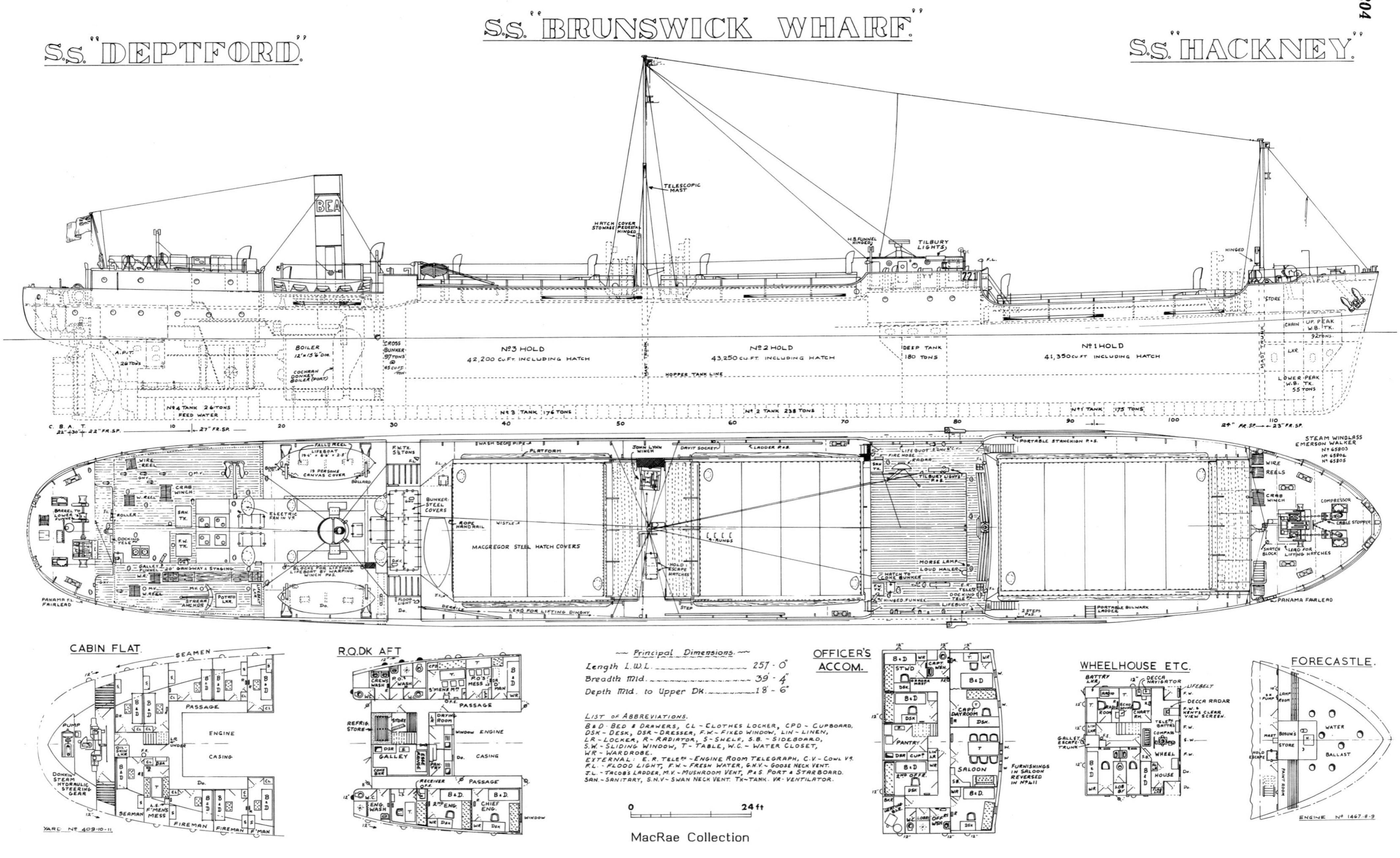
S.S. "DEPTFORD."
S.S. "BRUNSWICK WHARF."
S.S. "HACKNEY."
TELESCOPIC MAST
HATCH COVER STOWAGE PEDESTAL HINGED
H.B. FUNNEL HINGED
TILBURY LIGHTS
HINGED
BEA
BOILER 12'×15'6" DIA.
COCHRAN DONKEY BOILER (PORT)
CROSS BUNKER 97 TONS @ 45 CU.FT./TON
No 3 HOLD 42,200 CU.FT. INCLUDING HATCH
No 2 HOLD 43,250 CU.FT. INCLUDING HATCH
DEEP TANK 180 TONS
No 1 HOLD 41,350 CU.FT. INCLUDING HATCH
HOPPER TANK LINE
MAST TRUNK
STORE
CHAIN
UP. PEAK W.B. TK. 92 TONS
LKR.
LOWER PEAK W.B. TK. 55 TONS
A.P.T. 26 TONS
No 4 TANK 26 TONS FEED WATER
No 3 TANK 176 TONS
No 2 TANK 238 TONS
No 1 TANK 175 TONS
STEAM WINDLASS EMERSON WALKER No 65803 No 65806 No 65805
WIRE REELS
CRAB WINCH
COMPRESSOR
CABLE STOPPER
SNATCH BLOCK
LEAD FOR LIFTING HATCHES
PANAMA FAIRLEAD
PORTABLE STANCHION P. & S.
PORTABLE BULWARK LADDER
2 STEPS P. & S.
MORSE LAMP
LOUD HAILER
HATCH TO CONE BUNKER
HINGED FUNNEL
LIFEBUOY
FIRE HOSE
RADAR
TILBURY LIGHTS P. & S.
DOCKING TELE.
LADDER P. & S.
DAVIT SOCKET
JOHN LYNN WINCH
HOLD ESCAPE HATCHES
4 RUNGS
STEP
LEAD FOR LIFTING DINGHY
DERRICK
WASH DECK PIPE
PLATFORM
ROPE HANDRAIL
WISTLE
MACGREGOR STEEL HATCH COVERS
BUNKER STEEL COVERS
F.W. TK. 5½ TONS
FLOOD LIGHT
FALLS REEL
LIFEBOAT 19'6" × 6'6" × 2'5"
19 PERSONS CANVAS COVER
BOLLARD
ELECTRIC FAN IN V.R.
BLOCKS FOR LIFTING LIFEBOAT BY WARPING WINCH P. & S.
GALLEY FUNNEL
20' GANGWAY & STAGING
STREAM ANCHOR
POTATO LKR.
LIFEBOAT LKR.
SAN. TK.
F.W. TK.
ROLLER
DOCKING TELE.
BARREL TO LOWER FUNNEL
W. REEL
PANAMA F.L. FAIRLEAD
CABIN FLAT.
SEAMEN
PASSAGE
ENGINE CASING
PUMP
DONKIN STEAM HYDRAULIC STEERING GEAR
OIL-SKIN LKR.
L.R. UNDER
SEAMAN
F'MENS MESS
FIREMAN
F'MAN
YARD No 409-10-11
R.Q.DK AFT.
CREWS WASH
P.O.'s WASH
S'MENS M.
P.O.'S MESS
PASSAGE
REFRIG. STORE
STORE
DRYING ROOM
GALLEY
ESSE RANGE
WINDOW
ENGINE CASING
RECEIVER
ENG. WASH
2ND ENG.
CHIEF ENG.
~ Principal Dimensions ~
Length L.W.L. .... 257'-0"
Breadth Mld. .... 39'-4"
Depth Mld. to Upper Dk. .... 18'-6"
LIST OF ABBREVIATIONS.
B & D - BED & DRAWERS, CL - CLOTHES LOCKER, CPD - CUPBOARD,
DSK - DESK, DSR - DRESSER, F.W. - FIXED WINDOW, LIN - LINEN,
LR - LOCKER, R - RADIATOR, S - SHELF, S.B. - SIDEBOARD,
S.W. - SLIDING WINDOW, T - TABLE, W.C. - WATER CLOSET,
WR - WARDROBE.
EXTERNAL: E.R. TELEG. - ENGINE ROOM TELEGRAPH, C.V. - COWL V.R.
F.L. - FLOOD LIGHT, F.W. - FRESH WATER, G.N.V. - GOOSE NECK VENT.
J.L. - JACOBS LADDER, M.V. - MUSHROOM VENT, P & S. PORT & STARBOARD.
SAN. - SANITARY, S.N.V. - SWAN NECK VENT. TK - TANK. V.R. - VENTILATOR.
0 24 ft
MacRae Collection
OFFICER'S ACCOM.
STWD
CAPT. WASH
DAYROOM
PANTRY
SALOON
2ND OFFR.
FURNISHINGS IN SALOON REVERSED IN No 411
WHEELHOUSE ETC.
BATTRY LKR.
DECCA NAVIGATOR
LIFEBELT
DECCA RADAR
F.W. & KENTS CLEAR VIEW SCREEN.
GALLEY ESCAPE TRUNK
CHART RM.
WHEEL HOUSE
FORECASTLE.
BOSUN'S STORE
WATER
BALLAST
PAINT ROOM
ENGINE No 1467-8-9

205. Top left: **Hackney** under the Ellis Colski unloader at Woolwich Power Station (see page 178). Top Right a view from the **Hackney** about to pass under Westminster Bridge which was the narrowest and lowest of the Thames bridges between Tower Bridge and Wandsworth. Inches mattered when leaving Fulham Power Station on a Spring tide. Percy Carter, the bridge pilot used to assure masters new to the run that if they could not see the colour of the pedestrian's boots on the bridge then there was room to spare! Lower left: Crews mess of the **Hackney** showing bosun Jimmy Grey and able seamen Archie Anderson and Jan Gawlik. Bottom right: Second engineer Ridley and Chief engineer Scurr at work on the main engine. The photos were taken by Captain MacRae while master of the **Hackney** about 1972.

MacRae collection

was about 6 inches greater in beam. Deadweight was a little under 4,600 tons on average. They were essentially a post-war version of the **Mr. Therm** design and were very similar to the colliers built for the down-river power stations. The demand for gas was such that the sale of older colliers was not begun until 1958, but by this time plans for the importation of liquified natural gas were advanced and **Methane Pioneer** came into service delivering gas from Algeria. This and the advent of North Sea gas led to the sale of all the larger colliers between 1966 and 1968 but the last of all to go was the flatiron **Falconer Birks** in 1970.

The Brighton vessels were built from the outset to be oil fired and the others were later converted as stokers became difficult to get and oil proved cheaper overall. The trend to oil firing was also occurring on shore and both Poole and Portishead power stations were converted to oil and the 'Poole' type boats were sold in 1959/60 with the exception of **Mendip**, which was sold in 1966. The first news of the impending change was announced to crews in a letter dated 22 July 1958 stating the Authority's intention to dispose of about half its fleet and that only the most senior officer personnel could be sure of retaining their jobs. The large down-river colliers were mostly disposed of in the early 1970s, though last to go were **Cliff Quay** and **Sir William Walker** in 1983, as the sharp increase in oil prices led to a new lease of life for the coal-fired stations and the colliers which served them.

The last of the flatirons to be sold were **Battersea** and **Harry Richardson** when Battersea Power Station was finally closed. The position of large coal-fired stations in central London had always caused difficulties with smoke fumes even though the 337 feet high stacks had scrubbers fitted to remove sulphur dioxide. However the flats in Dolphin Square often found themselves getting the smoke as well as benefitting from the district heating scheme provided by the exhaust steam from the turbines. Barry loaded some 20,000 tons of coal a week for the Thames power stations but by 1955 a change was being made to foreign coal transhipped at ports such as Rotterdam and Antwerp into the flatirons.

Most of the British Electricity Authority colliers were managed by Stephenson Clarke and they continued to do this when the authority became the Central Electricity Authority in 1954. The 'B' was carefully removed from 50 or so funnels and replaced with a 'C' but when the name was changed yet again to the Central Electricity Generating Board the letters were removed entirely in 1958, so for much of their lives the ships had red funnels with a black top and two black bands.

Stephenson Clarke continued to expand their own fleet in the 1950s, concentrating for the most part on motor ships, though they acquired **Heyshott** 2918/49 from the winding up of Coastwise Colliers and had two new steamers delivered in the 1950s, **Borde** 3401/53 and **Arundel** 3422/56. One of the regular coal runs was to Fords at Dagenham, which was shared with France, Fenwick, who dropped out after some years. **Arundel** was placed on a ten-year time charter to the Central Electricity Authority and had no deck gear, whereas **Borde** was built for more general trading. They also purchased oil tankers as the change was made to oil-fired power stations. Some large steamers were purchased from other owners such as **Horsted** 2034/45 (ex Moorwood) of France, Fenwick, and **Bowcombe** 3332/54, which had been **Sir David II** of the North Thames Gas Board and which they had been managing. The fleet was often augmented in the 1960s by the purchase of managed ships and moved more into general trading.

Cory's colliers were fully employed in the latter part of the 1940s and the company was replacing the thirteen war-loss ships. Many others fought off attacks in the East Coast convoys. For example in June 1941, Mr. C. W. Davies won the M.B.E. for bringing **Cormount** into port after being attacked off Harwich by enemy aircraft. The cook won a British Empire Medal and a young D.E.M.S. gunner who died from his own wounds after selflessly carrying a wounded officer below received a posthumous George Cross. Several vessels were taken up for special tasks and **Corchester** 2374/27, **Corfirth** 1803/34, **Corcrest** 2373/18, **Corstar** 2337/18 and **Corfell** 1802/34 all served in the Mediterranean as cased petrol carriers. A hazardous task, especially as they were often under fire from enemy aircraft and in some cases had Cory crews. As the ships became more defensively armed they began to protect themselves better and the **Corfell** destroyed an E-boat off Lowestoft. A number of ships were managed on behalf of the Ministry of War Transport, including five Great Lakes steamers and five 'jeeps', American built 4-hatch vessels with engines amidships similar to Scandinavian timber ships. A number of other collier owners found themselves managing a variety of vessels for the Ministry during and immediately after the war.

206. Frederick John Evans
North Thames Gas Board.
Photo Alex Duncan

In order to replace losses during the war an associated company ordered the ferro-concrete motor collier **Lady Kathleen** 1832/43 which was traded until sold in 1946. A number of conventional colliers were added to the fleet throughout the war, especially those 315 to 317 feet long with a beam of about 44'6" and depth of 22'1". The series was begun before the war by the rather shorter **Cormount** 2841/36 which was mined and sunk off Harwich in 1943 and **Cormarsh** 2848/39. The first of the seven larger vessels was **Cormull** 2865/42, ending with **Cormist** 2886/46. They had deadweights up to about 4,350 tons. Seven years later the last steamers built for Cory's were **Cormoor** 3374/53 and **Corstream** 3375/55. They were closely similar to the 4,600 ton deadweight ships built for the British Electricity Authority and went on charter to them. **Cormoor** was renamed **Corsound** as she was so different from the earlier 'M' class vessels. This size was considered about the maximum the loading berths could handle without lengthy waiting periods. Only **Corstream** was built with oil firing, all the others were coal burners. The smaller vessels burned about 10 tons a day, while the larger ones burned 12 tons or more. English firemen after the war were happy as long as the runs were regular but did not like the continental voyages, and so the change to foreign firemen came about. By the time she was delivered coal imports were rising and imports from the U.S.A. and even India had reached 1.5 million tons a month. Cory's were rapidly diversifying and developing their interest in oil distribution and bunkering, towage and cargo handling. They also ordered ocean tankers and ore carriers as demand for coal fell. The first motor colliers **Corbrae** 2002/52 and **Corburn** 2059/53 proved successful and no further steamers were ordered although three motor colliers the same size as **Corsound** were built for the fleet. Last of the steam colliers to be sold was **Cormain** 2883/42.

The William Cory organisation had many berths on the Thames where coal was handled, the most famous of them being Albert Dock Hoists (220). Here in 1931, the record discharge of **Corbridge** had been achieved; 2,287 tons between 12.45 p.m. and 2.15 p.m. The berths had seven fast electric cranes which made short work of discharging four of the larger colliers every day. In fact, the only restriction which reduced the throughput was the inevitable truck shortage, but when this was foreseen, there were usually barges moored outside the ships to take care of that eventuality. The hoists and berth finally closed in March 1968. A few years later the last of the motor ships were sold and with them the black diamond on a white band which made the recognition of 'one of Cory's' so easy, had gone perhaps for ever from the coal trade.

Another great collier fleet of the Thames to disappear was that of the Hudson S.S. Co., a subsidiary of Samuel Williams of Dagenham Dock. Their fleet was decimated during the early part of the war and of the six ships only **Brasted** 1076/38 survived without serious damage. The only other survivor, **Dagenham** 2178/19, struck a mine on July 12th, 1940, whilst acting as convoy commodore ship. She was beached on Barrow sands, salved and her cargo discharged in London where she was repaired, but all this took six months. Replacements in the form of four second hand steamers were purchased in 1942, **Macbrae** 2117/24, **Philipp M.** 2085/24 and **Bramhill** 1821/23 from Cardiff owners, and **Hetton** 2714/24 from the Tanfield S.S. Co., of Newcastle. In June 1944 **Dagenham**, **Hetton** and **Bramhill** spent three months assisting in the Normandy landings, **Bramhill** suffering considerable grounding damage at the beach-head, but she was later repaired. At the end of the war, **Empire Lagoon** (191) and **Empire Pioneer** were purchased, becoming **Hudson Bay** and **Hudson Bank** respectively and beginning the use of 'Hudson' names.

Unlike the other collier companies, replacements were ordered from the Ailsa Shipbuilding Company. First to be delivered was **Hudson Strait** 3105/46 a collier of 4,465 tons deadweight with five holds and steel hatch covers. A sister, **Hudson River** 3128/49 followed as the first Ailsa built vessel, and a smaller four-hatch version of the design, **Hudson Cape** 2524/46, of 3,561 tons deadweight had proved very successful. The vessels were built without derricks and destined for the London coal trade where grab discharge was used. However with the nationalised utilities rapidly building up their own fleets, the company decided at a late stage to equip **Hudson Firth** 3117/49 with derricks and winches and with oil firing equipment (208). Oil fuel capacity was 382 tons giving her the range to carry bulk sugar from the West Indies. She proved very successful and carried more sugar than coal. It is interesting to note that her extra gear, mainly the derricks and winches reduced the deadweight of the design by 176 tons and this is why gear was often put ashore when a ship was time chartered to run in the coal trade.

Hudson Firth (and her sisters) had an unusual hatch layout with three hatches in the well deck. Most ships of this size had two hatches, but this arrangement allowed up to five different grades or consignments of coal to be carried. The accommodation was well laid out, but double cabins were retained for seamen and firemen. Last steamer to be delivered was **Hudson Sound** 2577/50, sister to **Hudson Cape**. The layout was almost identical except that the dimensions were 293.5' x 42.3' x 18.9' and four hatches sufficed as they were some 32 feet shorter than the five hatch vessels. Although MacGregor hatches had been fitted to the previous vessels, on **Hudson Firth** the shortest hatch behind the bridge was made shorter by having to leave space for the MacGregor hatch cover when open. To avoid this Mepco of Liverpool supplied the new vessel with units which could fold into a compact pile on the side decks, folding rather like a roller shutter. This allowed the hatch to be longer but were eventually replaced by a wooden hatch cover. She was fitted for oil fuel and an enlarged bunker to make her suitable for the Baltic and Mediterranean trades, but was also fitted with her Tilbury collier signal lights, white over red over white over blue, day number 107 so she could also work the coal run (front endpaper). The company built no more steamers and their next

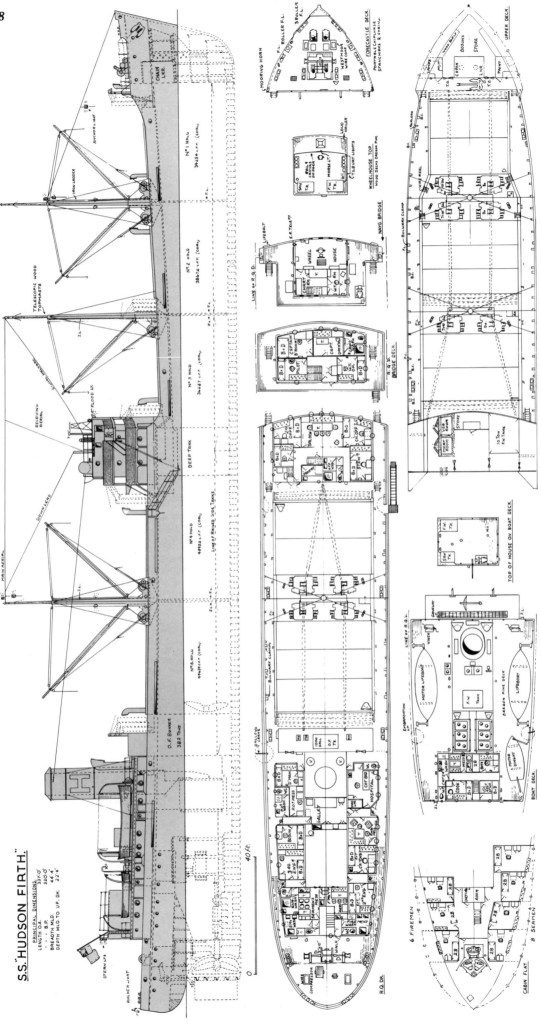

208. **Hudson Firth** *was fitted with oil firing and derricks at a late stage so that she could be used outside the east coast coal trade as there were already signs that the trade was changing by 1949. Her two sisters were both coal fired and gearless and so were essentially confined to shorter voyages.*

P. N. Thomas

vessel, **Hudson Deep**, was a bulk sugar carrier of 7,810 tons deadweight. She was later used with the Central Electricity Generating Board to develop large motor colliers. The steam colliers were sold during 1966 and 1967 because of their age and reduction in the coal trade. Charrington's only collier, **John Charrington**, survived the war and was joined by **Lady Charrington** 2154/52. The older vessel was later scrapped as was **Lady Charrington** in 1969.

William France, Fenwick had entered the war with some 20 ships of which 10 were to be lost, but perhaps the near loss of **Sea Fisher** 2950/40, mined in the North Sea soon after delivery alarmed the Admiralty most. She had been built for the associated Fenwick, Fisher S.S. Co., formed with James Fisher of Barrow. Her task was to carry gun turrets for the new battleships and to do this, was given a beam of almost 47 feet. Even then the hatch coamings had to be bulged outwards at the widest part of the turret. France, Fenwick employed her in the coal trade when not needed for carrying the turrets. The Admiralty, to be sure a ship would always be available, asked the company to build a sistership, **Sound Fisher** 2931/41. The company was dissolved at the end of the war and **Sound Fisher** became **Portwood**, continuing on the same power station coal runs to the Thames. She could easily be distinguished from the other colliers as she did not have masts between the hatches, but at the ends.

Some vessels were delivered during the war, in particular **Bushwood** 2842/42 of 4,300 tons deadweight and the first to have steel hatches in the fleet. The vessel was similar to the 'M' class of Cory's. Four sisterships were added ending with **Birdwood** 2862/45. Essentially they were a slightly larger version of the big engines aft colliers built for the fleet in the 1930s. Three smaller 'Empire' colliers were purchased at the end of the war to replace losses of that size. In 1948 **Bushwood** took the first cargo of coal to the new deep water jetty built to serve Cliff Quay Power Station and Kenneth R. Pelly reported to shareholders that export of coal to the continent had revived and the company were able to keep up the record of paying a dividend to shareholders as they had done for every year since the company was formed. In the same year two Baltic timber carriers were delivered and the company began to reduce their dependence on coal. Ocean tramps were also ordered. Last steamers to be delivered were **Bearwood** 3395/55 and **Helmwood** 3403/56. They were similar to the 4,600 deadweight colliers also built by Austin's for the British Electricity Authority and suitable for charter to them. **Bearwood** had no deck gear, but **Helmwood** had a full complement of 8 derricks and was immediately chartered for a season on the Canadian coast. During the latter part of the 1950s and early 1960s the fleet was rapidly reduced in numbers as the older colliers were scrapped or sold, though the old **Birdwood** of 1945 was converted by Smith's Dock to a motor ship suitable for ocean service and so remained in the fleet longer. **Bearwood** and **Helmwood** were the last to go at the end of the 1960s and the company continued in the ocean trades.

One of the smaller ships, **Kentwood** (ex-Empire Hearth) was sold after being laid up for a time. The purchaser was E. P. Atkinson's Ouse S.S. Co., in August 1956. All his coasters were scrapped by 1960, but they had participated in the boom years of the early 1950s when Goole was shipping as much coal as it had pre-war. **Kentwood** became **Mayfleet** (209), but although she visited Goole she was too big for the port on a regular basis and ran mainly from Newcastle for a few years before Mr. Atkinson gave up shipowning when freight rates fell at the end of the 1950s. Comben Longstaff had been in coasting prior to the war and now became more involved in the coal trade. Their new larger coasters like **Londonbrook** 960/46 were well suited to the Goole coal trade. His largest new steamer **Cardiganbrook** 1780/52 and her motor ship sister **Cardiffbrook** both had collier numbers for the Tilbury Hailing Station. Their last steamer was **Devonbrook** 1414/54. The company also managed the colliers of the Hargreaves Coal & Shipping Co. Ltd., who had several old coasters in the coal trade from Goole, all with names beginning 'Har' such as **Harfry** 936/21. They purchased the **Gwynwood** (ex **Lincolnbrook**) in 1958 which became **Harwood** 964/49 and was their last steamer when sold in 1964.

*209. E. P. Atkinson's **Mayfleet** at Southampton in the late 1950s.*   Courtesy F. Atkinson

210. Yokefleet *844/10, leaving the locks at Goole.*

Cooking on Colliers

Whereas Captains and Engineers were most important to the owners, the cook was most important to the crew. Alan Dowsland recalls what it was like to cook aboard some of the Goole colliers: "The first coaster I joined at Goole, my home town, was the coal-fired steamer **Saltfleet**. I was 17 years old and on the shipping pool at the time, as cabin boy cum galley boy. Ted Smith, the pool officer, knocked at our house door one December night, in 1947, at about 9 o'clock and said, "Join **Saltfleet**. Victoria Lock now!" I picked up my old kit bag I had been given, with my belongings in it, (they used to say just a pack of cards, and sweat rag!). I joined her at the lock, got aboard and found my cabin. The ship was loaded with about 1,600 tons of coal for Southampton Gas Works. The Skipper was Ratty Townsley, as he was then known. **Saltfleet** was ex-**Empire Cheyne**, wartime built, three masts, funnal aft, one hold forward, and one very large hold aft of the bridge; not a bad sea boat, as they go. I did a month in her, making trips from Goole and Blyth to Southampton Gas Works with coals and then paid off. At a later date the **Saltfleet** grounded and sank in a fog in the Ouse. She went down with no loss of life, near the village school of Reedness. She belonged to local shipowners Atkinson's of Goole, and was eventually cut up for scrap by a Dutch salvage firm, where she lay.

"Another coaster I sailed on was **Londonbrook**, a collier of about 1,300 tons loaded capacity. Dating from 1946, she was well built, riveted as they were then, a good sea boat. She was owned by Comben Longstaff's. From the Port of Goole, we sailed round the coast carrying coal to various power stations and gas works. The main ports of call at that time were Shoreham and Poole, where we tied up for the Gas Works at Town Quay, a very handy berth for provisions and stores. Yes, we all liked Poole as there were several local pubs along the waterfront, convenient for a quick pint. I usually settled for the Jolly Sailor, a good night out there too with piano, sing-song and plenty of local talent. While our cargo of coal was discharged we had our one night in port and sailed on the first morning tide, back to Goole again to load.

"Saturday night sailings at the port of Goole, in the steam coaster era, was an event in itself, in the coastal trade boom years after the war; a shipowner's headache, a Captain's nightmare! As usual, by 8 o'clock that evening most seamen were ashore for a drink before sailing so they said! Sailors, cooks, mates, engineers and firemen, most of the latter were still covered in coal dust and grime, a sweat rag round their necks. All were ready for sailing if it happens! Saturday night, my rendezvous was the George Hotel saloon bar, where cigarette smoke was so thick you could cut it with a knife, as it swirled up and outside through a small top window. The large black round coal bogey stove in the corner was glowing nicely with a couple of good size meat pies warming on its top and a few coal trimmers sitting round it. There were the ladies too, sailor's wives, girlfriends and others, out for a bit of fun. I had a look outside the George; it was a dark wet night with the Salvation Army Band playing across the road, on their pitch by the Clock Tower, under the light from the flickering gas street lamps. The rain was drizzling gently down on them and their music was familiar; for those in peril on the sea. "Buy a War Cry, Sir?" I put a tanner in her tin. "Thank you, Sir." She bravely pushed her way into the crowded bar. "Are they blowing yet?" someone in the bar shouts out. Of course they were blowing: steamers loaded with coal, waiting to sail, sounding off their whistles and hooters, trying to attract their crews back aboard. You could hear them all over town! Some would sail, some would not.

One sailing night in March 1949, most of the crew and myself were having our usual farewell drink in the Royal Hotel. Of course we drank as if we would never get another pint in our lives! We were ordered aboard for 8 o'clock. We could hear her blowing for us, on her steam whistle in the locks. Saying goodbye to the landlord, and the crowd in the Bar, we eventually made our way to the locks, got aboard, and sailed out of the locks into the River Ouse. On clearing the lock entrance the tide got hold of her and pushed us on to the wreck of another steamer, **Colwith Force**,

211. Londonbrook sinking off Goole after striking the wreck of **Colwith Force**, whose masts can be seen above water on the left. **Londonbrook** was later salvaged and returned to service with Comben Longstaff, her London managers.

until we were looking down on her masts and funnel. Our ship the **Londonbrook** was holed, settled down and sank alongside her, leaving the bow, bridge and stern end still well up from the swirling waters of the river (211). We required a knife at the lifeboat to cut away some rope lashings. Being the ship's Cook-Steward I fetched one from the galley which was now flooding with water. The lifeboat was lowered away, but not required as a local tug came alongside our vessel's stern and we all scrambled aboard. We were all at the locks and back ashore again within about one and a half hours of our sailing, with our lifebelts and any possessions we had salvaged. Typically seaman-like, someone said, "I could sup a pint!" It was only 9.45, so off we trooped, where to? Back to the Royal Hotel, of course, where we started out from. We caused quite an uproar in the bar! The landlord said, "Have you come back to finish your ale?" I must admit it did taste better than usual! Through the Shipping Federation and our Company, we were allowed one month's indemnity pay, after being shipwrecked on the doorstep, you might say!

"After having a few weeks off, up to the end of April 1949, on indemnity pay, the pool office of the Shipping Federation sent me to join the **Yokefleet**, as cook steward (210). She belonged to Atkinson's of Goole and had as Master Captain Bruce. She was a coal-fired steamer and carried about 1,000 tons. Her bottom was completely replated in dry dock in Goole after the Second World War. She was built about 1910 and had two masts, two holds, funnel aft, red with black topping. Once this funnel caught fire in the English Channel, and was glowing red from top to bottom. She was a popular design for coasters, very sturdy and a good sea boat. The **Yokefleet** really was ancient and the galley stove stood on four shapely cast-iron legs. My cabin was midships, under the bridge and I do not know how I slept as at every turn of the wheel on the bridge I could hear the chain steering gear rattling above me; not very restful! I thought I might get used to it, but I never did!

"The Captain's cabin, which I cleaned, reminded me of an old-time saloon bar. A big coal-fired bogey stove stood in it, all very Victorian, but having a lot of character. I enjoyed my job and what I was doing at 19 years of age was an adventure. In all coasters, early after the war years, we still used ration books. The crews were deducted, on average, one pound per week food money, which the ship's Master collected and handed to the Cook-Steward for victuals. The average number of crew being 14 to 16 men. The Butcher, Don Oldridge, and Ship's Chandler, Tommy Duckett, usually came aboard to collect the orders. Laundry was picked up by the Goole Steam Laundry.

Loading of the **Yokefleet**, at the coal hoists in Goole, generally took about 5 to 6 hours, followed by battening down her wooden hatch covers, sheeting and securing them. All coal dust was then hosed down off the ship and believe me there was some! We missed a tide and caught the next one, 24 hours in port, and ready for away. So on leaving the Victoria locks at Goole, which we went out of stern first, and alongside the Victoria Pier, we then butted our way seaward, into the tide,. With our funnel belching out big clouds of black smoke, it was full steam ahead. It was about 4 hours steaming to reach the sea. Gradually we got a good way of speed on, going nicely past the low villages, Swinefleet, Reedness, Whitgift and on to Blacktoft, past its jetty and the Hope and Anchor, a riverside pub; Trent Falls coming up; next Ferriby, Hessle and Hull, portside. Here we dropped the Goole River Pilot and took aboard the next River Pilot, in Hull Roads and so on to Spurn Point, passing Grimsby to starboard. We are steaming well now, with a following tide, Spurn ahead and the pilot cutter comes alongside. Hull Pilot away and we are on our own, sailing for Ipswich, 1,000 tons of coal for the Gas Works.

"Crew's wages on coasters were not high in the later 1940s, even with a small amount of overtime, of which, as Cook/Steward I booked myself two hours a day, and that was more than most. Our official working day was 10 hours, making up 70 hours a week, before overtime. There was never a lot of money about, as we had nearly every other night in port, and going ashore boozing was our way of life as long as we could afford it. Being single, I was always letting some of the ship's crew have small loans of money, though some of the married men could hardly afford to pay me back. Going to sea gave us a sense of freedom and we meant to have and try to enjoy that freedom.

"Well, we tied up early that evening at the Gas Works wharf, at Ipswich, ready to discharge after a rough entry into the harbour owing to bad weather and very high winds. So on being at our berth, for a change, I decided to have a shave, ready to go ashore for a few pints with my shipmates. At 19 years of age, I did not shave much, not much to shave really anyway! 'Just a bit of fluff' the lads told me. Anyway, I thought I had better do it while the electric lights were still on, which were kept going by a steam engine maintained by the Donkey man. As it happened, my brother had given me a Solingen steel cut-throat razor, which I thought I would have a shave with for the first time, though I was a bit scared of this razor really. I lathered my face with a piece of soap, and lifted the cut-throat razor with a trembling hand towards my throat, looking at the same time into the little mirror over the sink. And seeing the reflection of the electric light bulb hanging there without a shade on it, it did not look very bright either, but the privilege, even of that light, was to be denied me, because it started to fade and went out, in accompaniment to the generator whining to a stop. If the ship rolled, I could have cut my throat. So I looked out of the cabin door into the black alley way. "All lights out" shouts Big Peter, the Donkeyman. "I am not on overtime now, better light your paraffin lamp cookie," he said. I did so, only then my cabin looked like the 'Black Hole of Calcutta'.

Yokefleet even rolled in the harbour that night, caused by the heavy winds. The paraffin lamp moved about too, as it was on a pivot, to follow the ship's motion, and the mirror was now all shadows. Well, I had started shaving and intended to finish shaving now, even if it killed me. So I did my best as the present situation allowed, but I kept nicking my face. I stuck small pieces of newspaper on the cuts and then tried to wipe the blood away, which still trickled down from each cut. The wind buffeting **Yokefleet** about did not help much either. I think I should have packed the shaving up really, but it became a challenge. The blood did not bother me anyway, so I thought, but a few more razor cuts on my face and I said 'that will do, what a mess.' I should not have gone ashore, but I thought 'it's dark, nobody would see me.' I was dying for a pint of beer. So I went down to the Queens Hotel, where my mates off the ship Arnold, Mick, Big John and Bill Thorpe, were supping their beer. As I walked through the pub door towards their table, they burst our laughing at me, and were rolling about in their seats with laughter. The following morning aboard **Yokefleet**, there was a count-up by my interested shipmates - I had only cut myself sixteen times anyway! I never did use that razor again, only to cut a piece of carpet. The next and last time I had a shave in Ipswich, was in the safety of the local barber's shop.

"Some years later I returned for a few short weeks as Cook-Steward on **Yokefleet**. Unfortunately I had what we called a touch of the 'dropsies', meaning whatever I handled, or put down safely, like pans, trays, dishes and particularly crockery, somehow or other finished up on the deck. Fortunately **Yokefleet** was well stocked with crockery, as I found out! With me having been on a few deep sea trips, previously, and having reasonable weather, on bigger and more stable vessels, I had lost touch with coasters. Mind you, I was a bit speedier and a bit more reckless by this time. Dinner plates; put them on wet cloths and they slid off and smashed. I put them down all over the galley where they should have been safe but I was still losing them. Cups and mugs amidships; I washed them up and hung them on hooks for safety above my head. **Yokefleet** rolled slightly so I had a cup or a mug still in my hand leaving the handle still hanging on the hook! I hid them in lockers, but eventually I had so many mugs and cups stowed away without handles I started tossing them over the side.

Comments were made to me by the officers midships. "Seem to be short of mugs, cookie," the mate said to me. I said I had not noticed. Crews quarters aft; "not many plates about, steward", a sailor said. "Don't worry I'll get some more" pacified him for now, but I was getting a sweat on! So taking the bull by the horns, I said to the Captain, Mr. Bruce, that I had had a bad run on crockery lately owing to the weather, and I was willing to pay for it. "Don't worry, cook," he said, "there is a drawer with plenty of spare dinner plates locked in your cabin and spare mugs and cups and saucers in a box in the pantry." He gave me the key. "Thank you, Sir." Situation solved, but it was not, because I carried on my crockery breaking spree, getting through the spares as well! I did not feel very happy about it myself and as I was thinking of leaving the ship for various reasons this made my mind up. I put an order in for more crockery at the company's office and they said, "what have you been doing, eating them?" They would find out, and before they did, I paid off in Goole.

I started out on coasters in 1947 at Goole and finished up back on one, after having been seven years on the liners of the Cunard White Star fleet. The coaster was **Poole River**, a B.E.A. boat. I joined her as ship's cook, quite a change of environment! Another change was the ship itself (213). The **Poole River** was a well-built vessel, beamy, with a big red funnel aft, two holds, MacGregor type steel hatches and no masts to speak of. She also had good accommodation aft, well covered in against the weather, a good galley, and to me a revelation for a coaster. Her load capacity was about 1,600 tons. She had a crew of 16 men, some from Goole and some Geordies, while the four firemen were coloured, from North Shields. I never did settle down on the **Poole River**, as I was now married and we were picking up cargoes from further North, from Blyth and not Goole for the power stations at Shoreham and Poole. On one trip I received a telegram at Poole saying my wife was not well, so I paid off there which was not a usual practice and caught the first train home from Poole Station and so ended my last time in steam colliers."

213. Poole Sound.
Sketch John Bartlett

London and the Northern Fleets

A. F. Henry & MacGregor of Leith had continued to build up their coasting fleet which were mainly involved in carrying cement from the Thames area to Scottish ports with coal or stone southwards. After the Second World War there was less Scottish coal for the southward cargo and so larger vessels were acquired to carry coal from North East ports including two 'Icemaid' type colliers in 1949. They became **Kinnaird Head** 2066/44 and **Rattray Head** 2066/43 and along with **Dunvegan Head** 1434/21, purchased in 1947, entered the London coal trade. The latter vessel had been built as Maud Llewellyn (see page 80) for the Cardiff trade. A Norwegian steamer was added to the fleet and became **Denwick Head** 2006/47.

In the London trade they came into competition with the London collier owners one of which was the Shipping & Coal Co., who had two steam colliers at the end of the war, **Foreland** 1870/39 and **Queensland** 1628/28; both coal fired. Reliable English firemen became more difficult to recruit and they would not work short handed. Sometimes one would stay ashore and keep the ship in port and the others would contribute to cover his fine as they had all had an extra night in port. Eventually Arab firemen were taken on which worked well. The English fired better (when sober) whereas the Arabs would tend to panic when they saw the pressure gauge dropping, frantically shovelling on coal and producing clouds of black smoke which was not allowed on the Thames and the company were fined £40 on one occasion. They were replaced in the 1950s with new motor vessels and the new **Queensland** of 1958 could carry 3,500 tons on a draught of 18'6". Shipping & Coal had supplied London Transport pre-war and the company got this trade back after persuading the manager to put down special moorings for **Queensland** which was longer than the wharf. **Kinnaird Head** and **Rattray Head** could only carry about 2,650 tons on the same draught. The change to the bigger motor ship saved about a shilling per ton and so the less efficient steamers were squeezed out of the trade and were sold. Both companies developed motor colliers, but in 1973 Shipping & Coal purchased the old Electricity collier **Captain J. M. Donaldson** (192) which became **Highland** 3341/51 with the view to having her available for the power station trade, especially in the winter. She was sent to Seaham and was the largest collier to get in there for some years. She was only retained for a short period.

The northern owners found their coal exports much reduced or non-existent. Efforts were made in the late 1940s and early 1950s to get the trade going. Witherington & Everett had just three of their own ships, two of the old pre-war ships which were soon sold and **Granta** 2841/40. This 'Empire' collier was mainly employed running to Littlebrook or Barking Power Stations in the latter part of the 1940s, usually from Blyth. The rate was usually about 7/- per ton on the ships 3,900 tons. Cargoes became more varied in the 1950s including coal to Dagenham for Fords. Cargoes were also carried for Charrington's and Stephenson Clarke. By 1959 they were concentrating on the Mediterranean trade. The Pelton S.S. Co., had four of their old steamers left at the end of the war, **Zelo** 2294/21, **Spero** 1960/20, **Rondo** 2750/27 and **Lesto** 1893/18 oldest of the fleet. The **Lesto** was involved in an effort to get the export trade going again as Mr. C. L. Lovell, Marconi Radio Operator for the voyage recalls: "In May 1953 I was sent to join the **Lesto** which turned out to be a very old steam collier which had just finished loading coal. Everything was covered in coal dust, and there seemed little sign of life on board. A man wearing a coal-stained singlet appeared and informed me that he was the steward and that my cabin was 'up there', and that I would find some of the other officers in the saloon which was right aft. 'Up there' was a steel box rivetted on just behind the funnel; it was about eight feet by fifteen and had to be reached by climbing up a steel ladder which had slight treads and handrails. I lugged my suitcases up the ladder, and had a quick look round my new home. It only needed a quick look because there was just a radio room comprising a chair and a desk with very old equipment on it that was so simple that it did not need further examination. Slightly partitioned off was my sleeping cabin, which was very spartan. There was a washbowl on a stand but no taps or waste pipe; no lavatory or shower and no windows, only portholes (128).

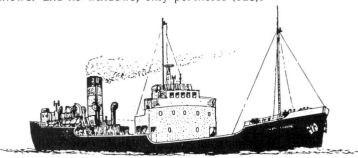

213. Poole Channel
Sketch John Bartlett

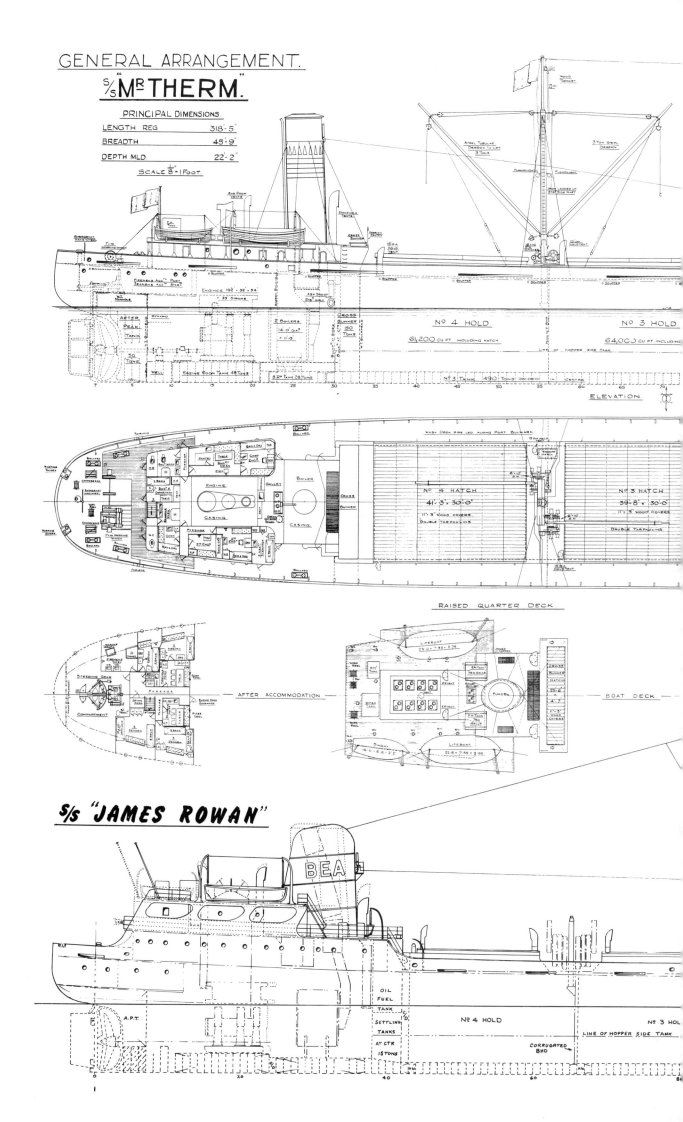

GENERAL ARRANGEMENT.
S/S "Mr THERM."

PRINCIPAL DIMENSIONS.

LENGTH REG	318'- 5"
BREADTH	45'- 9"
DEPTH MLD.	22'- 2"

SCALE ⅛" = 1 FOOT.

ELEVATION.

RAISED QUARTER DECK

AFTER ACCOMMODATION

BOAT DECK.

S/S "JAMES ROWAN"

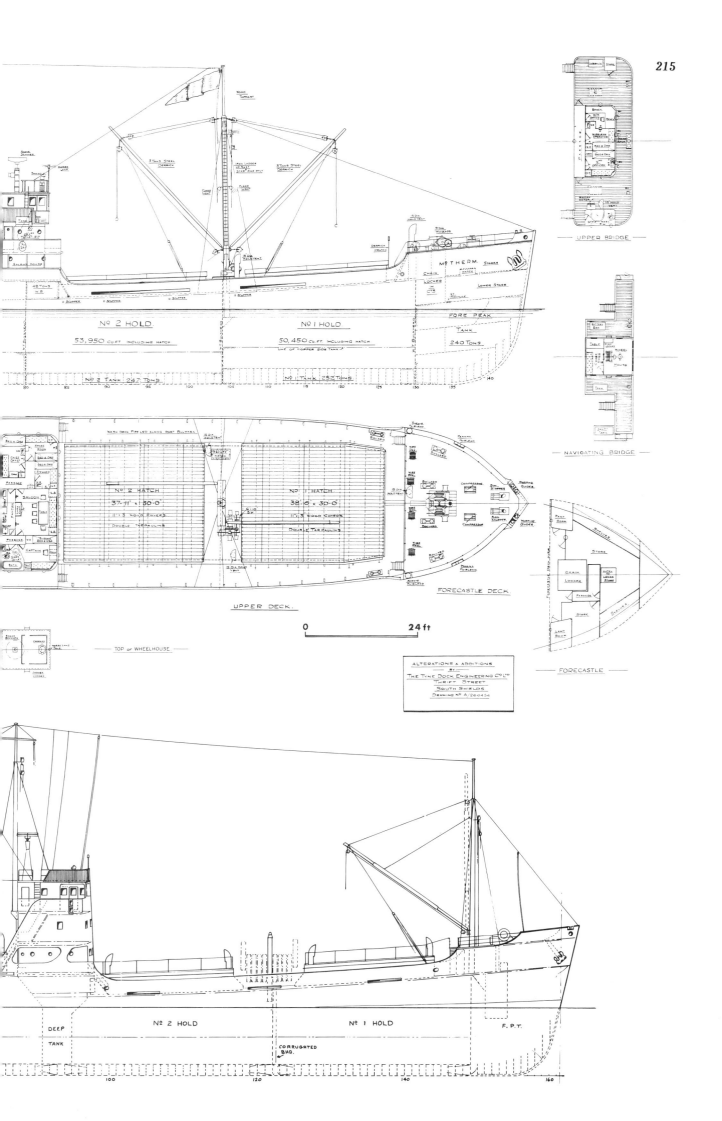

216. Fulham III
Sketch John Bartlett

I went aft to the saloon, it is only on very old ships that the saloon is located in the stern, usually accommodation for the navigating officers is amidships, especially when, as in the **Lesto**, the engine room was amidships. In the 1950s one expected the accommodation to be above the waterline rather than almost below it as in a sailing vessel! In the saloon were three or four others who welcomed me and no doubt gave me a drink. There was an old second mate, two or three engineers and the young first mate who was lying (fully dressed) on his bunk with his girl friend. They were quite visible, for the cabins of the mates and the Captain were ranged round the saloon, but their sides terminated in an ironwork grill for the top foot or so. I learned that we would leave later that evening and the ship belonged to the Pelton S.S. Co. I also learned that for the past 27 years she had been on the London coal trade, but that this voyage was to the Mediterranean. Conversation on this point went on for a long time and the old mate was quite indignant that he would not be home on the usual days which had become routine on the London run; others wondered about the provisions because there was no refrigerator and about the capacity of the water tanks and other such matters.

Soon after the Captain's arrival the crew staggered out from somewhere and started putting the hatch covers on. Whilst they were doing so, a man from Marconi's appeared and said to me, "I have not had a chance to check the transmitter because the aerial has been down during loading. There is an intermittent fault on the receiver which you will have to fix yourself. No one ever uses the direction finder so I haven't looked at it. The emergency transmitter needs new batteries so I will go and get some now, see you soon." I watched the crew drive home the wedges holding down the canvas hatch covers. Then they hoisted my aerial, hauled in the gangway and started to cast off the mooring lines. The Marconi man re-appeared as we pulled away from the berth, threw the batteries across the water to me and waved me goodbye. The steam engine gave us a marvellously smooth and vibrationless movement through the water as we headed down the east coast for the Mediterranean and it was not until we were off Lisbon that I received the vital message directing us to ports in Algeria where the cargo had been sold during our voyage southwards." **Lesto** and the other old steamers were sold soon afterwards and the export trade was never to become important again. The company's last ship **Rondo** 3410/57 was a motor ship of 4,600 tons deadweight suitable for the power station trade but with this declining too, she was sold in 1961 to Stephenson Clarke and the company wound up.

Stephenson Clarke had purchased **Greenbatt** 1968/54 from another Newcastle owner who chartered to them regularly, E. R. Newbigin, who had ordered the vessel when there had been a general up-turn in the coastal coal trade. Speaking at the launch of the **Greenbatt**, Mr. Haslam, Chairman of the owners said it was the first new vessel for the company in 28 years and he felt before long the ship would find employment with the great nationalised industries as a record 28 million tons of coal had been moved coastwise the previous year. The company had several pre-war steamers which were sold in the 1950s and the firm looked to their new motor ship **Greathope** 2750/58, but it was not to be, for she was delivered just as freight rates and coal demand were falling. The company struggled on for a while but eventually had to sell up. Constantine Lines, as they had become, built no more steamers during or after the war, concentrating on motor ships and developing the Golden Cross line to the Mediterranean. They purchased an 'Empire' steam coaster which became **Levenwood** 1058/45 which joined the other steamers on the coal trade to the Thameside cement works, but this trade too was ended when the works changed to oil firing and so the steamers were slowly sold from the mid-1950s. Last to go was **Southwood** in the early 1960s.

Closing of the Staiths and the end of the Steam Collier

Following the Second World War, exports were much reduced, and imports began. Coastwise coal shipments though had increased steadily to 8 million tons, mainly due to the rapidly expanding southern power stations. By 1964 no coal was being taken by France or Germany, with Scandinavia becoming the main export market.

By the mid-1950s on the Tyne only No.5 staith of the Commission's staiths was still in use, but No.1 had been replaced by a reinforced concrete jetty equipped with two loading booms with conveyors fed from two new wagon tipples, each capable of 500 tons per hour. The first staith to be fitted with this equipment was Pelaw Main, which with Derwenthaugh and Harton was under the control of the National Coal Board, while the British Transport Commission was responsible for Dunston Staiths. In Tyne Dock two of the staiths had been reduced to jetties, with the remaining two offering 4 berths only.

In common with the staiths at most of the other ports on the east coast of England, those at Dunston were constructed almost wholly of wood. Of substantial sizes and excellent quality, they were very carefully made and erected by skilled craftsmen, and could reasonably be expected to last about 100 years. They would have done this quite easily, with minor maintenance, had not the demand for shipping facilities fallen off at the beginning of the 1960s, consequent upon the closure of uneconomic pits throughout the whole of the Northumberland and Durham coalfields. So that by 1975 there were very few pits indeed in Northumberland and not many more in Durham. So it was decided to discontinue the use of the inside staiths and finally to demolish them. The Derwenthaugh staiths had closed some 15 years previously when **Birdwood** took the last cargo of coking and steam coal on the 25th of March 1960, bound for Ford's at Dagenham. The contract was awarded to Messrs. Grant, Lyon and Eagre of Doncaster who had successfully demolished the staiths belonging to the British Rail at North Blyth in 1974. Work was started in November 1974 and completed early in December 1975. A most gratifying aspect of the job was that not a single major mishap caused injury to any of the men employed on the task. The beautiful little cast steel footbridge over the railway lines at the shore end of the staiths was carefully dismantled and transported to the Beamish Open Air Museum at Stanley in Durham, where it can be admired for all time.

The timber was, in the main, in excellent condition and was immediately sold for further use, the verticals being in great demand. Most of the timber that had lain horizontally was very badly rotted in places, which had made it a little dangerous to wander far off the tracks. By 1976 only three wooden staiths were left in the country. They were the West Blyth Staiths belonging to British Rail, which were fitted with retractable belt conveyors; the outside staiths at Dunston, also the property of British Rail, and No.22 in the South Dock at Sunderland, now the property of the City of Sunderland. That at Seaham Harbour was made of reinforced concrete.

It would be wrong to leave Dunston without mentioning some of the places and perhaps one or two of the inhabitants who gave the seamen such good service. There was the Excelsior Club, the first place of call on the Staiths road. Here the facilities were excellent, billiards and dominoes, drinking and yarning, television and bingo in later years, to name a few of the distractions. There are three well known Public Houses in the near vicinity, the Anchor, the Cross Keys and the Keel. Yet another institution was Fred Parker. He kept a store at the entrance to the staiths proper for many years, at which anyone could buy practically anything from a packet of chewing gum to a complete outfit of clothing and rubber sea boots. Fred was a really good friend to all seamen using the staiths, and could always be relied upon to give a helping hand if need ever arose. Despite having been let down very badly more than once, he never refused help. He knew the history of everyone calling at his shop, yet he never told tales out of school. Anyone invited into the room at the back of the shop invariably was warned "Mind the steps" alluding to the staircase leading down to the rear yard of his premises. After a few years of the warning we could all chorus it with him, recalls Captain MacRae. There was an excellent Mission to Seamen at Dunston, but as with everything else, with the declining number of colliers it fell into disuse and was ultimately converted into a Community Centre, popular with the inhabitants of Dunston.

The conveyors at Jarrow continued in operation to the end of the steam era but those at Whitehill Point ceased operation in 1976. The conveyors at Harton were of much later construction and the supervisor had closed circuit television to help him keep an eye on loading operations, but Howden disappeared along with the Northumberland Dock and the conveyors of Pelaw Main Staith.

So the steam collier had lasted over a century and was now out, superseded by the motor ship. The long lived iron hulls and inefficient steam engines of the early years had given way to the much more efficient steel hulls and triple expansion engines using superheated steam. The steam colliers made possible a better and more prosperous life for those aboard and the country as a whole. This was not achieved without considerable vigilance as the colliers were often close to the shore in narrow channels used by many other vessels, without the aid of radar for most of the years of their service. Despite this they were expected to keep up a relentless schedule of deliveries and generally did so. They also fought in two world wars to maintain vital fuel supplies and won through despite many casualties, to be finally replaced by the motor bulk carrier.

217. Captain MacRae (bottom row, left) and the crew of the **Hackney,** *August 1972 on the occasion of her last voyage down the Thames.*
MacRae collection

LIST of FLATIRONS
(Up - River Colliers)

Appendix

Compiled by John Bartlett

Westminster 817/78. 220.0' x 32.2' x 13.8'. Palmers, for T. & C. Nicholls (later River Steam Colliers Co. Ltd.), London. Lost in collision with **Nerissa** off the Mouse Lightvessel 30.5.84 while on passage Tyne to London with coal.

Vauxhall 817/78. 220.0' x 32.2' x 13.8'. Palmers, for T. & C. Nicholls (later River Steam Colliers Co. Ltd). Foundered 21.1.15 after striking a sunken vessel.

Lambeth 923/79. 220.5' x 32.2' x 14.5'. Palmers, for T. & C. Nicholls (later River Steam Colliers Co. Ltd.). Lost after collision off the Gunfleet Sands 7.12.99.

Chelsea 1171/84. 230.0' x 33.2' x 14.9'. Palmers, for River Steam Colliers Ltd., London. Lost off Dudgeon 1903.

Vane Tempest 689/84. 185.0' x 30.0' x 13.5'. E. Withy & Co., for the Marquis of Londonderry, Seaham. Broken up for scrap May 1924.

Stepney 688/86. 160.0' x 35.0' x 14.6'. W. Gray & Co., for F. Green later H.C. Pelly/East London S.S. Co., London. 1901: Sm. France, Fenwick & Co., London. Sold out of service 1904.

Wapping 688/86. 160.0' x 35.0' x 14.6'. W. Gray & Co. for F. Green later H.C. Pelly/East London S.S. Co. Wrecked near Flamborough Head 20.11.91.

Poplar 886/86. 180.0' x 36.1' x 15.2'. W. Gray & Co. for F. Green later H.C. Pelly/East London S.S. Co., London. 1901:Wm. France, Fenwick, London. 1903: Commercial Gas Co., London. 1911: Sold to Keeps S.S. & Lighterage Co. 1912: Sold out of service to Italian owners.

Walker 606/90. 185.0' x 30.0' x 11.9'. Wood, Skinner & Co. for Lambert Bros. 1896: Wm. Cory & Son. 1903: Sold out of service.

Ratcliff 802/92. 170.0' x 36.0' x 13.7'. Short Bros. for H.C. Pelly/East London S.S.Co., London. 1901: Wm. France, Fenwick. 1906: Wandsworth & Putney Gas Co. 1908: Sold out of service to Irish owners.

Battersea 860/02. 215.0' x 32.1' x 15.4'. W. Dobson & Co. for River Steam Colliers Co. 1915: Gas Light & Coke Co. Sunk in collision with **Walton** in convoy 8.2.18 east of Scarborough. Tyne for London.

Limehouse 562/03. 165.0' x 30.0' x 12.9'. W. Dobson & Co. for Commercial Gas Co., London. 1919: Wandsworth, Wimbledon & Epsom District Gas Co. 1922: Commercial Gas Co. 1926: Sold to Gracechurch Transports and renamed **Yorkvalley**. 1928: W.A. Wilson, Southampton. 1935: Broken up.

Bow 565/04. 165.3' x 30.1' x 12.8'. W. Dobson & Co. for Commercial Gas Co. 1926: Sold out of service. Broken up 1935.

Bromley 565/04. 165.3' x 30.0' x 12.8'. W. Dobson & Co. for Commercial Gas Co. 1926: Harrison's (London) Colliers Ltd., renamed **Harley**. 1927: Sold out of service, wrecked 1940.

Ewell 1036/06. 220.0' x 34.2' x 13.4'. Dublin Dockyard for J. Harrison Ltd. as the coaster **Berne**. 1914: Renamed **Balham**. 1915: Wandsworth, Wimbledon & Epsom District Gas Co. 1919: Converted for up-river service. 1925: Sold out of service and wrecked 1936.

Ravonia 703/08. 182.7' x 27.9' x 12.3'. R. Williamson as a coaster for their own fleet. 1915: Commercial Gas Co. 1919: Wandsworth, Wimbledon & Epsom District Gas Co., and converted for up-river work. 1923: Stephenson Clarke, renamed **Lancing**. Sold to Italian owners 1933. Sunk 1944.

Wandle 889/09. 205.2' x 32.1' x 14.4'. J.P. Rennoldson & Sons, South Shields, for Wandsworth & Putney Gas, Light & Coke Co. Wrecked off Flamborough Head 12.12.17.

Mitcham (twin screw) 1125/13. 220.4' x 35.0' x 13.6'. W. Dobson & Co. for Wandsworth, Wimbledon & Epsom District Gas Co. 1926: Sold out of service. Torpedoed 1.7.43.

Avonwood 854/15. 198.1' x 30.7' x 12.4'. W. Harkess & Son for Constantine & Donkin. 1917: London Transport Co. Ltd. (Brown, Jenkinson & Co. managers). 1920: H. Rees Jones & Co., Cardiff. 1920: Wandsworth, Wimbledon & Epsom District Gas Co. and converted for up-river work. 1924: Sold out of service, converted back to a coaster and renamed **Broomfleet**. Lost 13/14 December 1933.

Flashlight 934/20. 216.5' x 32.0' x 13.4'. S.P. Austin & Son for Gas Light & Coke Co. Sunk by bomb 11.3.41.

Afterglow 936/20. 216.6' x 32.0' x 13.5'. J.P. Rennoldson & Sons for Gas Light & Coke Co. 1949: North Thames Gas Board. Broken up 1953.

Ethylene 936/21. 217.3' x 32.0' x 13.4'. Wood, Skinner & Co. for Gas Light & Coke Co. 1949: North Thames Gas Board. 1953: Sold to Hargreaves Coal & Shipping Co., renamed **Harfry**. Broken up Grays 1957.

Wandle 889/23. 209.3' x 31.4' x 13.3'. Burntisland Shipbulding Co. for Wandsworth, Wimbledon & Epsom District Gas Co. Sold Stephenson Clarke 1932 and renamed **Pitwines**. Lost in collision 19.11.41.

Woodcote 1242/24. 220.7' x 34.9' x 16.4'. Burntisland Shipbuilding Co. for Wandsworth, Wimbledon & Epsom District Gas Co. Sold Stephenson Clarke 1934 and renamed **Cerne**. Broken up 1955.

Fireglow 1261/25. 225.0' x 36.0' x 15.3'. S.P. Austin & Son for Gas Light & Coke Co. Sunk by mine 8.12.41 Thames Estuary.

Homefire 1262/25. 225.0' x 36.0' x 15.3'. S.P. Austin & Son for Gas Light & Coke Co. Sunk by bomb 1.7.41 off Cromer.

Ewell 1350/26. 226.0' x 36.4' x 16.5'. Burntisland Shipbuilding Co. for Wandsworth & District Gas Co. 1949: South Eastern Gas Board. 1958: Renamed **Ewell II** briefly and sold to Ditta Feruzzi Serafina to be a grain lighter at Ravenna. Renamed **Candiano**.

Sir David 1275/27. 225.1' x 36.0' x 15.2'. J. Readhead & Son for Gas Light & Coke Co. 1949: North Thames Gas Board. Sold Belgian breakers Dec. 1957.

Lady Olga 1266/27. 225.0' x 36.0' x 15.3'. S.P. Austin & Son for Gas Light & Coke Co. 1949: North Thames Gas Board. Sold Belgian breakers Dec. 1957.

William Cash 1186/29. 225.5' x 36.1' x 14.0'. Hawthorn Leslie & Co. for Stephenson Clarke & Associated Companies. Sold to Dutch breakers April 1958.

Suntrap 939/29. 217.5' x 32.0' x 13.5'. Hawthorn Leslie & Co. for Gas Light & Coke Co. 1949: North Thames Gas Board. 1954: Sold Ouse S.S. Co. (Atkinson). Renamed **Sunfleet**. Sold Dutch breakers Sept. 1958.

Torchbearer 1267/29. 225.0' x 36.0' x 15.3'. J. Crown & Sons for Gas Light & Coke Co. Sunk by mine 19.11.39 off Harwich. First flatiron casualty WW2.

Horseferry 951/30. 217.0' x 32.0' x 13.5'. J. Crown & Sons for Gas Light & Coke Co. Sunk E-boat torpedo 11.3.42 north east of Great Yarmouth.

Tolworth 1351/30. 226.0' x 36.4' x 16.5'. Burntisland Shipbuilding Co. for Wandsworth & District Gas Co. 1949: South Eastern Gas Board. 1958: Sold Ditta Feruzzi Serafino to be a grain lighter at Ravenna. Renamed **S.Apollinare**

Tyndall 1314/32. 235.0' x 36.4' x 15.4'. S.P. Austin & Son for London Power Co. 1948: British Electricity Authority. Sold to Dutch breakers July 1958.

Alexander Kennedy 1313/32. 234.5' x 36.4' x 15.4'. Burntisland Shipbuilding Co. for London Power Co. Sunk by submarine torpedo 22.2.45 south east of Falmouth.

John Hopkinson 1314/32. 235.5' x 36.4' x 15.4'. S.P. Austin & Son for London Power Co. 1948: British Electricity Authority. Broken up at Grays June 1959.

Wandle 1482/32. 236.0' x 38.0' x 16.5'. Burntisland Shipbuilding Co. for Wandsworth & District Gas Co. 1949: South Eastern Gas Board. Sold Dutch breakers Nov. 1959.

Ferranti 1317/32. 235.0' x 36.4' x 15.4'. Burntisland Shipbuilding Co. for London Power Co. 1948: British Electricity Authority. Beached after collision 8.6.55. Broken up Grays March 1956.

Colonel Crompton 1495/33. 237.0' x 38.2' x 15.9'. S.P. Austin & Son for London Power Co. 1948: British Electricity Authority. Broken up at Sunderland arriving 3.6.59.

Fulham I 1599/36. 238.1' x 38.3' x 16.5'. Burntisland Shipbuilding Co. for Fulham Borough Council. 1948: British Electricity Authority. Sold Dutch breakers August 1958.

Fulham II 1596/36. 238.1' x 38.3' x 16.5'. Burntisland Shipbuilding Co. for Fulham Borough Council. 1948: British Electricity Authority. Broken up at Sunderland arriving 28.6.60.

Charles Parsons 1535/36. 239.0' x 38.7' x 16.2'. S.P. Austin & Son for London Power Co. 1948: British Electricity Authority. Sold Belgian breakers March 1967, £10,000.

Fulham III 1594/37. 238.3' x 38.3' x 16.5'. Burntisland Shipbuilding Co. for Fulham Borough Council. 1948: British Electricity Authority. Sold Dutch breakers 1958.

George Balfour 1570/37. 239.2' x 38.7' x 16.2'. S.P. Austin & Co. for London Power Co. 1948: British Electricity Authority. Damaged by mine 17.10.40 and by E-boat torpedo 14.10.42. Sold Dutch breakers July 1958.

Wimbledon 1598/37. 250.0' x 39.6' x 16.6'. Burntisland Shipbuilding Co. for Wandsworth Gas Co. 1949: South Eastern Gas Board. Foundered Oct. 1956.

Leonard Pearce 1571/38. 239.0' x 38,7' x 16.2'. S.P. Austin & Son for London Power Co. Sunk in collision 11.1.1940 off Bull Point.

Joseph Swan 1571/38. 239.0' x 38.7' x 16.2'. S.P. Austin & Son for London Power Co. Sunk by E-boat torpedo 4.9.1940 off Cromer.

Fulham IV 1562/39. 247.5' x 39.6' x 16.6'. Burntisland Shipbulding Co. for Fulham Borough Council. 1948: British Electricity Authority. Damaged, sold to Dutch breakers in March 1959.

Fulham V 1562/39. 247.5' x 39.6' x 16.6'. Burntisland Shipbulding Co. for Fulham Borough Council. Sunk by E-boat 4.9.40 off Cromer.

Ambrose Fleming 1555/41. 239.0' x 39.6' x 16.6'. Burntisland Shipbulding Co. for London Power Co. Sunk by E-boat 28.4.41 off Cromer.

Capitol 1558/41, 247.0' x 39.7' x 16.6'. S.P. Austin & Son for Gas Light & Coke Co. 1949: North Thames Gas Board. Sold Belgian breakers August 1963.

Sir Leonard Pearce 1580/41. 247.0' x 39.6' x 16.6'. Burntisland Shipbulding Co. for London Power Co. 1948: British Electricity Authority. Broken up at Sunderland arriving 20.4.60.

Fulham VI 1552/41. 247.0' x 39.6' x 16.6'. Burntisland Shipbulding Co. for Fulham Borough Council. 1948: British Electricity Authority. Broken up at Rotterdam 29.5.59.

Fulham VII 1552/42. 247.0' x 39.6' x 16.6'. Burntisland Shipbulding Co. for Fulham Borough Council. Sunk in collision Feb. 1946 with S.S. **Alfred Victory.**

William Pearman 1552/42. 247.0' x 39.6' x 16.6'. Burntisland Shipbuilding Co. for London Power Co. 1948: British Electricity Authority. Broken up at Bruges 2.5.61.

Firedog 1557/42. 247.0' x 39.6' x 16.6'. S.P. Austin & Son for Gas Light & Coke Co. 1949: North Thames Gas Board. Sold Dutch breakers April 1959.

Fireglow 1549/44. 247.0' x 39.6' x 16.6'. S.P. Austin & Son for Gas Light & Coke Co. 1949: North Thames Gas Board. Sold to Dutch breakers May 1965.

Firebeam 1554/45. 247.0' x 39.6' x 16.6'. Hall, Russell & Co. for Gas Light & Coke Co. 1949: North Thames Gas Board. Sold to Sweden second quarter 1963, converted to barge.

Sir Joseph Swan 1554/45. 247.0' x 39.6' x 16.6'. Hall, Russell & Co. for London Power Co. 1948: British Electricity Authority. Sold German breakers March 1967, £10,000.

Chessington 1720/46. 260.0' x 39.5' x 16.6'. Burntisland Shipbulding Co. for Wandsworth Gas Co. 1949: South Eastern Gas Board. Sold 1966 to Gotebergs Bogserings & Bargnings A/R, Gothenburg, converted dumb barge.

Sir Alexander Kennedy 1714/46. 260.0' x 39.6' x 16.6'. S.P. Austin & Son for London Power Co. 1948: British Electricity Authority. Sold Belgian breakers May 1968.

Brixton 1635/46. 247.3' x 39.5' x 16.6'. S.P: Austin & Sons for South Metropolitan Gas Co. 1949: Southern Electricity Generating Board. Sold 1962 to Emilio Canale, Genoa and renamed **Brunetto.**

Brixton 1635/46. 247.3' x 39.5 x 16.6'. S.P. Austin & Son for South Metropolitan Gas Co. 1949: South Eastern Gas Board. Sold 1962 to Emilio Canale, Genoa and renamed **Brunetto.**

Brimsdown 1837/51. 258.0' x 39.3' x 18.5'. Burntisland Shipbuilding Co. for British Electricity Authority. Sold to T.W.Ward Ltd. for demolition June 1972. The last coal burner.
Brunswick Wharf 1782/51. 257.0' x 39.3' x 18.5'. S.P. Austin & Son for British Electricity Authority. Sold to Paul Christenson, Denmark in 1972 and renamed **Allan C.** Broken up 1974.
Deptford 1782/51. 257.0' x 39.3' x 18.5'. S.P. Austin & Son for British Electricity Authority. 1972: Sold V.O. Levy. Sold to T.W.Ward Ltd. for demolition Feb. 1973.
Hackney 1782/52. 257.0' x 39.3' x 18.5'. S.P. Austin & Son for British Electricity Authority. Last steamer built. Sold to Estrella Shipping Co. Ltd., Cyprus 1972, renamed **Bulk I.** Broken up 1973.

Motor Vessels: Mitcham 1787/46, Fulham VIII 1773/47, Fulham IX 1759/48, Fulham X 1759/48, Murdoch 1759/49, Adams Beck 1773/49, Wandsworth 1875/50, Samuel Clegg 1773/50, Accum 1771/50, Thomas Hardie 1771/50, Dame Caroline Haslett 1777/50, Harry Richardson 1777/50, Battersea 1777/51, Blackwall Point 1776/51, Sydenham 1871/51, Croydon 1871/51, Falconer Birks 1762/53, Thomas Livesey 1779/53, Kingston 1873/56, Dulwich 1873/57, Lambeth 1877/58, Ewell 1877/58 and Camberwell 1877/58.

*220. **Moorwood** discharging at Albert Dock hoists 27th May 1957.* MacRae Collection.

Polgrange covered in ice on a voyage from Hull to Bruges 10th of February 1932. From a photo by R.H. Hughes.

INDEX - Companies etc.

Cedarwood 899/33 John Bartlett